C000027337

Macroeconomic Policy and Adjustment in Korea 1970–1990

Harvard Studies in International Development

Other volumes in the series include:

Reforming Economic Systems in Developing Countries
edited by Dwight H. Perkins and Michael Roemer, 1991

Markets in Developing Countries: Parallel, Fragmented, and Black
edited by Michael Roemer and Christine Jones, 1991*

Progress with Profits: The Development of Rural Banking in Indonesia
by Richard Patten and Jay K. Rosengard, 1991*

Green Markets: The Economics of Sustainable Development
by Theo Panayotou, 1993*

The Challenge of Reform in Indochina
edited by Börje Ljunggren, 1993

Africa and Asia: Legacies and Opportunities in Development
edited by David L. Lindauer and Michael Roemer, 1994*

*Jointly published by the International Center for Economic Growth.

Macroeconomic Policy and Adjustment in Korea, 1970–1990

Stephan Haggard
Richard N. Cooper
Susan Collins
Choongsoo Kim
Sung-Tae Ro

Harvard Institute for International Development
and Korea Development Institute

Distributed by Harvard University Press

Published by Harvard Institute for International Development
June 1994

Distributed by Harvard University Press

Editorial management: Vukani Magubane
Editorial assistance: Sarah Newberry
Design and production: Editorial Services of New England, Inc.

Library of Congress Cataloging-in-Publication Data

Macroeconomic policy and adjustment in Korea, 1970–1990 / Stephan
    Haggard . . . [et al.]. — Rev.
        p. cm. — (Harvard studies in international development)
    Includes bibliographical references and index.
    ISBN 0-674-54085-9 : $30.00
    1. Korea (South)—Economic policy—1960–   2. Korea (South)–
–Economic conditions—1960–   3. Economic stabilization—Korea
(South)   I. Haggard, Stephan.   II. Series.
HC467.M33 1993
338.95195—dc20   94-10736
                                                                          CIP

Printed in the United States of America

Contents

Contributors   *vii*

Preface   *ix*

I. *Introduction*

1
Understanding Korea's Macroeconomic Policy   *3*
Stephan Haggard, Richard N. Cooper, and Susan Collins

II. *History: The Political Economy of Macroeconomic Policy in Korea*

2
Macroeconomic Policy Through the First Oil Shock, 1970–1975   *23*
Stephan Haggard

3
From the Heavy Industry Plan to Stabilization:
Macroeconomic Policy, 1976–1980   *49*
Stephan Haggard

4
The Political Economy of Adjustment in the 1980s   *75*
Stephan Haggard and Susan Collins

III. *Issues in Korean Macroeconomic Policy*

5
Fiscal Policy in Korea   *111*
Richard N. Cooper

6
Korean Monetary Policy   *145*
Sung-Tae Ro

7
Wage Policy and Labor Market Development   *185*
Choongsoo Kim

8
Saving, Investment, and External Balance in South Korea   *231*
Susan Collins

9
Korea's Balance of International Payments   *261*
Richard N. Cooper

10
Epilogue   *295*
Stephan Haggard and Richard N. Cooper

Select Bibliography *305*

Index *311*

Contributors

Stephan Haggard is Professor at the Graduate School of International Relations and Pacific Studies, University of California, San Diego. His research focuses on the political economy of development. He is the author of *Pathways from the Periphery: The Politics of Growth in the Newly Industrializing Countries* (1990), and co-editor of *The Politics of Adjustment* (1992), *The Political Economy of Finance in Developing Countries* (1993), and *Voting For Reform: The Politics of Adjustment in New Democracies* (1994). He has been a consultant to the World Bank and the OECD. He holds a Ph.D. in political science from the University of California, Berkeley.

Richard N. Cooper is Maurits C. Boas Professor of International Economics at Harvard University. He has written extensively on questions of international economic policy. He is the author of *The International Monetary System* (1987), *Can Nations Agree?* (with others, 1989) *Economic Stabilization and Debt in Developing Countries* (1992), and *Boom, Crisis, and Adjustment: The Macroeconomic Experience of Developing Countries* (with others, 1993). He has served on several occasions in the U.S. government. He was Under-Secretary of State for Economic Affairs from 1977 to 1981, and Chairman of the Federal Reserve Bank of Boston from 1990 to 1992. He holds a Ph.D. in economics from Harvard University.

Susan M. Collins is Senior Fellow at the Brookings Institution and Associate Professor of Economics at Georgetown University, where she teaches international macroeconomics and trade. She has served as Senior Staff Economist for the U.S. President's Council of Economic Advisers, and has been a consultant to the World Bank. Her research has included analyses of macroeconomic policy and performance in South

Korea, exchange rate policy in the European Monetary System, and implications for the global economy from developments in Eastern Europe and the Former Soviet Union. She holds a Ph.D. in economics from MIT.

Choongsoo Kim is Secretary to the President for Economic Affairs, Republic of Korea. He has worked as Senior Fellow and Director of the Center for Economic Education at Korea Development Institute. He has conducted extensive research on the topics of labor market policy, macroeconometric forecasting, and economic institutions. He received his B.A. in economics from Seoul National University and his Ph.D. from the University of Pennsylvania.

Sung-Tae Ro is President of First Economic Research Institute in Korea. He has worked as a Senior Economist at the Bank of Korea and Director of Research Coordination at Korea Development Institute. He has published widely on the subjects of monetary economics, forecasting modeling, international economics, and the economy of the Republic of Kazakhstan. He received his B.A. in economics from Seoul National University and his M.A. and Ph.D. from Harvard University.

Preface

Fifteen years ago the Korea Development Institute (KDI) and the Harvard Institute for International Development (HIID) jointly researched, wrote, and published ten book-length studies on the first three decades of Korean economic development (1945–1975). Several years ago, the reception of these volumes encouraged the two institutes to think of a sequel. In considering that sequel, we decided to focus on a number of studies that went in-depth into several of the key features of the post-1975 period.

We chose three themes that dealt with central features of Korean development, which were either not present in the pre-1975 period or were present in only muted form. The first of these studies deals with macroeconomic policy during the difficult period of the 1970s when oil prices were rising sharply, and with the aftermath of these macro problems in the 1980s. The second study deals with Korea's move away from generalized support for exports of manufactures to a policy of targeting specific industries, the heavy and chemical industry drive of the 1973–1979 period, followed by the retreat from industrial targeting in the 1980s. The final study deals with some of the strains of rapid economic growth. Special attention is paid to labor relations and the labor market in the 1980s when Korean democratization led to the end of government efforts to suppress the labor movement, and labor and management had to learn new ways of working together.

These three studies differ from the earlier ten-volume series in another important respect. The earlier series dealt only peripherally with the politics of the economic changes that were analyzed. The three recent studies include political economy issues as central themes. Technical economic analysis continues to play an important role, but many chapters are devoted to how and why key economic policy decisions were actually made, a process that involved more than purely economic considerations.

In completing this volume on macroeconomic policy in Korea, the authors are grateful for the assistance of Professor Chung-In Man. We owe special thanks to David Lindauer, who has borne the principal responsibility for managing the research and production of these volumes. We also want to thank the three past presidents of KDI who helped initiate these studies and bring them to fruition, Dr. Park Yung Chul, Dr. Koo Bon Ho, and Dr. Song Hee Yhon. Funding for these studies was provided from KDI funds and from the unrestricted income of HIID. The editorial process was under the overall direction of HIID's editor, Vukani Magubane.

DWIGHT H. PERKINS
Director, HIID

IN-JOUNG WHANG
President, KDI

*Macroeconomic Policy
and Adjustment in Korea
1970–1990*

Part I

Introduction

1

Understanding Korea's Macroeconomic Policy

Stephan Haggard, Richard N. Cooper, and Susan Collins

Because of the extraordinary performance of the Korean economy, economists have scrutinized it from every angle (Table 1-1). Trade and industrial policy have received particular attention, but several excellent studies are available on various aspects of macroeconomic policy and performance as well.[1] Given the plethora of material, what can yet another study add to our understanding of Korea's development?

This book, which examines macroeconomic policy and performance in South Korea from 1970 through the end of the Roh administration in 1992, makes two contributions. First, it provides a political economy perspective on Korean macroeconomic policy. Studies of Korea's rapid growth and successful adjustment in the early 1980s have given particular weight to credible and cohesive policies. Yet the work on Korea's macroeconomic performance provides a relatively narrow economic analysis of the adjustment experience, paying little attention to the institutional and political setting in which policy decisions were made. Part II of this book provides an analytic history of Korean macroeconomic policy over the past two decades that integrates political and economic analysis.

Our second contribution is to draw lessons from the past two decades that are of relevance to the performance of other developing countries; this study is thus implicitly, if not explicitly, comparative. The initial motivation for this project was both to update the original Harvard Institute for International Development–Korea Development Institute studies on Korean development and to examine Korea's experience in managing the external shocks that buffeted the world economy beginning with the first oil crisis. Although Korea is a large debtor and an extremely open economy, when measured by the share of exports in total output, it adjusted relatively smoothly to the international turbulence of the 1970s

Table 1-1. Korea: Basic Indicators of Economic Performance

	1970	1980	1990	1970–1980	1980–1990
				(Annual % Rate)	
GDP (trillion won)	2.72	37.9	169.7	30.1	16.2
Real GDP (trillion 1985 won)	23.74	52.4	121.7	8.2	8.8
Real GDP per capita (000 1985 won)	736.0	1,374.0	2,844.0	6.4	7.4
Labor force (million)	10.2	14.5	16.9[a]	3.5	2.2
Consumer price level (1985 = 100)	15.7	70.9	130.2	16.3	6.3
Real wage (1985 = 100)	34.4	76.7	219.3	8.3	8.2
Exchange rate (won/U.S.$)	311.0	607.0	708.0	6.1	1.6
Exports (U.S.$ billion)	0.88	17.2	63.1	34.6	13.9
External debt (U.S.$ billion)	2.24	28.8	33.1[b]	29.1	1.6
International reserves (U.S.$ billion)	0.61	2.92	14.8	17.0	17.6

[a]1987.
[b]1989.
Source: IMF, *International Financial Statistics;* World Bank, *World Debt Tables;* and author calculations.

and 1980s, maintaining robust growth in the face of external adversity. Given the disastrous experience of most Latin American economies in the 1980s, Korea's successful adjustment process raises important comparative policy issues.

The Political Economy of Macroeconomic Policy in Korea

Most studies of macroeconomic policy take policy choice as exogenous and examine the effects of policy on performance. Yet this begs the crucial question of why certain policies were chosen in the first place. Given that Korea managed to adjust quickly and efficiently, why was it able to do so?

To answer this question, Chapters 2 through 4 provide a historical narrative of Korea's macroeconomic policy since 1970. Chapter 2 focuses on the first half of the 1970s and the government's response to the first oil shock. Chapter 3 analyzes the development of the Heavy and Chemical Industry Plan of the second half of the 1970s, with particular emphasis on the emergence of the stabilization plan of April 1979 and the government's response to the second oil crisis. Chapter 4 outlines the developments of the 1980s, focusing on the stabilization and structural adjustment efforts of the first half of the decade. A brief epilogue to the book provides an overview of some of the political issues surrounding

Korea's adjustment to balance-of-payments surpluses, which occurred under the new democratic government of Roh Tae-Woo (1988–1992).

This historical narrative is built around two types of analyses that are generally foreign to purely economic treatments. The first is a historical reconstruction of the perspective of the policymaker. In analyzing a given policy juncture, analysts enjoy the luxury of knowing what ultimately transpired. The rationality or irrationality of a policy choice is easily gauged by subsequent events and performance. For the policymaker, though, the future is clouded in uncertainty. Decisions must be taken with less-than-perfect information and often pose high political as well as economic risk. Ex post facto, this drama of the policymaking process is easily lost.

In attempting to reconstruct events, the analyst must be particularly sensitive to both the information available to policymakers at the time and the theoretical frameworks they have at their disposal. We have therefore relied in part on interviews with a number of the principal policymakers who held office during the period under review. Their policy frameworks, as much as economic conditions per se, play a crucial role in explaining the logic of policy choice.

Although Korea's economic policy has been broadly outward oriented, the thinking of its top economic policymakers has departed in a number of ways from economic orthodoxy.[2] During the 1970s, two contending policy lines coexisted. A number of officials in the economic bureaucracy argued for a more market-oriented style of economic management. The top political leadership and advocates of an activist industrial policy supported a more dirigist approach, emphasizing exports but also industrial planning and the use of a variety of controls and direct interventions in order to deepen the industrial sector in heavy and chemical industries.

At the end of the 1970s, reformers took advantage of declining export performance and rising inflation to advance their liberalizing program. They gained ground within the economic bureaucracy, but their economic program was not fully realized until the 1980s under a new military government. Even during this period, certain policy areas, such as exchange rate management and financial market policy, continued to exhibit a penchant for state control and guidance that had characterized Korea's growth from the initiation of an export-led growth strategy in the 1960s.

The empirical reconstruction of the policy process provides the raw material for our second line of analysis: a focus on the institutional and political constraints on policy choice. Despite the emphasis that has been given to economic policy as an "input to development," economists generally treat the government as a black box.[3] When they do consider politics, it is assumed that the pursuit of economically optimal policies is also politically rational. An efficiency-enhancing economic reform may have distributional consequences in the short run, but the overall gains should permit the government to compensate the "losers" so that all are better off.

The emergence—or more accurately the reemergence—of a political economy has called these assumptions into question.[4] Electoral, interest-group, and international political pressures generate conflicts between economic and political rationality. Macroeconomic adjustment is particularly interesting in this regard, since it can involve the imposition of short-term costs that have important political consequences. To the extent that policy does show consistency and coherence in formulation and implementation, as it frequently has in Korea, this outcome constitutes an important puzzle to be explained.

Two broad theoretical insights guide our political economy analysis. The first grows out of the renewed interest in how institutions affect the coherence of decision making. The second, more traditional political economy approach focuses on the interests of relevant social groups and the process through which politicians build and sustain coalitions of support.

One theme in our analysis is the unusual degree of institutional centralization in Korea, of both political power and economic policymaking.[5] Prior to the transition to democracy in 1987, political power was strongly concentrated in the hands of two presidents, Park Chung Hee and Chun Doo Hwan, who took an active interest in economic management. Within the bureaucracy, economic decision-making authority was also centralized in a powerful Economic Planning Board (EPB).

This institutional structure had both advantages and drawbacks. On the one hand, the centralization of power permitted a high degree of flexibility in the formulation and implementation of policy. With little interference from interest groups, the legislature, local governments, or competing bureaucratic forces, the top leadership could respond swiftly to events if it chose. The centralized, authoritarian system also allowed tight control to be exercised over the operations of the government itself. Korea's unusual ability, among the developing countries, to control its fiscal policy has been an important factor in maintaining relative macroeconomic stability, an outcome that can be traced to a highly centralized budgetary process.

On the other hand, any centralized system is a captive of the outlook of its chief executive. In general, both Park and Chun chose to forge close working relations with top technocrats, giving the economic bureaucracy the political space to operate relatively free from political constraints. In the absence of institutionalized checks on executive power, however, the technocrats enjoyed little independence from the president. When the chief executive chose a certain course of action, such as Park's launching of the Heavy and Chemical Industry Plan, the technocrats' ability to resist was marginal, and influence could be wielded only when economic changes exposed the disadvantages of the chosen path.

An analysis of institutions can tell us about the capacity of government officials, but it provides few clues on what they are inclined to do. For insight into this question, we must examine not only the strategies of policymakers and the economic constraints they face but the political constraints that politicians face and their strategies for managing them.

For part of the period we are concerned with here (1964–1972), Korea was at least nominally a democracy. During that time, electoral strategy had an important influence on economic policy, affecting both the timing of policy measures (the delay and reversal of stabilization efforts in 1970) and their content (agricultural subsidies after 1969).

For much of the time we are concerned with, however, including both the Yushin constitution (1972–1980) and the Fifth Republic period (1980–1987), Korea was an openly authoritarian country. But even authoritarian leaders must build bases of political support—a coalition that benefits from the basic political and economic order and thus provides stability not only to the economy but to the polity itself.

In the absence of free interest-group and legislative representation, characterizing these coalitions is difficult. But we argue in Chapters 1 and 2 that Park Chung Hee constructed a growth coalition in the 1970s that included the military, large export-oriented firms, conservative rural constituencies, and at least some members of the growing middle class of professionals. Excluded or controlled were intellectuals, students, opposition politicians, and the growing urban working class. Although labor showed impressive real wage gains throughout the 1970s, the government severely curtailed the ability of workers to organize. This political equilibrium was sustained through policies that favored supporting groups, including extensive subsidies to farmers and large conglomerates. These measures, in turn, had implications for macroeconomic policy and efficiency.

Park's coalition proved politically unstable because of its distributive consequences and its authoritarian political assumptions. In 1979, the political order came under increasing pressure from a resurgent democratic opposition. Following Park Chung Hee's assassination and a brief political interregnum, Chun Doo Hwan faced the problem of constructing a new political coalition.

For several reasons, this proved extremely difficult to do. First, Chun came to power through a coup d'état, and thus his legitimacy was challenged from the beginning. Like Park, Chun faced steadily increasing pressure from democratic political forces in society. Second, because Park's policies had produced both relatively high inflation and various inefficiencies, there were strong internal and external pressures to stabilize the economy and move policy in a more market-oriented direction. These liberalizing initiatives involved both short-term costs and major dislocations for some groups.

We argue in Chapter 4 that the authoritarian political structure was at least one factor in the "successful" adjustment of the early 1980s. But stabilization and structural adjustment also had political costs, reducing the discretionary instruments with which Chun could secure bases of political support among farmers, portions of the bureaucracy, and even the private sector.[6] The regime was able to restore rapid growth with price stability, but Chun's economic program was the subject of virulent attack by opposition forces and contributed to his political downfall.

Political institutions and the coalitional base of politics underwent substantial change following the political opening in 1987. For the first time since the early 1970s, and arguably since the early 1960s, political leaders and economic policymakers had to operate in a democratic milieu. In contrast to the new Latin American democracies, however, Roh Tae-Woo enjoyed the political advantages of booming economic conditions and large external surpluses. Moreover, the early choice of an outward-oriented growth strategy created strong pressures for policy continuity.

Nonetheless, democratization did imply institutional changes, toward greater decentralization of power, and coalitional changes, as new groups articulated demands on the government for the first time. The resulting tension between political and economic imperatives was visible in a number of policy areas that had macroeconomic implications, including exchange rate management, wage policy, rice pricing policy, and trade liberalization; we discuss these briefly in the epilogue.

Korean Macroeconomic Policy and Performance: Some Lessons

Part III approaches the same period through the lens of specific issues. Chapter 5 outlines Korea's fiscal policy, paying particular attention to the puzzle of why the government was able to pursue a relatively consistent fiscal stance. Chapter 6 analyzes Korea's monetary and financial market policy, and Chapter 7 addresses the relationship between labor markets and inflation. Chapter 8 explores several alternative hypotheses concerning investment and savings behavior in Korea. Chapter 9 concludes this book by looking at the external accounts and the balance-of-payments adjustment process. Our findings both confirm and modify existing analyses. Yet even where we tread on familiar ground, the lessons are worth reiterating.

Fiscal Policy

It is important to emphasize that Korea was in many ways still a developing country as it entered the 1970s. Over half of the labor force was engaged in agriculture, and per capita national product was only $250 (about $750 in 1988 dollars), despite nearly a decade of rapid growth. The country's financial structure was primitive by the standards of developed countries, and by the standards that Korea itself was to attain by the late 1980s. Like many other developing countries, Korea pursued an activist industrial policy, though one oriented heavily toward the expansion of exports.

In its management of fiscal policy, however, Korea stands out sharply from other developing countries. First, both the development and the implementation of the budget were highly disciplined processes, framed with an eye to overall resource availability. Government spending was relatively small; total government expenditures equaled only 13 percent of gross domestic product (GDP) in the early 1970s, despite exceptionally heavy military expenditures. These rose over the subsequent fifteen years, as they did in both developing and developed countries, but still reached only 17 percent by 1988, well under levels in most other countries of roughly comparable income levels. Moreover, tax revenues grew more rapidly than expenditures in percentage terms, so the budget deficit generally declined relative to GDP.

The government was consistently a net saver, in the sense that total revenues exceeded the government's noninvestment expenditures. It is true that Korea typically ran budget deficits, reaching as high as 3.3 percent of GDP in 1981. But deficits were used either to finance government investment or for relending for private sector investment. By 1985 Korea had the fourth largest external debt among the world's developing countries—$44 billion. But the government's external borrowing was also typically directed toward project financing of some sort and was not used for general budgetary support. In short, although the government played a substantial role in steering the economy, it did so through policies that placed a high priority on investment.

Korea's budgetary discipline throughout two decades would not be remarkable except for the fact that it is so unusual among developing countries. Few others have a comparable record, and none with so much to show for it. How did such discipline come about? It may have been in part a reaction to the political and economic failures of periods of relatively high government spending during the 1950s under Syngman Rhee and in the early years of military rule. To be sure, a rapid growth in revenue made possible by a rapidly growing economy also made it easier to accommodate competing claims than would have been the case in a stagnant economy. But the key point is that honoring these claims was kept within the resources available.

Decision-making institutions appear to have played a central role. Spending by ministries was generally under tight control by the powerful EPB. Budgetary discipline was maintained by concentrating authority over total spending in the hands of a group of qualified EPB officials and, above all, providing them with continual presidential support.

The second noteworthy feature of Korean fiscal policy, related to the first, is that it was generally stabilizing from a macroeconomic point of view. Fiscal policy tended to damp down fluctuations in national income coming from a variety of sources, although stabilization of the economy was not the government's principal objective. Again, this feature is hardly remarkable to those trained in Europe, Japan, or the United States, where the stabilizing character of fiscal policy is taken for granted, mainly through the short-run elasticity of government revenues. But it is highly unusual among developing countries, where fiscal policy tends to be procyclical rather than countercyclical and is often a major source of macroeconomic disturbance.

A stabilizing fiscal policy arises partly from the structure of expenditure and taxation and partly from the priority policymakers accord to stabilizing the growth of income. Again, however, such a role presupposes a high degree of budget discipline. Higher-than-expected revenues must be protected from spending ministries and used to dampen exuberant growth.

Monetary Policy

Although the government generally did not need to borrow extensively from the central bank, monetary policy in Korea was not truly independent of fiscal policy. First, the banking system was the residual lender to the government; second, and more important, the Bank of Korea was under the direction of the ministry of finance, which, in turn, was under the control of the EPB. During the period under review, the most noteworthy pattern to Korea's financial and monetary policy was a long policy cycle from financial liberalization in the 1960s, to an aggressive use of credit for industrial policy purposes in the 1970s, back to a second wave of more substantial financial liberalization in the 1980s.

One of the noteworthy characteristics of Korea is that the government did not rely heavily on seigniorage—the gains from expanding the money supply—as a source of revenue. Seigniorage was substantial in Korea, as it is in any rapidly growing, mildly inflationary country, amounting in principal during the 1970s to 2 to 3 percent of GDP. But rather than being taken into government revenues, much of this seigniorage was dissipated in the form of low-interest loans by the Bank of Korea to commercial banks and, through them, to the favored sectors of the economy, especially export-oriented firms and, after 1973, the heavy and chemical industries. Thus, the government gave to favored sectors more fiscal support, indirectly, than shows up in budgeted expenditures. These subsidies exceeded 1 percent of GDP during the 1970s but gradually declined to less than 0.5 percent in the late 1980s.

During the mid- to late 1960s, Korean financial policy underwent a profound set of reforms that made it a model for other developing countries. Real interest rates were raised, and financial intermediation through the banking system increased rapidly, contributing to high levels of investment and growth. During the period under consideration in this book, however, these reforms were reversed and monetary policy was subordinated to the overriding goal of rapid growth of particular industrial sectors.

The reasons for this reversal were in part institutional, in part the result of the policy goals of the Park administration. The laws establishing the Bank of Korea in 1950 were written by American advisers to ensure a high degree of autonomy. Following the military coup in 1961, the central bank was formally subordinated to the minister of finance and the commercial banking system was nationalized. A variety of specialized banks were created that fell outside central bank control. Even before the launching of the Heavy and Chemical Industry Plan, the selective use of credit had become a major tool of industrial policy; in the 1970s it was used aggressively to promote the building of large, concentrated firms involved in exports and the new round of import substitution in favored sectors. With real interest rates at low, and even negative, levels, there was chronic excess demand for bank loans, which, in turn, created an excess demand for rediscounts from the central bank.

The use of credit for industrial policy purposes had a number of implications for the monetary and financial system. First, to mobilize resources for the big push of the 1970s, the government developed a variety of nonbank financial institutions. The process of financial market liberalization and freer entry is often dated to the 1980s, but these innovations had begun in the early 1970s in an effort to finance Park's ambitious industrial plans. Second, Korea continued to have a flourishing curb financial market designed to meet the short-term working-capital needs of firms. Finally, by Asian standards, Korea was a relatively high-inflation country in the 1970s; not until the 1980s did the objective of reducing inflation become paramount.

In the 1980s, the government gradually moved toward a liberalization of the financial system, including the privatization of the commercial banks, lowering barriers to entry, slowly moving toward freer interest rates, and slowly opening the financial sector to foreign investment and greater participation by foreign banks. Liberalization implied changes in the instruments of monetary management. With low real interest rates and in the absence of a working market for government bonds, the government was forced to devise a variety of other means for controlling the money supply, the most important of which were ceilings on credit extended by the banking system. As the financial system evolved, the focus of the Bank of Korea shifted from direct credit allocation to the broad monetary aggregates—from asset management to liability management. The large balance-of-payments surpluses of the late 1980s prompted the Bank of Korea to engage in extensive open market sales of claims against itself to soak up excess liquidity. Nonetheless, by the end of the decade, the processes of liberalization and deregulation were still impeded by the industrial policies of the 1970s, which left commercial banks holding large nonperforming loans. The Korean financial structure had still not reached the stage at which open market operations could become the principal channel for implementing monetary policy.

Labor Markets

During the period from 1970 to 1990, Korea experienced exceptionally rapid growth in employment, especially manufacturing employment, which was both encouraged and permitted by the extraordinary growth in exports of manufactured goods. Perhaps surprisingly, Korea also experienced a very rapid growth of productivity during this period, especially in manufacturing. This productivity growth both permitted and encouraged a steady but dramatic increase in real wages, exceeding 8 percent a year for two decades—the highest in the world. This growth occurred despite the large, underutilized surplus of agricultural labor at the beginning of the period and despite the absence of truly independent labor unions until the last few years of the 1980s.

The government program to build the heavy and chemical industries led to sharp upward pressure on the relative wages of skilled labor, especially professional and technical workers. This development called forth the first government-promulgated wage guidelines, in 1977. They were hortatory at first and never became mandatory. But during the anti-inflation program of 1981–1984, state-owned banks were asked to deny credits to companies whose wage increases exceeded their productivity growth and to companies that were running losses yet gave higher-than-average wage increases. In addition, to set an example for the private sector, the government significantly reduced pay increases for public employees, actually freezing wages and salaries during 1984.

It is difficult to judge the influence of the wage guidelines on actual wage growth; they are best regarded as a supportive component of the anti-inflationary program rather than as the essential element. A significant amount of wage drift occurred between 1981 and 1984, whereby actual wages increased more than negotiated wage increases. Nonetheless, nominal wage increases did drop significantly during this period, and both wage policy and the government's tougher stance toward labor organization no doubt played some role.

Politics played a role in the explosion of wages in the late 1980s. With the transition to democracy in 1987, particularly given the context of a large and stimulative trade surplus, labor mobilized actively, and nominal wages grew sharply. This wage growth focused especially on less skilled workers, so that labor costs rose and skill differentials declined.

Savings and Investment

Since the gap between investment and saving is equal to the current account deficit, the behavior of these two variables can be interpreted as the domestic counterpart to Korea's external performance. Because domestic macroeconomic policy is a key determinant of saving and investment, Chapter 8 provides a bridge between Chapters 5 and 6, which focus on policy, and Chapter 9, which addresses the balance of payments. Chapter 8 highlights three respects in which Korea stands out from other developing countries.

First, government saving and investment behavior has played a relatively minor role in leading to Korea's current account deficits. As has already been noted, Korea differs from other developing countries, where spurts in government consumption or investment, or both, have led to soaring external imbalances financed by accumulation of external debt. Instead, Korea's large current account deficits came about as private saving declined relative to investment. In fact, private saving—not public saving—accounts for most of the fluctuations in Korea's national saving.

A second distinguishing feature of Korea's experience has been that investment as a share of GDP, especially fixed capital formation, has been maintained at a consistently high level. This has been true even during periods of economic adjustment when the government was seeking to reduce price inflation and external imbalances. The high rates of investment help explain how Korean growth rates could recover so quickly following the negative growth in 1980, for example. In contrast, many heavily indebted countries slashed investment in order to reduce current account deficits and, as a result, found it extremely difficult to make the transition from stabilization to growth. An empirical analysis of investment behavior shows that credit availability and economic growth are the main determinants of private investment. Monetary restraint was short-lived during the adjustment of the early 1980s, which may help explain why private investment did not collapse in its aftermath.

A third finding of Chapter 8 is that Korea has experienced an impressive trend of rising private saving over the past two decades. In the 1960s, Korea saved little by international standards; by the late 1980s, it had one of the highest savings rates in the world. This increase enabled Korea to shift from persistent current account deficits to substantial surpluses in the late 1980s.

A central puzzle is why this enviable rise in saving came about. The empirical analysis in the chapter shows that aggregate private saving is strongly related to economic growth and that most of the rise in saving is attributable to the rise in real per capita income. Evidence from a survey of urban households suggests that household consumption is related to current, not expected lifetime, income and that the rise in saving may be due in part to slow adjustment of consumption patterns to the rapid rise in household wealth and prospective income over the past two decades. Little of the rise in saving appears to be attributable to changes in the real interest rate.

The Balance of Payments
On the external side, Chapter 9 confirms the oft-stated lesson that Korea's export orientation was critical in allowing the country to avoid the external constraints many other less developed countries faced in the 1980s.[7] Despite a large external debt, Korea was capable of securing external resources through both oil crises and, more telling, in the midst of an

international debt crisis that severely curtailed lending to many other developing countries. Although Korean officials did express concern about their ability to borrow at several points, particularly in 1974 and 1980–1981, Korea never faced the severe external constraints other debtors did and probably could have borrowed more than it did.

That Korea's export success allowed it to avoid the wrenching balance-of-payments adjustment problems faced by many developing countries is not controversial; less obvious is the fact that external borrowing was a critical component of Korea's export-led growth strategy. Until 1986, investment consistently outstripped domestic savings, and foreign borrowing was used to finance high and steadily increasing rates of domestic capital formation. High levels of investment proved critical not only in sustaining aggregate growth but in allowing Korea to exploit international market opportunities.

The openness of the economy also had an important consequence for policy, and even for politics. Korea's reliance on exports provided an important check on the range of policy options. In the late 1970s, President Park Chung Hee attempted to pursue an ambitious program of industrial deepening. Despite some successes, the misallocation of resources under the Heavy and Chemical Industry Plan, and its inflationary consequences, translated into a loss of competitiveness in international markets—an important signal to decision makers that policy adjustments were required. Korea's export orientation not only contributed to economic growth directly; it also contributed to a virtuous policy cycle. Significant departures from the pursuit of comparative advantage quickly became apparent to both business and the government. In political terms, the aggressive pursuit of export-led growth gave rise to the very forces in the private sector that acted to sustain that policy course.

Conclusion

Like many other countries, Korea was subjected to a number of serious shocks during the turbulent 1970s and 1980s: the large world oil price increases of 1974 and 1979–1980, the sharp rise in world interest rates over 1980–1982, and the strong appreciation of the dollar between 1981 and 1984. It also experienced the decline in the dollar, in oil prices, and in interest rates in 1986. In addition, Korea had two internally generated disturbances: the investment boom of 1976–1978 and the large harvest shortfall of 1980. Yet compared with most other developing countries, Korea's overall macroeconomic performance was outstanding during this period. Was it possibly due to the fact that the shocks hitting Korea were smaller in magnitude than those hitting other countries?

On the contrary, among large developing countries Korea experienced the largest external shocks relative to GDP in both 1974 and 1979–1981, 4.0 and 6.8 percent of prior-year GDP, respectively, taking into account movements both in the terms of trade and in interest rates during the second period (Table 1-2). Korea's ability to overcome these shocks relatively smoothly arose in part because it enjoyed a higher ratio of exports to GDP, reflecting its earlier export-oriented development strategy. As a result, the shocks were lower relative to exports than in some other countries. But Korea's performance was due mainly to its skillful handling of the adjustment process, including fiscal and exchange rate policy and the maintenance of high levels of investment.

Ironically, Korea's greatest difficulty arose in coping with the one major *positive* shock it experienced: the large payments surpluses of 1986–1988, arising in part from favorable external developments and in part from depreciating the won sharply in 1985. The emergence of large export surpluses stimulated a sharp increase in economic growth. The government was unable to neutralize the full effects of the export boom through monetary and fiscal action, which led to high wage demands and a resumption of inflation. It is admittedly difficult to separate these influences from those of political liberalization that occurred during the same period, which for the first time in many years allowed labor to organize and strike for higher wages and improved conditions of work.

Three broad themes run through our analysis. The first is the consistent tension between the political commitment to promote and sustain growth and the need—political as well as economic—to maintain price stability. As the history in Part II argues, Park Chung Hee sought to

Table 1-2. External Shocks (percentage of prior-year GDP)

	1974	1979–1981
Korea	−4.0	−6.8
Argentina	−0.9	−1.8
Brazil	−2.6	−5.2
Colombia	+0.9	−4.3
India	−0.9	−0.6
Mexico	−0.9	−0.3
Pakistan	−3.0	−1.8
Thailand	−0.8	−6.1
Turkey	−1.1	−1.9

Source: I.M.D. Little, R. Cooper, W.M. Corden, and S. Rajapatirana, *Boom, Crisis, and Adjustment: The Macroeconomic Experience of Developing Countries* (New York: Oxford University Press, 1993), Table 3.1, p. 30; Table 4.2, pp. 78–80, reproduced with permission.

legitimize an authoritarian style of rule by providing rapid growth. Yet there were also critical moments, particularly in 1979, when price increases themselves constituted a political liability, resulting in a shift in policy focus toward the reduction of inflation. Interestingly, President Chun Doo Hwan's pursuit of this new policy goal rested on political and administrative structures that showed surprising continuity with his successor. Not until the mid-1980s did new political constraints arise with the transition to democratic rule.

As the analysis in Part III shows, the focus on maintaining economic growth, even at the cost of rising inflation and growing external imbalances, was at the heart of the country's willingness to borrow to finance investment and to pursue countercyclical policies in the 1970s. Again, the shift in policy emphasis during the 1980s is evident.

A second broad finding is that Korea's macroeconomic policy was not wholly orthodox in its orientation. It is true that Korea stands out from many other developing countries in maintaining a relatively competitive and stable real exchange rate and in its fiscal conservatism, but the government also used the financial system to encourage high levels and particular patterns of investment. The reliance on various direct controls is also a striking feature of policy. The distinguishing feature of Korean macroeconomic management was the willingness to change policies—to adjust relatively quickly when a course appeared to be failing or creating serious collateral problems.

Korea also provides evidence of a virtuous cycle in policymaking that distinguishes it from other developing countries. Precisely because of the country's export-oriented strategy and high levels of investment, traditional stabilization measures during periods of adjustment were generally short-lived. After the 1979–1980 economic crisis, for example, Korea could afford to relax monetary and fiscal policies to restore growth; only after the economy revived did they turn more restrictive. Korea thus provides policy lessons for other developing countries, but it is important to underline that it does not provide an example of a country that restored economic growth after long periods of policy austerity, low investment, and poor performance, the situation facing many heavily indebted countries today.

A final theme returns us once again to politics: the role of disciplined centralized control in Korean policymaking. Centralized control helps account for Korea's disciplined fiscal and exchange rate policy, as well as the use of rationing and direct allocation as the means of conducting monetary policy. The major political challenge for Korea during the current period is to devise institutional arrangements that relax centralized control and increase the accountability of public officials, while also providing a new political basis for the continuation of sound policy.

NOTES

1. Among the most important studies that address macroeconomic policy for the period in question are E. Mason et al., *The Economic and Social Modernization of the Republic of Korea* (Cambridge: Harvard University Press, 1980); B. Aghevli and J. Márquez-Ruarte, *A Case of Successful Adjustment: Korea's Experience During 1980–84* (Washington, D.C.: International Monetary Fund, 1985); S. Collins and Won-Am Park, "External Debt and Macroeconomic Performance in South Korea," in J. Sachs and S. Collins, eds., *Developing Country Debt and Economic Performance,* vol. 3 (Chicago: University of Chicago Press, 1989), pp. 183–91; Soon Cho, *The Dynamics of the Korean Development Model* (Washington, D.C.: Institute of International Economics, forthcoming); V. Corbo and Sang-Mok Suh, eds., *Structural Adjustment in a Newly Industrialized Country: The Korean Experience* (Baltimore/London: Johns Hopkins University Press, a World Bank publication, 1992); R. Dornbusch and Yung-Chul Park, "Korean Growth Policy," *Brookings Papers of Economic Activity,* 2 (1987): 389–444; Il Sakong, *Korea in the World Economy* (Washington, D.C.: Institute for International Economics, 1993); Yung Chul Park, "Foreign Debt, Balance of Payments, and Growth Prospects: The Case of South Korea, 1965–1988," *World Development,* 14, 8 (1986): 1019–58; A. Amsden, *Asia's Next Giant* (New York: Oxford University Press, 1989), particularly pp. 79–114; B. Balassa and J. Williamson, *Adjusting to Success: Balance of Payments Policy in the East Asian NICs* (Washington, D.C.: Institute of International Economics, 1991); and Byung-Nak Song, *The Rise of the Korean Economy* (Hong Kong: Oxford University Press, 1990).

2. For a broad reconstruction of the Korean model that emphasizes its unorthodox elements, see A. Amsden, *Asia's Next Giant* (New York: Oxford University Press, 1989).

3. For an excellent view of contending political economy models, including those used by economists, see R. Bates, "Macropolitical Economy in the Field of Development," in J. Alt and K. Shepsle, eds., *Perspectives on Positive Political Economy* (New York: Cambridge University Press, 1990), pp. 31–54.

4. For surveys of political models of macroeconomic policy by economists, see A. Alesina, "Macroeconomics and Politics," in S. Fischer, ed.,

Macroeconomics Annual (Cambridge: MIT Press, 1988), pp. 13–51; and A. Alesina, "Political Models of Macroeconomic Policy and Fiscal Reforms," in S. Haggard and S. Webb, eds., *Voting for Reform: The Politics of Adjustment in New Democracies* (New York: Oxford University Press for the World Bank, forthcoming). For a sample of recent work by political scientists, see S. Haggard and R. Kaufman, eds., *The Politics of Economic Adjustment* (Princeton: Princeton University Press, 1992).

5. This factor is emphasized in a number of accounts of the Korean political economy. See Tun-Jen Cheng, "Political Regimes and Development Strategies: South Korea and Taiwan," in G. Gereffi and D. Wyman, eds., *Manufacturing Miracles* (Princeton: Princeton University Press, 1990), pp. 139–78; J. Cotton, "Understanding the State in South Korea: Bureaucratic Authoritarian or State Autonomy Theory?" *Comparative Political Studies,* 4, 4 (1992): 512–31; S. Haggard, Chung-In Moon, and Byung-Kook Kim, "The Transition to Export-led Growth in Korea, 1954–1966," *Journal of Asian Studies,* 50, 4 (1991): 850–73; C. Johnson, "Political Institutions and Economic Performance: Government-Business Relations in Japan, South Korea, and Taiwan," in F. Deyo, ed., *The Political Economy of the New Asian Industrialism* (Ithaca: Cornell University Press, 1987), pp. 136–64.

6. Chung-In Moon, "The Demise of the Developmentalist State? The Politics of Stabilization and Structural Adjustment," *Journal of Developing Societies,* 4 (1988): 67–84.

7. For a recent statement of this point, which links macroeconomic policy, the exchange rate, and export-led growth, see J. Sachs, "External Debt and Macroeconomic Performance in Latin America and East Asia," *Brookings Papers on Economic Activity,* 2 (1985): 523–64.

Part II

History:
The Political
Economy of
Macroeconomic
Policy in Korea

2

Macroeconomic Policy through the First Oil Shock 1970–1975

Stephan Haggard

Korea's strategy for adjusting to the first oil shock must be understood in the context of politically driven policy cycles that date to the late 1960s. Park Chung Hee justified military intervention in 1961 on economic grounds, and following the return to a nominally democratic system in 1964, he consistently sought electoral support on the basis of the government's economic record. This strategy served him well. The second half of the 1960s was a period of extremely rapid growth, and Park was reelected in 1967.

By 1969, however, Park Chung Hee's high-growth strategy faced important economic limitations: increasing pressure on real wages, a decline in international competitiveness, increasing current account deficits, and a sharp increase in external indebtedness. With assistance from the International Monetary Fund (IMF), an adjustment effort was launched in 1970.

Largely for political reasons, the stabilization effort proved to be short-lived. It occurred at a sensitive moment in the electoral cycle, prior to the hotly contested and highly controversial presidential election of 1971. Additionally, it contributed to broader political challenges to Park's rule and raised substantial protest from the private sector as well. The government quickly returned to a Keynesian approach to promoting growth, using an array of controls to keep prices in check.

As protest against the government continued, Park restructured politics in an explicitly authoritarian direction in late 1972 with the imposition of the Yushin, or "revitalizing," Constitution. This political change was followed by two major economic policy initiatives designed to secure new bases of political support: an ambitious Heavy and Chemical Industry Plan that benefited the largest Korean firms, or *chaebol,* and an expansion of the Saemaul (New Village) Movement, which improved rural welfare and cemented Park's standing among his conservative rural constituents.

The oil shock thus came at a sensitive point in Korea's political history, and the government chose the relatively risky strategy of borrowing heavily in international capital markets in 1974 and 1975 to maintain growth. Although Korea experienced some difficulty in borrowing, the strategy was vindicated by the recovery in Korea's major markets that began in the second half of 1975. This recovery set the stage for the resumption of the aggressive pursuit of heavy industrialization after 1976.

The Political Context of Adjustment

In 1961, the military came to power under Park Chung Hee's leadership, displacing the democratic but ineffectual government of Chang Myon.[1] Park launched far-reaching institutional reforms that centralized decision-making authority in the executive, including the creation of the Economic Planning Board (EPB), a purge of the bureaucracy, and an attack on the rent-seeking relationships that had developed among the bureaucracy, the ruling Liberal party, and the private sector during the 1950s.[2] Park returned the country to nominally democratic rule in 1964, but the legislature's role was limited and the opposition hampered by the government's use of emergency powers to quell dissent.

Under strong pressure from the United States, including the prospect of declining assistance, Park undertook difficult stabilization measures in 1963 and 1964.[3] These paved the way for the devaluation and unification of the exchange rate, crucial reforms in the turn toward an export-oriented strategy. Park used government control over the allocation of domestic credit and expanded foreign borrowing to support the turn to export-led growth, a strategy that also cemented political support for Park in the private sector.[4]

These policies were economically successful (Table 2-1). Initially, they also yielded political rewards. Park exploited the country's strong economic performance to justify his rule and argued explicitly that development should take precedence over fully democratic politics.[5] Park narrowly defeated a badly divided opposition in 1963; he ran on successful economic performance in 1967 and won 51.4 percent of the popular vote to 40.9 percent for the main opposition party.

Beginning in 1969, public disenchantment with the government once again increased. A major factor in the growth of the opposition was the passage of a constitutional amendment in 1969 that removed the two-term

Table 2-1. Background of Main Economic Indicators (percentages)

	1964–1965	1966–1967	1968–1969
Real GNP growth	7.8	11.1	13.5
Real GDP growth	7.7	9.0	12.6
Inflation	20.8	11.4	10.6
Real manufacturing wage growth	−0.1	7.8	17.6
Current account/GNP	−6.6	−8.6	−10.9
Real export growth	39.0	26.0	43.0
Debt/GNP	6.9	15.1	27.2
Debt service	5.0	5.4	8.6
Gross fixed capital formation/GDP	13.2	21.2	25.7
Private gross fixed capital formation/GDP	9.5	16.3	18.5
General budget deficit/GNP (−)	1.4	1.3	0.5
Central budget deficit/GNP (−)	N.A.	−0.6	−0.8
M2 growth[a]	52.7	61.7	66.7
Domestic credit growth[a]	40.1	54.3	72.0
Terms of trade (1980 = 100)	113.3	130.0	135.2

[a] 1964 only.
Source: EPB, *Korean Statistical Yearbook,* various issues; debt, Bank of Korea.

limit on the presidency.[6] The amendment increased fears (which ultimately proved valid) that Park was planning to seize political power on a permanent basis. A second issue of concern was the close relationship that had developed among the government, the ruling party, and the largest private enterprises. A series of political scandals in the mid-1960s confirmed that firms receiving government favors, particularly through the state-owned banking system, provided financial support for the ruling party.[7] The corruption of the business-government nexus *(chungkyung yuchak)* became a major opposition theme, and remained so into the 1990s.

Park's political difficulties were compounded by the slowdown in economic activity in 1970 and 1971 associated with the government's stabilization efforts as well as several broader socioeconomic trends associated with the growth strategy of the 1960s. These trends had two important political effects: they increased antigovernment protest, and they challenged Park's electoral strategy of relying on secure rural votes.

One source of challenge to the government was from the rapidly growing urban working class.[8] Real wages grew extremely rapidly from 1967 through 1969 but slowed beginning in 1970 (Table 2-2). Official data on the total number of labor disputes does not indicate a trend toward growing labor militancy. The number of strikes reached a high for the 1960s of 135 in 1968, dropped to 94 in 1969 and 90 in 1970, and increased somewhat to 104 in 1971. But these figures are misleading, since the number of participants in strike actions increased sharply and the nature of the conflicts changed.[9] A number of politically and emotionally

Table 2-2. Main Economic Indicators, 1969–1976 (percentages)

	1969	1970	1971	1972	1973	1974	1975	1976
Real GNP growth	13.8	7.6	9.1	5.3	14.0	8.5	6.8	13.4
Real GDP growth	13.8	8.8	9.2	5.9	14.4	7.9	6.5	13.2
Inflation[a]	10.0	12.7	12.3	11.8	3.1	23.6	26.3	15.3
General budget deficit/GNP (−)[b]	0.3	0.2	−0.9	−3.2	−0.1	−2.0	−1.7	−0.9
Central budget deficit/GNP (−)	−2.0	−0.8	−0.3	−3.9	−0.5	−2.2	−2.0	−1.4
Fiscal impulse[c]	N.A.	N.A.	1.3	1.7	−2.2	2.1	0.2	−1.2
M2 growth[d]	61.4	27.4	20.8	33.8	36.4	24.0	28.2	33.5
Domestic credit growth[d]	59.2	26.5	31.1	30.4	31.7	54.2	32.2	21.7
Consumer price index deflated wage[e]	N.A.	4.7	2.8	5.0	8.1	6.7	2.5	17.6
Current account/GNP[f]	−10.6	−9.1	−10.5	−5.1	−3.7	−12.1	−10.3	−2.6
Real export growth[g]	40.3	27.7	29.2	51.8	55.8	9.5	23.2	35.4
Real exchange index[h]	N.A.	N.A.	N.A.	106.6	89.9	91.1	91.0	100.6
Debt/GNP[i]	N.A.	24.6	27.1	30.2	29.3	27.2	31.2	27.9
Terms of trade: (1980 = 100)[j]	132.8	134.2	132.9	132.2	125.4	102.1	92.2	105.2
Gross fixed capital formation/GDP	26.1	23.0	21.5	19.9	23.2	25.1	24.9	24.0
Private gross fixed capital formation/GDP[k]	18.2	16.8	15.8	14.7	18.2	21.2	18.8	19.3

[a]The change in the Seoul CPI, which is year average prices.
[b]The total public sector deficit, general government plus nonfinancial public enterprises.
[c]From V. Corbo and Sang-Woo Nam, "The Recent Economic Evolution of the Republic of Korea," in Corbo and Sang-Mok Suh, eds. *Structural Adjustment in a Newly Industrializing Country: The Korean Experience* (Baltimore: Johns Hopkins University Press, 1992), p. 47.
[d]M2 and domestic credit are year-end to year-end.
[e]Real wages are all industry monthly earnings deflated by CPI.
[f]Current account is the national accounts exports of goods and services less imports of goods and services less net factor payments abroad.
[g]Real exports is the export quantum index.
[h]Real exchange rate is the Morgan Guaranty real exchange rate index; 1980/82 = 100.
[i]Debt is year-end total long- and short-term debt, both private and public.
[j]The terms of trade is the ratio of the export unit value index to the import unit value index.
[k]Gross fixed capital formation (GFCF); private GFCF is total less government GFCF.
Sources: Economic Planning Board, *Korean Statistical Yearbook* and *Major Statistics of the Korean Economy,* various issues; International Monetary Fund, *International Financial Statistics,* various issues; and World Bank, *World Bank Tables,* various issues.

charged labor actions occurred during this period, including two highly visible disputes with foreign-invested electronics firms in 1968, an industry-wide strike by textile workers, a prolonged strike by metal workers at the government-run Korean Shipbuilding Corporation, and most dramatic, the self-immolation by Tai-il Jeon in November 1970 in protest of poor working conditions in the small factories in the Seoul Peace Market area.[10]

Business leaders and technocrats expressed concern about the effects of rising real wages and labor activism on competitiveness and foreign direct investment.[11] The government responded by forming a committee on labor policy in 1969. The committee recommended even greater government supervision of unions, which were already informally penetrated by the government and management, and Park called on workers to exercise restraint in the name of continued export growth. The Federation of Korean Trade Unions, under increasing pressure from its shop-floor base, not only openly rejected the plea but threatened to create "political education" committees to increase labor's power.

The government feared that labor militancy would upset the investment climate, and on January 1, 1970, a law established separate settlement procedures for industrial disputes in foreign-invested firms that included compulsory arbitration and limits on the freedom to strike. The 1970 law presaged the tight restrictions on strikes and collective bargaining that followed the declaration of a state of emergency in December 1971.

Urban marginalism posed a second political threat to the government, particularly given the growing interest of church groups, such as the Urban Industrial Mission, in organizing in the urban slum areas. Industrialization induced migration from the countryside, and though employment growth was rapid, settlement in Seoul's slum districts increased. The government cleared several slum areas by force, resettling their residents in Kwangju, a suburb south of Seoul. In August 1971, a riot erupted in this area that involved an estimated 30,000 people. Protesting poor infrastructure and the lack of job opportunities, the rioters attacked government facilities, including police stations.

From an electoral perspective, perhaps the most daunting challenge to the government was the combination of a declining rural vote share and the widening gap in incomes between the rural and urban areas. Park's electoral strategy had centered on courting conservative rural voters. In the 1967 election this strategy worked, but poor agricultural performance threatened to erode the margin of rural electoral support needed to offset the growing middle- and working-class opposition in the cities.

Electoral concerns about the loyalty of rural areas had clear policy consequences. In an important decision, the government reversed its grain pricing policy in 1969, paying increasing prices to farmers for rice and barley.[12] This decision to subsidize producers had long-term implications for fiscal policy (see Chapter 5). Although central government accounts tended to balance, the Grain Management Fund was consistently in substantial deficit, financed by borrowing from the Bank of Korea. Concern about rural support was also responsible for the launching of the Saemaul Movement in 1971, an effort to channel resources to self-improvement projects in selected villages.[13] In combination, these policies did appear to have some effect on the welfare of farm households. The percentage of the population on farms stabilized between 1970 and 1974, and the gap between urban and rural household incomes steadily narrowed.[14]

These economic grievances and the fear that Park Chung Hee was amassing near-dictatorial powers were exploited by Kim Dae-Jung in his bid for the presidency in 1971.[15] Kim's campaign was explicitly populist. In addition to political reforms that would move the country in a more openly democratic direction, Kim pressed an economic program that included a more equitable distribution of income, a workers' stock ownership plan, agricultural reforms, and new taxes on the wealthy.

Kim also played on emerging regional disparities. Although extremely rapid growth can be expected to generate regional imbalances, government appointments, the allocation of resources, and planning decisions, such as the location of industrial estates, made them worse because they favored the growth of Park's native Kyongsang provinces over the less-developed Cholla region. The two Cholla provinces showed the slowest rate of overall growth in the late 1960s, and became a bastion of the opposition.[16]

The 1971 elections, criticized by the opposition and outside observers for large-scale government interference and fraud, showed a narrowing base of support for Park. In 1967, Park had led in both the rural and urban areas, but in 1971, Park lost narrowly in the urban areas.[17] The National Assembly elections in May proved a further setback to the government. Despite the financial and organizational weaknesses of the opposition New Democratic party, it managed to capture all but one seat in Seoul's nineteen districts and forty-six of sixty-five seats in all urban areas. The ruling party's legislative majority rested on large margins in the rural areas (sixty-seven to nineteen), and overwhelming victories in Park's native Kyongsang provinces.

Emboldened by its stronger electoral showing, the opposition party demanded a greater role in, and for, the legislature. A variety of groups— students, professors, and judges, among them—showed their displeasure with the Park regime. In December 1971, Park Chung Hee declared a state of emergency, and on October 17, 1972, martial law.[18] Citing the irresponsibility of political parties, military threats from the north, and changes in the regional security setting following President Richard Nixon's opening to China, Park dissolved the National Assembly, banned all political parties, closed the colleges, and instituted a tight system of press censorship. An Extraordinary State Council took over all legislative functions. A referendum on a new constitution was held in November under martial law conditions; with a virtual ban on opposition, Park received an overwhelming 92.3 percent of the votes. The new Constitution mixed presidential and parliamentary systems along French lines, but Park gained the power to appoint one-third of the National Assembly delegates and to dissolve the legislature at any time. In 1974 and 1975, a series of emergency decrees limited still further the range of political activity and moved the regime in a more openly repressive direction.

The features of the political setting that are important for understanding macroeconomic policy during the early 1970s can now be summarized. First, rising political opposition and electoral pressures were an important constraint on macroeconomic policy and contributed to the turn away from the stabilization policies adopted in 1970. Second, Park's powers were dramatically strengthened following the state of emergency and declaration of martial law. As will be shown in more detail in the next chapter, the Yushin system also affected the nature of decision making within the government, reducing the checks on executive discretion that had previously come from the economic ministries and high-ranking technocrats.

Nonetheless, political calculations continued to affect economic decision making after the state of emergency and transition to martial law, in part because Park himself justified the Yushin system on developmental grounds. This political context generated strong pressures for expansionist policies.

From Rapid Growth to Short-Lived Stabilization

To understand the government's response to the first oil shock demands a reconstruction of trends in the economy dating from the late 1960s, when Korea began to face several major economic difficulties (see Table 2-2). The first was a precipitous rise in the burden of external debt.[19] Despite Korea's exemplary export performance, the debt service ratio on long-term debt jumped from 7.8 percent in 1969 to 18.2 percent in 1970, an increase that mirrored consistently high levels of investment relative to savings. Gross fixed investment increased from less than 15 percent of gross national product (GNP) in 1965 to 26 percent in 1969. Although fixed investment declined slightly as a share of GNP in 1970 and 1971, inventory accumulation increased and remained high through 1971.[20] Domestic savings dropped by 3 percent of GNP between 1969 and 1970 and remained roughly constant for three years.

Another complex of problems centered on wage and exchange rate developments. Between 1966 and 1970, nominal wages rose by over 160 percent and real wages by 65 percent.[21] The nominal exchange rate depreciated by less than 15 percent, however. Gauging the resultant loss of competitiveness depends on the productivity series used. The Korea Productivity Center (KPC) measures show productivity increasing by 101.1 percent during the period, implying a 14.4 percent increase in unit labor costs, measured in dollars. Using the value-added index, however, productivity grew much more slowly, implying a 50.8 percent increase in unit labor costs.

In response to these problems, a number of prominent foreign-trained economists argued that greater emphasis should be placed on price stability. Nam Duck Woo, who became finance minister in 1969, and Mahn-Je Kim, first head of the Korean Development Institute, argued for a 3 percent cap on price increases, to be achieved by a variety of measures, including a freeze on the prices of public services.[22] In 1970, stabilization measures were launched to reverse the expansion of credit and money that had accompanied the 1969 referendum on Park's ability to stand for a third term of office. The rate of domestic credit expansion was cut from nearly 95 percent a year in 1969 to 29 percent in 1970, and foreign borrowing limits were imposed. Real growth rates declined, as did the growth of imports, particularly capital goods imports, resulting in a dampening of capital formation. Export growth, although still unusually high by comparative standards, slowed from its average 36 percent increase in 1968–1969 to 27 percent in 1970–1971.

Under standby agreements with the IMF in 1970 and 1971, fiscal and monetary policy were constrained. In June, after the presidential and National Assembly elections, the exchange rate was devalued. After an initial 13 percent devaluation relative to the dollar, the won was allowed to depreciate gradually until June 1972, when the exchange rate was fixed at 400 won to the dollar, still above the 450 won to the dollar that the IMF had sought in its June 1971 review of Korea's standby.[23] Given the adjustments of the dollar in relation to other currencies in the wake of the breakdown of Bretton Woods, the won depreciated by 11.9 percent in real terms between 1970 and 1972, and a further 15.6 percent in 1973. Although unit labor costs continued to rise when measured in won, in dollar terms they fell by 19 percent from 1970 to 1973 using the KPC index, or 5 percent using the value-added index.

The Return to an Emphasis on Growth

Beginning in 1972, political and economic pressures combined to reverse the stabilization effort, and monetary and fiscal policies turned in a more expansionist direction. The growing volatility of Korean politics in the postelection period no doubt affected the judgment of a government that had relied on economic performance to gain political support. In 1972, the growth rate, 5.8 percent, fell far short of the government's 9 percent target. Pressures on macroeconomic policy also came from two specific quarters. First, food grain production was low between 1970 and 1973, with harvests in 1971 being particularly disappointing. As a result, the government's Grain Management Fund ran large deficits, financed by domestic credit expansion.

The second set of pressures came from business. Korean firms have historically been highly leveraged. They were encouraged to borrow abroad to finance imports by the interest rate differential between local and foreign loans and corporate tax provisions that made interest payments on business borrowings deductible. But they were forced to borrow locally on the curb market, usually short term, because of the absence of any financial institutions that provided long-term finance.

The combination of stabilization efforts and devaluation forced many firms with foreign debts close to bankruptcy. Business uncertainty was compounded by the "Nixon shock" of August 15, 1971, which marked the beginning of the end for the fixed exchange rate system, followed in September by new American restraints on East Asian textile exports. Fixed investment for the fourth quarter of 1971 dropped precipitously—nearly 18 percent from the corresponding period in 1970. In the latter part of 1971, the Federation of Korean Industries (FKI), representing the largest Korean firms, lobbied against the "dogmatic" efforts to achieve price stability, calling the top technocratic team, and Nam Duck Woo in particular, "contractionist."[24]

In January 1972, the government approached the United States, Japan, and the World Bank for financial assistance, arguing that Korea's problems were the result of external circumstance, including increased debt service costs associated with currency realignments, declining invisible receipts from Korean troops in Vietnam, and the slowing of world trade following the Nixon shock. The U.S. view, however, was that Korea's own policy was partly to blame. The United States would extend further assistance but wanted to see increased IMF involvement and changes in policy.[25] In consultations in March, the IMF argued that progress could not be made without further depreciation and a dismantling of import restrictions and export subsidies. The United States sided with this assessment but nonetheless agreed to extend additional assistance, in part as compensation for new limits on Korea's textile exports.

Despite improvement in the balance of payments by mid-1972, profits declined and business debt mounted. Partly to avoid jeopardizing

Korea's standing in international credit markets, the government elected to bail out ailing firms as part of the wide-ranging Emergency Measures Regarding Economic Stability and Growth of August 3, 1972.[26] The government adopted proposals from the FKI and replaced all existing agreements between firms and unofficial lenders with new ones more favorable to the borrowers. The measures mitigated the difficulties of debt-ridden firms and effectively shifted the burden of the financial crisis onto the highly dispersed curb market.[27] At the same time, however, reformers within the economic bureaucracy took advantage of the crisis to develop domestic financial markets by providing the legal foundation for the creation of short-term finance companies, credit unions, and mutual savings banks.

To stimulate investment, controlled bank loan rates were lowered significantly, on the assumption, debated at the time, that prices would stabilize. The rate on loans up to one year was dropped from 19 percent to 15.5 percent and deposit rates from 16.8 percent to 12 percent. Approximately 30 percent of the short-term commercial bank loans to business were rescheduled, with longer terms and lower rates. Over the longer run, the disparity in interest rates between the formal and informal markets and the return to more active credit rationing provided new opportunities for the informal financial sector. In the short run, however, the curb market, which accounted for 34 percent of outstanding domestic credit in the banking system, virtually disappeared.[28]

Addressing the weakened financial structures of major firms was only one motivation behind the emergency measures. A second was stabilizing prices, which had not responded to government stabilization efforts. The rate of growth of the consumer price index fell modestly from 15.9 percent in 1970 to 13.5 percent in 1971 to 11.7 percent in 1972, but food and beverage prices were increasing at a much more rapid rate—21.4 percent in 1970, 18.9 percent in 1971, and 13.3 percent in 1972—and wholesale prices actually rose more rapidly in 1972 than in 1971.

In controlling prices, the emergency decree is striking for the emphasis it placed on direct controls. A freeze on the prices of all commodities was announced, with cost-push pressures to be offset by indirect subsidies. The Office of National Tax Administration set up an extensive network of price checkers, with violators subject to special tax audit, curtailment of credit, and excess profits taxes.[29]

When producers resorted to various measures to circumvent the controls, production quotas were attempted with daily checks on the activities of major producers. In March 1973, a law on price stability was passed prohibiting sales at greater than ceiling prices and prohibiting restricted shipments. Not until February 1974, in response to the oil shock, were these restrictions eased, and even then prior approval was still required for price increases and a number of items remained subject to direct controls.

The emergency measures also sought to rationalize the industrial structure.[30] Criteria were established to target certain industries for preferential credit, tax, and administrative treatment. These criteria were extremely wide, leaving discretion to the new Industrial Rationalization Council, established under the prime minister's office, in supporting particular firms and projects. Seventy-two percent of the total 50 billion won Industrial Rationalization Fund was released by the end of 1973, and of that, 75 percent went to facility expansion in key industries such as electric power, steel, polyvinyl chlorides, and sectors producing intermediates. Only 4 percent of the fund went to small- and medium-sized industries. Despite the rhetorical emphasis placed on the importance of the small enterprise sector, industrial policy leaned toward greater concentration and emphasis on heavy and chemical industries.[31]

This bias toward big business became clear with the announcement of the Heavy and Chemical Industry Plan in early 1973, the first economic initiative of the new Yushin system. In his new year's address in January, typically a major political statement, Park outlined an ambitious vision for the Yushin regime: $10 billion in exports and a per capita income of $1,000 by the early 1980s. The key to the new phase of growth was an emphasis on heavy and chemical industries: iron and steel, machinery, nonferrous metals, electronics, shipbuilding, and petrochemicals.

The emphasis on an expansion of the heavy industry sector was not new and had been a prominent feature of the third five-year plan (1972–1976), issued in 1971. Yet the economic justification for the new heavy and chemical plan drew on a more pessimistic assessment of the slowdown in growth of the early 1970s. Rather than reflecting a cyclical pattern, the Korean economy was seen to face basic structural problems, including rising protection, increasing competition from low-wage producers in export markets, and inadequate firm size.[32] By diversifying aggressively into heavy industries, Korea would not only substitute for imports in intermediate goods but could achieve the scale economies required for competitive exports.

The plan also had a domestic political rationale as the first initiative of the new Yushin regime. Yet as a number of studies of the plan have noted, military calculations probably weighed most heavily in Park's own calculations.[33] Nixon's Guam Doctrine of 1969 appeared to signal American retreat from East Asia and was followed closely by the withdrawal of one infantry division from Korea in March 1971. Heavy industries such as steel and machinery would form the core of a defense-industrial complex capable of guaranteeing Korea's defense self-reliance.

The decision-making structure surrounding the plan deserves close scrutiny, since it established the key intrabureaucratic cleavages of the late 1970s, contributed to the incoherence of macroeconomic policy, and was an important factor behind the increasing intervention of the state in the economy.[34] During the first half of 1973, the Heavy and Chemical Industry Plan (HCIP) was drafted by a small working group centered in the Blue House. Working closely with the industry-oriented Ministry of Commerce and Industry, the formulation of the plan bypassed both the EPB and the Ministry of Finance. The plan was released in May, at which time a Heavy and Chemical Industry Promotion Committee was formed under the Office of the Prime Minister. This organizational arrangement was unusual. The committee included all the major economic ministers but departed from the usual practice of centering economic policy coordination around the chairman of the EPB, who concurrently held the position of deputy prime minister.

In September, the Heavy and Chemical Industry Planning Council was formed, which later came under the direction of Second Presidential Economic Secretary Oh Won Chul, an engineer with a decade of experience in the industrial bureaucracy. Oh was a strong advocate of an extremely activist, even mobilizational industrial policy that would involve the government in detailed sectoral planning. The planning council was an extremely powerful body. Designed to provide staff work to the committee, it also was the center of various interministerial working groups designed to assist implementation of the plan and the main point of contact for consultations with big business over specific projects.

Numerous instruments were deployed in support of the plan, but the central policy instrument was preferential credit.[35] Although managed by the banks, the allocation of funds was largely in the hands of the planning council and, ultimately, with the president himself, who exercised final approval over major projects. The plan, and the system for managing it, thus had important implications for the conduct of macroeconomic policy, since crucial decisions affecting the level and allocation of credit took place outside the normal planning channels in which EPB and the Ministry of Finance played a more central role (see Chapter 6).

Scheduled investments far outstripped anticipated savings and existing sources such as the government pension fund. In 1974, the Ministry of Finance created a massive National Investment Fund through mandatory deposits from financial institutions. Modeled on the Japanese postal savings system, the immediate aim of the fund was to finance the HCIP. For the Ministry of Finance, however, it also served the political function of setting some limits on the ambition of the industrial planners in a bureaucratic context in which direct opposition to the initiative was impossible.

Several features of Korean policy prior to the first shock are noteworthy. The country had launched a stabilization episode in 1970, but political pressures contributed to its reversal and the return to a countercyclical policy stance. The style of economic management moved to emphasize direct controls and intervention, including a reversal of the financial liberalization that had characterized the economy since the mid-1960s and across-the-board price controls. A new level of government intervention was particularly visible in the ambitious effort to diversify into energy-intensive heavy and chemical industries.

The Response to the First Oil Shock

The year 1973 was an extremely favorable one for the Korean economy. Exports and output boomed, the debt situation improved, domestic savings rose, and the current account deficit as a share of GNP continued to fall. This outstanding performance can be attributed in part to the lagged effects of depreciation and expansionary monetary policies, but high levels of investment in export industries allowed Korea to exploit favorable external conditions when they returned during 1973.

Nonetheless, concerns about increases in the prices of raw materials and the growth of resource nationalism were apparent by mid-1973, even though oil price increases were not visible until October. In December, the government encouraged the import and stockpiling of raw materials by extending special financial assistance to importers and reducing tariffs on a number of essential goods, including crude oil, raw cotton, wheat, and logs. In late December, the Blue House economic secretariat began an effort to produce a more comprehensive policy response. The work involved only a handful of advisers from the Korean Development Institute and selected technocrats; at the ministerial level, it is said that only the finance minister was aware of the policy exercise.[36]

The precise sequence of policy measures is worth elaborating in some detail, since it suggests a close relationship between economic and political considerations. The response to the shock demonstrates both the ability of the government to act swiftly and decisively in undertaking unpopular measures, such as raising revenue and passing on price increases, and a clear concern to limit political damage by compensating those hardest hit by the adjustment.

On January 8, Emergency Decrees Nos. 1 and 2 were promulgated, aimed at halting a growing nationwide movement for a revision of the authoritarian Yushin Constitution.[37] The first decree made it illegal to defame the constitution or to advocate its revision, and the second set up a system of courts-martial for arresting and trying violators, with penalties ranging up to fifteen years' imprisonment. The authoritarian Yushin regime was clearly entering a phase of more directly repressive rule.

Within a week, on January 14, Park announced Presidential Emergency Decree No. 3, a curious mixture of stabilization measures and a commitment to address the distributional consequences of pending price increases.[38] This decree, entitled the Presidential Emergency Measures for the Stabilization of National Life, announced the intention to cut the 847 billion won budget for fiscal 1974 by 50 billion won, a decrease of nearly 6 percent. On February 25, a $40 million IMF standby also committed the government to hold money supply increases to 30 percent and domestic credit expansion to 32.2 percent.

These announced austerities were matched in Decree No. 3 by policies to reduce the effects of the price shocks on low-income households and small- and medium-sized businesses. Income taxes were eliminated for low-income workers, and contributions to a compulsory national welfare pension scheme aimed at providing for social welfare and increasing the pool of funds available for the Heavy and Chemical Industry Plan were deferred. Government salaries were increased 10 percent, and a 10 billion won fund was established to increase employment. The purchase price for 1973 rice was also increased. Employees having claims for back wages, a growing source of labor discontent, would be paid and strong punitive measures taken against violators of regulations on working conditions.

To finance these measures, new taxes were imposed on individuals in upper-income brackets and to capture windfall profits for the government. Customs duties on alcohol and autos were increased by two-thirds, and commodity taxes raised on a number of "luxury" items that included not only jewelry, furs, and expensive watches but virtually all consumer durables. Although price controls subsequently were lifted, the decree underlined a commitment to maintain stability in the prices of rice, barley, coal briquettes, and other necessities and outlined broad discretionary measures against illegal price increases, including a 100 percent excess profits tax. The new revenue measures more than offset the cost of the measures designed to assist lower-income workers and the incentives to small- and medium-sized firms.[39]

On February 1, Gulf, Caltex, and Union, the three groups that controlled Korean oil imports and refining, were granted an immediate 82 percent price increase on petroleum products.[40] Large price adjustments were also permitted in electricity rates and transportation charges.

The government's expectations of the effects of the oil price increases on the balance of payments were spelled out in the annual overall resource budget for the year. Announced in February, the resource budget provided the government's projections for investment, external payments, and public finance based on a target growth rate. The target growth rate of 8 percent demanded a ratio of investment to GNP only slightly lower than that in 1973: 26.4 percent versus 25.8 percent. Government investment—in forestry and agriculture, heavy and chemical industries, and social overhead—would compensate for an anticipated fall in private investment. The government anticipated that domestic savings to GNP would drop from 21 percent to 18 percent, however, meaning a rise in required foreign savings from 4.9 percent of GNP to 7.8 percent.

The shortfall in domestic savings showed up in the projected balance of payments as an increase in the current account deficit of $1 billion. To cover this deficit while increasing reserves by 10 percent, $1.4 billion of foreign capital was to be sought, consisting of $900 million in long-term loans, $200 million in direct investment, and the remaining $300 million from short-term capital and trade credits. In late March, the Consultative Group on Development Assistance to Korea, a multilateral group including aid donors and representatives of international financial institutions, reviewed these projections. While expressing concern about the effects of the oil crisis, the consultative group supported Korea's plans.[41]

The rapid pace of growth in 1973 carried over to the first half of 1974. Aided by continuing demand for exports, the anticipation of price increases, and the relatively smooth management of raw materials imports, the economy grew at a rate of 15.3 percent in the first half. The government's projected economic policy for the second half of 1974 announced continued aggregate demand restraint, but signs of weakening in the economy and the fact that the increase in the money supply was only 6.9 percent in the first half led to an announcement that monetary policy would be more flexible in the second half.

With growing evidence of a slowdown in growth, Korean macroeconomic policy once again turned in a countercyclical direction. The government planned an early release of 40 billion won of the government's 100 billion won fall crop purchase fund during September and October, generally a slack period in the government's crop purchase activity. The budget deficit as a share of GNP jumped from 1.6 percent of GNP in 1973 to 4.0 percent in 1974 and 4.6 percent in 1975. Adjusted measures of the fiscal impulse show a particularly strong expansion in 1974.[42] Monetary policy for the year managed to remain within the IMF guidelines, partly because of the contraction in the foreign sector in the second half. Domestic credit, however, increased at 53.8 percent, well above IMF targets, as a result of the large deficit in the Grain Management Fund, the substantial preferential financing of raw material inventory accumulation, and an increase in the special funds for low-income employment and small- and medium-sized firms.

By the late spring and early summer of 1974, it had become clear that initial balance-of-payments targets would not be met. Exports would ultimately exceed the annual target, but imports and invisible payments were $800 million more than projected. The decision was made to borrow through the crisis.[43] The debt stock increased by $4.2 billion from 1973 to 1975, pushing the debt-to-GNP ratio from 31.5 percent to 40.6 percent.

The government's borrowing strategy had both a short-term and a long-term component. In 1973, the EPB had planned to reduce Korea's short-term borrowing, which moved from 10.8 percent of total borrowing in 1969 to an average of 16.8 over 1970–1973. In 1974, this ratcheted up again to 20.9 percent, reaching 28.5 percent in 1975. Reserve policy also changed. In 1973, the goal was to maintain levels of reserves at 19 percent of current transactions. This plan was revised to maintain reserves at 15 percent of current transactions.

Efforts to induce longer-term capital proved more mixed. Despite new sectoral and equity restrictions on foreign direct investment in 1973, the inflow of foreign direct investment exceeded projections in both 1973 and 1974. Historically, however, Korea was not particularly open to foreign direct investment; the share of direct investment in long-term capital flows in 1974, for example, was only 12 percent. Over time, efforts to induce long-term capital from the oil exporters led to a range of lucrative construction contracts and joint ventures, particularly with Saudi Arabia, but these efforts yielded little in 1974.

A renewed effort to secure long-term finance from the commercial banks began in the spring of 1974 when Finance Minister Nam Duck Woo began to explore the possibility of major balance of payments financing through the Eurodollar markets. Nam hoped that Korea would be able to borrow at 1 percent over the London interbank offered rate (LIBOR), a rate that Korea had been able to secure in 1973. But South Korean firms seeking project finance were already paying higher rates, and the presence of other South Korean borrowers in the market constrained the government; subsequently, a Ministry of Finance steering committee was formed to coordinate public and private sector borrowing.

In mid-August, Nam once again opened discussions with Chase Manhattan.[44] The negotiations were continued at the IMF meetings and at presentations to major New York banks by Nam's successor at the Ministry of Finance, Yong Hwan Kim. Negotiations were protracted by the banks' demand for detailed information on the assumptions underlying balance-of-payments forecasts and over a series of issues concerning the loan itself: the loan's rate and term and the identity of the borrower. As the banks ran into difficulties completing the syndication, it became clear that the loan would not be approved before year's end, and Korea persuaded the major banks to advance a $100 million bridge loan. The $200 million syndication was finally signed in March 1975, with a rate of 2 percentage points over LIBOR.

Although the loan was viewed as a success at the time, it reflected the general difficulty developing countries faced in raising commercial balance-of-payments lending. In addition to general economic conditions, the borrowing effort was probably hurt by the diplomatic conflict with Japan over the kidnapping of Kim Dae-Jung, the leading figure in the opposition; there was no Japanese participation in the $200 million syndication. The draconian nature of Park's emergency decrees and continued opposition to his rule were also concerns. The opposition was gaining congressional sympathy in the United States, and calls were made for a review of U.S. military assistance. Dependence on the IMF, including the Oil Facility, and assistance from major allies, including a large $207 million Export-Import Bank loan for construction of a fertilizer plant in August 1973, remained crucial to balance-of-payments financing.

In October 1974, the cabinet was reshuffled, bringing Nam Duck Woo to prominence as the deputy prime minister. New controls were placed on foreign exchange, but on December 7, the won was devalued 21 percent against the dollar, a move pressed for several months by the private sector.[45] A new round of countercyclical policy measures were also announced. Sixty percent of the total budget appropriations for 1975 were to be released early in the year, an additional 50 billion-won fund was opened for investment in plant and equipment, and 90 percent of all government procurement for the year would be undertaken during the first six months. Firms borrowing abroad on a long-term basis would be granted special loans to meet additional debt-servicing burdens, a move designed to preempt the problems associated with the previous devaluation. As in the past, the Grain Management Fund recorded a substantial deficit. Price policy also followed the previous mixed pattern; on the one hand, further increases of 42 percent were allowed in electricity rates, 31 percent for petroleum products, and 39 percent in railways fares, but fifty-eight items needed prior government approval for price increases.

In addition to the devaluation, a wide array of new supports were granted to exporters. Before the devaluation, a six-month tax deferment was granted to troubled export industries. In late April, a new round of measures was announced, including further cuts in the interest rates on local currency export finance and an extension of the maturing on loans to finance raw materials imports. In September, an ambitious program was announced to create general trading companies along the Japanese model through a variety of incentives.

Given the policy stance of the government in the face of the first oil shock, there has been some debate over the determinants of the balance of payments during this period. In a provocative analysis, Y. C. Park argues that the terms-of-trade deterioration was not the most important factor in accounting for the current account deficit, which went from 2.9 percent of GNP in 1972–1973 to 10.8 percent and 9.1 percent of GNP in 1974 and 1975, respectively. He finds that increased nonoil imports were almost twice as important.[46] Because many of these imports are attributable to the "big push" of the Heavy and Chemical Industry Plan, Park concludes that this internal policy shift outweighed external factors in explaining the poor current account outcome.

Park's results probably overestimate the contribution of increased nonoil import volume effects and underestimate the contribution of external price developments. Park relies on indexes for unit value and volume for capital goods and other imports that are not reliable. Alternative decompositions by Collins and Park and Corbo and Nam show that the terms-of-trade deterioration is, in fact, a major factor explaining the 1974–1975 current account imbalance. In the Collins and Park study, the rise in oil and commodity prices accounts for 90 percent of the imbalance in 1974 and over 100 percent in 1975. The impact of the import volume changes is quite small in 1974 (6 percent) and even contributes to an improvement in the 1975 current account equivalent to 14 percent of the imbalance.[47] In the Corbo and Nam study, the recession in the advanced industrial countries and the terms-of-trade deterioration accounted for 49 percent and 57 percent, respectively, of the total cumulative impact of the first oil shock on the current account between 1973 and 1975 and were responsible for an increase in Korea's external debt of $2.2 billion and $2.6 billion, respectively, by the end of 1975.[48]

Nonetheless, the intuition behind Y. C. Park's analysis is worth exploring: Why did the government adopt such an aggressive adjustment strategy? We turn to this issue by way of conclusion.

Conclusion

This chapter has suggested that macroeconomic policy was influenced by recurrent, though shifting, political pressures. Political challenges were one reason for the reversal of the short-lived stabilization effort of 1970 and the turn toward a growth strategy that relied heavily on direct controls, a more interventionist industrial policy style, and renewed foreign borrowing. This strategy was designed in part to support a political system that had moved in a more explicitly authoritarian direction; this system, in turn, had important implications for the content and conduct of subsequent economic policy.

The oil shock naturally called into question the assumptions behind the heavy industry plan. The World Bank had expressed skepticism about the HCIP in early 1974, particularly the plan's export projections. An economic advisory board formed by Park Chung Hee that was composed mostly of university professors argued that growth targets should be lowered, greater emphasis should be placed on price stability, and the Heavy and Chemical Industry Plan should be scaled back.[49] The EPB, though skeptical, accommodated itself to the plan, arguing for greater flexibility in the implementation of particular projects.[50] The Ministry of Commerce and Industry, though arguing for the expansion of the electronic and shipbuilding portions of the plan, also recognized that greater emphasis would have to be given to energy conservation.[51]

There were, inevitably, some adjustments in the plan. In February 1974, the plans for a second steel mill were scrapped, and the Japanese firm Mitsui announced its intention to withdraw from its plan to participate in the Ryochun petrochemical facility.[52] Overall, however, both the HCIP and the government's commitment to a countercyclical policy remained intact. This was a course pursued by a number of developing countries, and the availability of international finance in itself constitutes a powerful explanation for this policy choice. Nonetheless, the domestic decision-making structure and political setting contributed to the outcome.

There can be little doubt that Park Chung Hee personally made the decision to go for an aggressively pro-growth adjustment strategy; no individual or group within the government was in a position to challenge Park, and he had personally rejected recommendations to scale back the heavy industry plan. The reasons are necessarily somewhat speculative, however.

First, Park had linked the heavy industry drive to national security concerns, making purely economic cost-benefit calculations partly, if not wholly, irrelevant to its pursuit. The fall of Vietnam, debates about U.S. troop withdrawal, congressional efforts in the United States to tie economic and military assistance to human rights conditions in Korea, and the continued arms buildup in North Korea all seemed to vindicate the government's concerns with national security.

The overall political setting was of undeniable importance, however. In this regard, the metamorphosis of Nam Duck Woo from a proponent of price stability in the early 1970s to an advocate of rapid growth is revealing. In a 1976 interview, Nam explained the change in terms suggesting the comparative fragility of the Korean political system:

> According to a KDI calculation, prices rose by 44 percent in 1974. If the government had kept the price increase to 20 percent, the growth rate would have been minus two percent. If that happened, quite a large number of people would have lost their jobs. The same logic can be applied to 1975. If the government pushed price increases from 20 percent to 10 percent, we could have faced enormous unemployment. We are different from Japan, Taiwan, and other developed countries. . . . Low growth rates increase unemployment, which would in turn reduce household income and precipitate social and political instability. This is not to deny that high inflation does not become a source of social and political instability. But high inflation is more manageable than unemployment.[53]

In the second half of 1975, the recovery in the advanced industrial states began to be felt in Korea, and exports revived. The government was still concerned with securing external finance, but GNP growth for the year was a remarkable 8.3 percent, the balance of payments improved, and prices stabilized. This outcome had an important effect on subsequent policy, since it appeared to justify the expansionist line within the government. This strategy rested on a willingness to borrow to maintain planned levels of investment, aggressive countercyclical policy, and extensive supports for the largest exporters and heavy manufacturers. Not until 1978 would this strategy again be challenged.

NOTES

1. For an account of the regime change, see John Kie-Chiang Oh, *Korea: Democracy on Trial* (Ithaca: Cornell University Press, 1968).

2. See S. Haggard, Byung-Kook Kim, and Chung-In Moon, "The Transition to Export-led Growth in Korea, 1954–1966," *Journal of Asian Studies,* 50 (1991): 850–73.

3. Accounts of these early reforms can be found in G. Brown, *Korean Pricing Policies and Economic Development in the 1960s* (Baltimore: Johns Hopkins University Press, 1973); and C. Frank, Kwang Suk Kim, and Larry Westphal, *Foreign Trade Regimes and Economic Development: South Korea* (New York: National Bureau of Economic Research, 1975).

4. Wontack Hong and Yung-Chul Park, "The Financing of Export-Oriented Growth in Korea," in A. Tan and B. Kapur, eds., *Pacific Growth and Financial Interdependence* (Sydney: Allen & Unwin, 1986), pp. 163–82.

5. This is a theme of Park Chung Hee, *Our Nation's Path: Ideology of Social Reconstruction* (Seoul: Hollym, 1963).

6. For various interpretations of this crucial event, see C. Kim and Young Whan Kihl, *Party Politics and Elections in Korea* (Silver Spring, Md.: Research Institute on Korean Affairs, 1976).

7. See S. K. Kim, "Business Concentration and Government Policy: A Study of the Phenomenon of Business Groups in Korea," unpublished Ph.D. dissertation, Harvard Business School, 1988, chap. 3, for evidence of the business-government relationship in the 1960s.

8. The share of unionized workers in the manufacturing labor force declined slightly over the 1960s and was only 14.4 percent in 1973. The dramatic expansion of the total labor force meant a large increase in labor union membership, though it was concentrated in the larger establishments in the major cities. On the development of labor politics in the 1960s, see Jang Jip Choi, "Interest Conflict and Political Control in South Korea: A Study of the Labor Unions in Manufacturing Industries, 1961–1980," unpublished Ph.D. dissertation, University of Chicago, 1983; and G. Ogle, "Labor Unions in Rapid Economic Development: The Case of the Republic of Korea in the 1960s," unpublished Ph.D. dissertation, University of Wisconsin, 1973.

9. See Hyug Baeg Im, "The Rise of Bureaucratic Authoritarianism in South Korea," *World Politics,* 39, 2 (1987): 231–57.

10. Ibid.

11. See Inwon Choue, "The Politics of Industrial Restructuring: South Korea's Turn toward Export-led Heavy and Chemical Industrialization," unpublished Ph.D. dissertation, University of Pennsylvania, 1988, pp. 242–43.

12. See Sung Hwan Ban, *The Growth of Korean Agriculture, 1968–1971* (Seoul: Korean Development Institute, 1974); Pal Yong Moon, "A Postive Grain-Rice Policy and Agricultural Development," in Lee Jay Cho and Yoon Hyung Kim, eds., *Economic Development in the Republic of Korea: A Policy Perspective* (Honolulu: University of Hawaii Press, 1991), pp. 371–404.

13. See Pal Yong Moon, "The Saemaul (New Community) Movement," in Cho and Kim, eds., *Economic Development in the Republic of Korea,* pp. 371–404.

14. See E. Mason et al., *The Economic and Social Modernization of the Republic of Korea* (Cambridge: Harvard University Press, 1980), Table 127, p. 428.

15. See C. Kim, "The 1971 Elections and the Transformation of the DRP," in Kim and Kihl, eds., *Party Politics and Elections in Korea.*

16. The Cholla provinces also had the slowest agricultural growth in the period 1960–1974; see Sung Hwan Ban, Pal Yong Moon, and D. Perkins, *Rural Development* (Cambridge: Harvard University Press, 1980), p. 127.

17. The following draws on ibid.

18. For a review of interpretations of the turn toward authoritarianism, see Hyug Baeg Im, "The Rise of Bureaucratic Authoritarianism in South Korea," *World Politics,* 39, 2 (1987): 231–57; J. Palais, " 'Democracy' in South Korea, 1948–72," in F. Baldwin, ed., *Without Parallel: The American-Korean Relationship since 1945* (New York: Pantheon Books, 1973), pp. 318–58.

19. For a comprehensive analysis of Korea's debt during this period, see S. Collins and Won-Am Park, "External Debt and Macroeconomic Performance in South Korea," in J. Sachs and S. Collins, eds., *Developing Country Debt and Economic Performance,* vol. 3 (Chicago: University of Chicago Press, 1989), pp. 183–91.

20. Much of the 1969 increase in inventories was accumulation of agricultural products arising from high grain imports and a large rice harvest. The increases in 1971 were primarily manufactured goods, in response to increasing overvaluation and expected depreciation.

21. Data from Collins and Park, "External Debt and Macroeconomic Performance in South Korea," Table 10.1, p. 273.

22. Duck-Woo Nam, interview with author, Seoul, May 1984.

23. U.S. Congress, House of Representatives, Subcommittee on International Organizations, Committee on International Relations, *Investigation of Korean-American Relations* (Washington, D.C.: U.S. Government Printing Office, 1978), p. 187.

24. The FKI also sought the conversion of curb market loans into bank claims, a reduction of the corporate tax burden, and lower interest rates. See Federation of Korean Industries, *Chungyungryun Isipnyonsa* (History of FKI: Twenty years) (Seoul: FKI, 1983), p. 267.

25. *Investigation of Korean-American Relations*, p. 189.

26. Wan-Soon Kim, "The President's Emergency Decree for Economic Stability and Growth," in Cho and Kim, eds., *Economic Development in the Republic of Korea*, pp. 163–82.

27. Borrowers could repay curb market loans over 3 million won over a five-year period, with three years of grace, at 16.2 percent annual interest, 2.8 percentage points less than prevailing bank rates. Lenders were given the option of shifting loans into equity holdings, and some were forced to do so.

28. Kim, "President's Emergency Decree for Economic Stability and Growth." See also the discussion in D. Cole and Yung-Chul Park, *Financial Development in Korea, 1945–1978* (Cambridge: Harvard University Press, 1983).

29. L. Jones and Il Sakong, *Government, Business, and Entrepreneurship in Economic Development: The Korean Case* (Cambridge: Harvard University Press, 1980), p. 125.

30. For a re-creation of the extensive internal debate on how to respond to the recession, see Inwon Choue, "The Politics of Industrial Restructuring: South Korea's Turn toward Export-led Heavy and Chemical Industrialization, 1961–1974," unpublished Ph.D. dissertation, University of Pennsylvania, 1988, pp. 225–64.

31. A final set of provisions in the special measures concerned the sharing of central government revenues with local governments. This had previously been fixed at 17.6 percent of the budget. This restriction was lifted, a centralizing move that gave the government greater discretion in the distribution of revenues. Following the decree, the local governments' share of government revenue fell steadily, reaching 13.3 percent by 1982.

32. Choue, "Politics of Industrial Restructuring," pp. 253–56.

33. See J. Stern et al., "Industrialization and the State: The Korean Heavy and Chemical Industry Drive," unpublished manuscript, Harvard Institute for International Development, 1992.

34. The following draws on Byung-Sun Choi, "Institutionalizing a Liberal Economic Order in Korea: The Strategic Management of

Economic Change," unpublished Ph.D. dissertation, Harvard University, 1987; and Jong-Chan Rhee, "The Limits of Authoritarian State Capacities: The State-Controlled Capitalist Collective Action for Industrial Adjustment in Korea, 1973–87," unpublished Ph.D. dissertation, University of Pennsylvania, 1991.

35. See particularly Cole and Cho, *Financial Development;* Collins and Park, "External Debt and Macroeconomic Performance in South Korea," pp. 295–97.

36. Jones and Sakong, *Government, Business, and Entrepreneurship in Economic Development,* p. 61.

37. R. Campbell, "Everything's Illegal," *Far Eastern Economic Review* (January 21, 1974): 19–20.

38. Yoon Hyung Kim, "Policy Response to the Oil Crisis and the Presidential Emergency Decree," in Cho and Kim, eds., *Economic Development in the Republic of Korea,* pp. 183–206.

39. For a discussion of the measure, see Ministry of Finance, *Jaijung Gumyung Samsipnyonsa* (Thirty-year history of finance and banking) (Seoul: Ministry of Finance, 1978), pp. 236–37.

40. "Oiling Inflation," *Far Eastern Economic Review* (February 11, 1974): 36.

41. Subcommittee on International Organizations, *Investigation of Korean-American Relations,* pp. 196–97.

42. V. Corbo and Sang-Woo Nam, "The Recent Economic Evolution of the Republic of Korea," in V. Corbo and Sang–Mok Suh, eds., *Structural Adjustment in a Newly Industrialized Country: The Korean Experience* (Baltimore/London: Johns Hopkins University Press, a World Bank publication, 1992), pp. 35–67.

43. See Collins and Park, "External Debt and Macroeconomic Performance in South Korea," p. 295.

44. For the details on Seoul's borrowing efforts, see Chang Doo Sung, "Enter the Opposition," *Far Eastern Economic Review* (September 13, 1974): 13–14; Kim Sam-O, "South Korea's Bid to Attract Capital," *Far Eastern Economic Review* (January 10, 1975): 36; Norman Pearlstine and Seth Lipsky, "Seoul and the Banks: A $200 Million Connection," *Far Eastern Economic Review* (February 21, 1975): 36–44; "Seoul Loan Signed," *Far Eastern Economic Review* (March 14, 1975): 42.

45. R. Spurr, "Beloved Kim's New Asian Force," *Far Eastern Economic Review* (July 8, 1974): 77.

46. Young Chul Park, "Korea's Experience with External Debt Management," in G. Smith and J. Cuddington, eds., *International Debt and the Developing Countries* (Washington D.C.: World Bank, 1985), pp. 289–328.

47. Counterfactual simulations using the KDI Quarterly Macroeconomic Model and holding oil prices at their 1973 level show a more modest terms-of-trade effect, however, due to the fact that lower oil prices would have implied faster domestic growth, with strong effects on investment and imports. See Collins and Park, "External Debt and Macroeconomic Performance in South Korea," pp. 205–212.

48. See V. Corbo and Sang-Woo Nam, "The Recent Macroeconomic Evolution of the Republic of Korea: An Overview," in Corbo and Suh, eds., *Structural Adjustment in a Newly Industrialized Country*, pp. 35–67. The individual effects do not add to the total because of the compounding of various effects.

49. *Dong-A Ilbo,* June 15, 1974.

50. Byung Yoon Park, "Jungwhahak Gongupoi Naimak" (Inside story of the heavy and chemical industry), *Shin Dong-A* (May 1980): 197.

51. *Dong-A Ilbo,* February 5, 1974.

52. J. Stentzel, "A Check to Seoul's Grand Plan," *Far Eastern Economic Review* (December 6, 1974): 42–43.

53. *Seoul Shinmun* (Seoul daily news), January 3, 1976.

3

From the Heavy Industry Plan to Stabilization: Macroeconomic Policy 1976–1980

Stephan Haggard

Korea's successful adjustment to the first oil shock, assisted by the recovery in the world economy in the second half of 1975, appeared to vindicate the ambitious targets of the 1973 Heavy and Chemical Industry Plan. Although some projects were temporarily suspended as a result of the oil crisis, the basic direction of the 1973 plan was incorporated into the fourth five-year plan (1977–1981). A distinctive feature of this period was a marked increase in the extent of government intervention in the allocation of resources, particularly through control of credit.

Economic growth in the early years of the plan was extremely rapid, inflation fell, and the current account achieved rough balance in 1977 (Table 3-1). By 1978, however, the economy showed signs of overheating. This was due in part to unanticipated capital inflows from Middle East construction and rising agricultural prices but was primarily the result of an investment boom and resulting wage pressures. Since the government remained committed to a fixed exchange rate, increased inflation translated into a real appreciation and a slowing of export growth.

The puzzle for comparative analysis is why the Korean government moved relatively quickly to adjust. Two reasons proved important. First, the country's outward orientation and the growing dependence of large firms on export markets made decision makers especially sensitive to the interests and concerns of the export sector. Second, in the absence of indexing, inflation became a broader political issue, particularly in the cities, where the regime faced its most vociferous opposition. In December 1978, the government suffered an electoral setback following a heated campaign in which rising prices played an important role.

Table 3-1. Main Economic Indicators, 1976–1980 (percentages)

	1976	1977	1978	1979	1980
Real GNP growth	13.4	10.7	11.0	7.0	−4.8
Real GDP growth	13.2	10.9	9.7	7.4	−2.0
Inflation	15.3	10.3	14.2	18.2	28.5
General budget deficit/GNP(−)	−0.9	−1.8	−1.7	−1.6	−2.6
Central budget deficit/GNP(−)	−1.4	−1.8	−1.3	−1.8	−2.3
Fiscal impulse	−1.2	−0.1	0.0	−1.1	−0.1
M2 growth	33.5	39.7	35.0	24.6	26.9
Domestic credit growth	21.7	23.6	45.9	35.6	41.9
Consumer price index deflated wage growth	17.6	19.8	18.2	8.5	−4.0
Current account/GNP	−2.6	−2.1	−4.8	−8.5	−11.2
Real export growth	35.4	19.3	14.4	−1.0	11.3
Real exchange rate index	100.6	100.2	98.3	100.8	97.8
Debt/GNP	27.9	39.2	33.7	37.3	48.9
Terms of trade (1980 = 100)	105.2	112.5	117.9	115.4	100.0
Gross fixed capital formation/GDP	24.0	28.2	32.5	33.8	32.1
Private gross fixed capital formation/GDP	19.3	22.4	27.3	29.8	28.0

Notes and sources: see Table 2–2.

This combination of economic and political problems provided an opportunity for technocrats on the Economic Planning Board (EPB) to gain the president's attention and to regain some of the authority they had lost with the creation of special institutional mechanisms for promoting heavy industries. The EPB gradually developed an alternative analysis of the economy and argued not only for greater attention to price stability but for broader reforms in the style of economic management. Following the election of December 1978, a major reshuffling of the cabinet brought in a new team, which ultimately convinced the president of the need for a stabilization plan, which was announced in April 1979. Unlike many other developing countries, therefore, Korea's decision to adjust was driven initially by internal rather than external developments.

The implementation of the adjustment plan was almost immediately interrupted by the second oil crisis and a series of political changes, including growing opposition to the Yushin regime, the assassination of Park Chung Hee in October 1979, a coup within the army in December, and the seizure of power by Major General Chun Doo Hwan in May 1980. These political changes overlapped with, and contributed to, a serious deterioration in the economy beginning in the second half of 1979.

The profound political uncertainties of 1979–1980 were reflected in vacillating policies. After accepting the April 1979 stabilization plan, Park initially resisted a number of its key measures. The transitional government, while undertaking a major devaluation in January 1980, was generally too weak to sustain major policy initiatives. The new military government initially adopted an expansionist macroeconomic policy stance to counter the severe recession, particularly in the agricultural sector. With the consolidation of political power by Chun Doo Hwan in late 1980, however, the government returned to the stabilization and structural adjustment measures outlined in early 1979; these initiatives are the subject of Chapter 4.

This chapter focuses on the major policy initiatives of the heavy industry drive and their macroeconomic consequences. The major change to be explained is the gradual shift in policy orientation toward stabilization and structural adjustment within the bureaucracy, the effort to sell these policies to Park, and the response of the government to the economic crisis of 1979–1980.

The Heavy Industry Plan: The Policy Instruments

The Heavy and Chemical Industry Plan reflected the belief that Korea's competitiveness could be improved by upgrading exports and moving into an emerging niche for relatively standardized intermediate and capital goods. The plan was supported, however, by a variety of policy instruments generally associated with a strategy of import substitution. With a fixed nominal exchange rate that appreciated in real terms, the level of effective protection fell. To offset this, protection was used as a "surgical tool for advancing sectoral priorities and investment programs."[1] For example, a Machinery Localization Program announced in early 1976 had as its goal achieving 70 percent "self-sufficiency" by 1979; 942 product categories were deemed "domestically producible" and subject to discretionary import prohibition; and local-content requirements obliged firms to keep the ratio of domestically produced equipment to imports above a certain level.[2]

Fiscal incentives were also discriminatory. A Tax Exemption and Reduction Control Law in 1975 granted tax holidays, investment tax credits, and accelerated depreciation to favored industries, while other industries, including traditional export industries, faced heavier tax burdens.[3]

By far the most important instrument for advancing the heavy industry drive was government-controlled finance, and as Sung-Tae Ro argues in Chapter 6, this had important implications for monetary policy.[4] Financial market developments from 1973 through 1980 contrasted sharply with the growth and liberalization of the late 1960s and reflected a deepening government intervention in the allocation of credit. During the "big push" period, commercial and special banks were increasingly regulated, real loan rates turned negative, and M2 did not grow relative to gross national product (GNP). Preferential loans increased from less than 40 percent of total bank credit in 1971, to over 55 percent during 1976–1977 and almost 70 percent in 1978.

The average cost of borrowing for sixty-eight manufacturing industries fell from 18 percent during 1970–1971 to a low of 12 percent during 1973–1974, before gradually rising to 17 percent in 1979.[5] The variance in borrowing costs across sectors also fell. In 1970, the variance in borrowing costs for sixty-eight manufacturing sectors was 83 percent, dropping to 14 percent in 1973, and rising gradually to 21 percent in 1979. Yet these figures do not capture the fact that many firms wanting to borrow from the banking system were unable to do so because of the growing share of preferential policy lending in total bank lending.

Incremental bank credit increasingly was allocated to heavy industries.[6] During 1973–1974, 66.1 percent of incremental credit allocation went to light industries, in which Korea had established its comparative advantage. During the 1975–1979 period, this ratio was nearly reversed, and 59.1 percent of new credit went to heavy industry.[7] The cost of capital to heavy industry was also less than to light industries. This pattern of credit allocation no doubt contributed to an acceleration of structural change. In 1975, heavy industry accounted for only 42 percent of value-added in manufacturing; by 1979 its share had risen to 51 percent, the target initially set in the fourth five-year plan for 1981. Nearly all of the investment in heavy industry projected by the plan for the 1977–1981 period had been completed by 1979, while the investment targets for other industries were less than half complete. This imbalance had supply-side effects; the capacity expansion of other industries, including those supplying a variety of basic commodities, was reduced.

Lending practices increasingly favored import-substituting activities over exporters. Between 1976 and 1979, the ratio of the average borrowing costs of export versus domestic industries rose steadily, and in both 1978 and 1979 this ratio exceeded one. The share of total credit allocated to domestic industries, though less than that going to the export sector, also increased steadily during the plan period.

Although aggregate government lending appeared to shift toward support of heavy and import-substituting industries in the late 1970s, the export performance of targeted sectors seemed to support the assumption that industrial deepening could occur side by side with export expansion. Exports of chemicals and machinery, key sectors under the Heavy and Chemical Industry Plan, and transport equipment, designated a strategic industry in 1977, grew from 14 percent of exports in 1973 to 24 percent in 1978.

These exports were supported by a variety of new initiatives, again usually involving preferential credit. The establishment of an export-import facility provided preferential medium- and long-term financing for the export of large-scale products such as ships and whole plant. Export promotion was also supported by the creation of general trading companies (GTCs).[8] In the early 1970s, Korean traders began to press the government to support trading houses that could challenge the dominant position of the Japanese *sogo shosha* (GTCs), which, it was believed, periodically boycotted competing Korean goods. Small manufacturing firms would benefit from the economies of scale of larger trading companies serving as windows to international markets. In 1975, the GTCs were established as legal entities. Qualifying as a GTC led to numerous privileges, including guaranteed letters of credit, easier access to foreign exchange, and an easing of administrative restraints on imports. GTC status was restricted to a limited number of firms, however, and thus contributed to the overall increase in concentration.[9]

Another export initiative that followed the first oil shock was the aggressive promotion of overseas construction, particularly in the Middle East.[10] Overseas construction had received its initial boost during the Vietnam War but had a relatively small effect on the balance of payments. Oil payments averaged $300 million annually in 1972–1973 and revenues from overseas construction a mere $14 million. During the 1974–1978 period, oil payments averaged almost $1.2 billion, but foreign exchange inflows from construction offset an average of $800 million of this expense each year.

This outcome was facilitated by extensive government intervention, including, once again, the manipulation of bank credit. In December 1975 a comprehensive strategy for penetrating the Middle East, and particularly Saudi Arabia, was formulated. Saudi Arabia followed the practice of demanding various bank guarantees on all contracts, such as bid bonds and performance bonds, as protection against possible losses and to guarantee performance. Given the gigantic scale of Saudi contracts, these guarantees, usually amounting to 20 percent of the contract, threatened to place substantial strains on Korean banks.

Park Chung Hee intervened personally in 1976 to overcome a bureaucratic stalemate created by the banks' and Ministry of Finance's reluctance to support the construction firms. Under a government-sponsored Agreement on Payment Guarantees for the Construction and Service Business Activities in the Middle East a bank consortium was formed, the statutory limits on banks' contingent liabilities were loosened, and banks were allowed to cover payments guarantees for Korean firms operating in the Middle East up to 600 percent of bank capital. Through the end of 1982, total guarantees extended by Korean banks equaled $7.8 billion, 70 percent of which was for Saudi contracts.[11]

Financing the Big Push: Domestic Savings and Foreign Debt

If the investment targets and financing needs of the fourth five-year plan were ambitious, the savings targets were equally so, and were one source of skepticism concerning the plan on the part of both foreign donors and portions of the economic bureaucracy, particularly the Ministry of Finance.[12] The government projected a sharp increase in gross domestic savings from 18 percent of GNP in 1975 to 26 percent by 1981. The ability to meet the domestic savings targets is partly attributable to rapid income growth and the strong performance of the external sector, including both a continuing expansion of exports and earnings from overseas construction.

Nonetheless, important policy changes also played a role in mobilizing savings. In early 1976, Park Chung Hee announced a trillion won savings goal, and over the course of the year, a battery of extremely attractive savings programs targeted at the household sector were announced, including a "property formation" savings deposit scheme with annual interest rates of over 20 percent.[13] Household savings went from just over 11 percent of GNP in 1976 to 15.6 percent of GNP in 1978, before falling dramatically in the recession year of 1980 (see Chapter 8).

Even with the ambitious targets for investment, the projected rise in domestic savings implied a sharp reduction in the reliance on foreign savings, from a high of 11.4 percent of GNP in 1975 to only 0.5 percent in 1981. The government was particularly intent on reducing its reliance on short-term foreign borrowing, which had increased dramatically in 1974 and 1975. Short-term capital inflows, mostly to finance imports, dropped from $972 million in 1975 to $540 million in 1976 and were actually reversed in 1977. With the achievement of virtual balance in the current account in 1977, a variety of controls were instituted to reduce short-term borrowing further.

This did not mean a reduction of overall foreign borrowing. The fourth plan predicted the trade balance for 1977 quite accurately, but a much stronger service account from foreign construction resulted in a current account that was $650 million larger than expected. Despite this windfall, Korea borrowed almost $600 million more than projected, accumulating substantial reserves.

In 1978 and the first half of 1979—prior to the oil shock—the trade deficit was worse than projected, primarily as a result of an unforeseen surge in imports of machinery and transport equipment associated with the Heavy and Chemical Industry Plan and a modest effort to liberalize imports. Korean monetary authorities did not offset this development through reserve depletion but took advantage of the favorable climate in international credit markets to continue to accumulate reserves. The government prepaid $114 million on the $200 million loan it had contracted during the first oil shock in April but simultaneously raised $300 million in Europe at only seven-eighths above the London interbank offered rate (LIBOR), in effect, a refinancing of the debt incurred during the first oil shock.[14] In July 1979, the state-owned Korea Development Bank (KDB), a major channel for supporting the Heavy and Chemical Industry Plan, was able to borrow $600 million in a single syndication— double the KDB's initial target—at the best terms Korea had received up until that time.[15]

Korea's external performance thus diverged from plan projections, particularly during the boom years of 1977 and 1978. As Table 3-2 shows, however, this divergence was in the direction of higher investment than projected, smaller domestic savings, and a larger deterioration in the current account, covered by the country's strong ability to borrow.

The real test of confidence, however, came in 1980. The second half of 1979 and the first half of 1980 not only marked a significant downturn in the Korean economy but a year of substantial political upheaval. Because of its successful borrowing and accumulation of reserves, Korea did not need to borrow further in 1979 following Park's assassination. In 1980, however, the government projected a current account deficit for 1980 of $4.7 billion and total financing needs of $6.3 billion.

The government quickly turned to the International Monetary Fund (IMF) for support as part of a strategy to raise funds and bolster confidence. With a long history of close relations with the IMF, Korea

Table 3-2. External Balance: Actual versus Planned (US$ million)

	1977		1978	
	Plan	Actual	Plan	Actual
Current account	634	−12.3	237	1,085.2
Reserve accumulation	711	1,346	611	631
Errors and omissions	—	31.7	—	312
Increase foreign debt	1,542	2,129	1,667	2,174

Source: Government of the Republic of Korea, *Fourth Five Year Economic Development Plan 1977– 1981;* EPB.

had little difficulty negotiating a standby. Going to the Euromarkets in March, the Korea Exchange Bank was able to borrow $500 million at 0.75 percent over LIBOR for the first three years and 0.875 for the remaining five years. The next time Korea came to the market for long-term money was in November, after the seizure of political power by Chun Doo Hwan and following a weak year in terms of economic performance. Nonetheless, Korea was still able to raise $500 billion through the KDB at 0.875 percent over LIBOR for an eight-year loan.

Although the terms of the first loan compared somewhat unfavorably with those for comparable borrowers and the second loan carried spreads that were slightly higher than the first, it does not appear that Korea had difficulty raising money (see Chapter 9).[16] There were, however, several troubling signs, and a reduction of the debt was to become a major concern of policymakers, as well as a larger political issue, in the early 1980s. First, Korea relied heavily during 1979 and 1980 on short-term debt. Gross long-term debt increased 27.5 percent in 1979 and 19.4 percent in 1980, but short-term debt grew 73 percent in 1979 and 72 percent in 1980. This borrowing resulted in a shift in the composition of Korea's external indebtedness. Short-term debt accounted for over 26.9 percent of Korea's debt in 1979 but over 34 percent in 1980. Second, Korea relied heavily on public sources of international finance in 1980. Public loans and IMF facilities accounted for only 22 percent of the increase in long-term debt in 1979; in 1980, this share jumped to 66 percent.

Macroeconomic Policy and Inflation during the Big Push

In comparative perspective, the most striking feature of Korean macroeconomic policy during this period is its conservatism. In contrast to virtually all other developing countries, Korea did not use foreign borrowing to expand the size of the government. Despite the ambitions of the fourth five-year plan, fiscal policy in the 1976–1979 period was countercyclical. Expenditure as a share of GNP stayed roughly constant over the period, and the budget deficit as a share of GNP declined in every year, from 2.9 percent of GNP in 1976 to 1.4 percent of GNP in 1979. The IMF's fiscal impulse measure even shows a slightly contractionary fiscal stance during these years.[17] Fiscal balance was achieved by steadily rising revenues and a profitable state-owned enterprise sector but also by extremely tight control over expenditures.

The one exception to this rule concerns agricultural policy and Park's decision to subsidize farmers. The implementation of the two-price system for rice and barley in 1969 and the creation of a fertilizer account in 1970 resulted in substantial losses to the government, financed through overdrafts with the central bank. One measure of the size of these losses is the net expenditures on subsidies for major cereals, fertilizer, livestock raising, and farm machinery as a share of the fiscal deficit:[18]

1974:	47.2%
1975:	29.1
1976:	0.9
1977:	4.7
1978:	9.5
1979:	26.3
1980:	10.8

Losses on these accounts were substantial in 1974, 1975, and 1979. These figures do not fully capture the total cost of the program, since they reflect only losses due to negative price differentials. In 1984, for example, only 46.8 percent of total losses was due to price differentials; another 9.7 percent was due to handling and 41.7 percent from interest payments on long-term borrowings from the central bank. On the other hand, these expenditures were relatively modest in 1977 and 1978, the period when concerns about inflation reappeared, and were offset by the government's aggregate fiscal stance.

The government's conservatism is reflected in the modest growth of claims by the banking system on the government (Table 3-3). The government borrowed from the central bank during the two oil shocks, but this was viewed as unusual. Any time the government seeks to borrow from the central bank (outside of borrowing within the fiscal year to smooth the mismatch between tax receipts and expenditures) it must get approval from the National Assembly. By custom, there is no government borrowing from commercial banks. Unlike the United States and other developing countries, these institutional arrangements appear to constitute a barrier to greater government borrowing.

Thus, unlike other developing countries, government deficits were not the source of inflationary pressures; other factors were at work. Table 3-3 shows the development of major price indexes during the second half of the 1970s and traces the movements of their major determinants.[19] In the aftermath of the first oil shock, Korea benefited substantially from the stabilization of the prices of its imports, though this is in part an artifact of increasing real appreciation that had other undesirable consequences.

Table 3-3. Annual Price Changes and Their Determinants, 1974–1980
(percentages)

	1974	1975	1976	1977	1978	1979	1980
Inflation							
Consumer price index	24.3	25.3	15.3	10.1	14.4	18.3	28.7
Wholesale price index	42.1	26.5	12.2	9.0	11.6	18.8	38.9
Determinants							
Wages[a]							
Nominal	35.3	27.0	34.7	33.9	34.3	28.6	22.7
Real	8.8	1.4	16.8	21.5	17.4	8.7	−4.7
Productivity	2.4	2.2	2.4	10.3	12.6	16.0	−3.9
Food prices[b]	33.6	36.1	17.8	15.5	24.4	11.2	27.7
Import prices	43.8	−4.8	3.0	0.9	4.3	26.7	27.6
Mineral fuel	228.0	5.5	6.4	6.8	3.8	38.3	40.4
M2	24.0	28.2	33.5	39.7	35.0	24.6	26.9
Domestic credit	53.1	31.9	22.9	23.6	45.9	35.6	41.9
Of which:							
Government	5.3	6.8	−1.1	−2.2	1.2	−1.5	3.1
Government agencies	−1.2	3.0	0.0	2.1	0.5	0.0	0.2
Private	49.1	22.1	24.1	23.7	44.2	37.1	38.5
Foreign assets[c]	12.4	47.8	86.8	61.1	5.8	15.1	65.2

[a]Manufacturing wages.
[b]Wholesale prices.
[c]Includes gold and silver bullion, subscriptions to international financial institutions, and Special Drawing Rights holdings.
Source: Bank of Korea, *Economic Statistics Yearbook*, various issues. Numbers may not add up due to rounding.

One source of inflationary pressures during 1976–1977 was an explosive growth in foreign assets associated with unanticipated inflows of foreign exchange from Middle East construction projects. Food prices also rose faster than inflation from 1974 through 1978. As in the late 1960s, this rise became a major political issue in late 1978. (In Chungsoo Kim's expanded discussion of inflation in Chapter 7, he underscores the sharp rise in real wages between 1976 and 1978.)

Yet a striking fact that emerges from Table 3-3 is the sharp increase in credit to the private sector. From the launching of its export-led growth strategy in the early 1960s, Korea had a history of using preferential credit as an industrial policy tool, and this tendency became even more marked during the heavy industry push. Private credit rose an average 23.3 percent a year between 1975 and 1977 and then accelerated to just under 40 percent a year in 1978, the peak of the investment boom.

Construction of industrial facilities and housing played an important role in the boom of the late 1970s, but investments associated with the Heavy and Chemical Industry Plan were a crucial component of the inflation story of the late 1970s.[20] The share of gross domestic capital formation (GDCF) in GNP went from 26 percent in 1976 to 37 percent in 1978. In the same period, the share of machinery and capital goods in GDCF increased from 26.5 to 35 percent.

The expansion of bank credit that financed this investment, in turn, was supported by central bank operations. Lacking independence, the Bank of Korea was instructed to engage in lending operations to support the state-owned banks, which were devoting an increasing share of their portfolios to policy loans reflecting government priorities. Such support was necessary given the negative margin between deposit and loan rates and the continual excess demand for credit that resulted.

The growth of credit-financed investment naturally had consequences for employment and wages (see Chapter 7). Beginning in 1976, both nominal and real wages showed sharp increases, partly as a result of the severe shortages for skilled workers in construction and the heavy and chemical industries associated with the plan. Moreover, wage gains far outstripped the impressive gains in productivity, contributing to a decline in export competitiveness.

Reconsideration: Toward the Stabilization Plan of April 1979

The leadership of the EPB accommodated itself to the expansionist premises of the heavy industry initiative after the first oil shock. Despite the ambition of the plan and its potentially inflationary consequences, Korea's successful adjustment to the first shock appeared to remove any basis for skepticism. The domestic price adjustment to international inflation had apparently been completed.[21] The fourth five-year plan (1977–1981) targeted inflation, as measured by the GNP deflator, to drop from 15 percent in 1976, to 10 percent in 1977, before reaching the 7 percent goal for the remainder of the plan period.

Although annual policy statements in 1976 and 1977 announced limits on money supply and credit expansion consistent with these price targets, the characteristic feature of the government's annual stabilization efforts during these years was—as it had been in the early 1970s—the use of direct price controls (Table 3-4). Following a presidential Law Concerning Price Stabilization and Fair Trade in 1976, the EPB established an interministerial Price Stabilization Committee to enforce controls on 136 "monopoly" or "oligopoly" items. Direct controls were supplemented by a monitoring system that would allow the government to tailor specific tax and financial incentives to relieve supply bottlenecks, a stockpiling system for a variety of basic foodstuffs and items subject to seasonal or

Table 3-4. Number of Products under Government Price Controls (at year end)

	1976	1977	1978	1979
Monopolistic and oligopolistic items	148	157	148	35
Factory price ceilings	2	25[a]	22	2
Administrative guides or price monitoring	—	407	54	25

[a]During the year, ceilings were imposed on 251 factory prices, 150 wholesale prices, and 45 retail prices in Seoul in anticipation of inflationary consequences from the introduction of the VAT. These controls were lifted by the end of the year.
Source: Sang–Woo Nam, "Integrated Stabilization Programs (1979)," East–West Population Institute, Korean Economic Policy Studies 16, November 1984, from unpublished EPB data, with permission.

international price fluctuations, and export controls on select items that were in great demand because of the building boom.

The first sign of a more comprehensive effort to address the inflation problem appeared in the announcement on June 14, 1977, of a major policy review for the second half of the year.[22] The review was motivated by two concerns: the problems generated by the rapid rise in reserves in the middle of the year that resulted from Korea's success in breaking into the Middle East construction market and the anticipated inflationary effects of the introduction of a value-added tax (VAT) on July 1.

The idea of a VAT had been explored years earlier at the Ministry of Finance, but its introduction had been interrupted by the first oil shock.[23] Although simplification of the tax system was one reason for introducing it in 1978, a major motivation was the expectation that it would generate additional revenue that could be used to finance industrial plans.

Despite efforts by the government to consult widely with major peak associations through a special Deliberation Committee, the introduction of the VAT became a charged issue that fueled inflationary expectations. Labor leaders opposed it as regressive, but the private sector was opposed as well and called for a delay in its introduction. Small businesses feared that the costs of compliance would be excessive, and within the economic ministers' meeting, in which major policy measures are debated, the measure was opposed by the minister of commerce and industry. Moreover, leaders of the ruling Democratic Republican party expressed their opposition on the ground that its inflationary consequences would weaken the standing of the party in the upcoming general election, an interesting sign of the growing political salience of inflation.[24]

The mid-1977 policy review introduced a variety of new short-term controls.[25] Yet as Byung-sun Choi has argued, several of the announced measures indicated an effort on the part of the EPB to use the concern over the VAT and inflation to reassert control over the investment decision-making process and economic policy more generally.[26] Under the oversight of a revived Industrial Rationalization Deliberation Committee (IRDC), the review called for a survey of Korean industry involving the KDB, the Federation of Korean Industries, and various industry associations. The EPB created eight new subcommittees and twenty-nine task forces under the IRDC, drawing on representatives from industry associations as well as government officials. The stated purpose of the task forces was to assess the competitiveness of Korean industry, but the EPB also sought information that would allow a thorough assessment of the heavy industry plan.

Finally, the EPB attempted to exploit the concern with inflation and the improvement in the current account to press for the liberalization of imports, joining a debate that has characterized Korean economic policy both inside and outside the bureaucracy ever since. The advocates of import liberalization in the EPB initially linked liberalization to the stabilization of prices, but the EPB's proposals for a new trade policy decision-making structure also sought to check the authority of the Ministry of Commerce and Industry, whose power had expanded under the Heavy and Chemical Industry Plan.[27]

The 1977 review focused solely on short-term measures that were easily reversible, such as a relaxation of controls on specific items in the Import Notice for the second half of the year. In March 1978, however, the EPB circulated a document for internal discussion, "Current Tasks of the Korean Economy and Countermeasures," which summarized previous debates within the bureaucracy.[28] The document argued explicitly that inflation was a potential source of social instability and attributed price increases to three major factors: supply bottlenecks caused by shortages of housing, construction materials, and food; monetary expansion caused not only by the increase in foreign assets but by domestic policy; and increasing labor costs. To counter these trends, the EPB argued for a wide-ranging import liberalization program, a reduction of the deficits in the Grain Management Fund, and a liberalization of the banking sector.

Despite the first steps toward liberalization and the continuation of a number of controls, strong pressures continued on the prices of food, real estate, and a variety of other basic commodities during the first half of 1978. With confidence in the government's 10 percent inflation target undermined, Deputy Prime Minister Nam Duck Woo called a press conference in June to announce that the government would "establish a base of price stability within two years."[29] More rapid stabilization was ruled out in part due to concerns about upcoming elections in December. The new measures included a temporary acceleration of import liberalization, a hike in interest rates, and government stockpiling of a variety of agricultural products, construction materials, and coal.

Nam's statement had virtually the opposite of its intended effect; inflation, which averaged 1.5 percent a month from January through May, jumped to 2.8 percent in June. The opposition New Democratic party quickly attacked the government for allowing rapid price increases and called for a special session of the National Assembly to address the problem of inflation.[30] In response to the public outcry, the EPB put together a more comprehensive stabilization effort that included a special $500 million import plan, new measures to curb real estate speculation, and a number of other structural reforms. In the short run, however, the EPB's plans called for a number of one-time price adjustments that would have added to inflation, including a readjustment of electricity fees and rice and coal prices. These policies were blocked by interministerial conflicts that resulted in an extraordinary Blue House meeting with the president on August 29, 1978, and ultimately led to the resignation of Nam Duck Woo.

The general election of December 1978 did not appear to pose any direct threat to Park's rule. Under the Yushin system, one-third of the 261-seat National Assembly is appointed by the president. The election was nonetheless significant in that turnout was high and the major opposition party, the New Democratic party, polled more votes than the ruling party.[31] Moreover, the elections played a crucial role in gaining the president's attention, and thus provided an opportunity for the EPB to voice its concerns about the distortions of the big push strategy.

Immediately following the elections, Park reshuffled the cabinet, placing former Minister of Health and Social Welfare Hyun-Hwack Shin in the position of deputy prime minister and head of the EPB. Shin's appointment substantially increased the EPB's power within the government, providing critical political support for a number of economists who had argued for a more market-conforming strategy, including Mahn-Je Kim, Chong Jae-Sok, Kyung-Shik Kang, and particularly Jae-Ik Kim, who was to play a particularly important role in subsequent reforms. In contrast to Nam Duck Woo, Shin was a veteran politician who had survived three different changes of political regime and was a prominent figure in the Taegu-Kyungbuk group from Park Chung Hee's native Kyongsang province, which constituted the core of political power under Park.

Within a month of taking office, Shin presented Park with a major report on the economy.[32] Previous EPB analyses had treated the country's problems as cyclical and skirted the issue of the responsibility of the Heavy and Chemical Industry Plan. The new report tackled the issue head on. It argued not simply for discrete reforms but for a broader change in the style of economic management, away from the dirigism of the heavy industry drive and toward a more balanced strategy emphasizing comparative advantage, the lifting of controls, and the liberalization of markets, including the financial market.

In introducing the report, Shin found support among the other ministries, with the exception of the Ministry of Commerce and Industry, which had the closest links to the private sector and the greatest stake in the heavy industry plan. Park himself was also skeptical and called on the Korean Development Institute (KDI), the Bank of Korea, and the Economic and Science Examination Council to submit independent studies on the problems in the economy. The studies varied subtly in emphasis but basically shared the diagnosis that had been elaborated by the EPB. The most critical of the three reports, that of the KDI, argued that the crisis was the result of monetary expansion linked to the heavy industry plan and that the government needed to avoid stop-go policies, raise interest rates, and fundamentally restructure duplicative investments in the heavy industry sector, many of which were running at a small fraction of capacity.[33]

With bureaucratic forces increasingly aligned against the heavy industry plan, Park relented at a special Blue House meeting on March 31, 1979, specifically instructing Shin that growth, export, and investment targets could all be reexamined. Two weeks later, on April 17, Shin announced the Comprehensive Measures for Economic Stabilization. Although the Comprehensive Measures focus on the problem of stabilization, the diagnosis of inflation could be called structural in the sense that it involved not simply changes in policy instruments but basic changes in the style of economic management.[34] To control excess liquidity, the plan proposed lower targets for credit expansion, to be achieved through a reduction of support to the heavy and chemical industries and higher interest rates and a realignment of the entire system of monetary management away from direct credit controls toward an indirect monetary management, greater independence for the central bank, and the privatization of the banking sector. Current government expenditure would be cut by 5 percent and a variety of changes in the tax system considered in order to improve the system's efficiency.

Inflation was not simply seen as a consequence of lax credit policies, though; the measures gave substantial attention to market structure and the rigidity in prices resulting from increasing industrial concentration. The plan criticized the previous system of price controls as ineffective, since they encouraged hoarding and speculation, led to production and sales boycotts and black markets, and ultimately resulted in price adjustments that stimulated inflationary expectations. In the future, the government would address problems of market structure directly by regulating mergers, takeovers, and noncompetitive business practices, particularly of firms in monopolistic and oligopolistic sectors. This task would prove particularly difficult since it put the government on a collision course with the largest firms.

Finally, the Comprehensive Measures called for a realignment of industrial policy toward greater emphasis on comparative advantage and the market. The plan would shift investment decisions back toward the private sector, make planning indicative, liberalize imports, and support exporters through realistic exchange rate policy rather than targeted financial support. The government would rationalize the complex system of industrial incentives and move toward more general, rather than targeted, forms of support.

Reform Interrupted: The Political Transition and the Response to the Second Oil Shock

The decision to stabilize and launch a structural reform program was a crucial turning point in the history of Korean economic policy. At the same time, it was also a severe blow to Park Chung Hee, not only because of the personal prestige he had invested in the heavy industry plan but because of the political costs inevitably associated with implementing the stabilization plan. The problems confronting the regime in 1979 were not solely economic in nature, but economic difficulties exacerbated Park's political dilemmas, which in turn weakened his commitment to the stabilization effort.

The problems Park faced can be seen by reviewing the government's base of political support during the heavy industry push of the late-1970s. First, Park relied heavily on the military and security and intelligence apparatus, including particularly the Korean Central Intelligence Agency. Not only were they used for coercive and surveillance purposes, but external military threats were a major justification for both the Yushin system and the Heavy and Chemical Industry Plan. In 1970, defense accounted for 24 percent of government expenditures. In 1974, this went over 30 percent, peaking in 1978 at 38 percent.[35]

A second pillar of support was big business.[36] Specific companies had been close to the government and received policy favors in the early years of Park's rule, but the promotion of labor-intensive manufactures encouraged small- and medium-sized firms, and support was extended to exporters on a nondiscretionary basis. By contrast, the capital-intensive projects associated with the heavy industry drive, the promotion of overseas construction, and the establishment of general trading companies all favored the large industrial conglomerates, or *chaebol.* The result was an increase in the level of industrial concentration during the late 1970s.

The increase in concentration and targeted incentives required to make large projects work fostered an increasingly close relationship between the government and the largest firms. In addition to the biases already created by the channeling of credit to heavy and chemical industry projects, deepened government intervention in financial markets increased opportunities for rent seeking and the diversion of preferential credit into speculative activities such as real estate. Close business-government relations were associated in the public mind with corruption, the authoritarian nature of the Yushin system, and the deterioration in the distribution of income that occurred in the late 1970s.[37]

The final component of the Yushin coalition was rural. Although agriculture typically is hurt by government intervention in favor of industry, Park used protection, subsidization, and traditional political appeals to retain rural support. As in the 1960s, conservative rural constituencies continued to provide a counterweight to the growing urban opposition.

The political presumptions governing the regime's relationship with other groups revealed the coercive underpinnings of the Yushin structure. Particular attention was paid to restricting the organizational capabilities of the growing number of industrial workers. The groundwork for the increased level of labor control was laid under the Special Measure Law Concerning National Security and Defense that accompanied the declaration of the state of emergency in 1971. Under the Special Measure Law and implementing measures that followed, the government suspended the right to strike and undertake collective bargaining, moved to settle all disputes by administrative arbitration that was beyond judicial review, and shifted labor-management negotiations into "cooperative councils" that distinctly favored management, allowed for close government monitoring and input, and were designed to "seek improvement of productivity through mutual cooperation."[38]

Park thus counted on political acquiescence from the growing middle class and those portions of the working class that benefited from rapid growth, while making all efforts, including direct repression, to prevent the formation of horizontal alliances among disaffected groups: students, intellectuals, opposition politicians, urban marginals, and the poorer segments of the working class and agricultural sector.

Until 1979, the opposition leadership chose to work within the narrow rules set by the Yushin structure. In May, with crucial backing from the recently freed opposition leader Kim Dae-Jung, Kim Young Sam captured the presidency of the NDP by arguing for the pursuit of a more confrontational political strategy. Kim Young Sam pressed for a full review of the operation of the Yushin system and openly sought to bring U.S. pressure on Park to liberalize politics by capitalizing on President Jimmy Carter's commitment to human rights.

His appeals also stressed economic concerns and sought to attract support from segments of the population that had been disadvantaged under the Yushin system, the heavy industry plan, and the subsequent stabilization effort.[39] A crucial incident that underlined the possibility of new political alignments and more militant opposition tactics occurred on August 9, when 178 female textile workers occupied the headquarters of the NDP, calling on the party to assist them in resolving a labor dispute. The YH Trading Company, for which they worked, was typical of many small- and medium-sized firms driven to bankruptcy or temporary closure by rising labor costs and the squeeze on credit, often leaving workers unpaid. After two days, the police launched an assault on NDP headquarters to break up the protest. The YH incident, which left one woman dead and thirty wounded, received wide coverage in the press and broad political resonance. The sit-in protest appeared to mark the formation of a coalition linking opposition politicians with disaffected workers and farmers, church groups, and increasingly militant students, precisely the combination Park had sought to avoid.

In the wake of the YH incident, the government adopted a hardline stance toward the opposition. As the judiciary invalidated Kim Young Sam's election to the presidency of the NDP on a technicality, Kim moved in a more radical direction, calling for the overthrow of Park and the Yushin system. When the ruling party ousted Kim from the National Assembly on October 4, it sparked violent demonstrations in Pusan and Masan. Internal disagreements between hardliners and softliners with the security apparatus over how to handle mounting protest were the proximate cause of Park's assassination on October 26.

This political environment was clearly not amenable to undertaking significant reforms, particularly those such as the restructuring of the heavy and chemical industry sector, which required extensive business-government coordination. The measures that were introduced, including a squeeze on credit, resulted in a substantial outcry from business, particularly small and export-oriented businesses. Despite the apparent consensus around the new course, Park's preoccupation with politics and the lack of overall direction following the abandonment of the previous strategy created a vacuum within the economic bureaucracy. The minister of commerce and industry, Jai-Suk Jung, openly attacked the stabilization plan as doctrinaire and divorced from day-to-day economic problems, comparing the stabilizers to Buddhist monks reading from texts in a remote mountain retreat.[40] In June, the government restored preferential finance to export industries that had been cut under the stabilization plan. This policy was initiated by the Ministry of Commerce and Industry in collaboration with a trusted aide of President Park and approved by the president while Deputy Prime Minister Shin was abroad; journalists referred to the incident as an "economic coup d'état."[41]

Finally, the deteriorating situation in the economy itself raised some doubts about the wisdom of fully implementing the plan. Prices continued to increase following the announcement of the stabilization program, even prior to the second oil shock, and in September, the KDI argued strongly for continuing to implement the stabilization measures.[42] But equally, if not more, troubling was the serious deterioration in export performance and overall growth. As will be shown in more detail in Chapter 9, the terms of trade and higher interest rates were major causes of the external imbalance in 1980, but in both 1979 and 1980, poor export performance was also a major contributor. This resulted not only from weakened world demand but from declining competitiveness associated with continuing wage pressures and the real appreciation of the won.

The original projection for domestic credit for 1979 was 22.4 percent, but this goal was abandoned as a result of the need to support the banking system in the wake of the failure of a large trading company in April, the restoration of preferential financing for exporters in the summer, and efforts to offset the sharp downturn in the economy in the second half of the year.[43] Total credit increased 35.6 percent for the year.

The assassination of President Park on October 26 compounded political uncertainty. On December 12, 1979, Major General Chun Doo Hwan arrested General Seung-Hwa Chung, army chief of staff and martial law commander, thus effecting a coup within the army.[44] Chun urged interim president Kyu-Ha Choi to reshuffle the cabinet, elevating Hyun-Hwack Shin to prime minister and bringing in Lee Hahn Been to take over the EPB. The change of leadership and the drafting of the Annual Management Report for the president's State of the Union Address provided the opportunity for a reassessment of policy. The economic puzzle was how to solve simultaneously the problems of rising unemployment, widening current account deficits, and persistent inflation. There was consensus in the EPB, the Ministry of Finance, and the KDI on the need to continue, and even strengthen, tight money policy, though this was bitterly opposed by the Ministry of Commerce and Industry. In January, lending rates were raised sharply, and though a KDI proposal to eliminate policy loan differentials was rejected, rates were realigned to narrow somewhat the differential between preferential and non-preferential loans.

There was sharp internal debate about the wisdom of devaluation.[45] The EPB and Ministry of Finance were concerned about the inflationary consequences of devaluation. The Ministry of Commerce and Industry, with its close ties to business, favored the opposite policy mix of devaluation and lower interest rates. In fact, the interests of the private sector were mixed: Firms would be favored by increased export opportunities, but large firms with foreign obligations would face increasing debt service costs. The decisive argument concerned exports. The KDI argued strongly that exports could not be expanded through additional incentives, which were, in any case, extremely costly. Although the KDI had initially sought a devaluation from 480 to 630 won to the dollar, the final figure of 580 was personally chosen by the president.

The full political history of the turbulent years of 1979 and 1980 has yet to be constructed. For our purposes, the important feature of the period is that the promise of a democratic opening and the lack of clarity surrounding the precise role of the military in the political system stimulated the mobilization of a wide array of political and social forces. Student demonstrations for democratization were widespread and virtually continuous in the spring of 1980. Within the first five months of 1980, over 900 strikes occurred, more than had taken place in the entire Yushin period. On May 17, Chun Doo Hwan declared full martial law. This was followed by an insurrection in the southern city of Kwangju that was bloodily repressed with regular army troops, signaling Chun's intention to consolidate power at any cost.

This political setting and the interest of the military in consolidating power and support naturally influenced the assessment of planners. On June 5, the EPB prepared its first report to the National Security Council. The report pointed out that although the stabilization policy was basically sound, it had contributed to social unrest, which was undermining economic confidence. It was therefore imperative to address unemployment through a series of countercyclical policies, subsequently known as the June 5 measures. These included the release of public works moneys that had been frozen as part of the stabilization effort and a massive road paving project, carried out by expanding the ability of local governments to borrow from the central bank. Other measures included a small (1 percent) reduction of interest rates, tax concessions to depressed industries, and increased financing for exporters. As the economy continued to worsen, further stimulus was applied. Interest rates were lowered two percentage points in September, and an additional two points in November,[46] and the money supply was allowed to grow by 27 to 28 percent, breaking the ceiling of 25 percent in June, though remaining within the targets of the IMF standby. The special consumption tax, an excise tax on a number of consumer durables, was lowered by 30 percent to activate sales of depressed sectors, including autos and televisions.

The structure of the new government disrupted established patterns of economic policymaking and provided new channels for military involvement. Under the interim military government (May 1980–March 1981), the National Security Council became the highest ruling body. The council's economic committees began to take over decision-making authority from the economic bureaucracy. The subcommittees were composed of an odd mix of populist military officers, middle-level technocrats recruited to perform staff functions, and market-oriented technocrats, such as Jae-Ik Kim, who had been brought in to tutor the top military leadership on economic questions.

Seeking to distance themselves from the politics of the Park era, the younger officers criticized the corruption and decadence of big business and launched a wide-ranging "social purification" campaign that included deep purges of the press and attacks on, and internment of, labor union and student leaders. They launched a range of economic initiatives, including a sweeping reorganization of a number of troubled heavy and chemical industries, the announcement of new social programs, including medical insurance, and a commitment to the construction of a welfare state.

Conclusion

As the period of political transition came to a close and the National Security Council was dissolved and the Fifth Republic formally established, a more conservative policy line reemerged. Reformist officers were either returned to the barracks or reassigned, losing the influence they had temporarily gained over economic policy. Immediate economic problems—inflation, severe recession, increasing debt, and rising balance-of-payments difficulties—overshadowed plans to launch welfare state initiatives. In addition, business viewed the new government with skepticism, particularly given the lack of economic expertise at the top.

These economic difficulties and the decline in private sector confidence provided the reformers with a second opening. The economists responsible for the earlier stabilization plans gradually gained in authority. Economic policymaking was once again centralized in the EPB. Kihwan Kim assumed the presidency of the KDI, Kyung-Shik Kang became minister of finance, and Jae-Ik Kim assumed the post of chief economic secretary to the president, a position from which he was to wield substantial influence until his death in the Rangoon bombing of 1983.

Yet the pursuit of stabilization was once again delayed, this time by a combination of scandals in the curb market and the deepening financial difficulties of a number of the largest *chaebol*. It is to these problems, and the ultimate triumph of the reformers, that we now turn.

NOTES

1. World Bank, *Korea: Managing the Industrial Transition,* vol. 1, *The Conduct of Industrial Policy* (Washington D.C.: World Bank, 1987), p. 42.
2. "Machinery Localization Program Laid Out," *Monthly Review,* 10, 3 (1976): 15.
3. See World Bank, *Korea: Managing the Industrial Transition,* vol. 1, pp. 42–44.
4. See D. Cole and Yung-Chul Park, *Financial Development in Korea: 1945–1978* (Cambridge: Harvard University Press, 1983); Wontack Hong and Yung-Chul Park, "The Financing of Export-Oriented Growth in Korea," in A. Tan and B. Kapur, eds., *Pacific Growth and Financial Interdependence* (Sydney: Allen & Unwin, 1986), pp. 163–82. Data in the following paragraphs draw from Yoon-Je Cho and D. Cole, "The Role of the Financial Sector in Korea's Structural Adjustment," in V. Corbo and Sang-Mok Suh, eds., *Structural Adjustment in a Newly Industrialized Country: The Korean Experience* (Baltimore/London: Johns Hopkins University Press, a World Bank publication, 1992), pp. 115–37.
5. See S. Collins and Won-Am Park, "External Debt and Macroeconomic Performance," in J. Sachs and S. Collins, eds., *Developing Country Debt and Economic Performance,* vol. 3 (Chicago: University of Chicago Press, 1989), p. 296.
6. Ibid.
7. Heavy industry is defined here as the chemical, petrochemical and coal; basic metal; and fabricated metal products and machinery sectors. World Bank, *Korea: Managing the Industrial Transition,* vol. 2, Table 2.5.

8. See K. Fields, "Developmental Capitalism and Industrial Organization: Business Groups and the State in Korea and Taiwan," unpublished Ph.D. dissertation, University of California, 1991, chap. 6.

9. The criteria for being designated as a GTC included overall capital and detailed export requirements. For example, GTCs had to export at least $10 million worth of goods to at least ten markets and had to have ten foreign branches. These requirements, which clearly separated the ten to twelve largest trading firms, were periodically raised, keeping the number of GTCs roughly constant. Moreover, since all of the GTCs were affiliates of the major industrial groups, the program contributed to the concentration of industry. The GTCs accounted for 12 percent of Korea's exports in 1975 and 20.7 percent in 1976. In early 1977, additional policy favors were announced with the objective of pushing the GTC share of total exports to 65 percent by 1981. "Strengthening International Competitiveness and Promotion of Investment," *Monthly Review,* 11, 3 (March 1977): 3, and "General Trading Companies in Korea, *Monthly Review,* 13, 3 (1979): 1–17; Korean Traders Association, "Background to the GTC System" (mimeo., n.d.).

10. The following account draws on Chung-In Moon, "Political Economy of Third World Bilateralism: The Korean–Saudi Arabian Connection 1973–84," unpublished Ph.D. dissertation, University of Maryland, 1983, chap. 5.

11. A variety of other supports were also extended to construction firms, though the government also closely monitored their activities to control competition and monitor contract performance that might have injured Korea's overall reputation. Construction firms gained access to credit on the same terms extended to exporters. A $400 million fund supported their activities, foreign exchange controls were relaxed, and the Saudi riyal was even designated as an accepted currency of payment. See Moon, "Political Economy of Third World Bilateralism," chap. 5.

12. "Marshalling the Small Savers," *Far Eastern Economic Review* (May 13, 1977): 55–56.

13. The Workmen's Property Formation Savings System was an installment savings scheme for workers earning up to 300,000 won a month, a limit that extended the scheme well into the ranks of the salaried middle class. Workers contracted to pay set amounts into the scheme for a fixed period up to five years. At maturity, the government promised to pay a "bounty" on the basic interest rate, and employers paid a "voluntary" premium of 2 to 5 percent of the total accumulation, raising the five-year return to as high as 30 percent a year. Interest was exempt from taxes. Other programs included a medical installment savings system, a rural

household savings system, a doubling of the number of school savings banks, and several new insurance and savings bonds schemes.

14. Restraints were placed on swap arrangements. Under a scheme devised in 1974 to encourage capital inflow, foreign banks, which were restricted in their taking of deposits, could swap hard currency for won without exchange risk and lend the won to domestic borrowers at lucrative spreads. New restrictions tied the level of swaps to outstanding foreign currency loans. In mid-1977, the government imposed ceilings on the rates payable on short-term foreign borrowings, compensating importers by increasing access to local foreign currency loans. See P. Weintraub, "Seoul's Test of Faith," *Far Eastern Economic Review* (March 17, 1978): 38.

15. The terms of the loan were 0.625 percent over the London interbank offered rate (LIBOR) for the first five years of the ten-year loan and 0.75 over LIBOR for the remainder.

16. The terms of the first loan compared unfavorably with the Philippines, which borrowed $200 million at 0.75 over LIBOR over ten years. See R. Richardson, "About Face Is the Order for Seoul's Economy," *Far Eastern Economic Review* (June 13, 1980): 90. On the second loan, see R. Richardson, "Seoul Takes the Temperature," *Far Eastern Economic Review* (November 7, 1980): 104.

17. See V. Corbo and Sang-Woo Nam, "The Recent Macroeconomic Evolution of the Republic of Korea: An Overview," in Corbo and Suh, eds., *Structural Adjustment in a Newly Industrialized Country*, pp. 35–67.

18. Includes price subsidies for major cereals, fertilizer, farm machinery, and livestock raising, net of tariffs and profits from sales of nongrain agricultural commodities. Pal-Yong Moon and Bong-Soon Kang, *Trade, Exchange Rate, and Agricultural Pricing Policies in the Republic of Korea* (Washington, D.C.: World Bank, 1989), p. 126.

19. This follows closely Corbo and Nam, "Recent Experience in Controlling Inflation," in Corbo and Suh, eds., *Structural Adjustment in a Newly Industrialized Country*, pp. 95–114.

20. The following draws on P. Kuznets, "The Dramatic Reversal of 1979–80: Contemporary Economic Development in Korea," *Journal of Northeast Asian Studies*, 1, 3 (1982): 71–87.

21. See, for example, Mahn-Je Kim, director of Korean Development Institute, in *Euromoney* (April 1977), special supplement on Korea, p. 34.

22. "General Trends of the Economy During the First Five-Month Period of 1977 and Major Economic Policy for the Second Half of the Year," *Monthly Review*, 11, 7 (1977): 1–14.

23. Kwang Choi, "Introduction of the Value Added Tax," in Cho and Kim, eds., *Economic Development in the Republic of Korea,* pp. 273–302.

24. Ibid.

25. Firms would be allowed adjustments based on price lists drawn up at the end of May, and price ceilings would be placed temporarily on 95 major commodities and 157 monopolistic products.

26. The following paragraph draws on Byung-Sun Choi, "Institutionalizing a Liberal Economic Order in Korea: The Strategic Management of Economic Change," unpublished Ph.D. dissertation, Harvard University, 1987, pp. 205–21.

27. This argument is made in ibid., chap. 5.

28. Korean Development Institute (KDI), *Gyungje Anjunghwa Sichaek Jaryo Jip* (Collection of materials on economic stabilization policies) (Seoul: KDI, 1982), pp. 125–46.

29. The following draws from Choi, "Institutionalizing a Liberal Economic Order," pp. 239ff.

30. See *Dong-A Ilbo,* June 16, 1978.

31. The opposition gained nine seats, increasing its total to sixty-one. The Yushin Constitution established two-member districts, in which the top two vote getters in each district gain seats.

32. See KDI, *Gyungje Anjunghwa Sichaek,* pp. 221–56.

33. Ibid.

34. The following is drawn from Economic Planning Board, *Economic Survey: Annual Report of the Korean Economy in 1979* (Seoul: EPB, 1980), pt. 2.

35. International Monetary Fund, *Government Financial Statistics Yearbook, 1980* (Washington, D.C.: International Monetary Fund, 1980), p. 311.

36. See K. Fields, "Developmental Capitalism and Industrial Organization: Business Groups and the State in Korea and Taiwan," unpublished Ph.D. dissertation, University of California, Berkeley, 1990.

37. On the evolution of the distribution of income in this period, see G. Fields, "Changing Labor Market Conditions and Economic Development in Hong Kong, Korea, Singapore and Taiwan," unpublished ms., Cornell University, 1993, p. 22.

38. E. Baker, "Within the Scope Defined by Law: The Rights of Labor under the Yushin Constitution," unpublished manuscript, Harvard University, n.d., p. 23, which provides a succinct summary of the system of industrial relations under the Yushin Constitution.

39. In an interview in June 1979, Kim noted, "Inflation has become worse. The economic position in general has become much more

unstable. . . . A handful of entrepreneurs . . . have profited far more than the man in the street from our economic growth. The time has come to stand up and confront the government." *Far Eastern Economic Review* (June 8, 1978): 13.

40. *Dong-A Ilbo,* January 9, 1982.

41. See In-Joung Whang, "Korea's Economic Management for Structural Adjustment in the 1980s," paper presented at the World Bank/Korea Development Institute Working Party Meeting on "Structural Adjustment in the NICs: Lessons from Korea," Washington, D.C., June 19–20, 1986.

42. KDI, "Forecasting for Forthcoming Twelve Months and Countermeasures," September 1979 report to the Monthly Economic Trend Meeting.

43. On the Yulsan failure, see *Far Eastern Economic Review*, R. Richardson, "Yulsan Rocks the Boat" (April 17, 1979): 104; R. Richardson, "Yulsan Exposes the Flaws" (May 11, 1979): 52; R. Richardson, "Korea Learns the Hard Way" (June 22, 1979): 84.

44. On the government's efforts to restore the confidence of foreign business, see Deputy Prime Minister Hyon Hwack Shin's speech at a special meeting of representatives of foreign companies operating in November. R. Richardson, "Damping Waves of Uncertainty," *Far Eastern Economic Review*, 106, 46 (1979): 65.

45. Koo Bon Ho, interview with author, Seoul, May 1989.

46. Discounts on bills.

4

The Political Economy of Adjustment in the 1980s

Stephan Haggard and Susan Collins

Korea's successful adjustment in adapting to the shocks of the early 1980s has been held up as a model for other countries to emulate. The record is impressive (Table 4-1). Following the deep recession of 1980, gross national product (GNP) growth rebounded quickly in 1981, in part because of an improved harvest. Growth of GNP and exports fluctuated substantially over the next five years, but output growth never dropped below 5 percent. This performance was achieved while dramatically reducing the level of inflation, allowing the resumption of real wage growth, steadily improving the country's balance of payments, and stabilizing, and then reducing, the level of external indebtedness. A different set of adjustment problems emerged in the second half of the 1980s, centered on the management of large current account surpluses. Yet the main focus of this chapter is on the early 1980s, a period not only of successful stabilization but also of profound changes in Korea's overall style of economic management.

The controversy over the economics of Korea's rapid adjustment is substantial. Given that strong growth had in the past typically been associated with higher inflation and a deterioration in the balance of payments, several accounts have stressed the importance of the traditional tools of demand management and appropriate exchange rate adjustments. For example, the Morgan Guaranty Survey argues that Korea's adjustment experience demonstrates that "shock therapy can yield quick and major benefits."[1] An International Monetary Fund (IMF) study calls Korea an "excellent example of how orthodox stabilization policies, effectively implemented, can help a country adjust to domestic and external shocks."[2]

A brief review of the sequencing of the stabilization effort suggests that this account is misleading and that a distinction has to be drawn

Table 4-1. Main Economic Indicators, 1979–1985 (percentages)

	1979	1980	1981	1982	1983	1984	1985
Real GNP growth	7.0	−4.8	5.9	7.2	12.6	9.3	7.0
Real GDP growth	7.4	−2.0	6.7	7.3	11.8	9.4	6.9
Inflation	18.2	28.5	21.3	7.3	3.6	2.2	2.5
General budget deficit/GNP (−)	−1.6	−2.6	−4.0	−3.3	−0.9	−1.1	−1.4
Central budget deficit/GNP (−)	−1.8	−2.3	−3.5	−3.2	−1.1	−1.2	−1.2
Fiscal impulse[a]	−1.1	−0.1	1.6	−0.5	−2.1	0.1	0.0
M2 growth	24.6	26.9	25.0	27.0	15.2	7.7	15.6
Domestic credit growth	35.6	41.9	31.2	25.0	15.7	13.2	18.0
Consumer price index deflated wage growth	8.5	−4.0	−0.5	7.9	7.2	6.4	6.6
Current account/GNP	−8.5	−11.2	−9.5	−7.0	−3.9	−3.6	−2.2
Real export growth	−1.0	11.3	17.6	6.6	16.2	15.7	7.5
Real exchange rate (1980–1982 = 100)	100.8	97.8	100.3	101.9	97.6	96.6	89.3
Debt/GNP	37.3	48.9	49.8	53.9	50.8	48.4	52.6
Terms of trade (1980 = 100)	115.4	100.0	98.0	102.2	103.2	105.4	105.9
Gross fixed capital formation/GDP	33.8	32.1	28.0	28.4	29.2	28.9	28.2
Private gross fixed capital formation/GDP	29.8	28.0	24.3	24.0	23.8	24.5	23.9

[a]IMF measure starts with a base year in which actual and potential real output are assumed to be the same. A more than proportionate increase is defined as expansionary, and a less than proportionate increase is contractionary. The measure uses potential GNP obtained from a regression equation.
Sources: Economic Planning Board, *Korean Statistical Yearbook* and *Major Statistics of the Korean Economy*, various issues; International Monetary Fund, *International Financial Statistics*, various issues; and World Bank, *World Debt Tables*, various issues.

between two subperiods: the initial response to the crisis over 1980–1982 and the introduction of more orthodox measures thereafter. The IMF's fiscal impulse measure shows a contractionary stance in 1979; the budget deficit was cut from 2.5 percent of GNP in 1978 to 1.4 percent in 1979. From 1980 through the end of 1982, however, a series of economic events delayed the further implementation of stabilization measures, including a deep recession in 1980, crises in the curb market in 1982 and 1983, and the dramatic slowdown in world trade growth in 1982. These shocks occurred on top of ongoing structural problems in a number of heavy and chemical industries and the political uncertainty associated with the assassination of Park Chung Hee and the transition to a new government under General Chun Doo Hwan in mid-1980. The budget deficit increased by 2 percentage points of GNP in 1980, and fiscal policy continued to be strongly expansionist in 1981. Credit policy was particularly loose in 1980, interest rates were lowered to counteract the effects of the recession, and monetary policy remained expansionary in 1981 and 1982.

During this first phase of adjustment, therefore, Korea's macroeconomic policy was characterized by a mix of conventional stabilization measures with a number of expansionist policies.[3] This can be traced partly to important political constraints on the government but also to the views of important policymakers. Jae-Ik Kim, in particular, voiced skepticism about the merits of using monetary instruments for stabilization purposes. Korea also came into conflict with the IMF in 1981 and 1982 over the real appreciation of the exchange rate.

It was not until 1983 and 1984 that the government resumed strong stabilization measures and began to accelerate the pace of structural reform. As we show, stabilization was initiated and carried out by a military government that had fully consolidated its power and was even more authoritarian in its leadership style than the government of Park Chung Hee. This new policy direction was sustained through 1985, despite growing political opposition and sharp conflicts between the government and the private sector, particularly over credit policy.

Since orthodox adjustment measures were not consistently launched until 1983, other factors besides macroeconomic policy must be important in explaining the reduction in inflation and the improvement in the current account, which had begun prior to that time. Three interrelated factors help explain the dramatic decline in inflation.

The first was a change in the external environment (see Chapter 9). Unlike many other developing countries, Korea adjusted oil prices swiftly in the face of the second oil shock. Beginning in 1982, Korea's terms of trade underwent a steady improvement due to the real decline of oil and raw materials prices on which the country is heavily dependent. The results of a modeling exercise by Corbo and Nam suggest that the slowdown in prices was mostly the result of the slowdown in the rate of increase in the won prices of raw materials.[4]

The second factor affecting inflation was the slowdown in wage growth, which helped translate the sharp drop in the won price of raw materials into lower inflation (see Chapter 7). Real wages fell in 1980 and 1981, remarkable for Korea, and though they resumed their upward march in 1982, the wage pressures of 1978–1979 were not replicated.

The third factor was the exchange rate (see Chapter 9). The devaluation of 1980 was a major source of inflationary pressures, but the real effective exchange rate was allowed to appreciate slightly in 1981 and 1982 before being gradually depreciated through 1984. The period of appreciation helped to dampen price increases, and the subsequent real depreciation contributed to improved export growth following the sluggish performance in 1982. Real wages measured in dollars fell by 30 percent over the 1979–1984 period.

Positive developments in the terms of trade after 1981, an easing of international interest rates, and the effects of the devaluation of 1980 help explain why Korea's external position improved so rapidly, though it was not until the sharp oil price drop of 1986 that the country's terms of trade recovered their 1979 level. Nonetheless, in the second half of 1984, the country experienced a slowdown in export growth. Given the political leadership's continuing commitment to tight monetary and fiscal policies, currency depreciation was seen as the best available instrument for providing an economic stimulus. In mid-1985, the won was depreciated against the dollar and then depreciated substantially throughout the year as the dollar weakened against the yen.

The depreciation of the won and the unanticipated declines in world oil prices and interest rates opened a third policy phase (1985–1987), during which the emergence of large current account surpluses and the accumulation of substantial reserves constituted the main adjustment problem. These economic problems coincided with the transition to democratic rule, and thus raised a number of sensitive political issues, including how to manage trade and exchange rate policy, macroeconomic policy, and labor relations in the face of increasing political demands from a long-repressed civil society.

We now turn to an outline of the political context of stabilization and structural adjustment under Chun Doo Hwan. In the following sections we trace the evolution of macroeconomic policy, distinguishing among three subperiods. During the first two years of the Chun government, economic and political constraints blocked the full implementation of stabilization and adjustment measures. In the second phase, 1983–1985, government power was fully consolidated. Orthodox stabilization measures came to the fore and structural adjustment efforts accelerated. Finally, we analyze the problem of managing growing current account surpluses.

The Political Context of Adjustment, 1980-1984

Stabilization and structural adjustment raise interesting puzzles for political economy analysis.[5] Despite the longer-term social benefits to be gained from economic reform, these policies impose short-term costs, as well as permanent losses for some groups, and are thus politically difficult to implement. The Chun government was politically constrained at both the beginning and end of its tenure, which helps account for some of the nonconventional components of the early adjustment program and some important policy changes in 1985. When compared to other developing countries, however, Korea is more striking for the vigor with which adjustment was undertaken. Why was Korea able to stabilize and launch such wide-ranging reforms when so many other countries failed to do so?[6].

Upon seizing office in May 1980, Chun adopted a strongly moralistic stance, promising a purification *(jonghwha)* of society that would eliminate the "three negative attitudes" of corruption, lack of civic-mindedness, and inflation.[7] Chun believed that inflation had been responsible for the erosion of living standards of farmers and workers, which in turn had contributed to the social unrest of 1979 and 1980. He thus saw inflation not simply as an economic problem but as reflective of a deeper social malaise.

In pursuit of his goal of purification—and the consolidation of his own personal power—Chun aggressively repressed all social opposition. The government was more direct and harsh in the controls it extended over the labor movement than Park had been. Students challenged the legitimacy of the Chun regime almost from its inception, but the government effectively squashed these early protests. The press experienced a wide-ranging purge in the early years of the Chun government that virtually eliminated published criticism of the administration.

Chun's views were also reflected in changes within the economic bureaucracy and policymaking machinery in the early 1980s. As a result of the debate over stabilization policy in 1978 and 1979, the Economic Planning Board (EPB) regained some of the influence it had lost to the industrial planners. For example, the creation of the Industrial Policy Deliberation Committee in 1981 increased the power of the deputy prime minister and the EPB over industrial policy, at the expense of the ministries of commerce and industry and of finance.

More important than an institutional resurgence of the EPB was a rise in the power of the Blue House economic staff and close personal relations forged between Chun and a small group of technocratic reformers. Following the declaration of martial law in 1980, several EPB technocrats, particularly Kihwan Kim and Jae-Ik Kim, became advisers to the military. Jae-Ik Kim chaired the economic subcommittee of the National Security Council, became Chun Doo Hwan's economic tutor, and in March 1981 was elevated to the position of chief adviser to the president on economic affairs. Because of Jae-Ik Kim's close position to the president, the Blue House became even more important in the formulation of policy than it had been under Park; in effect, the position of presidential adviser became more important than that of deputy prime minister and head of the EPB. Moreover, Kim influenced appointments in other parts of the government, for example, moving EPB personnel into top positions in the Ministry of Finance in order to secure active support for his efforts at financial liberalization. Despite the turnover of personnel at the ministerial level, including changes of the deputy prime minister, Kim provided policy continuity from 1981 through the Rangoon bombing in October 1983. He was followed by an intellectual ally, IL Sakong, who also wielded substantial influence.

As the late Park period shows, authoritarian regimes are not invulnerable to opposition, and during the early part of his tenure, Chun faced political constraints that help explain both the timing and content of adjustment measures. His seizure of power through a coup d'état and the violent suppression of the Kwangju uprising undercut the basic legitimacy of the government. In an attempt to secure support, Chun promised to address the inequality that had arisen during the late 1970s by giving greater attention to issues of social development. Although the fifth five-year plan (1982–1986) emphasized stabilization and structural adjustment and generally reflected the priorities of the 1979 stabilization program, it also placed greater weight on social development; indeed, the plan's name was changed to the Five-Year Economic *and Social* Development Plan.

The government also faced short-term political challenges. In the six months between October 1980 and March 1981, Chun and his party faced a referendum on the Constitution and separate presidential and legislative elections, all held against the backdrop of a severely depressed economy. The referendum was held in October 1980. The Constitution was drafted by the martial law leadership and was not subject to meaningful public debate. Major opposition figures and student leaders had been held in detention, and the month before the referendum, Kim Dae-Jung, the most prominent opposition leader, had been sentenced to death for plotting to overthrow the government.[8] The Constitution was supported overwhelmingly at the polls, allowing Chun to stand for election to the presidency in February, which he won against token opposition.[9]

The lifting of martial law prior to the presidential election permitted the formation of new political parties. With severe limitations on campaign activities, a political ban on key opposition leaders, and new controls on the press, Chun's Democratic Justice party (DJP) received 69.4 percent of the votes cast in the March legislative elections.[10] The DJP won ninety seats out of ninety-two two-member districts. In contrast to previous elections, it did surprisingly well in the cities, gaining the highest number of votes in half of Seoul's electoral districts. Chun's control of the legislature was guaranteed by a system of proportional representation that allocated only two-thirds of the assembly seats on the basis of constituency elections, with the remainder allocated on the basis of total votes. This system, and the conciliatory stance initially taken by a weakened opposition, provided the government with a comfortable margin of legislative support.

In sum, despite Chun's efforts to differentiate the new government from its predecessor, there were a number of political and institutional continuities between the authoritarian Yushin system and its successor Fifth Republic that provided the government substantial leeway in pursuing its program of stabilization and structural adjustment. These included a powerful executive, a weak legislature, a politically strengthened core of technocrats, and a president willing to suppress all opposition in order to achieve his political and economic goals. When the government undertook fiscal and wage policy initiatives, particularly in 1983 and 1984, they rested not simply on government will and commitment but on an authoritarian structure that insulated the government from opposition, both inside and outside the legislature.

The main political constraint on the implementation of economic policy was the private business sector, and particularly the largest *chaebol.* The junta had taken a number of actions that increased business uncertainty, including the wide-ranging restructuring by fiat of several heavy and chemical industry sectors. The populist stance of a number of the younger officers also raised doubts about the stability of the business environment. Shortly after his inauguration, Chun signaled that the close relationship that existed between government and the *chaebol* was subject to revision. The government devised a credit administrative system for big business whereby firms with large bank debts, including all of the *chaebol,* were required to sell subsidiaries not related to their main lines of business and to liquidate "unproductive" real estate investments. The government also announced that the allocation of credit would henceforth favor small- and medium-sized firms and that relief loans for large firms involved in the heavy and chemical industries would not be forthcoming unless companies undertook financial reforms.[11]

A number of structural adjustment measures taken early in Chun's presidency also attempted to reduce the privileged position of big business. The enactment of the Monopoly Regulation and Fair Trade Law in April 1981 sought to challenge the dominant position the *chaebol* enjoyed in the domestic market by promoting competition. An accelerated program of import liberalization had the same effect. Finally, the EPB fought to revise the system of industrial policy toward more arms-length incentives. Measures to achieve this objective included doing away with industrial assistance targeted on an industry or sectoral basis, expanding general supports such as incentives for research and development and training, and enhancing the role of tax incentives while reducing the use of policy loans.

The attitude of the *chaebol* toward the government's stabilization and structural adjustment initiatives was ambivalent. On the one hand, liberalization promised greater managerial autonomy from government directives. The privatization of the banking sector opened new opportunities for business. Following the initial period of political consolidation, the Chun government also sought to repair its relations with the private sector. For example, in January 1982, the cabinet was reshuffled to improve business ties.[12]

On the other hand, the government's effort to reverse the bias Park had shown toward big business posed risks. The government's stabilization policies were particularly unpopular given that many of the largest firms experienced severe financial difficulties in the early 1980s and vacillating fortunes in export markets. This very weakness, coupled with the high level of industrial concentration, made the large business sector, represented by the Federation of Korean Industries, a politically powerful lobby. The early 1980s were thus characterized by ongoing tension between the Chun government and big business, with the government oscillating between attempts to discipline the *chaebol* and to offer the concessions required to facilitate growth and financial stability.

Phase One: Crisis Management, 1980-1982

Despite Chun's personal commitment to stabilization, the new government faced severe constraints on fiscal policy in 1980 due to the severity of the recession and unemployment. Budgetary expenditures were increased several times following Chun's seizure of office in May 1980, accomplished in part through a supplementary budget that included a large public works program, a doubling of the share of expenditure going to housing, and cuts in sales taxes. These policies, and more important the loss of revenue associated with the recession, contributed to an increase in the budget deficit from 1.4 percent of GNP in 1979 to 3.2 percent in 1980.

In contrast to the expectation that new governments will exploit honeymoons to undertake fiscal adjustments, the budget turned in an even more decisively expansionist direction in 1981, as can be seen in the measure of fiscal impulse in Table 4-1. Expenditure increases played the major role in the expansion and appeared to reflect a concern to offset the losses in agricultural incomes that had resulted from the severe crop failure in 1980.[13] Grain price increases were cut somewhat from their trend growth in the 1970s, but the Grain Management Fund increased the volume of its purchases in 1981 in order to replenish stocks that were released during the poor harvest of 1980. Public spending on rural projects also continued, and several temporary tax reduction measures were targeted at poorer groups, including cuts in income taxes for low-income workers.

Government plans, including the fifth five-year plan issued in September 1981, called for a return to stabilization objectives in 1982, and in mid-1981, there were revisions in the budget to cut expenditures. The government issued bonds to reduce its borrowing from the central bank. But the fiscal deficit remained high—4.4 percent of GNP—due to poor revenue performance, the slowdown in growth that accompanied a slump in export performance,[14] and failure to restrain the growth of public sector wages, which increased nearly 12 percent in real terms. It was not until 1983 that fiscal policy became restrictive.

Given the government's fiscal stance, monetary policy was left as the main instrument of stabilization policy. Broad money (M2) grew no faster in 1980 than it had in 1979 despite the currency depreciation (Table 4-1), implying a slowdown in real terms. However, in the early years of the Chun administration, credit policy was quite expansionary. In the fall of 1980, the government used its control of the commercial banks to increase the amount of export loans per dollar of letter of credit and allowed a massive increase in local government borrowing for the purpose of road construction. The government also announced an expansion of credit to small- and medium-sized industries, though the data do not indicate that such a shift was in fact accomplished.[15] Critics argued that the burst of credit in late 1980 and early 1981 was used to finance the presidential and legislative campaigns.[16] But base money declined for 1980 as a whole and grew very slowly in 1981–1982 due to a sharp drop in reserve requirements.

In January 1980 in conjunction with the devaluation, interest rates were raised substantially, both to dampen expected inflationary pressures associated with the devaluation and to improve the efficiency of the financial system. Beginning in June, the new government began a gradual reduction in interest rates, consistent with the expansionary stance adopted in mid-1980. This action was undertaken well before any sign of a slowing of inflation (Table 4-2).

This policy might be viewed simply as a response to the recession and business pressure; as can be seen in Table 4-3, business experienced severe difficulties even after the upturn in the economy in 1981. As early as June 1979, immediately after the April 17, 1979, package, the four

Table 4-2. Interest Rate Changes, 1980–1982

Date of Rate Change	Discount on Bills[a]
September 7, 1979	18.5
January 12, 1980	24.5
June 5, 1980	23.5
September 16, 1980	21.5
November 8, 1980	19.5
November 9, 1981	18.5
November 30, 1981	17.5
December 29, 1981	16.5
January 14, 1982	15.5
March 29, 1982	13.5
June 28, 1982	10.0

[a]Discount to prime borrowers.
Source: Bank of Korea, *Money and Banking Statistics 1984*, Table 40, p. 386.

major business associations issued a policy statement opposing any increase in interest rates, the opening shot in a conflict over credit policy that would persist over the 1980s. In fact, there were important divisions within the government on interest rate policy. The EPB and the Bank of Korea believed the financial system had been distorted by the pervasive use of preferential credit as an instrument of industrial policy and that targeted credit was being diverted into real estate and curb market speculation. A realignment of interest rates was thus seen not only as a component of stabilization and balance-of-payments policy but as the beginning of structural reform of the financial system.

Jae-Ik Kim agreed that industrial targeting had resulted in credit misallocation and argued vigorously for financial market reform. Yet he also viewed high interest rates as a cost-push factor contributing to inflationary pressures and thus ineffective as an instrument of inflation control.[17] Over the next two years, his views tended to prevail. Table 4-2 suggests that reductions in interest rates led, rather than followed, the

Table 4-3. Major Business Indicators, Manufacturing Sector

	1978	1979	1980	1981	1982	1983	1984	1985	1986
Normal profit/net assets	5.0	3.4	−0.2	0.0	1.0	3.3	3.4	3.0	4.5
Normal profit/net worth	22.9	15.6	−1.3	0.1	5.3	15.5	15.2	13.2	20.2
Normal profit/net sales	4.0	2.7	−0.2	0.0	0.9	2.7	2.7	2.5	3.6
Financial costs/total costs	4.9	5.9	7.1	7.8	6.4	5.2	5.0	5.3	4.9
Debt/equity ratio	366.8	377.1	487.9	451.5	385.8	360.3	342.7	348.4	350.9
Private investment/GNP[a]	27.4	31.0	26.9	25.3	23.3	24.6	26.5	25.8	25.3

[a]Private gross domestic captial formation, all sectors.
Source: Bank of Korea, *Money and Banking Statistics,* various issues.

slowdown in inflation in 1980 and 1981. Real interest rates did not turn positive until the fourth quarter of 1981. Moreover, the lowering of domestic interest rates was faster than the decline in (exceptionally high) international rates, which opened a differential in favor of foreign assets that was not closed until the second half of 1982.

The structural problems in the financial sector were revealed clearly by a series of curb market scandals beginning in May 1982.[18] When two large companies defaulted on debts, confidence in nonbank financial institutions dropped, and a number faced severe runs. Given that even the *chaebol* relied on the informal credit markets for operating funds, the crisis also posed problems for nonfinancial firms. As Table 4-3 shows, the crisis came at a time of particular vulnerability. Firms in manufacturing showed low and declining profitability, rising financial costs, and extremely high debt burdens.

The scandal had serious political implications, coinciding with a phase of Korean politics during which economic issues came to play an increasing role. At the center of the scandal was a woman named Yong Ja Chang who was distantly related by marriage to President Chun. Chang had played on supposed connections to the Blue House in order to borrow extensively on the curb market. The opposition immediately seized on the incident as evidence of government corruption, charging that illicitly obtained funds had been used to finance the ruling party. The depth of the crisis was signaled by Chun's decision to replace not only the finance minister but the prime minister as well.

On June 28, the government announced a wide-ranging plan to counter the crisis. Bank interest rates were lowered by four percentage points, a controversial move that reflected Jae-Ik Kim's concern that real rates were becoming too high. The government announced that it would not hold itself to the credit target of 25 percent set at the beginning of the year. Although they did in the end succeed in doing so, the growth of broad money in the second half was expansive, approaching 50 percent on an annualized basis. Moreover, a corporate tax cut was announced for 1983, from 33–38 percent to a uniform 20 percent, a new credit line was opened for small businesses, and collateral requirements on these loans were relaxed.

The curb market scandal provided an opportunity for reformers to advance their plans for financial market liberalization. In a Blue House meeting in November 1980, Chun had decided to reduce policy loans and restrictions on the managerial autonomy of the commercial banks, with the ultimate aim of privatizing them altogether. The Ministry of Finance established a commercial paper market, lowered required reserve ratios, and in January 1982 shifted the major instruments of monetary management by replacing direct credit controls with more active use of reserve requirements and open market operations.

Prior to the curb market scandal, however, support for financial market liberalization and bank privatization was tepid.[19] The Finance Ministry considered liberalization as premature given that the state-owned banks held substantial nonperforming assets associated with the Heavy and Chemical Industry Plan and the lingering effects of the recession. Jae-Ik Kim exploited the crisis to push through a number of reforms, however: the lowering of interest rates in June; a substantial revision in the interest rate structure, replacing a complex system of differential rates for different activities and classes of borrowers with more nearly uniform rates; efforts to reform the curb market itself;[20] privatization of the remaining commercial banks; opening of the banking sector to foreign joint ventures; and a dramatic deregulation of the nonbank financial sector, which quickly mushroomed into the most dynamic segment of the market.[21]

If fiscal and monetary policy were both expansionary during the first two years of the new government, exchange rate policy was a third area in which expansionist views prevailed. As we saw in Chapter 3, the won was devalued by 17 percent by the interim government in January 1980, though by the end of 1980, the real effective depreciation was only 7 percent due to inflation. Business attitudes toward the devaluation were mixed. Exporters naturally favored a competitive exchange rate, but business associations also expressed concerns about rising costs of imported inputs associated with the depreciation.[22] This concern was not limited to those selling in the domestic market; the Korean Traders Association estimated that the average import requirement for each unit of manufactured exports in 1980 was 42.3 percent.

In 1981, the government restricted the pace of depreciation.[23] The result of this policy, can be seen in the real exchange rate index (Table 4-1), which showed an appreciation in 1981 and 1982. Three reasons were advanced against further devaluation. The first was that it would contribute to inflation; exchange rate policy was seen as an important component of stabilization. Second, the Ministry of Finance argued that since the current account was improving, there was no reason for the government to increase the local currency servicing burden on its dollar-denominated debt.

An additional factor, however, was a structural one advanced by Jae-Ik Kim. Kim believed that devaluation provided a quick fix and eliminated the incentives for firms to improve productivity through cost cutting and technological improvement. By allowing a slight overvaluation of the won, firms were forced to enhance their competitiveness, including through tight controls on wages.

These views led to an open conflict with the IMF, which called for more rapid depreciation in 1982.[24] As export growth began to slow in 1982 as a result of the world recession, exporters became more vocal in opposition to government policy.[25] The Korean Traders Association publicly called for more flexible management of the exchange rate. Other exporters argued for an additional devaluation against the dollar of from 5 to 20 percent as well as more substantial reforms, such as decreasing the weight of the strong dollar in the basket of currencies used to manage the float and the liberalization of the foreign exchange market altogether. Not until the slowdown in export performance became fully apparent in the second half of 1982 did the government act to adjust the exchange rate in a more competitive direction. By this time, the damage had been done, however. Annual export growth was lower than it had been in any other year since the transition to export-led growth in the early 1960s, and though this was largely attributable to the global recession, exchange rate policy made matters worse.

Phase Two: Stabilization and the Acceleration of Structural Adjustment, 1983-1984

By the end of 1982, Korean authorities could point to economic accomplishments that would have been the envy of other developing countries. Inflation had fallen dramatically, growth had recovered, though it remained below both trend and targets, and the current account deficit had steadily narrowed from its high of over 11 percent of GNP in 1980 (Table 4-4). Yet despite these favorable trends, the top economic planners focused their attention on a number of outstanding economic problems in order to push forward a new set of policy initiatives for 1983. These initiatives reflected a return to the objectives of stabilization that had been interrupted by the political and economic crises of 1979–1980.

One justification for the program was external. Despite the current account improvement, total debt had grown from $20.3 billion in 1979 to $37.1 billion in 1982, an increase from 32.5 percent of GNP to 53.5 percent. The maturity of debt had shifted toward greater reliance on short-term borrowing, from 26.9 percent of total debt in 1979 to 33.5 percent in 1982. The debt-service ratio increased from 16.3 percent in 1979 to 20.6 percent in 1982. None of these numbers appears particularly

Table 4-4. Quarterly Economic Performance, 1980–1984

	Consumer Price Index (1980 = 100, period average)	Real GNP Growth	Current Account/ GNP
1980 I	90.5	2.1	−13.9
1980 II	97.5	6.3	−11.2
1980 III	102.2	0.8	−9.1
1980 IV	109.8	10.6	−8.2
1981 I	114.2	1.6	−10.7
1981 II	119.4	4.1	−10.0
1981 III	125.3	5.8	−6.4
1981 IV	126.1	13.9	−6.1
1982 I	127.6	5.6	−2.8
1982 II	129.7	4.1	−3.2
1982 III	131.4	7.1	−4.5
1982 IV	131.6	4.8	−6.5
1983 I	134.1	8.5	−8.7
1983 II	134.5	9.9	−3.3
1983 III	134.7	10.4	2.0
1983 IV	134.7	8.7	−2.7
1984 I	136.7	12.5	−4.7
1984 II	137.4	9.0	−3.3
1984 III	137.9	5.6	−2.9
1984 IV	138.3	5.1	0.3

Source: Exports, imports, GNP, and CPI: International Monetary Fund, *International Financial Statistics,* various issues; real GNP growth: Bank of Korea, *Statistical Yearbook,* various issues.

alarming when compared with the problems facing the Latin American debtors, nor was there evidence that Korea experienced a worsening in the terms of its borrowing in 1983.[26]

Nonetheless, the onset of the debt crisis and the slowdown in exports raised fears that contagion effects might limit Korea's ability to access the market on the favorable terms it had enjoyed in the past. At the broader political level, the opposition argued that rapid debt accumulation reflected the mismanagement, if not corruption, of the Chun government. In April 1984, the fifth five-year development plan, which covered the years 1982–1986, was revised to call for increased exports and savings (from 24 percent of GNP in 1983 to 28.6 percent) and a ceiling on external debt of $50 billion by the end of 1986.[27] President Chun personally lowered the proposed target from $60 billion proposed in the draft plan.

The second goal of the plan was to consolidate the stabilization in prices that had occurred since 1981. Despite the fact that inflation had dropped substantially in 1982, policymakers were not convinced that inflationary expectations had been broken. Budget deficits were historically high, and the curb market scandals, ongoing problems of ailing firms, and business pressures had forced the government to relax monetary policy. Thus, in the absence of any apparent inflation problem by past Korean standards, the government initiated a stabilization program based on the standard policy instruments: fiscal, wage, and monetary policy. Each of these measures demanded confronting and overcoming particular sources of political resistance.

Korea's fiscal structure is relatively rigid. Under a bilateral defense burden-sharing agreement with the United States, Korea allocates 6 percent of GNP to defense, which normally accounts for around 30 percent of the budget. Debt service, grants to local governments, which do not have extensive independent sources of revenue, educational financing, and public sector wages account for another 40 percent. The EPB controls the remaining 30 percent, the bulk of which goes for economic services and large public investment projects.

The squeeze on the budget began in 1983 with zero-based budgeting but was carried into 1984 by a decision to freeze government expenditures. This idea was pushed by Jae-Ik Kim and given full backing by President Chun.[28] An IMF study confirms that although cyclical factors contributed to the dramatic improvement in the fiscal picture in 1983, the bulk of the adjustment was associated with discretionary measures.[29] To higher indirect taxes were added a 5 percent surtax on foreign oil as world prices fell from their 1981 high. Expenditure measures accounted for the bulk of the fiscal adjustment, however. The government subjected the general administrative sector to a dramatic squeeze and imposed a wage freeze on public sector workers in 1984. Promotions were delayed and hiring frozen. An organizational reform of the government sector was implemented and redundant and overlapping agencies either eliminated or merged.

The most politically difficult expenditure-reducing measure was the decision to freeze the support prices of rice and barley. This move halved the deficit of the Grain Management Fund to 0.4 percent of GNP. Although the deficit of the fund increased once again in 1984 due to a large crop and a decision to ease somewhat the earlier price freeze, the new direction of policy was clear; the dual rice pricing policy that had been a critical mainstay of Park's political strategy would be phased out.

The government saw wage policy as a component of the stabilization package, although the ability of the government to control wages was limited (see Chapter 7). Top technocrats had consistently argued that the rapid real wage growth of the late 1970s, which outstripped productivity growth, was a critical component of the country's economic difficulties. Beginning in 1981, state-owned banks were called on to enforce guidelines on wage increases. Banks were to do this by insisting that their borrowers, mostly large firms, reduce debt-equity ratios to specific targets before granting raises. Wage increases were also to be limited to increases in productivity. The public sector wage squeeze was designed as a way of setting a range for wage increases in the private sector. Public sector wages from 1980 through 1986 were consistently held below the growth of private sector wages, though this could be interpreted as either an indication of government commitment to slow the pace of wage growth or of the failure to achieve this objective.

Also difficult to assess is the influence of the larger political milieu in which labor operated.[30] During the brief political opening in 1980, labor unions pursued internal organizational reforms in order to reduce the pervasive governmental interference in their operations. These attempts ended when the military government launched an extensive purge of top union leaders, amended the trade union law, and once again restricted strike activity. The new industrial relations regime weakened the power of the trade union confederation by decentralizing the union system, prohibiting third-party intervention in labor disputes, and limiting unions' ability not only to strike but even to negotiate independently. The repressive stance toward labor ultimately backfired, but in the short run, the new system of industrial relations significantly weakened labor's political power and probably had some effect on its market power as well.

The final component of stabilization policy concerned credit. The new fiscal stringency reduced the government's borrowings from the Bank of Korea in 1984, but these were in any case small, and the real squeeze on credit fell on the private sector beginning in 1983. The growth rate of domestic credit had declined from 31.2 percent in 1981 to 25 percent in 1982 but fell dramatically to 15.7 percent in 1983. For 1984, the government announced that the growth of credit would be held to the 1983 level; in fact, credit for the year grew less—13.2 percent.

In reducing credit growth to the private sector, the government targeted preferential financial schemes that had previously been extended to particular industries. In 1978, such preferential finance accounted for 51 percent of total domestic credit. The ratio was cut to 40 percent between 1982 and 1984. This drop partly reflects the dramatic growth of the unregulated nonbank financial sector, despite government limitations on the share of loans that nonbank financial institutions could make to their parents, usually large *chaebol.*

The ratio of preferential loans to total bank loans showed a different trend, however. In 1982, this ratio was 62 percent but increased to 68 percent in 1983 and 70 percent in 1984. These figures suggest that while overall domestic credit to the private sector was being cut and preferential financing was falling as a share of total credits, banks were still playing the role of providing special loans to certain classes of borrowers.

The reasons for this trend were several. The government was forced to act as the lender of last resort during the financial scandals of 1982. These scandals did not prove to be the last, however. At least three other major financial irregularities resulting in problems in the curb market occurred in 1983 and 1984. Although the precise details varied from case to case, these scandals usually involved the rapid expansion of a business group through illicit borrowing, guarantees based on personal connections, or outright fraud. Rapid expansion was followed by financial collapse and subsequent reverberations in the unregulated curb market. In all cases, the government was forced to provide additional liquidity to the system.[31]

The problems in the financial sector were not limited to illicit behavior in the curb market; they also stemmed from past patterns of government targeting, cyclical and structural problems in specific industries, and the highly leveraged nature of the Korean firms. Beginning in late 1983, the Federation of Korean Industries (FKI) began a campaign to reverse the government's tight money policy.[32] The arguments are interesting, since they reflect the political difficulties the government faced in seeking to liberalize the economy given past patterns of policy. First, the FKI argued that controls on credit to large firms would depress investment and limit the pace of recovery. Investment by big business was crucial not only because of its direct role in exports and employment but also because of the dependence of small and medium businesses on larger ones through marketing and subcontracting relations. Thus, the effort to tilt credit toward smaller firms was seen as misguided.

Second, the FKI argued that the inefficiency and weak financial structures of large firms were not the result of poor financial management but of past government policy. In some cases, business conglomerates had been forced to take over delinquent firms, particularly in the restructuring of the heavy and chemical industry sector. Moreover, many of the investments made by the *chaebol* reflected government priorities.

A third constraint was the health of the commercial banking system. The difficulties faced by the industrial sector were reflected in the growth of nonperforming assets, just as the government was seeking to privatize and liberalize the financial system.

These factors left the government in a double bind. Despite the strong commitment of the technocratic team and of Chun himself to the goal of price stabilization, the very size of the *chaebol* and their close links with the banking system made it impossible for the government to ignore their financial difficulties.[33] Although the curb market scandals had raised this problem before, the Kukje Group provided the most serious test case. Kukje, the sixth largest business group in the country, began to experience severe cash flow problems in mid-1984. Shrinking Middle East markets, ambitious corporate expansion, and poor export performance had put the group under strain. When Kukje requested financial relief, the government decided to let the firm go bankrupt. Rumors circulated that Daewoo, the second-largest group, was next.[34]

In fact, the political cost of allowing further bankruptcies among the largest firms would have been prohibitively high. Over the course of 1984, the government periodically used the Korea Exchange Bank to extend relief to troubled firms. By the summer of 1985, these measures proved to be inadequate. The commercial banking sector was saddled with nonperforming assets in the construction and shipping industries, as well as other sectors previously targeted by the government. Systematic rescue financing and adjustment plans were developed for a number of sectors, including overseas construction, shipping, textiles and apparel, and plywood.[35] The government committed additional resources to normalize several heavy and chemical industry sectors, such as shipbuilding, that had been the object of earlier promotional efforts. In July 1985, the Monetary Board amended the Bank of Korea regulation to allow the bank to grant loans at 3 percent interest in order to finance industrial structural adjustment and to continue sound management of the financial institutions. The exact size of the fund was closely guarded, and later became politically controversial, but was believed to total approximately $1.7 billion.[36] In part as a result of these policies, total domestic credit eased somewhat in 1985, and the growth of loans and discounts to the private sector rose to 20 percent.

Despite these political and economic difficulties with the private sector concerning credit policy, the commitment of the government to stabilization during the 1983–1984 period is undeniable. A technocratic team led initially by Jae-Ik Kim initiated politically difficult fiscal adjustments, such as cuts in rice subsidies and public employment, attempted an incomes policy to slow wage growth, and launched a number of structural adjustment measures, including financial market reform and trade liberalization. The reasons for Korea's success with adjustment are both economic and political. As we have noted, favorable shocks after 1981 contributed to the stabilization of prices, and as Table 4-3 demonstrates, investment did not suffer during the stabilization episode, and even increased from a low point in 1982.

Yet it appears undeniable that political and institutional factors played a crucial role in Korea's adjustment. With strong backing from the president and little scope for organized opposition to coalesce, technocrats were free to pursue a reform agenda that would prove difficult under the more pluralist political setting that characterized the second half of the 1980s.

Phase Three: Macroeconomic Policy, 1985-1987

The Emergence of Democratic Politics

The legislative elections of February 1985 were a turning point in Korean political history, opening a period of turbulence that culminated in the transition to democratic rule in 1987. The election revealed a typical pattern of opposition to the government in the cities being offset by support in the countryside. But cuts in grain subsidies, growing farm debt, and the threat of liberalization of trade in agricultural products provided new opportunities for the opposition in the rural areas. The ruling Democratic Justice party retained its control of the National Assembly because of the proportional representation system but received only 35.3 percent of the popular vote,[37] a stunning upset, particularly given that the New Korea Democratic party, the main opposition force, was formed only just prior to the election. Moreover, it was founded by former members of the Korea Democratic party (KDP) who had rejected the KDP's conciliatory stance toward the government.

The vote largely reflected popular dissatisfaction with Chun's military rule, the slow pace of political reform, and the government's unwillingness to negotiate changes in the Constitution that would allow for the direct election of the president. Unexpectedly, however, economic policy also became a key election issue. The opposition appealed to those disadvantaged by the stabilization and structural adjustment measures and emphasized the government's continuing links with big business at the expense of workers, farmers, and the less developed regions of the country. The opposition also managed to capitalize on public aversion to the country's large foreign debt, using special legislative hearings to their tactical advantage.

The strong showing in the 1985 election encouraged opposition forces to organize around the issue of constitutional revision.[38] As a group, students had the most staunchly antigovernment stance and played a leading role in organizing antigovernment protests both before and after the elections. Although their interests were primarily political, they also developed an increasingly radical critique of Korea's economic development and sought to forge alliances with worker and farmer groups, in part under the umbrella of the churches.

Although there were periodic signs of a political thaw, the government vacillated between an accommodating and repressive stance toward the opposition in 1985 and 1986, and little progress was made on negotiating constitutional revisions. On April 13, 1987, President Chun suspended the debate, sparking a wave of nationwide antigovernment protests. In June, the DJP officially nominated ex-general Roh Tae-Woo as the ruling party's presidential candidate. Given that the electoral college system all but guaranteed that he would gain the presidency, this nomination sparked the largest and most prolonged demonstrations until that time, with broad participation from middle-class professionals in Seoul. On June 29, Roh made a declaration of political reform that included direct presidential elections and guarantees of political and civil liberties, threatening to resign if Chun failed to support the proposals. Chun's assent set the stage for presidential elections in December 1987 and National Assembly elections the following April, marking the country's transition to democratic rule.

Economic Policy during the Political Transition: The Emergence of Surpluses

By the end of 1984, Korean economic planners should have had a number of reasons for satisfaction. Stabilization measures had consolidated the gains in reducing inflation and improving the external balance made in 1981–1982, and a number of structural adjustment initiatives were underway. Two interrelated constraints operated on the government beginning in late 1984, however. The first was political, and came as much from within the ruling party as from the opposition. Prior to the 1985 elections, ruling party politicians strongly urged Chun to back away from some elements of his stabilization plan. After the elections, the government was placed even more squarely on the defensive, as the legislature and press provided more open forums for debate on the economy.

The second constraint was economic (Table 4-5). In the second half of 1984, the domestic economy began to slow. Export orders slackened, and export volume actually declined briefly in the first quarter of 1985, largely as a result of the slowdown in world economic recovery. For the year as a whole, Korea would register export growth that was only marginally better than in 1982, and gross domestic product growth of "only" 5.4 percent.[39] Although 5 percent real growth would be considered robust in most other countries, Korean planners considered 5 percent a minimum threshold, and plan targets routinely topped 7 percent. A major concern was unemployment and labor absorption, particularly of the rapidly increasing number of college graduates.

The slowdown in exports and growth put the government in a policy bind. Chun was reluctant to yield on his commitment to stabilization, despite mounting political pressures. Credit remained extremely tight through the first quarter of 1985. Moreover, for the year as a whole, the budget deficit fell to 1 percent of GNP, resulting in a neutral stance in terms of fiscal thrust. During the course of 1985, however, as export performance continued to worsen, two policy initiatives gained ground within the government. First, the notion of accelerated currency depreciation was seen as a way to improve the cash flow of export-oriented firms. Second, some of Chun's advisers began to advance supply-side arguments that credit policy should be loosened in order to increase investment that would allow Korean manufacturers to exploit the growth in world trade that was forecast for 1986. Business clamored loudly for additional stimulus through lower interest rates, and Chun himself was sympathetic to arguments that a greater share of credit should be channeled to small- and medium-sized firms.

Thus, despite government pronouncements of a commitment to relaxing direct controls over interest rates and the use of credit, a package of measures was announced on July 13 that included expanded export credit financing, an increase in credit lines to small companies, and

Table 4-5. Main Economic Indicators, 1984–1988 (percentages)

	1984	1985	1986	1987	1988
Real GNP growth	9.3	7.0	12.9	12.8	12.2
Real GDP growth	9.4	6.9	12.4	12.0	11.5
Inflation	2.2	2.5	2.8	3.0	7.2
General budget deficit/GNP(−)	−1.1	−1.4	0.0	1.1	2.2
Central budget deficit/GNP(−)	−1.2	−1.2	−0.1	0.5	1.6
Fiscal impulse	0.1	0.0	−0.9	1.0	N.A.
M2 growth	7.7	15.6	18.4	19.1	21.5
Domestic credit growth	13.2	18.0	15.9	14.5	10.9
Consumer price index deflated wage growth	6.4	6.6	5.3	6.9	7.7
Current account/GNP	−3.6	−2.2	3.1	5.9	7.0
Real export growth	15.7	7.5	12.2	23.8	13.0
Real exchange rate index	96.6	89.3	76.3	75.6	82.3
Debt/GNP	48.4	52.6	45.5	31.4	21.5
Terms of trade (1980 = 100)	105.4	105.9	115.3	118.1	121.4
Gross fixed capital formation/GDP	28.9	28.2	27.8	28.7	29.2
Private gross fixed capital formation/GDP	24.5	23.9	23.8	24.8	25.5

Source: see Table 2–2.

changes in depreciation schedules.[40] This did not arrest the escalating conflict between the "stabilizers" within the government and the business community, however; the chairman of the FKI, Chung Ju-Yung, called for a more general stimulus through a reduction of interest rates. A major cabinet shake-up in January 1986 resulted in tacit concessions to the private sector position. Mahn-Je Kim, long a supporter of the use of credit for industrial policy purposes, was made deputy prime minister and the head of the EPB. Although postponing a number of large infrastructural projects, Kim quickly announced plans to increase concessional loans for export and small- and medium-sized businesses.

The emergence of current account surpluses in 1986 may be approached through an examination of the external sector or through the savings-investment balance (compare Chapters 8 and 9). Korean exports responded relatively quickly to the depreciation, jumping 28 percent in 1986. However, this export surge coincided with an unexpected decline in world oil prices, which accounted for almost half of the turnaround in the current account between 1985 and 1986 and a sharp drop in world interest rates. Moreover, the won was being depreciated against the dollar, which in turn was dropping rapidly against the yen and the European currencies (Table 4-6). Viewed from the perspective of the savings-investment balance, the unexpectedly rapid growth of incomes and profits associated with the export boom led to a sharp increase in savings. Savings outstripped even the rapid growth in investment, but continued restrictions on capital flows impeded directing the private savings surplus into the acquisition of foreign assets.

An interesting puzzle is why the Koreans depreciated the won so far and so fast; the factors that contributed to this outcome demonstrate the importance of analyzing the indicators and information that policymakers themselves used at the time their judgments were made.[41] The first reason had to do with developments in the current account. The main purpose of the depreciation was to stimulate the export sector. But as late as August 1985, both the government and business press were issuing alarmist statements concerning adverse developments in the current account.[42] The recovery in exports did not begin until the early months of 1986, and not until the middle of the year did the current account move into surplus (see Table 4-6). Second, officials involved in the decision admitted that their attention was focused almost exclusively on the won-dollar rate. Although the bilateral exchange rate index showed a sharp depreciation of the won between the fourth quarter of 1984 and the first quarter of 1985, the rate was surprisingly stable over the next year. In fact, however, the effective depreciation accelerated sharply after

Table 4-6. Quarterly Exports and Exchange Rates, 1984–1986

	Exports (US$ million)	Real Effective Exchange Rate (1980 = 100)	US$/Won Rate (1980 = 100)	Yen/Won Rate (1980 = 100)
1984 I	5,861	93.2	76.3	77.8
1984 II	6,602	92.5	76.1	77.1
1984 III	6,647	94.0	74.9	80.5
1984 IV	7,225	93.4	74.1	80.4
1985 I	5,790	94.2	72.4	82.3
1985 II	6,673	88.9	70.1	77.5
1985 III	6,772	85.0	68.8	72.4
1985 IV	7,207	78.7	68.1	62.2
1986 I	6,804	76.1	68.5	56.7
1986 II	8,337	73.1	68.5	51.4
1986 III	8,959	N.A.	N.A.	N.A.
1986 IV	9,834	N.A.	N.A.	N.A.

Source: Exports US$ from monthly data, Bank of Korea, same as IFS 77aad, merchandise export fob. Exchange rate indexes from International Monetary Fund, *Korea: Recent Economic Developments* (Washington, D.C.: IMF, September 1986).

March 1985 when the dollar began its steep decline against the yen and the deutsche mark, trends that continued into early 1986.

It should also be noted that the judgment of Korean policymakers was validated by international financial institutions. In early 1985, the IMF staff believed that the won was overvalued, and in the consultations leading to the IMF standby of July 1985, they urged an even greater depreciation than occurred, as they had done also in 1974 and in 1980. Protectionist pressures in the United States peaked in the fall of 1985, but it was not until the following year that the United States moved to open discussions with Korea on exchange rate issues.

The sharp depreciation of the won created a set of adjustment problems that were novel for most large debtors and resembled the "Dutch disease" difficulties associated with natural resource booms. Without some policy response, adjustment would occur, but through a decline in saving, wage-price pressures, and inflation. During 1986 and 1987, however, the choice of adjustment policies was complicated by the emergence of broad political pressures, ongoing tensions between business and government, and the emergence of particular cleavages between large and small firms, industry and agriculture, and management and labor. These political constraints can be illustrated by analyzing briefly three policy dilemmas associated with the emergence of surpluses: the question of trade and exchange rate policy; macroeconomic, and particularly monetary, policy; and wages and labor relations.

The first, and most obvious, problem was that relative prices strongly favored the traded goods sector, widening the bilateral imbalance with the United States and exacerbating trade conflicts (Table 4-7). The emergence of surpluses thus raised politically sensitive issues about the pace and extent of trade liberalization and exchange rate management, and the mix between the two.

Technocratic efforts to liberalize trade can be traced to the late-1970s opposition within the EPB to the Heavy and Chemical Industry Plan. At that time, freer trade was seen as important not only for improving efficiency and lowering the cost of critical inputs but as a tool of stabilization policy. These earlier efforts were interrupted by the economic and political shocks of 1979–1980 and their aftermath. Not until 1983 did the Ministry of Finance elaborate a five-year scheme for liberalizing imports. It was able to do so in part because of the strategic positioning of liberals, notably Kihwan Kim, at the traditionally more protectionist Ministry of Commerce and Industry. Despite strong presidential support, the gradual design of the liberalization program and the order in which sectors were to be opened reflected compromises, both with affected firms and with the more dirigist elements of the bureaucracy.[43]

Liberalization efforts were complicated by foreign pressure. President Reagan approached the Korean government with a list of specific market-opening requests on his visit to Seoul in 1983, the first year Korea's current account position with the United States moved into surplus. Protectionist pressures in the United States surged in late 1985, and the Reagan administration responded with an aggressive trade policy initiative that emphasized opening foreign markets to U.S. exports of goods and services. At the same time, under pressure from Congress, the Treasury Department opened discussions with Korea and Taiwan over

Table 4-7. Bilateral Trade Balances in the 1980s (US$ million)

	Korea–United States	Korea–Japan
1980	−266	−2,819
1981	−362	−2,871
1982	329	−1,900
1983	1,984	−2,856
1984	3,651	−3,030
1985	4,235	−3,011
1986	7,372	−5,443
1987	9,621	−5,220
1988	8,719	−3,843

Note: Trade balance is exports minus imports.
Source: IMF, *Direction of Trade Yearbook*, various issues.

exchange rate issues, calling for a more rapid appreciation of the won and for a liberalization of the Korean financial market.

Overall, the government's record in liberalizing trade was impressive, reflecting the same institutional capabilities that allowed it to pursue its stabilization objectives. Between 1984 and 1987, the government liberalized 65 percent of the items requested by the United States, particularly in the manufacturing sector. Some of the items were already on the Ministry of Finance's liberalization schedule, which reduced the share of items subject to quantitative restrictions from 20 percent at the end of 1983 to about 5 percent in 1988. Average tariff rates were cut during the same period, from 23.7 percent to 18.1 percent. In addition, the government undertook a series of more targeted actions to alleviate bilateral tensions with the U.S.: foreign currency loans to promote imports of capital goods, the announcement of voluntary export restraints on ten products in 1987, and both compulsory and voluntary measures to diversify the geographic sources of imports, particularly away from Japan.

The main points of controversy concerned services but particularly agriculture. As U.S. pressure on the exchange rate mounted, a split emerged between the large export-oriented *chaebol* and smaller businesses and agriculture. From mid-1986, the *chaebol* argued vociferously against won appreciation. They openly expressed support for import liberalization as a way of deflecting political pressure from the United States. Small- and medium-sized businesses, by contrast, joined agriculture in calling for continued protection. It is a testimony to the pivotal political importance of the rural sector that negotiations between the United States and Korea on beef and other agricultural items were completely stalled in 1986–1987. Nor was the controversy limited to sectoral concerns. Opposition to free trade became a broader rallying cry, particularly of the student movement. In 1986, Deputy Prime Minister Mahn-Je Kim abolished the International Economic Policy Council, an organ designed to manage trade issues with foreign governments, because of both bureaucratic and broader political resistance to the free trade stance of its liberal head, Kim Kihwan. In the second half of 1987, implementation of the import liberalization program virtually ceased, and not until after the political transition in 1988 did the government launch a new liberalization effort, both as a response to continuing foreign pressures and in an effort to dampen inflationary pressures associated with the accumulation of reserves.[44]

The second problem was that large current account surpluses threatened price stability because of the difficulty of offsetting the large net export earnings. The policy problems of macroeconomic management were both technical and political. Given that the economy was operating near capacity during the boom years of 1986–1987, there was little scope to adjust through expansionary demand policies. In 1986, the consolidated government account moved from a slight deficit to balance and maintained this stance in 1987, despite the accommodation of political pressures from farmers. The freeze on prices paid by the Grain Management Fund was lifted in 1984. The political significance of farmers to the ruling party was once again revealed in March 1987, when the government undertook a large debt relief operation for farmers, who swapped farm debts carrying high interest rates for preferential loans from public financing sources. This action was initiated by members of the ruling party in cooperation with the Ministry of Agriculture and Fisheries and over the opposition of the EPB, the Ministry of Finance, and the Bank of Korea.

The main macroeconomic policy dilemmas centered on monetary policy. By late 1986, the government was struggling to keep the rapid growth in net foreign assets from pushing money supply growth above targets. The main instrument of adjustment was sale of monetary stabilization bonds by the Bank of Korea. During 1987, the central bank offset the equivalent of 16 percent of the broad money stock through sale of these instruments, incurring losses estimated by the IMF to equal 0.6 percent of GNP.

These actions posed two further dilemmas. On the external side, the resulting upward pressure on interest rates further widened the differential with international rates. When coupled with expectations of further appreciation, this induced speculative capital inflows that complicated monetary management. The Bank of Korea attempted to manage this problem in part by encouraging firms to prepay their external debt. But the central bank was able to exercise influence over only financial institutions and state-owned enterprises, and in the latter case, only by actually providing these enterprises with foreign currency loans. Private sector borrowers were, predictably, unwilling to repay external obligations because of their lower interest costs and anticipated appreciation; to the contrary, large firms pressed for more rapid liberalization of the capital account.

The second dilemma concerned interest rates and once again exposed the rift between the government and the credit-dependent *chaebol*. Concerns about excessive monetary growth led to cutting some concessional credit lines, including to exporters. Increases in the rediscount rate (in 1986 and again in 1988) and reserve requirements, together with the sale of stabilization bonds, increased the cost of credit. Repeating a line of argument that they had advanced over the 1980s, the Federation of Korean Industries argued that "interest rates should be set from the viewpoint that they are an ingredient of the production cost rather than a tool for allocating or controlling funds."[45] Business pressed the government throughout 1986 and 1987 to lower rates, particularly following the generous wage settlements forced on the private sector by labor actions in the second half of 1987. Yet the dictates of stabilization policy, concern that lower interest rates would trigger real estate speculation, and a broader political effort by the government to distance itself from the demands of the *chaebol* led to a firm stance through the end of 1987.

Pressure on prices came not only from the external sector but also from wages; this constituted a third axis of policy conflict. Even without the dramatic political opening of mid-1987, the high profitability of the export sector in 1986–1987, the emergence of large surpluses, and the relatively tight labor market would have invited workers to rewrite their contracts. Yet the political opening was quickly followed by a massive surge in strike activity and generous wage settlements; these are reflected in the rapid increase in the growth of nominal and real wages. (See Table 4-5.)

In 1981 and 1982, labor disputes dropped sharply under new labor laws.[46] After 1983, this trend was reversed. Labor actions also began to take on a more political cast, due in part to the penetration of the labor movement by radical students. In the two months from July 4 to September 4, 1987, however, there were more labor disputes in Korea than there had been in the previous ten years. Labor demands centered on wage increases and improved conditions but also raised more fundamental political issues, including a reduction in government intervention in union affairs, greater freedom to organize independent unions, and changes in the structure of dispute settlement. While the Federation of Korean Trade Unions and various industrial unions were vying to regain support and influence after a period of relative quiescence by demanding reforms in the labor law, independent labor unions sprang up to defy both the government and the quasi-official labor establishment. In the two months following Roh Tae-Woo's historic June 29 announcement, over 1,000 company-level unions were formed.

Given the government's announced intention to move toward more democratic politics and the interest of politicians in responding to a core electoral constituency, the government had little choice but to respond to rising labor pressures. In 1986 and 1987, the ruling party itself introduced legislation that guaranteed collective bargaining, the right to strike, and the freedom to form new unions. In 1987, firms were informed that they would have to resolve labor disputes on their own and could not rely on government intervention in support of management that had been typical during both Park's and Chun's presidencies.

Conclusion

The period of political transition from 1985 through 1987 presaged the types of dilemmas policymakers would face under democratic rule. First, the liberalization of politics provided new channels for groups to air grievances. In a more open political context, opposition parties quite naturally sought to exploit economic issues for electoral gain. Second, political liberalization forced the government to abandon the coercive means of adjustment that had been used in the past, for example, with reference to labor, and to pay greater attention to building coalitions and bases of support. In some cases, such as trade policy, this meant slowing the process of reform or providing compensation to potential losers. Finally, the broad political changes began to erode the independence of the economic bureaucracy. Certain ministries, such as Commerce and Industry or Agriculture and Fisheries, had traditionally maintained close ties with constituents. In the past, however, these could be overridden by the centralized power of the EPB and the Blue House itself. Now, technocrats had to pay greater attention to the role of politicians, including within the ruling party itself.

These developments did not necessarily point to a reversal of the reforms of the 1980s, however. Because of the close, and often corrupt, nature of business-government relations, many liberalizing measures, such as financial market liberalization and a reduction of government intervention in support of industry, were taken up by both the private sector and the opposition. In 1987 and 1988, a wide-ranging political debate took place on the independence of the central bank, with the Bank of Korea making a strange alliance with Center-Left politicians who argued that government interference in the conduct of monetary policy should be reduced. Second, the coherence of Korea's economic policy was in part a function of institutional characteristics that will survive the transition to democracy, including a well-trained bureaucracy and a relatively centralized economic policymaking process.

Finally, our analysis provides support for an important piece of conventional wisdom: the economic and political significance of an outward-oriented development strategy. Although there was a concern with the growth of foreign debt throughout the period of Korea's adjustment in the 1980s, the country was able to borrow through the crisis because of its proved export record. It did not have to cut investment, despite a fall in domestic savings (Chapter 8). When world growth resumed in 1983, Korea was well positioned to exploit export opportunities. This cycle repeated itself on a less dramatic scale in the middle of the decade. When export growth slowed in 1985, the government moved quickly to provide incentives to exporters, through both the exchange rate and the provision of concessional credit. Again, investment did not suffer.

This pattern is in stark contrast to the experience of the Latin American countries in the early 1980s. Unable to service their obligations through exports, they were forced to compress their current accounts when international lending was withdrawn. Investment suffered accordingly, contributing to their economic difficulties.

The export thrust also had important political effects. First, it made government officials sensitive to competitiveness; exposure to international markets itself acted as a check on economic policy. Second, the large and growing share of the economy that was connected with exports provided a political or coalitional base of support for the continuation of those policies. No doubt, democratization will give rise to important debates about the distribution of income and the need for a more equal relationship between labor and capital. As in Japan, the weight of rural constituencies will guarantee some subsidization of agriculture. It is unlikely, however, that Korea will fundamentally reverse course or even return to the dirigist policy experiments that characterized the late 1970s.

NOTES

1. "Korea: Adjustment Model of the 1980s?" *World Financial Markets* (Morgan Guaranty Trust) (March 1984): 8.
2. B. Aghevli and J. Márquez-Ruarte, *A Case of Successful Adjustment: Korea's Experience During 1980–84,* IMF Occasional Paper 39 (IMF: Washington, D.C., August 1985), p. 1.
3. Our analysis here is similar to that by T. Casse, *The Non-Conventional Approach to Stability: The Case of South Korea: An Analysis of Macro-Economic Policy, 1979–1984,* Research Report 5 (Copenhagen: Centre for Development Research, 1985), chaps. 4, 5.
4. V. Corbo and Sang-Woo Nam, "Recent Experience in Controlling Inflation" in V. Corbo and Sang-Mok Suh, eds., *Structural Adjustment in*

a Newly Industrialized Country: The Korean Experience (Baltimore: Johns Hopkins University Press, 1992), pp. 95–114.

5. See S. Haggard and R. Kaufman, eds., *The Politics of Adjustment: International Constraints, Distributive Politics and the State* (Princeton: Princeton University Press, 1992).

6. For other treatments of this issue, see S. Haggard and Chung-In Moon, "Institutions and Economic Growth: Theory and a Korean Case Study," *World Politics,* 42, 2 (1990): 210–37, and Chung-In Moon, "The Demise of a Developmentalist State? The Politics of Stabilization and Structural Adjustment," *Journal of Developing Societies,* 4 (1988): 67–84.

7. Shim Jae Hun, "Seoul's Leader for All Seasons," *Far Eastern Economic Review* (May 14, 1982): 46–47.

8. Under pressure from the United States, his sentence was commuted to life imprisonment.

9. Unlike the Yushin system, deputies could campaign for specific candidates. New rules stipulated that the president be elected through an electoral college system; opposition to the system of indirect election was to become the rallying cry of the opposition.

10. For example, ballot sheets contained names but no party affiliations.

11. The measure was directed at the twenty-six largest groups, which held 631 subsidiaries.

12. The new team was made up wholly of technocrats but included several figures with strong links to the business community, including Chang Soon Yoo, who became prime minister, and Woo Bae Rah, who assumed leadership of the Ministry of Finance.

13. The following draws on Aghevli and Márquez-Ruarte, *A Case of Successful Adjustment.*

14. The deep recession in the United States reached bottom in the fourth quarter of 1982.

15. The share of bank loans going to small and medium industries was 43.9 percent in 1980, 45.2 in 1981, 43.3 in 1982, 44.3 in 1983, and 44.0 in 1984. Casse, *Non-Conventional Approach to Stability,* p. 70.

16. Shim Jae Hun, "Chun Wins Another One," *Far Eastern Economic Review* (April 3, 1981): 19.

17. For a characterization of Jae-Ik Kim's views, see Kihwan Kim, "Jae-Ik Kim: His Life and Contributions," in L. Krause and Kihwan Kim, eds., *Liberalization in the Process of Economic Development* (Berkeley: University of California Press, 1991), pp. xi–xxiv.

18. See Yoon-je Cho and D. Cole, "The Role of the Financial Sector in Korea's Structural Adjustment," in Corbo and Suh, *Structural Adjustment in a Newly Industrialized Country,* pp. 115–37.

19. See Byung-Sun Choi, "Institutionalizing a Liberal Economic Order in Korea: The Strategic Management of Economic Change," unpublished Ph.D. dissertation, Harvard University, 1987, pp. 297–300.

20. On July 3, in the wake of the scandal, the government also launched an attack on the curb market through the so-called real name system. Kyung Shik Kang announced his intention to seek legislation that would allow taxation of curb-market loans secretly advanced to companies or anonymously deposited in banks. The plan required those opening a new deposit over a certain limit to identify themselves with a passport and those with deposits to do so by June or face differential taxation on interest income. The objective was to limit the ability of curb market lenders to hide behind anonymous deposits, though the benefits of operating on the curb market were actually increased by the lowering of interest rates.

21. The interbank call market, on which only South Korea and foreign banks and large investment trusts could heretofore operate, was opened to smaller secondary banking institutions.

22. G. Woodfield, "Restricting the Pace of Depreciation in '81," *Far Eastern Economic Review (May 15, 1981): 52.*

23. Ibid., p. 51. The managed float following the 1980 devaluation was determined by a secret central bank equation using the trade-weighted basket of currencies principle, but, in fact, the government maintained substantial discretion over the rate. Two components of the equation were public: the special drawing rights (SDR) basket formulated by the fund and the "Korea basket" composed of the SDR currencies but with the Canadian dollar replacing the French franc. The currencies are weighted according to both actual trade values and export targets. There are, however, two other variables in the equation: a "B" factor linked to government growth and export goals and a "P" factor that allows the central bank authorities significant discretion. See T. Chesser, "High Noon for the Won," *Far Eastern Economic Review* (December 17, 1982): 47–48.

24. *Wall Street Journal,* May 10, 1982, p. 34.

25. See T. Chesser, "High Noon for the Won," *Far Eastern Economic Review* (December 17, 1982): 47–48.

26. Ibid., (June 30, 1983): 65–66.

27. In fact, as will be analyzed in more detail below, debt reached only $45 billion by the end of 1986, thanks to the "three blessings" of 1986: the sharp drop in oil prices, the sharp drop in the value of the dollar relative to the yen (thus increasing Korean export competitiveness with respect to Japan), and a further decline in world interest rates.

28. On October 9, 1983, seventeen high-ranking Korean officials were killed in Rangoon by a bomb planted by North Korea. A number of senior economic officials, including Jae-Ik Kim, were among the dead. The successor cabinet also showed a strong technocratic bias, however, including Kyung Shik Kang, Mahn-Je Kim, Il Sakong, and Kihwan Kim, all supporters of reform if not protégés of Jae-Ik Kim's.

29. Aghevli and Márquez-Ruarte, *A Case of Successful Adjustment,* p. 15.

30. The following paragraph draws on S. Haggard and Chung-In Moon, "Institutions and Economic Growth: Theory and a Korean Case Study," *World Politics,* 42, 2 (1990): 224.

31. On the case of the Myongsong group see *FEER,* September 3, 1983; on the Choheung bank irregularities that involved the Yongdong Group and Soeil Construction Co., see ibid., October 20, 1983; on the collapse of the Kwangmyong Group, see ibid., August 23, 1984.

32. See Federation of Korean Industries, "Anjunghwa Sichaek gwa Giup ui Jakum Sajung" (The stabilization policy and the financial situation of corporations), *Chun Gyung Ryun* (December 1983): 28–34. The following draws from S. Haggard and Chung-In Moon, "Institutions and Economic Growth," pp. 228–29.

33. See Haggard and Moon, "Institutions and Economic Growth."

34. *Hankuk Ilbo,* February 23, 26, 1985; *Business Korea* (August and September 1985).

35. Construction provides an example of the dilemmas the government faced. By the end of 1983, the government had extended $5.81 billion in payment guarantees on behalf of Korean contractors operating overseas. As the Middle East construction boom slowed as a result of the decline in oil prices, firms began underbidding one another to secure work, and a number of small firms failed. Under a new construction industry law, the government sought to rationalize the finances of construction firms, including through the disposal of land and affiliates. See "Government Steps In as Construction Crisis Looms," *Business Korea* (April 1984): 31.

36. *Hankuk Ilbo,* March 25, 1987.

37. See B. C. Koh, "The 1985 Parliamentary Election in South Korea," *Asian Survey,* 25, 9 (September 1985): 883–97.

38. The best account of the political events leading up to the presidential elections of December 1987 is James W. West and Edward J. Baker, "The 1987 Constitutional Reforms in South Korea: Electoral Processes and Judicial Independence," *Harvard Human Rights Yearbook,* 1 (Spring 1988): 135–77.

39. In 1985, exports contributed only 1 percentage point to GNP growth compared to their 4 percent contribution to growth in 1984 and their 6 percent contribution in the boom year of 1983.

40. See *Business Korea* (August 1985): 16.

41. The following draws on an interview with Mahn-Je Kim, Seoul, October 1991.

42. See, for example, *Business Korea* (August 1985): 24.

43. See Hee-Jung Shin, "Korea's Trade Liberalization Strategies: Reconciling Political and Economic Difficulties," A.B. thesis, Harvard University, 1988.

44. See "A Basic Change in Policy," *Business Korea* (June 1988): 16.

45. Interview with Dae-Joo Chun, Federation of Korean Industries, *Business Korea* (November 1987): 20.

46. The following is drawn from S. Haggard and Chung-In Moon, "Institutions and Economic Policy: Theory and a Korean Case Study," *World Politics*, 42, 2 (1990): 233–34.

Part III

Issues in Korean Macroeconomic Policy _____

5

Fiscal Policy in Korea ———

Richard N. Cooper

Government budgets serve a variety of different and occasionally conflicting functions. The now-classic distinction by economists is the role the budget plays in allocation, distribution, and stabilization. The allocative function is the redirection of the output of the economy, through either public spending on goods and services, such as defense and infrastructure, or the influence of the tax structure on private economic decisions. The distribution function is the redirection of national income from one group of residents to another, such as from the rich to the poor or from the average citizen to the well-placed lobbyist, and may operate through either expenditures or taxes. The stabilization function is the use of taxes and expenditures to attenuate fluctuations in overall economic activity.

From the vantage point of financial officials, however, a different set of distinctions is more meaningful. They seek to maintain administrative control over the expenditures of other parts of the government, to collect revenues with reasonable administrative efficiency, and to finance any difference between total expenditures and total revenues. Financing deficits requires the allocation of resources over time, since servicing the public debt represents a charge on future taxpayers for expenditures, including investments, that have been made in the current period.

The most serious function of a finance ministry is to persuade the political leadership to keep total expenditures within the vicinity of expected revenues. Otherwise, budgetary discipline is lost, which leads to inefficiency in the use of resources through carelessness and waste and to macroeconomic instability through excessive government spending, which can lead to a buildup of public debt. Beyond some point, public debt can be financed only through monetary expansion and, hence, higher inflation, which, if it proceeds far enough, can undermine the foundations of an efficient economy.

The various aspects of budgetary policy occasionally clash. Budgetary controls are most effective when expenditures are not permitted to exceed revenues. Raising tax revenue is almost always politically unpopular, and therefore a balanced budget requirement exerts a strong discipline on expenditures, even when the proposed expenditures are themselves popular. Yet from a social point of view it may make sense to spend in excess of current revenue in some circumstances, for example, on investment projects that have high rates of return but heavy up-front costs. Government deficits may also be used to cushion a downturn in the economy, by smoothing public expenditure despite a fall in government revenue, or even increasing public expenditure to compensate for a fall in private demand. Raising tax revenues in practice always has some allocative costs, and usually some unwanted distributional consequences as well. Political management of the budgetary process is accomplished by striking trade-offs among these various conflicting considerations; successful management ensures that the trade-offs stick.

This chapter addresses the Korean approach to budgetary and fiscal policy during the period 1973 through 1988. It reviews public expenditures and revenues for 1987, in order to provide a profile of the budget; describes the budgetary process and outlines trends in expenditures, revenues, and public debt since 1973; discusses the instrumental, or policy, uses of the budget, with special attention being paid to stabilization policy; provides a short survey of Korean tax policy; and offers a brief overall evaluation of the use of fiscal policy in Korea since the first oil price shock.

The major point to emerge from this survey of fiscal policy is that throughout the period Korea maintained a relatively tight rein on the budget, using it when appropriate for economic stabilization and other purposes but never losing budgetary discipline. Korea thus differs in this respect from many other developing countries, which at one point or another effectively lost budgetary control and ran deficits, typically financed through credit creation, that could not be easily justified under any economic objective.

Korea was not entirely immune from political pressures on fiscal policy, particularly following the oil price increases of 1974 and 1979–1980 and as a result of the extremely ambitious investment requirements of the Heavy and Chemical Industry Plan of the 1970s. Still, Korea addressed these disturbances earlier and more effectively than did most other countries and coped more firmly and more decisively with the residual imbalances following these major disturbances. While several dimensions of economic policy were involved, part of the response was through the budget.

A Profile of the Budget, 1987

Until 1990 Korea was a highly centralized country, with little autonomy for the provincial and local governments; since the transition to democratic governance, there has been a move to devolve greater control to local authorities. Prior to this development, the bulk of local revenues were grants from the central government with specified purposes. Local and provincial tax revenues were the equivalent of 12 percent of the central government revenues in 1987. Thus, the bulk of public expenditure is captured by looking at the central government.

The fiscal condition of the central government is made complex by the fact that in addition to the general account there are numerous extra-budget accounts, as well as (in 1987) twenty-seven nonfinancial state-owned enterprises, some of them performing governmental functions, and nine financial state-owned enterprises, mostly specialized banks of various kinds. The general account and the extra-budget accounts are typically consolidated for presentation, and that practice will be followed here. Most of the nonfinancial state-owned enterprises, significantly, are run on commercial lines and are appropriately excluded except for dividend and interest payments to the government, and loans or capital subscriptions from the government, both of which are included in the government accounts. Several of the off-budget enterprises, most notably the Grain Management Fund and the Bank of Korea, perform governmental functions and will be discussed separately.

Table 5-1 shows the level of expenditures, by major expenditure category, in 1987 and, for historical comparison, for a decade earlier. In 1987 the Korean government spent 16.9 trillion won, nearly 16 percent of gross domestic product (GDP), and had net lending of another 1.2 trillion won. It took in 18.7 trillion won in revenues, of which 16.7 trillion, or 15.4 percent of GDP, were tax revenues. For the first time since 1968, the government ran an overall surplus—478 billion won. Surpluses were also run in 1988 and 1989 before a deficit returned in 1990.

The most important categories of expenditure were defense (27 percent), education (18 percent), economic development (17 percent), and interest on the public debt (7 percent). Total expenditures in relation to GDP rose slightly over the decade, and all major categories of expenditure except defense rose even more rapidly, while defense declined both as a share of public expenditure and as a share of GDP, from 5.6 percent in 1977 to 4.3 percent in 1987.

Including the five most government-like state-owned enterprises—the Grain Management Fund, the Supply Fund, railways, communications

Table 5-1. Profile of Expenditure by Consolidated Central Government

	1977		1987	
	Billion Won	Percentage	Billion Won	Percentage
General public services	297	10.6	1,693	16.0
Defense	1,008	35.9	4,628	27.3
Education	470	16.8	3,108	18.3
Health	48	1.7	398	2.3
Social security and welfare	141	5.0	1,091	6.4
Housing and community services	44	1.6	300	1.8
Economic development	443	15.8	2,812	16.6
Other	353	12.6	2,914	17.2
(of which, interest payments)	132	4.7	1,166	6.9
Total expenditure	2,804	100.0	16,944	100.0
Percentage of GNP		15.7		15.6
Net lending	470		1,236	
Total revenues	2,958		18,658	
Taxes	2,657		16,690	
Nontax revenues	281		1,820	
Sales of assets	20		148	
Overall surplus	−316		478	
Percentage of GNP		−1.8		0.4

Source: IMF, *Government Finance Statistics Yearbook* (1988, 1990).

(mainly the post office after telecommunications was removed in 1982), and the Office of Monopoly, which controls sales of tobacco and ginseng—would add 3 to 4 percent to both revenues and expenditures in the mid-1980s. The timing of revenues and expenditures is not always synchronized, however, and in 1981, when economic expansion was sought, these five enterprises added about 1 percent of GDP to the overall budget deficit.

Total revenue exceeded total expenditures in 1987, resulting in a surplus amounting to 0.4 percent of GDP. Taxes accounted for 89 percent of total revenue, with the remainder coming from enterprise profits, fines, sales of assets, and other miscellaneous sources.[1] Table 5-2 shows the main sources of tax revenue, with income and corporate profits taxes amounting to over 30 percent of the total, a value-added tax plus selective excise taxes accounting for 43 percent, and taxes on foreign trade (mainly import duties) for nearly 20 percent. Over the decade 1977–1987, the relative importance of direct taxes increased somewhat, and that of taxes on goods and services receded.

The overall tax incidence rose from 14.9 to 15.4 percent of GDP, implying an overall ex post tax revenue elasticity with respect to total output of 1.06. In addition, local taxes in 1987 amounted to about 2 percent of GDP, for an overall tax incidence of 17.4 percent, rather lower than the average for middle-income countries, where the overall incidence is generally in the range of 22 to 35 percent; Mexico, Thailand, and Turkey have an incidence around that of Korea, and Colombia's is notably lower. It is much lower than that for high-income countries, where the incidence ranges from 32 percent in the United States to 52 percent in the Netherlands.

The Budgetary Process

Management of the budget in Korea is concentrated in the hands of the Economic Planning Board (EPB), which reports to the deputy prime minister, a super-minister responsible for overall economic policy. This system has been in effect since the 1960s. The EPB makes a forecast early in each year of the growth of the economy and the rate of inflation, in part on the basis of assumptions about prospective developments in the world economy. Growth in the industrialized countries, the likely growth of world trade, and interest rates in the world money market all influence the economic prospects of Korea and are forecast explicitly. On the basis of this information and the historical performance of Korea's tax system, the EPB makes an estimate of revenues for the coming year.

Government ministries and agencies are asked to submit their plans for new programs for the following fiscal year (which coincides with the calendar year) by the end of February. By the end of March, the Budget Office of the EPB promulgates budget guidelines to all ministries and

Table 5-2. Profile of Central Government Taxes

	1977		1987	
	Billion Won	Percentage	Billion Won	Percentage
Direct taxes	736	27.7	5,295	31.7
Individual	353	13.3	2,856	17.1
Corporate and other	383	14.4	2,439	14.6
Social security and wages	29	1.1	314	1.9
Property	20	0.8	176	1.1
Value-added and excise taxes	1,310	49.3	7,243	43.4
Import and export taxes	475	17.9	3,205	19.2
Other and unallocable	88	3.3	457	2.7
Total tax revenues	2,657	100.0	16,690	100.0
Percentage of GDP		14.9		15.4
Note: Local tax revenue			978[a]	

[a]Budgeted.
Source: IMF, *Government Finance Statistics Yearbook* (1988, 1990).

agencies, which then submit their formal budget requests to the EPB by the end of May. Following discussions with the various ministries, a draft budget is submitted to the deputy prime minister and to the president by the end of August. Final adjustments are made in response to pleas by ministers and the ruling party in September, and the final budget is submitted to the National Assembly in early October. During September any discretionary adjustments in tax rates that may be needed are agreed upon.

An unusual feature of the Korean budgetary process is that the National Assembly must pass the budget, as revised, by four weeks before the beginning of the fiscal year—that is, by December 3. Absent such passage, authorization for the continuation of operating expenditures at the level of the current year is automatic. The National Assembly may reduce the budget, but it may not increase it without presidential approval. No expenditure can be made without the approval of the National Assembly, except on default. But within statutory limits, some existing tax rates may be increased or reduced without the approval of the National Assembly.[2] This set of institutional arrangements is conducive to a high degree of budgetary control.

The EPB also has responsibility for monitoring expenditures during the course of the year. Ministries must report quarterly and for the year just concluded by the following spring. Apparently Korean officials adhere rigorously to the approved budget; they have not developed the habit, prevalent in some other developing countries, of spending in excess of the approved budget. The EPB may advance or retard expenditures, especially the inauguration of new projects, during the course of the year by issuing guidelines to that effect. Macroeconomic considerations sometimes indicate the use of this authority. Supplementary budgets have typically also been submitted, usually in the late summer or early fall, for approval by the National Assembly.

The EPB thus has broad powers with respect to fiscal policy in Korea, going well beyond the powers, for instance, of the Office of Management and Budget in the United States. These powers have generally been exercised to keep budgetary expenditures within the ability of the government to finance comfortably. Budgetary control seems to have been the principal objective, supplemented on occasion by macroeconomic considerations, mainly in the direction of stimulus when the economy seemed to be slowing inappropriately, and periodically by a desire to influence the magnitude of private wage settlements through wage increases adopted for government employees.

State Enterprises

The International Monetary Fund records Korea as having thirty-six public enterprises in 1988, not counting the Bank of Korea. Five of these, however, are more appropriately regarded as specialized governmental agencies. That leaves twenty-two nonfinancial public enterprises, in which the government owns over 50 percent of the equity, and nine financial public enterprises.[3] With the exception of a coal mining company and a chemical company, these enterprises are devoted to public goods or natural monopolies, such as electric power, telecommunications, broadcasting, the post office, and the railroads, activities undertaken by public enterprises in many countries.[4]

The financial public enterprises include a commercial bank with many branches in small towns; a housing bank; the Korea Development Bank (KDB), which mediates between the international capital market (including multilateral lending institutions) and local private enterprises; two specialized savings institutions (for workers and farmers); and a postal insurance agency. There was little change in these lists during the 1980s. In 1980 a number of government-owned commercial banks were privatized, and early in the decade so was the Pohang Iron and Steel Company. Much insurance was also made private, but the government entered the gas business. In 1988 a number of public enterprise subsidiaries, of which there are quite a few, were sold to the public, and the general thrust of policy has been toward more privatization.

In contrast to many other developing countries, Korea's state-owned enterprises as a group ran operating surpluses throughout the late 1970s and 1980s, including the recession year of 1980. In the 1980s, these surpluses ran around 3 percent of GDP. But they also ran cash deficits, due to heavy investments, until 1986. Their investments ran around 5 percent of GDP early in the decade, gradually declining to around 3 percent. Some of their net borrowing was directly from the government and some from public financial enterprises (especially the KDB, with its foreign sources of funds), but most was from Korea's nonbank financial institutions.

In financial terms, the Korea Electric Power Company and the Korea Telecommunications Authority dominate the nonfinancial public enterprises. In the late 1980s, together they accounted for nearly half the total revenue of these enterprises and for essentially all of the operating surplus. (In several years, the other nonfinancial public enterprises taken as a group ran small operating deficits.) These two enterprises ran sufficiently large surpluses from 1986 to 1988 to cover not only their own investment requirements but also those of all other nonfinancial public enterprises, putting the whole group into overall cash surplus. The rate of return on their activities, calculated crudely, seems to be in the range of 20 to 30 percent a year.[5]

Until 1984 the budgets of the public enterprises were under tight control of the EPB, and their operations were under the control of the ministry directly responsible, an arrangement that did not encourage innovation or operational efficiency. A new law passed in 1984 gave considerable autonomy to public enterprises and made their officers responsible to boards of directors appointed by the government. Senior managers (but not the president) had to be drawn from among those with technical skills within the organizations—the appointments, that is, could no longer be used for retired generals or government officials—and a system of incentive bonuses based on performance was established. Price changes still required government approval, so performance was not based on profit alone but rather on a series of criteria tailored to each enterprise. Major investments must still be approved by the EPB.

The reform came about in a curious way. President Chun noticed in the early 1980s that the Korea Electric Power Company ran a surplus. He wondered how that came about and whether it could be encouraged in subsequent years and in other enterprises. Economists at the Korea Development Institute were consulted, and by coincidence Dr. Il Sakong had been working on a nine-country comparative project on state enterprises and was thus prepared to address the issue of appropriate structure and incentives in Korea. He outlined a plan that, with some modification, became the reform of 1984. This history illustrates the interest of President Chun in economic issues as well as his willingness to listen to practical-minded academics even when it meant changing practices that had benefited his colleagues. It also illustrates the role that chance or coincidental matching of supply with demand for ideas can sometimes play.

Trends in Expenditure and Revenue, 1973-1988

Government expenditures grew by a factor of twenty-seven, or over 24 percent a year, over the fifteen-year period 1973–1988. This is a startling rate of growth, but it must be set against the fact that the economy as a whole grew by a factor of twenty-one over this period, or by nearly 23 percent a year. On average, 13.6 percentage points represented inflation (measured by the GDP deflator), leaving real growth of 8.7 percent a year, an astonishing rate for a period that was disrupted by two sharp oil price increases and two sharp world recessions.

Government expenditures grew more rapidly than GDP over the period as a whole, and indeed the ratio of government expenditures to GDP increased from 13 percent in 1973 to 15.2 percent in 1988. In fact, government expenditures grew even more rapidly early in the period, reaching a peak of 18.5 percent of GDP in 1982, and then dropped sharply in 1983 and more gradually thereafter (Table 5-3). During this period, government investment varied between 2.1 and 3.6 percent of GDP, reaching the higher figure only in 1976. The share of total government spending has been substantially lower than that in industrialized countries and some 5 to 10 percent lower than that in other middle-income developing countries.

Government revenues also grew rapidly in Korea, by a factor of twenty-nine over the period as a whole, or 25 percent a year, slightly faster than government expenditures. Revenue grew from 12.5 percent of GDP in 1973 to 17.9 percent in 1988. Indeed in every year since 1975 except for 1982, revenue has exceeded expenditure, apparently leaving

Table 5-3. Consolidated Government Expenditures and Revenues in Relation to GDP (percentage)

	Current Expenditure	Capital Formation	Revenues	Budget Deficit
1973	13.1		12.5	0.5
1974	11.8	2.3	13.6	2.2
1975	12.3	3.4	15.2	2.0
1976	12.9	3.6	16.6	1.4
1977	13.2	2.5	16.4	1.8
1978	13.3	2.4	16.9	1.2
1979	13.5	3.3	17.4	1.7
1980	14.9	2.4	18.0	2.2
1981	14.6	2.3	18.1	3.3
1982	15.2	3.3	18.3	3.0
1983	14.3	2.4	18.1	1.0
1984	14.1	2.3	17.4	1.2
1985	14.3	2.2	17.2	1.2
1986	13.7	2.3	17.0	0.1
1987	13.2	2.4	17.2	−0.4
1988	13.1	2.1	17.9	−1.6
1989	14.0	2.6	18.2	−0.2
1990	14.3	2.5	17.1	0.7

Note: Rows do not sum to zero because of net lending.
Source: Calculated from IMF, *Government Finance Statistics Yearbook* (1988, 1990, 1992).

the government with a budgetary surplus. But the government has also acted as a financial intermediary, borrowing from the public and abroad and relending to the Korean public, mainly to financial institutions. So the government typically ran a cash deficit, varying from 0.1 to 3.3 percent of GDP. Net lending by the government reached a peak of 4.5 percent of GDP in 1981.[6]

In short, a rapid growth in GDP combined with an elastic revenue system (supplemented from time to time with discretionary increases in taxes) permitted a rapid growth in government expenditures to be comfortably financed. Indeed, the strong sense of fiscal rectitude that prevailed during most of this period required that growth in government expenditures be held generally to the growth in revenues. These in turn were typically estimated conservatively, such that in most years actual revenues exceeded projected revenues by 2 to 3 percent. A supplementary budget was typically introduced during the 1970s as the revenue became available, and during the 1980s as well. A supplementary budget was skipped in 1983, however, so the additional revenues could be devoted to reducing the borrowing requirement of the government, and in 1986 and 1988 the supplementary budget was devoted in part to paying interest on government debt held by the Bank of Korea, not the usual practice.

The Korean government ran a current account surplus (revenues less noninvestment expenditures) in every year during the period under discussion, including the difficult years 1980 and 1982, when the surplus declined but remained substantial. The current surplus was devoted to financing government investment, generally 2 to 4 percent of GDP, and to lending to other institutions, which was supplemented by additional borrowing by the government. Government loans went to public enterprises and to both banks and nonbank financial institutions for on-lending to private enterprises. Very little government lending was directly to private nonfinancial institutions (less than 2 percent of outstanding government loans of 7.8 trillion won in 1986). In addition, the government provided equity capital (totaling 9.2 trillion won outstanding at the end of 1987), mainly to public enterprises.

The growth of revenues that permitted continuing current surpluses was due less to the elasticity of the tax system, whereby growing incomes and expenditure would lead automatically to a somewhat more than proportional increase in tax revenues, than to additional taxes, most notably the defense surtax levied on a number of existing taxes in 1975 and the education surtax introduced in 1982.

In addition, there was a substantial and controversial tax reform in 1977, when a value-added tax was introduced to replace a hodgepodge of excise taxes. The main objective of the reform was to rationalize the tax system and to build a sounder revenue base for the future rather than to raise additional revenue at the time of its introduction, though considerations of financing the Heavy and Chemical Industry Plan no doubt were present to some extent. The introduction of the tax at that time was influenced by the strong view of Japanese Finance Ministry officials of the superiority of a value-added tax, as well as by European experience. Ironically, the Japanese were unable to make their own tax reform until 1989, over a decade later, and even then amid so much controversy that it played some role in toppling Prime Minister Takeshita's government.

Since the Korean government is a net lender, interest earnings are a substantial source of revenue, amounting to over 5 percent of total revenues during the 1980s. One consequential source of revenue that the government might have had, but did not, was seigniorage on the issuance of new currency. This brings us to the distinctive role of the Bank of Korea.

Seigniorage and the Bank of Korea

The Bank of Korea is a separately incorporated government enterprise that performs the role of central bank, including banking for the government, issuing currency, serving as lender of last resort to the commercial banks, and supervising the prudential behavior of the commercial banks with respect to their lending and deposit activities. It reports to the Monetary Board, which is chaired by the minister of finance. (Further institutional detail can be found in Chapter 6.) Two features of the Bank of Korea are especially noteworthy as far as fiscal policy is concerned. First, the government cannot borrow from the bank without the express permission of the National Assembly. In practice, this means that the government has relied relatively little on borrowing from the central bank, in sharp contrast to many other developing countries and a number of developed countries. For example, in 1987 only 12 percent of the domestic assets of the Bank of Korea represented claims on the government and government agencies, and even during the period of large budget deficits in the early 1980s, only 30 percent of the bank's domestic assets represented claims on government and government agencies.

Put another way, of the large 1.6 trillion won budget deficit in 1981, only 183 billion won, or under 12 percent, was financed directly by the Bank of Korea, and despite a modestly larger budget deficit in 1982, the government made net repayments to the bank in that year. However, a substantial part of the financing in each year was done with foreign loans, which were in part converted into won at the Bank of Korea, and a further substantial part was financed by loans from the commercial banks, which in turn could and did borrow from the Bank of Korea, so its indirect role in financing budget deficits was substantial.

Second, the Bank of Korea, like any other bank of currency issue, should generate a source of income as seigniorage. Strictly speaking, seigniorage is the value of new money less the cost of producing and issuing it. It represents a command over resources by the money-issuing authority. In practice, central banks issue currency (bank notes) on demand from the banking system and possibly other financial institutions in exchange for interest-bearing claims on those institutions. So a note-issuing central bank exchanges non-interest-bearing liabilities (bank notes) for interest-bearing claims. Central banks should therefore run a substantial profit on their operations, even after allowing for expenses, and this profit is typically turned over to the government as a source of revenue. That in practice is how seigniorage accrues to the government.[7]

The Bank of Korea, in contrast to the Federal Reserve System of the United States, purchases mainly claims against private entities, particularly the deposit money banks and other financial institutions, as well as claims against foreign banks and governments in the form of foreign exchange reserves. But the principle is the same: It issues non-interest-bearing liabilities against interest-bearing assets and therefore should show a substantial net income. But the bank typically showed only modest net income during the 1970s and typically ran losses in the 1980s. In 1987 the bank issued currency that amounted to 0.86 percent of GDP. Had this accrued directly to the government, it would have augmented revenues by 4.4 percent; instead, this new currency was exchanged for assets, on the model of the Federal Reserve. But the assets did not result in commensurate net earnings. Evidently the seigniorage has been used for subsidies to the private (and perhaps public enterprise) sector, in the form of low interest loans or even write-offs of nonperforming claims.

A rough estimate of the magnitudes can be made by supposing that the domestic assets of the Bank of Korea earned an interest rate 1 percent below the three-month time deposit rate at deposit money banks and that foreign reserves earned the U.S. Treasury bill rate. The hypothetical interest earnings of the bank on these assumptions are shown in Table 5-4,

Table 5-4. Calculated versus Actual Earnings of the Bank of Korea
(in billion won)

	Hypothetical Net Interest Earnings	Reported Surplus	Difference[a]	Percentage of GDP
1973	85	2	83	1.5
1974	107	35	72	1.0
1975	142	1	141	1.4
1976	175	51	126	0.9
1977	205	36	169	0.9
1978	359	64	295	1.2
1979	513	160	353	1.1
1980	820	502	318	0.8
1981	765	175	590	1.3
1982	591	−132	723	1.4
1983	430	−109	539	0.9
1984	422	−195	539	0.9
1985	356	−131	487	0.6
1986	328	−57	385	0.4
1987	498	−87	585	0.6
1988	334	37	297	0.2
1989	1,578	365	1,213	0.9

[a]Hypothetical net interest earnings – reported surplus.
Sources: Bank of Korea, *Annual Report* (various years), and author's calculations.

along with the actual reported surplus of the bank and the discrepancy between the two. The difference is substantial: around 1.5 percent of GDP in the mid-1970s and early 1980s, falling gradually to around 0.5 percent of GDP in the mid-1980s, although rising to 0.9 percent in the high interest rate environment of 1989. Of course, these estimates exaggerate somewhat the earnings that could have been paid to the government, considerably enhancing revenues, because they do not allow for the operating expenses of the bank. At the Federal Reserve, expenses amounted in 1987 to $1.1 billion, or about 0.4 percent of the Fed's total assets. Expenses of the Bank of Korea exclusive of interest paid on outstanding liabilities, mainly for stabilization, which have been allowed for in the calculations shown in Table 5-4, amounted to 123 billion won in 1987, or 0.5 percent of its total assets and 0.1 percent of GDP. The shortfall of earnings thus does not arise from exceptional operating expenses but rather from exceptionally low interest rates charged on Bank of Korea loans.

To the extent that these loans are to the government, they represent an alternative way to transfer seigniorage to the government; but as we have seen, loans to the government account for a relatively small portion of Bank of Korea assets. Instead, the seigniorage was transferred to favored sectors or favored activities in the private sector. In short, a consequential portion of the influence on the structure of the economy that in other countries was influenced directly by the budget in Korea was accomplished by the diversion of seigniorage to the private and public enterprise sector.

Public Debt

The financing requirements of the central government from 1973 through 1990 are shown in Table 5-5, along with various sources of finance. The government relied relatively little on central bank financing during this period and indeed on balance repaid previous obligations to the Bank of Korea. Rather, most financing came, in equal measure, from three sources: deposit money banks, other domestic sources (mainly nonbank financial institutions, although some debt in the late 1980s was sold directly to the public), and foreign sources. All of these sources

Table 5-5. Financing of Budget Deficits (in billion won)

| | Deficit: | Financing | | | | |
| | | Domestic | | | Foreign | |
	Total Required	Bank of Korea	Deposit Banks	Other	International Institutions and Governments	Other
1973	27	−41		3	64	
1974	168	15	8	60	75	10
1975	202	−53	49	49	122	33
1976	192	−147	82	43	222	−7
1977	316	−113	140	11	216	62
1978	300	−147	36	47	14	351
1979	545	127	124	20	715	−442
1980	849	117	317	89	170	156
1981	1,585	183	204	659	449	90
1982	1,656	−144	524	594	570	111
1983	663	−123	8	375	394	9
1984	841	−305	751	81	314	—
1985	943	95	370	36	377	65
1986	86	−255	429	59	57	−204
1987	−478	−1,206	181	536	320	−309
1988	−2,009	−2,118	1,651	−830	−469	−243
1989	−285	−557	190	682	−495	−105
1990	1,207	597	290	648	−328	

Source: IMF, *Government Finance Statistics Yearbook* (1988, 1990, 1992).

involve the Bank of Korea indirectly, since foreign loans that are not used directly for import financing are converted into won at the Bank of Korea, and deposit banks and other financial institutions have access to the Bank of Korea through its lending and rediscount operations.

Nonetheless, Korea has by and large avoided a principal weakness in most other developing countries: financing budget deficits at the central bank, resulting in direct monetary expansion. One inhibition on such financing is the requirement for approval by the National Assembly, that is, subject to public debate. This feature was put into Korea's basic monetary law, dating from 1950, apparently at the suggestion of Professor Arthur Bloomfield, who was then working for the Federal Reserve Bank of New York.

Despite only modest direct use of the central bank as a source of finance for the budget deficit, Korea did from time to time rely extensively on commercial bank loans. The commercial banks were government-owned enterprises until the early 1980s and remained under strong government influence even after they became private. In six years during the period under study, a third or more of the government deficit was financed by the deposit money banks (see Table 5-5). During the high deficit period of 1979–1982, bank financing (Bank of Korea plus deposit money banks) of the deficit contributed to a growth in the money supply (M1) in excess of 9 percent a year, an amount that was typically augmented by additional lending to the private sector. The budget was not without influence on monetary expansion, but it had a significant impact in relatively few years, and even then its influence was restrained compared with that in many other developing countries at roughly the same level of per capita income.

A second noteworthy feature of the structure of financing is that relatively little of the foreign financing was at commercial banks (1978 was the most notable exception). Rather, the Korean government arranged loans from international financial institutions such as the World Bank and the Asian Development Bank, and from export-credit agencies of foreign governments, such as the Japan Export-Import Bank. These credits were overwhelmingly related to investment projects with import content. The government did not borrow abroad for general budget support but rather to finance investment projects, particularly those that could be expected to increase exports or conserve foreign exchange by substituting for imports. This represented sound practice, since the foreign debt would have to be serviced in foreign exchange, a fact that many indebted developing countries apparently neglected. The Korean government did draw foreign exchange from the International Monetary Fund on three occasions—in 1974–1975, 1980–1981, and 1984—and these funds were not directly related to projects (see Chapter 9). But except in 1980–1981, the amounts were relatively small. From 1986 onward there was substantial repayment of commercial bank debt.

A rough measure of the financial prudence of Korea is that total outstanding government liabilities (including local governments but excluding commercial-type public enterprises) at the end of 1987 were 14.0 trillion won, or 13 percent of GDP. This was a lower ratio than that prevailing in most developed countries (federal debt held by the public in the United States, for instance, amounted to 42 percent of gross national product [GNP], and state and local debt amounted to another 10 percent of GNP), and much lower than that prevailing in most other middle-income developing countries.

Total external debt of Korea followed a somewhat more conventional pattern than direct government debt and is discussed in more detail in Chapters 8 and 9. Both public and private enterprises borrowed extensively from private lenders abroad, mainly commercial banks. The debt grew most rapidly between 1976 and 1978, during the period of large investment associated with the Heavy and Chemical Industry Plan, but it continued to grow more rapidly than GDP, reaching a peak of 42 percent (excluding short-term debt) in 1985, after which it declined sharply due to prepayments undertaken as a matter of policy. At its peak, Korea was the fourth largest indebted developing country, after Brazil, Mexico, and Argentina. But Korea's exports had also grown rapidly, so the interest burden on long-term debt reached a peak, in 1982, of only 8.7 percent of exports of goods and services, low by the standards of most heavily indebted countries.[8]

Use of the Budget as an Instrument of Policy

Thus far, this chapter has mainly described the Korean fiscal system and the principal trends in expenditures, revenues, and debt. We now turn to the budget—specifically, the extent to which it was used as an active instrument of policy. The conventional headings under which to address this question are growth, distribution, stabilization, and allocation. Each of these will be taken up in turn, although the principal emphasis will be placed here on the stabilization function, since allocation and distribution are covered in other books and growth is covered in part in Chapter 8.

Growth

An important contribution of the budget toward economic growth was in the customary provision of public goods, most notably hard and soft infrastructure, such as highways and educational expenditures. In the mid-1980s, for instance, the government (at all levels) spent about 1.2 percent of GDP on transportation infrastructure and 3.8 percent of GDP on education; by comparison, the United States spent about 1.5 percent and 2.9 percent, respectively. Second, the current budget was always in surplus, so the government contributed to national savings. Third, the government was a financial intermediary, borrowing at home or abroad and relending for investment, to either public enterprises or other financial intermediaries. The principal role of government in steering the growth of the economy, however, was not through the budget but through EPB approval or guidance to favored investments, backed up early in the period by the use of exchange controls and throughout the period through the direction of credit given by the banking system, often with concessional loans or other support from the Bank of Korea. (This system of credit guidance and support is discussed more fully in Chapter 6.)

Distribution

All government expenditures have a distributional influence. Although this is not the main subject of study here, it is important to underline one redistributional scheme concerning agriculture because of its relatively large fiscal impact. The agricultural sector has been the object of special treatment at least since the early 1970s, when President Park singled out the rural sector for special attention. Rural population growth in Korea, as in many other developing countries, pressed on the limited arable land. Korea created substantial higher productivity employment in the cities, and substantial rural-urban migration occurred. This migration created demand for urban infrastructure, including housing, which competed for the limited investable funds with the directly productive (mainly manufacturing) sector of the economy, and in particular it competed in the 1970s with the heavy investment requirements of the Heavy and Chemical Industry Plan. Hence, programs were introduced to raise incomes from farming and to encourage the development of small-scale industry in rural areas in order to create nonfarm sources of income and employment outside the large cities, thus reducing the need for expensive urban infrastructure.

The principal instrument for raising farm income was protection against competition from lower-cost imports. In addition, however, the government subsidized heavily the distribution of fertilizer, and in 1969 it created the Grain Management Fund (GMF), both to raise and to stabilize income from grain production, mainly rice, but also barley and some less important products. Rice produced in Korea comes in two qualities. The majority is of the higher-quality, traditional rice and moves through commercial channels. About 20 percent of rice production is of the lower-quality, high-yield varieties, and this rice is purchased from farmers by the GMF at a fixed price, stored, transported to market, and sold in urban areas at a lower fixed price.[9] During the period 1982–1984, the selling price was about 94 percent of the purchase price, although in 1974 this ratio had reached a low of 83 percent. In addition, the GMF covered storage and distribution costs that represented another 20 to 25 percent of the value of the rice.

Thus, the GMF raises prices to farmers without raising them correspondingly to urban consumers, and it also puts a floor on rice prices since the market price of the higher-quality rice is related to the controlled price of the lower-quality rice. It has been estimated that total transfers to the agricultural sector, direct and indirect, amounted to 24 percent of gross value-added in agriculture in 1984, down from a high of 32 percent in 1978.[10]

Since the GMF fixes a target price, it represents (at least for each season) an entitlement program, expenditures from which, being influenced by the volume of the harvest, introduce an unpredictable element into the budget—or would do so to the extent it is directly carried as a budget item. But the GMF is run as an independent agency, with direct access to the Bank of Korea for its (largely seasonal) financing. The subsidy element is covered by low interest charges on its extensive seasonal borrowing, plus an accumulation of debt over the years, which by the end of 1983 exceeded 2 trillion won. Up until 1984, financing for the GMF represented the principal lending by the Bank of Korea to the government, and indeed in many years over the decade 1973–1983 such net lending represented about a quarter of the growth in M1. Since actual expenditures depended on the harvest as well as on the target prices, this procedure also introduced a somewhat unpredictable component into monetary policy. In 1984 the GMF switched from Bank of Korea financing to a direct budget subsidy, which in that year amounted to 330 billion won.

A rapid growth in total and per capita incomes, such as Korea has had over the past two decades, eases all problems of choice and should reduce the problems of income distribution, apart from the special problem of farmers. But income distribution became a contentious political issue in Korea in the 1980s because of the emergence of more open and democratic politics and because of cultural views concerning the accumulation of wealth. "Excessive" wealth and income in Korea are often attributed to luck or venality rather than to reward for effort, skill, or risk taking. Most Koreans work hard, few have skills so special as to warrant huge increases in income, and risk taking is (or is thought to be) cushioned by the government and therefore not warranting exceptional reward. These attitudes prevail even though by international standards Korea seems to have a remarkably even distribution of income.[11]

A public social security system was introduced before 1974, in part to mobilize public savings, and a public welfare system was introduced in 1979, but following the transition to democracy in 1985, the Roh government committed itself to improve income distribution in various ways. As a result, much more weight has been placed recently on public support for urban housing, and medical insurance coverage was extended from rural to all citizens in 1989. In addition to rural-urban discrepancies and growing concerns about income distribution, differences in regional incomes, particularly the relative poverty of the southwest, have become important political issues.[12] In the future, these distributional issues could clearly exert a strong influence on both the composition and the level of government spending.

Stabilization

The Korean budget has not been used mainly for economic stabilization, but occasionally it has been manipulated with that objective in mind. The rapid growth of GDP and nonagricultural employment has resulted in little need for conscious countercyclical adjustment of fiscal policy much of the time. Moreover, the budget cycle in Korea, as elsewhere, does not give a lot of scope for fine-tuning. However, the recurrent possibility for a supplementary budget gives some scope for short-term adjustment of expenditures, as does the possibility for accelerating or retarding within-year expenditures, which are evaluated quarterly from a macroeconomic as well as from a management perspective by the EPB. There have been supplementary budgets in almost every year. Moreover, the EPB has retarded or accelerated the quarterly release of funds in response to economic developments. Finally, there is some scope for tax rate adjustment by the government, which has used this authority on occasion, particularly during economic slowdowns.

The budget has always been framed with the macroeconomic characteristics of the economy in mind; it is based on conservative revenue projections, which in turn are based on forecasts of GDP growth, inflation, and international interest rates. Moreover, it is also framed with the overall resource balance of the economy in view, and indeed during the 1970s an explicit estimate was made of the overall resource balance of the economy, that is, the total expenditures (including exports) in relation to total supply (including imports) that is likely to be available to the economy in the coming year. In view of expected resource imbalances, major adjustments were made in the budget in 1973, 1979, 1980 through 1982, and 1984 and 1985. The contractionary budget of 1979 was designed to help combat inflation, which with its correlative deterioration in international competitiveness (under the fixed exchange rate that then prevailed) was seen to be a major problem. An expansionary supplementary budget was introduced in mid-1980 to combat the economic decline and rising unemployment of that unusual year and was continued into 1981. Emphasis returned to stabilization when a zero-base contractionary budget was introduced in 1983. In 1984 a tight budget was accompanied by the drastic step of a wage freeze for all government employees, not so much to combat inflation, which was already declining rapidly, as to ratify the anti-inflation program by setting an example for private sector wage settlements and to reduce the growth of public and external debt, which was low by international standards but was thought to be excessive.

It is useful to have a summary measure of the influence of fiscal policy on the overall economy. The ex post budget deficit in principle is marred for this purpose by the fact that it responds in part to changes in GNP directly, through changes in tax revenues that are linked to income and consumer spending, for instance. Moreover, government spending may be linked to prospective or potential GNP, taking on something of its own trajectory, rather than to actual GNP insofar as it deviates from potential GNP. Both of these weaknesses are corrected by a measure called fiscal thrust, which represents the difference between the actual budget deficit and the deficit that would prevail if government expenditures grew proportionally with potential GNP and tax revenues are proportional to actual GNP. Fiscal thrust thus attempts to measure the deviation from a presumed normal pattern; a positive thrust—that is, an excess of expenditures over revenues compared with the normal pattern—would be expansionary. The fiscal impulse, in turn, measures change in fiscal thrust and presumably captures the changes in tax rates and government expenditures that the authorities have made in response to short-run economic developments, or possibly for other reasons but which will have an influence on macroeconomic developments.

Table 5-6 presents one measure of fiscal impulse in Korea over the period 1971 through 1988. Several points are noteworthy. First, the fiscal

Table 5-6. Fiscal Impulse in Korea

	Fiscal Impulse[a]	Change in Actual Deficit (percentage of GDP)
1971	1.3	–0.4
1972	1.7	3.6
1973	–2.2	–3.4
1974	2.1	1.7
1975	0.2	–0.2
1976	–1.2	–0.6
1977	–0.1	0.4
1978	–0.0	–0.5
1979	–1.1	0.5
1980	–0.1	0.5
1981	1.6	1.1
1982	–0.5	–0.3
1983	–2.1	–2.0
1984	0.1	0.1
1985	–0.8	0.0
1986	–0.9	–1.1
1987	0.0	–0.5
1988	0.7	–1.2

[a]Fiscal impulse is the change in fiscal thrust, defined as the difference between the actual budget deficit and a cyclically neutral budget deficit calculated on the assumption that government expenditure grows in proportion to potential GNP and tax revenues grow in proportion to actual GNP, where potential GNP is measured from peak to peak, with 1970 and 1979 taken as peak years. This measure of fiscal impulse incorporates the effects of the so-called automatic stabilizers (e.g., in the responsiveness of tax revenue to changes in GNP), but in fact this component is negligible for Korea.
Sources: Table 5-3. and Vittorio Corbo and Sang-Mok Suh, eds., *Structural Adjustment in a Newly Industrialized Country: The Korean Experience* (Baltimore/London: Johns Hopkins University Press, 1992). A World Bank publication, reproduced with permission.

impulse is negligible in many years, particularly after the early 1970s, indicating that fiscal policy was not influencing changes in aggregate demand significantly. Second, however, in a few years, fiscal impulse changed markedly. The expansionary program of 1974, the year of the first oil shock, was substantial, amounting to over 2 percent of GDP. The swing from the previous, contractionary, policy is especially noteworthy. The stabilization program of 1979 is discernable, at about 1 percent of GDP, as is the expansionary program of late 1980–1981. The stabilization program of 1983 amounted to about 2 percent of GDP in terms of fiscal action. Moreover, these fiscal programs are generally negatively correlated with contemporaneous GNP growth. That is, exceptionally rapid growth of GDP, putting pressure on the economy and generating inflationary or balance-of-payments pressures, evoked a contractionary response, while an overall economic slowdown evoked an expansionary one. In short, Korea generally used fiscal action to help stabilize the economy.[13]

Third, there seems to be little in the way of automatic stabilizers in the Korean fiscal system, whether in the form of revenue response or government expenditure (for example, unemployment compensation). A comparison of measures of fiscal impulse that both include and exclude such automatic stabilizers reveals almost no difference between the two measures, and indeed, there is little cyclical response of tax revenues in Korea, at least within the year-to-year variation that has existed in Korean GDP growth.[14]

Finally, since the Korean economy has generally run close to its economic capacity, changes in the actual budget deficit have been, in most years, a reasonable approximation of fiscal impulse; that is, the need for the more refined measure of fiscal policy is less applicable to Korea than to many other countries. The notable exception is 1980, when GDP dropped, largely, but not solely, because of the agricultural sector. The budget deficit rose sharply, but fiscal impulse was still negative from the stabilization program of 1979 until the expansionary program was launched in mid-year.

The major macroeconomic problem from 1986 through 1989 was to neutralize the expansionary effects of the large current account surpluses, which (in terms of the national accounts) moved from a small surplus in 1985 to 6.1 percent of GDP in 1986, 8.0 percent in 1987, and 8.2 percent in 1988, receding to 2.7 percent in 1989 and into deficit in 1990. There were several logically possible courses of action to accomplish this objective, and each had somewhat different political implications. First, the government could have reduced sharply the budget deficit by increasing taxes. Second, it could have substantially liberalized imports, which were still subject to substantial restraint, with a view to siphoning off purchasing power without putting further inflationary pressure on the economy. Third, the government could have liberalized private capital outflows, so residents could invest some portion of their rapidly growing incomes abroad. Fourth, it could have appreciated the currency, with a view to retarding export growth and stimulating imports, thus reducing the current account surplus in that way.

All of these possible courses of action were difficult in the Korean context, especially at a time of political liberalization and democratization. Raising taxes is always unpopular. Government expenditures had been severely squeezed since 1983, and the political imperative was not for less but for more government expenditures, especially of a social character. The economic technocrats were largely committed to import liberalization, but that program had already been announced in 1981 to cover the period 1982 thorough 1986 (later extended to 1987–1988). It was associated with the unpopular Chun regime and with pressure from the United States, a politically sensitive issue, especially but not exclusively with respect to liberalization of imports of agricultural products.

Relaxation of exchange controls on capital outflows, which was done modestly for business activities, would have been seen as favoring the rich at the expense of the ordinary Korean. Finally, in 1989, the Korean government did remove the restrictions on foreign travel by young Koreans, an extraordinarily late move given the progress of the Korean economy and balance of payments over the preceding decade. Again, concern for the apparent preference to the well-to-do seems to have been the important inhibiting factor.[15] In 1988 Korea formally accepted Article VIII (convertibility) obligations under the International Monetary Fund, and in late 1989, four years after the emergence of a surplus, it formally dropped balance-of-payments grounds for maintaining trade restrictions under the General Agreement on Tariffs and Trade (GATT). Both moves reflected the extreme caution of Korean officials regarding foreign exchange earnings and expenditure.

Currency appreciation was seen as reducing export competitiveness, always unwelcome in Korea, and as an explicit policy it had the unwelcome consequence of encouraging capital inflow, or discouraging outflow, the opposite of what was wanted for stabilization.

The course of action undertaken by the government involved a series of expedients as well as some basic changes. The government built up its balances at the Bank of Korea (by 2 trillion won in 1987), thus reducing liquidity in the hands of the public. It also encouraged financial institutions and public enterprises to prepay their external debt, a particular form of capital outflow. Deposit banks cut their liabilities to foreigners in half from the end of 1985 to the end of 1988, by 7 trillion won. In all, Korea repaid $16.6 billion in long-term external debt during these three years and another $2.7 billion in short-term debt.

Third, the Bank of Korea issued 15 trillion won in stabilization bonds between 1986 and 1988, also to soak up liquidity in the hands of the public, although these bonds had the long-term disadvantage of creating interest flows from the central bank to the public.

Fourth, the won was appreciated against the U.S. dollar by 23 percent from the end of 1985 to the end of 1988. This was a period, however, in which the dollar depreciated against the Japanese yen by 37 percent, so the won actually depreciated against the Japanese currency, probably Korea's major competitor in export markets. On a Korean trade-weighted basis, the won depreciated by 8 percent, although that was the net effect over the three years of a 15 percent depreciation (1985–1987), followed by appreciation in 1988.

Some further trade liberalization and tariff reduction also occurred, raising the liberalized list of nonagricultural imports from 81 percent in late 1983 to 95 percent in late 1988 and reducing the average (unweighted) tariff from 24 to 18 percent over the same period.

The total effect of these measures was inadequate to prevent a sharp increase in nominal demand and in GDP. But the Korean economy showed remarkable elasticity: Real GDP grew by 12 percent a year in each of the three years 1986, 1987, and 1988. While the growth in the M1 increased from being negligible in 1984 and 11 percent in 1985 to 16 percent a year in 1986–1987 and 20 percent in 1988, inflation remained extremely low in all three years; consumer prices rose only 2 percent over the entire period. Wage settlements accelerated sharply in 1989, however, although it is difficult to sort out the influence of the macroeconomic environment from the political liberalization that took place in the late 1980s.

Tax Policy

Korea went through a period of tax experimentation and tax reform from 1960 through 1977, culminating with the adoption of a more or less comprehensive income tax in 1975 and the replacement of a host of excise taxes with a value-added tax plus a series of luxury consumer taxes in mid-1977. Particularly in the mid-1960s, considerable attention was paid to improving tax enforcement.[16]

Since 1977 there has been no major change in tax structure, although there have been extensive moderate changes in tax rates and some reorientation of the secondary objectives of the tax system. Until 1983 there were almost annual increases in personal exemptions and changes in brackets in the personal income tax, for instance, both to allow for the influence of inflation on nominal incomes—and, hence, on taxes in the presence of a progressive rate structure—and to exempt increasing numbers of relatively low-income workers from the income tax. By the late 1980s, only 45 percent of Korea's wage and salary workers paid income taxes, since the exemptions and deductions amounted to over one and a half times per capita GDP.[17] Moreover, in 1982, various tax reductions and exemptions designed to stimulate business activities began to be shifted from a sectoral to a functional basis—for example, from supporting fertilizer production or petroleum refining to supporting research and development expenditures by any industry—although some sectoral support remained. This same principle was applied as well to import tariff exemptions and combined with a five-year program for the reduction of schedular tariff rates.

The major sources of revenue in 1977 and 1987 have already been presented (see Table 5-2). Total tax revenues, including the tobacco monopoly profits and local taxes, came to about 19 percent of GDP, a figure that is low not only by the standards of developed countries but also in comparison with many other developing countries except the poorest. Of total tax revenues, about one-eighth were local in origin, mainly from business licenses and property taxes. At the national level, import duties accounted for about one-fifth of revenue, direct taxes (including a nascent payroll tax) for about one-third, and indirect taxes for most of the remainder (just under one-half). Personal incomes are taxed on a progressive basis, with tax rates for the 45 percent of workers who are taxable ranging from 7 to 70 percent, inclusive of the defense surcharge; the top rate was reduced to 55 percent in 1989. In principle, almost all income is taxable as part of global income, but the widespread use of bearer bonds makes it difficult in practice to capture taxes on interest, dividends, and capital gains. Interest and dividends are subject to a 10 percent withholding tax (plus an education surcharge), and capital gains on securities sales are exempt from taxation. Farmers are also subject to a special tax regime.

Basic corporate income tax rates range from 20 to 33 percent (5 percent on the income from public enterprises), which with the defense and other surcharges brings the maximum corporate rates to 43 percent. Somewhat lower rates are applicable to corporations that list their shares and allow public trading in them. The basic value-added tax rate is 10 percent, but many items are exempt on grounds of administrative difficulty or to relieve the tax burden on low-income families. However, the defense surcharge plus the special consumption tax levied on forty items bring total excise tax rates on these items from 15 to 153 percent, and even higher on liquor.

The principal objective of the tax system has been to raise revenue, which in the Korean fiscal context is seen as a precondition for current (as opposed to capital) expenditure. Subject to that, however, the tax system has also been called upon to serve a variety of other public policy objectives: encouragement to national savings, influence on the structure of investment, fostering a more equitable distribution of income, and stabilization of the economy, more or less in that order of importance.

The overall ex post elasticity of national revenues with respect to GDP between 1977 and 1987 was 1.06, implying that revenues grew about 6 percent more rapidly than nominal GDP. This figure, however, conceals some tax reductions, especially in terms of exemptions and bracket adjustments, as well as reductions in the top corporate and personal income tax rates in the early 1980s and reductions in import tariffs, such that without those, the elasticity might have been even higher. On the other hand, the education surcharge was imposed in 1982, the only major tax increase in tax rates; and the tariff reductions may themselves have stimulated imports, such that some of them actually increased revenue.

A somewhat surprising feature of the Korean tax system is that revenues do not seem to be especially responsive to downturns in economic activity, such as occurred in 1980 (admittedly most significantly in agriculture), or to slowdowns, such as in 1985. In 1980 revenue rose 4 percent more rapidly than nominal GDP, about the same elasticity as the 3 percent average for the decade. In many economies, tax revenues typically grow less rapidly than GDP in a weak year, due to a downturn in corporate profits (corporate income taxes did decline 1.9 percent in 1980), a rise in unemployment, and a decline in consumption of highly taxed goods.

Part of the explanation lies perhaps in the target revenue approach adopted by Korea's Office of National Tax Administration (ONTA). ONTA is given a target revenue for the year (conservatively estimated), and revenue agents in turn are given target revenues to achieve. Since compliance is not generally self-enforcing in Korea, this approach means that more stringent efforts by revenue officials can generate higher revenues.

The central importance of revenue to the Korean authorities can be illustrated by the introduction of two special surcharges on taxes to finance increases in expenditures above trend that were perceived to be desirable or necessary. The first was the defense surcharge, introduced as a temporary measure in 1975 in the wake of the withdrawal of the United States from Vietnam, the collapse of the South Vietnamese government, and the general disaffection by the American public with foreign military commitments. Korea, which relied on U.S. forces to help deter adventurism by an unpredictable North Korea, felt the need to strengthen its own forces, and in particular to modernize its air force. To this end, a surtax ranging from 0.2 to 30 percent was added to taxes on incomes, commodities, imports, telephone charges, and advertising rates, for a period of five years. It was twice extended and finally expired in 1990. By the mid-1980s it accounted for about 12 percent of total tax revenues, roughly the same as local taxes. The proceeds were earmarked for defense spending, but the normal budgetary processes were not altered, so the earmarking was political rather than administrative; that is, the Ministry of Defense still had to persuade the budgetary authorities and the president of its need for funding in the annual budget cycle.[18]

A similar development occurred in education. Classrooms, particularly in elementary schools, had become over-crowded, and pupil-teacher ratios, often around sixty to one, were considered too high. In 1981 the Korean authorities introduced an education surcharge on interest and dividend taxes and on certain items of consumption, at rates varying from 0.5 to 10 percent, plus a 0.5 percent gross receipt tax on banking and insurance. By the mid-1980s this surtax accounted for 2.4 percent of total tax revenues. As with the defense surtax, the earmarking was political rather than administrative. Political opposition to these tax increases was minimal.

With revenues typically running ahead of current government expenditures, including those for defense and education, the Korean government has been a net saver since 1964. The tax system has also been used to encourage private savings. Interest and dividend income during the 1970s were taxed at 5 percent; the rate was raised to 10 percent in 1980 when the authorities wanted to limit the budget deficit while encouraging an increase in domestic demand. Most capital gains are taxed at rates varying from 30 percent (on structures) to 50 percent (on land), but capital gains on securities are not taxed, nor are interest earnings in the Wage and Salary Workers Fortune Formation Savings Fund, created in 1976 to encourage savings by workers.

The tax system has been used as well to influence the structure of the economy, mainly by encouraging exports and by influencing the pattern of investment. Under the Tax Exemption and Reduction Control Law, as amended from time to time, tax relief has been extended to favored activities in a variety of ways. Firms with substantial export earnings enjoyed a 50 percent reduction in corporate profits tax in the 1960s. In 1973 this was abolished in favor of several tax-free reserves related to foreign market opening and potential losses on exports. In 1977 a tax-free reserve could also be established for price fluctuations. Throughout the period, export firms could depreciate their machinery investments 30 percent more rapidly than that normally allowed.

Apart from export industries, certain key or strategic industries have benefited from various forms of tax relief, generally some combination of tax holidays, investment tax credits, and accelerated depreciation on their investments. In line with the move toward a more market-oriented style of economic management, the two former incentives were abolished in 1981, leaving only special depreciation allowances during the 1980s.

Strategic industries included those covered by the Heavy and Chemical Industry Plan during the late 1970s. The list was narrowed somewhat in 1982, when the emphasis began to shift from favored sectors to favored activities, such as small- and medium-sized firms, which since 1982 have enjoyed a variety of tax breaks, and research and development expenditures, which enjoy a 10 percent tax credit and a variety of other tax favors.

Discretionary tax breaks within the framework of the Tax Exemption and Reduction Control Law were used in 1985–1986 to help overcome the financial crisis that plagued many Korean firms, particularly those in overseas construction and in shipping, coming out of the 1982 world recession. They were also used to help banks with nonperforming loans to the troubled firms. For a variety of reasons, having to do with foreign policy and Korea's reputation abroad, previous government incentives to some of the insolvent firms, and public confidence in the financial system, the Korean authorities felt that many of the insolvent firms should not be allowed to go bankrupt; indeed, officials did not want their insolvent condition to become public knowledge until a solution was in hand. The preferred solution was to find viable firms to acquire the insolvent ones, many of which still had solid assets and operating contracts.

But viable firms were not likely to take over insolvent firms without some incentive. The incentives were found in some combination of write-offs of old bank loans to the insolvent firms, new loans to the acquiring firms at favorable interest rates, and exemption from capital gains taxes on sale of acquired assets. Similarly, the banks that agreed to write off loans to insolvent firms were encouraged to do so through similar incentives, where the lender in this case would be the Bank of Korea. The strictly financial aspects of these arrangements were probably more important than the exemption from capital gains tax and are discussed more fully in Chapter 6. Altogether over seventy firms were helped out of insolvency in this way, a matter that later became the source of charges of favoritism by the Chun administration toward those firms, generally large ones, that undertook the acquisitions. But economic officials who conceived the arrangements saw an important public purpose in doing so. Until 1985, the banks had simply been encouraged to continue lending money to the insolvent firms, thus postponing the problem.

The total magnitude of all of these tax favors can be approximated by relating the revenue forgone to total national tax revenues; this ratio fell from 28 percent in 1975 to 8.6 percent in 1984, rising to 11.8 percent in 1985.[19] The tax breaks designed to influence resource allocation were thus substantial, although less in the 1980s than in the 1970s, when they were used for industrial policy purposes. Moreover, these tax favors were probably less important in influencing resource allocation than were the controls over credit at favored interest rates.[20]

Tax policy was not used extensively for purposes of stabilizing the Korean economy, but on several occasions it played a role. The Emergency Decree on Stabilization and Growth of August 1972, for instance, introduced a 10 percent tax credit for investments using domestic capital goods manufactured by the end of 1974, in order to stimulate the sluggish domestic economy. Following the sharp rise in oil prices in early 1974, the Emergency Measure for the Stabilization of National Life promulgated in January 1974 lowered personal income tax rates so as to offset in part the contractionary impact of the oil price increase. And in the slump of 1980–1981, capital gains tax rates on real estate transactions were lowered from 50 to 80 percent (to which they had been raised in 1978 to discourage real estate speculation) to 35 to 75 percent in order to encourage residential construction. Selected consumption tax rates were also cut by 30 percent to encourage consumption, and the withholding tax rate on interest and dividend income was raised from 5 to 10 percent to recoup revenue without reducing consumption.

The tax system of Korea has been called upon over the past two decades to perform a variety of functions—to redistribute income, to stabilize the economy, to encourage savings—but generating revenue has always been the predominant concern of the economic officials, and of the government.

Overall Appraisal

By comparison with the industrialized countries and many developing countries, Korea has a relatively low level of governmental activity as measured by government expenditures—less than 20 percent of GNP.[21] Within this total, Korea has had a larger than average share of military expenditures—between 4 and 6 percent of GNP. Military expenditures (relative to GNP) have fallen slowly over the past decade, while nonmilitary expenditures have grown, for a slow net increase in the size of the government sector.

The dominant impression left by an examination of the Korean fiscal system, whatever the trends, is one of tight budgetary control, in both framing and executing the budget. This control might be thought to arise in the first instance from the tight budgetary process, held closely in the hands of skilled economic officials with broad powers and extensive continuity. But these officials are just that: officials. They have not controlled the political process. Without the strong support of successive presidents, they would not have prevailed. Moreover, the spending ministries and the National Assembly have shown considerable concern for fiscal discipline even while urging particular programs. There seems to be a general understanding of the need for fiscal discipline, especially for a country as open and as dependent on the world economy as Korea is. Even when officials would have encouraged greater foreign borrowing rather than economic retrenchment, political sentiments, expressed by both the opposition and pro-government members of the National Assembly, held external indebtedness in disfavor and pressed to reduce it in the early 1980s.

There is no doubt that a rapid rate of growth eases many problems (while creating problems of adaptation and adjustment). With rapidly growing revenues, competition for limited funds is less acute than it would otherwise be, and all parties can be accommodated to some extent, even if their full desires are not satisfied. But the high rate of growth itself was influenced by the government budget: the high rate of public savings, the focus on education, the encouragement to private saving and investment, and the establishment of the principle of accountability in public enterprises as well as in the ministries, which set an example for the private sector.

At the same time, contrary to widespread impressions about Korea promulgated by strong advocates of weak and small government, the Korean government was intimately involved in many of the key economic decisions, private and public, that have generated the Korean economic miracle over the past three decades. The nature of these involvements evolved over time and by the late 1980s were less concerned with detailed economic structure than with broad institutional development and establishment of general rules for economic behavior. But despite heavy involvement in the economy, the government generally resisted committing large budget support to private economic activity. In fiscal matters, the Korean government remained stingy throughout the period, compensating to some extent with generous use of low interest loans from the Bank of Korea.

Within the context of relatively tight fiscal discipline, the budget was used regularly to help stabilize the overall economy. Throughout the period, the budget was framed in the setting of overall resource availability and use. Conservative revenue estimates combined with rapid growth gave Korean economic policymakers more scope for midyear corrections through supplementary budgets than is true of many other countries. Moreover, the persistence of revenue underestimates implies that the various parties involved in the process, including the National Assembly, seem to accept the conservative approach to fiscal affairs, an acceptance that doubtless helped to make the process work.

One can only speculate on why a relatively conservative fiscal tradition was established and maintained in Korea. It was not due mainly to the fact that Korea was under authoritarian rule, since several democracies, such as Colombia and India among developing countries, also have had conservative fiscal traditions, not to mention the Netherlands, Germany, and Japan among developed countries. And many authoritarian leaders have not supported a conservative fiscal system. Japan's conservative fiscal tradition undoubtedly played an important role, less as former colonial power than as modern model for emulation. Having two ex-generals as president for sixteen years probably reinforced the disciplinary training of financial officials, especially after what was considered the profligacy of the Syngman Rhee administration during the 1950s. Although regional feelings run strong in Korea, there are no marked ethnic, linguistic, or religious divisions within the country, hence no need to placate such groups through the budget, a problem that exists in many other developing countries.

Most important, however, is the record of success since the mid-1960s and the association of that success with Korea's budgetary behavior: conservative revenue forecasts, public savings, and low central government access to central bank financing. It remains to be seen whether the pressures of vociferous democracy that emerged in the late 1980s will eventually undermine the practice and tradition of tight control over the budget.

NOTES

1. Foreign aid, which had been an important part of government revenue in the 1950s and early 1960s, declined gradually and had disappeared by the late 1970s.
2. The permissible range for the value-added tax is 8–13 percent, a reduction from the initial range of 10–16 percent introduced in 1977. In fact, the actual rate was set at 10 percent in 1977 and remained there.
3. The same IMF source records, by way of comparison, fifteen nonfinancial public enterprises in the United States and thirty financial public enterprises, plus state and local public enterprises in both cases.

4. They also include a textbook publisher and agencies for the development of petroleum, minerals, land, housing, and tourism.

5. Calculated from net operating revenues (before payment of interest) relative to cumulated investment over the preceding ten years.

6. Government consumption in the national accounts is considerably smaller than current government expenditures shown in Table 5-3. The latter figures, from the consolidated central government budget figures, include transfer payments to local government and to individuals; the national accounts figures cover only government purchases of goods and services.

7. For example, in 1987, currency in circulation increased by $15.9 billion in the United States, or about 0.35 percent of GNP. The cost of producing this currency, including the cost of replacing worn notes, was $171 million, or just over 1 percent of the net increase. The Federal Reserve System issues the notes against earning assets, mainly Treasury securities but also some foreign exchange and some claims on the banking system. Total Federal Reserve earnings in 1987 came to $17.6 billion, less $1.1 billion in expenses, plus $1.8 billion in revaluation gains on foreign exchange and net gains on sales of Treasury securities. After paying a statutory dividend to member banks and adding to its own reserves, the Federal Reserve paid $17.7 billion in net profits to the U.S. Treasury. This is recorded as a receipt to the government, a partial offset to interest paid on the public debt (including that held by the Federal Reserve). This payment amounted to 2.1 percent of total U.S. federal government revenues in 1987.

8. Apart from the usual problems of measuring external debt adequately—World Bank figures do not exactly agree with national figures when the latter are converted at plausible exchange rates—the measurement problem is complicated in Korea's case by the fact that a consequential portion of Korea's external debt—perhaps 15 percent—is denominated in yen rather than dollars, combined with the fact that there were large exchange rate movements between the yen and the dollar in the 1980s. Thus, the depreciation of the yen against the dollar would, by itself, lower the dollar value of Korea's external debt between 1980 and 1984, and the subsequent appreciation of the yen would tend to raise the dollar value of the debt, as recorded by the World Bank, in 1985–1987.

9. The government purchase program for high-yield rice was introduced in 1969, when the government was encouraging farmers to introduce the new high-yield varieties, even though they lacked the taste and the consistency of traditional rice.

10. Pal-Yong Moon and Bong-Soon Kang, "Trade, Exchange Rate, and Agricultural Pricing Policies in the Republic of Korea," Washington, D.C.: World Bank, Comparative Studies, 1989, p. 282.

11. In Korea the top fifth of income earners earned 7.9 times the bottom fifth of income earners in 1976, as reported in World Bank, *World Development Report, 1988* (New York: Oxford University Press, 1988), p. 273. This ratio compares with 7.5 in the United States and 4.3 in Japan (the lowest ratio recorded for any country), but with 8.7 in Hong Kong, 8.9 in Thailand, 16.1 in Turkey, 20 in Mexico, and 33 in Brazil. By standards of developing countries, Korea seems to have achieved a relatively even distribution of income. The comparison is marred, however, by the fact that the survey on which Korean data are based imposed a ceiling on incomes, so the very high-income families were not recorded as such. Of course, there may be serious problems with the data for other countries as well. Moreover, like Japan, Korean firms give perks to their senior managers that in the United States and some other developed countries are counted as income.

12. See D. Lindauer et al., "Korea: The Strains of Economic Growth," unpublished manuscript, Cambridge: Harvard Institute for International Development, 1991, chap. 7.

13. In a study of fiscal policy in eighteen major developing countries, Korea stands out, with Brazil, as having used its budget to stabilize the year-to-year growth in output. In many developing countries, the budget, in contrast, contributes to destabilization of output. See I. Little, R. Cooper, W. Corden, and S. Rajapatirana, *Boom, Crisis and Adjustment: Macroeconomic Experience in Developing Countries* (New York: Oxford University Press, 1993), chap. 10.

14. V. Corbo and Sang-Woo Nam, "The Recent Macroeconomic Evolution of the Republic of Korea: An Overview," in V. Corbo and Sang-Mok Suh, eds., *Structural Adjustment in a Newly Industrialized Country: The Korean Experience* (Baltimore: Johns Hopkins University Press, 1992), p. 53, Table 8.

15. Some officials argued that it was especially important for young Koreans to travel, not least to see how well Korea was doing compared with most other developing countries, and indeed they suggested that such travel should be subsidized.

16. It has been estimated, for example, that over half of the increase in revenues in the late 1960s was due to better enforcement. See Wan-Soon Kim and K. Y. Yun, "Fiscal Policy and Development in Korea," *World Development* 16, 1 (1988): 65–83.

17. Kwang Choi, "Tax Policy and Tax Reforms in Korea," unpublished paper, World Bank, 1990.

18. By longstanding convention, Korea is thought to devote 6 percent of GNP to defense spending. This figure seems to have originated with the Carter administration of the United States, which was trying to persuade Korea to increase its defense spending in order to modernize its forces and to relieve the obligations on the U.S. forces stationed in Korea. Six percent seemed a suitable target. This figure subsequently became the starting point of the Ministry of Defense in annual budget negotiations, from which grudging retreats were made. The Korean armed forces were mainly worried about North Korea, which spent about a quarter of its GNP on the military; since South Korea was in a defensive posture, it did not need to match North Korean expenditures but strove toward a sufficiency of 75–80 percent of North Korean expenditures. In fact, because of the rapid growth of the South Korean GNP, the 6 percent target was rarely achieved, and during the late 1980s, defense spending fell below 5 percent of GNP.

19. Choi, "Tax Policy and Tax Reforms in Korea," Table IV-3.

20. For a rough comparison of financial versus tax incentives for export firms, see ibid., Table IV-7, where it is suggested that tax breaks were only about one-fifth as important as financial incentives in the 1970s, and one-third as important—at a much lower level of total incentive—in the mid-1980s.

21. All OECD countries are above 30 percent, and most of the European countries are above 40 percent.

6

Korean Monetary Policy

Sung-Tae Ro

In pursuing its industrialization objectives, the Korean government has depended heavily on monetary and credit policies. To promote investment and exports, it has typically pursued an accommodative monetary policy coupled with fixed interest rates, supplying firms with bank credits at low cost. In general, this strategy has contributed to Korea's rapid economic growth. Yet the government's intervention in the allocation of financial resources has also had undesirable side effects: chronic inflation, an underdeveloped financial sector, and concentration of economic power among a few conglomerates.

These effects became particularly apparent during the late 1970s, when industrial strategy moved to support the growth of heavy industry. Top governmental policymakers understood that economic policies should aim at price stability and balance-of-payments equilibrium and that there exists a trade-off between these goals and rapid growth, and many believed that greater attention should be given to macroeconomic stability through monetary targeting. Yet for both political and economic reasons, the Park government generally placed the highest priority on growth.

In 1979 and the 1980s, government policy objectives shifted toward the achievement of price stability. At the same time, monetary authorities came under a variety of pressures, political as well as economic and foreign as well as domestic, to deregulate the financial sector. The conflict between the objectives of growth and stability, and the efforts to move toward financial market liberalization constitute the major themes of this chapter.

The Institutional Setting

The Monetary Authorities

Formally, the Bank of Korea and the Ministry of Finance share responsibility for Korean monetary policy. As in most other countries, the two institutions have not been on the friendliest terms, though no serious confrontations have occurred except in the early 1960s and again in the late 1980s when the central bank sought to exert greater independence from the government.

The Bank of Korea was established in 1950 under the Bank of Korea Act, which was drafted by two economists from the Federal Reserve Bank of New York.[1] The original legislation postulated that the bank should be given a high degree of autonomy. The bank's nine-member Monetary Board was the supreme policymaking organ—even more powerful than its U.S. equivalent—with formal responsibility for the formulation and execution of monetary policy and supervision over the activities of banking institutions.

In 1962, the military government of Park Chung Hee amended the Bank of Korea Act to strengthen the government's control over monetary policy and the bank itself.[2] In the series of minor amendments of the act that followed, bank independence steadily weakened, to the point that the minister of finance has come to have ultimate authority over monetary policy.

The finance minister is the chairman of the Monetary Board, which holds regular biweekly meetings to discuss policy issues and select the policy actions. The board is typically criticized for being a rubber stamp for government initiatives.[3] Virtually all of its members, including the Bank of Korea governor, are appointed by the finance minister, who has the power to overrule board decisions.[4] The minister's power is augmented by the existence of special banks and nonbanking financial institutions that are supervised by the Ministry of Finance and are effectively beyond the control of the Monetary Board.

Most important policy measures have been proposed by the government, to be approved by the board.[5] In the case of monetary targeting, annual target growth rates for monetary aggregates were announced in the financial stabilization program, or in later years, in the economic management program of the government, which resulted from discussions and consultations among the Economic Planning Board, Ministry of Finance (MOF), and the economic adviser in the Blue House. Other contemplated policy actions of some importance are usually contained in the ministry's *Annual Project Report* to the president.

During President Park's administration, the president himself sometimes took personal policy initiatives, for example, in response to business requests at the monthly export promotion meetings. In the case of some important reforms, even the minister of finance and the Bank of

Korea governor were excluded from the policymaking process. Policies were formulated under the leadership of the senior economic councilor to the president in the Blue House. One example of such policies, discussed in more detail below, was the presidential emergency measure to abolish the curb loan market in August 1972.

Still, the power of the Monetary Board and the Bank of Korea cannot be dismissed; indeed, it has probably increased since the transition to democracy in 1987. Most of the instruments of monetary policy are in the bank's hands now, and it is equipped with a large and reliable research staff. The bank also houses the powerful Office of Bank Supervision and Examination. Since the minister of finance has only a small number of staff specialists in monetary policy, some delegation of authority is inevitable.

Financial Institutions

Financial intermediaries in Korea can be divided into banking and nonbanking institutions (Figure 6-1). The banking institutions consist of commercial and specialized banks. Commercial banks regularly engage in short- and long-term financing, sales of commercial bills, securities investments, foreign exchange business, and other financial services with funds acquired through deposits, securities, or debt. At the end of 1990, the commercial banks were eleven nationwide banks, ten local banks, and sixty-nine branches of foreign banks.

Nationwide banks are the most important of the commercial banks, accounting for three-quarters of the total assets of the commercial banks. Throughout the 1970s, there were only five nationwide commercial banks (the Big Five), and they were under tight government control, in spite of only partial government ownership.[6] Now all of them are privately owned, although government control persists. At the end of 1990, almost 40 percent of the nationwide commercial banks' total assets were in the form of loans and discounts, acceptances on behalf of customers accounted for 17 percent, and investment or securities holdings accounted for 8 percent (Table 6-1). The major source of funds for commercial banks is deposits, which account for around 50 percent of total financial resources. Another important source of funds is borrowing from the Bank of Korea, which comprises 8.1 percent of the total.

Most local banks opened in the late 1960s to foster regional development. Branching of local banks was limited to specific provinces or prefectures, but otherwise government intervention was not as strong as

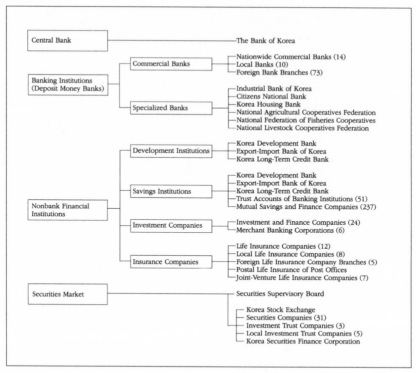

Figure 6-1. *Korea's Financial System (as of the end of 1992)*

in nationwide banks, and the local banks were permitted to charge higher loan rates. The financial structure of local banks is generally similar to that of the nationwide commercial banks except for the relatively large proportion of securities and small holdings of foreign currencies.

Foreign bank branches have been relatively free from government intervention. For a long period, they have lent money out of what they brought in from abroad. Because of a large interest rate differential and swap agreements with the Bank of Korea, most of the foreign banks have made handsome profits, particularly in the 1970s and in the first half of the 1980s.[7] Foreign banks were immune from most government intervention but at the same time subject to discrimination. For example, they were not allowed to utilize the rediscount facilities of the Bank of Korea until March 1985.

Most specialized banks were established in the 1960s in order to provide funds to particular sectors, such as agriculture, having no access to commercial banks because of restrictions specified in the

Table 6-1. Principal Accounts of Nationwide Commercial Banks, 1990
(in billion won)

Assets	Amount	Percentage of Total	Liabilities and Net Worth	Amount	Percentage of Total
Currency and checks	17,060.0	16.9	Deposits in won currency	39,256.7	38.9
Foreign exchange	3,875.7	3.8	Demand	16,402.3	16.3
Deposits with the Bank of Korea	2,376.5	2.4	Time and savings	22,854.5	22.7
Deposits with other banks in foreign currencies	1,333.9	1.3	Deposits in foreign currencies	7,993.3	7.9
Securities	8,202.5	8.1	Borrowings from the Bank of Korea	8,189.9	8.1
Loans and discounts	33,352.4	33.1	Borrowings in foreign currencies	2,410.4	2.4
Loans in foreign currencies	5,924.8	5.9	Acceptances and guarantees	17,000.3	16.9
Personal and real estate	2,791.2	2.8	Other liabilities	17,216.3	17.1
Customers' liabilities on acceptances and guarantees	17,000.3	16.9	Paid-in capital	5,101.0	5.1
Others	8,919.8	8.8	Capital surplus	2,232.7	2.2
			Earned surplus	1,436.5	1.4
Total	100,837.1	100.0	Total	100,837.1	100.0

Source: Bank of Korea, *Economic Statistics Yearbook* (1992).

General Banking Act. Initially, these banks were expected to rely mainly on the issuance of their own debentures and borrowing from the government for loanable funds. Gradually they became more dependent on deposits from the public. Since most of the specialized banks engage in business similar to that of commercial banks and compete with them, the government is planning to privatize some of them. At the end of 1990, specialized banks held 36.9 percent of the total assets of the banking institutions. Loans and discounts made up 51.6 percent of their total assets, and deposits accounted for 54.5 percent of total liabilities.

Nonbank financial intermediaries were introduced in the 1970s to attract curb market funds into the organized market and thereby help finance economic development plans. This sector has grown rapidly in both number and volume, and recently their share in total deposits outstripped that of deposit money banks. Nonbank financial institutions can be broadly classified into five categories according to their business activities. Development institutions, raising funds by borrowing abroad, from the government, or through issues of special bonds, provide

Table 6-2. Market Share of Financial Institutions (in percentage at the end of period)

	1975	1980	1985	1990
Deposits				
Commercial banks	54.6	43.8	31.4	25.9
Specialized banks	24.3	26.4	22.3	16.6
NBFI[a]	21.1	29.8	46.3	57.5
Total	100.0	100.0	100.0	100.0
Loans and discounts				
Commercial banks	47.2	39.6	34.4	29.9
Specialized Banks	25.9	25.0	24.4	19.5
NBFI[a]	26.9	35.4	41.2	50.6
Total	100.0	100.0	100.0	100.0

[a]NBFI = nonbank financial institutions.
Source: Bank of Korea, *Economic Statistics Yearbook* (1992).

medium- and long-term loans or credit for development of favored activities such as exporting or production in the heavy or chemical industries. Savings institutions grant small loans with funds mobilized in the form of time deposits. Investment companies are concerned with short-term financing business, such as the purchase and sale of commercial paper issued by business firms with funds raised through the issuance of their own paper or debentures, the management of cash management accounts, and so on. In addition, there are insurance companies and a fifth residual category of other institutions, such as securities companies and lease companies, that function as supplementary financial institutions.

There have been enormous changes in the structure of the financial system in recent decades, and these are reflected in the market shares of different types of institutions (Table 6-2). The market share of banking institutions, measured in terms of deposits in local currency, contracted from about 79 percent in 1975 to around 42 percent at the end of 1990, while that of nonbank financial institutions increased from about 21 percent to around 58 percent in the same period. The share of investment companies increased particularly rapidly. Similarly, the market share of banking institutions for loans and discounts dropped sharply from about 73 percent to about 49 percent during the period. This rapid change in market share was caused largely by differences in regulatory treatment: Nonbank financial institutions have been allowed greater freedom in their management of assets and liabilities and, most important, have been permitted to apply higher interest rates on their deposits and loans than those of banking institutions.

Government Control over Financial Institutions

The government exercises tight control over financial institutions in Korea. Private institutions like commercial banks, and especially the special banks, are subject to extensive government intervention and supervision.[8] Interest rates on deposits and loan rates have ceilings, and banks' lending portfolios are controlled through government directives. The government has also restricted competition among financial institutions by setting entry barriers. For almost two decades, from the early 1960s to the early 1980s, no new nationwide commercial bank was allowed to open, a situation providing existing institutions oligopolistic benefits.

Special laws and regulations have restricted the private ownership of commercial banks, making the government de facto owner of the banks. The government has the power to intervene in the appointment of high-ranking bank officers. Until quite recently, major bank management issues, such as budget planning, wage increases, branch opening plans, and dividend payments, were subject to implicit or explicit government approval. De facto government ownership also affects prudential regulation; since the government stands behind the banking institutions, there is no formal deposit insurance system. Whenever banks have experienced trouble, however, the monetary authorities have come to their rescue; there have been no incidents of bank failure in Korea.

The Instruments of Monetary Policy

Monetary authorities typically attempt to control particular financial variables, such as monetary aggregates or market interest rates, that are believed to be linked reliably to ultimate target variables. These financial variables are called intermediate targets, monetary indicators, or monetary policy indicators. As will be explained in more detail in the next section, Korean monetary authorities have employed various monetary aggregates as policy indicators at different times. Since 1979, broadly defined money (M2), or the sum of currency in circulation and deposits of banking institutions, has served as the principal target of monetary control.

The literature on monetary policy distinguishes between direct and indirect policy instruments. The charter of the Bank of Korea envisioned that it would depend on indirect instruments such as open market operations, changes in legal reserve requirements, and changes in the rediscount rate for the purpose of monetary control. In actuality, these instruments did not function effectively because of the underdevelopment of the financial structure, the existence of persistent excess demand for bank funds, the excessive borrowing by commercial banks from the central bank, and government deficits. As a result, the authorities resorted to direct controls, including control over domestic credit, fixing of interest rates for loans and deposits, and the use of the Monetary Stabilization Account.

Open Market Operations

The Bank of Korea is authorized to buy or sell securities representing government obligations, other securities fully guaranteed by the government, and special negotiable obligations of the Bank of Korea called monetary stabilization bonds (MSBs) in the open market for the purpose of controlling the quantity of money. However, open market operations have been used only sporadically, mainly through the compulsory sale and repurchase of MSBs by the Bank of Korea. In the 1970s, the government depended on borrowing from the Bank of Korea for most of its fiscal deficits rather than on the issuance of government securities (Table 6-3).[9] Therefore, there was an insufficient supply of eligible securities. Even when the government started to increase its issuance of securities in the 1980s, they were not marketable because of their long-term maturity and low interest rate.

Table 6-3. Deficits and Public Sector Financing (in billion won)

	Public Sector Deficit	Net Borrowing from the Bank of Korea	Net Issue of Government Bonds
1971	54.4	−7.8	−2.9
1972	222.1	115.3	19.3
1973	90.4	34.4	0.1
1974	231.8	191.4	−9.3
1975	197.4	268.0	−7.7
1976	164.9	130.0	69.7
1977	149.3	100.3	192.9
1978	49.8	110.2	69.2
1979	664.6	−155.8	7.0
1980	423.5	265.0	123.2
1981	930.8	526.0	194.5
1982	2,222.1	196.5	869.0
1983	950.6	245.3	302.9
1984	922.9	−1.3	−163.6
1985	713.3	−6.5	−417.9
1986	64.9	−10.0	−31.0
1987	−259.7[a]	3.0	799.1
1988	−1,642.7[a]	−655.0	1,333.3
1989	19.1	−860.0	1,438.7

[a] Public sector surplus. The public sector includes the central government, government funds, and government enterprises such as railroads and procurement. To finance the deficit, the public sector has also depended on borrowings from commercial banks and from abroad.
Source: Bank of Korea, *Annual Report* (various issues).

MSBs were first issued by the Bank of Korea in 1961. Initially they were not offered to the general public but assigned to nonbanking financial institutions because their discount rates did not fully reflect the market interest rates and the capital market was not well developed. With the effort to shift toward indirect credit controls after 1982, however, MSBs were publicly offered, with interest rates raised nearly to the market level.

The volume of MSBs increased sharply, especially after 1986, in order to alleviate the pressure toward monetary expansion from the foreign sector that followed the emergence of current account surpluses (Table 6-4). However, the increase in bond issues imposed burdensome interest payments on the Bank of Korea and generated another source of pressure for monetary expansion.

Reserve Requirement Policy

The Bank of Korea sets reserve requirements for the deposit liabilities of banking institutions. The reserve ratio may not exceed 50 percent, but in a period of pronounced monetary expansion, the bank is authorized to impose a marginal reserve requirement from 50 to 100 percent on any increase in deposits. In late 1991, the reserve requirement ratio for most bank deposits was set at 11.5 percent. For Worker's Savings for Housing and other long-term deposits, however, the Bank of Korea imposed a 3 to 7 percent reserve requirement.[10]

In calculating the required reserves, a lagged accounting method has been adopted. Required reserves are calculated every two weeks based on deposits, and commercial banks are required to hold the reserves in the two-week period that begins one week after the calculation period. In case the actual reserves fall short of the required reserves, the commercial bank is subject to a penalty of 1 percent of the deficient reserves.

Until 1980, the reserve requirement policy was used frequently as an instrument for monetary control. In addition, reserve requirement ratios used to be relatively high. For instance, in the mid-1960s when an improvement in the balance of payments generated excess liquidity in the financial market, the Bank of Korea raised the ratios to 35 percent for demand deposits and 25 percent for time and savings deposits. Moreover, from October 1966 to March 1967, marginal reserve requirement ratios of 50 percent for the increase in demand deposits and 45 percent for time and savings deposits were temporarily imposed. Even in 1979, reserve requirements remained as high as 27 percent for demand deposits and 20 percent for time and savings deposits (Figure 6-2).

The rationale for maintaining high reserve requirements was undermined considerably, however, when banks facing excess demand for

Table 6-4. Issuance of Monetary Stabilization Bonds (in billion won)

	1981	1982	1983	1984	1985	1986	1987	1988	1989	1990
MSBs issued (net)	—	−25	150.5	408.1	−59.5	2,754.5	4,915.9	7,199.0	1,931.9	−2,064.9
MSBs outstanding	30	5	155.5	563.6	504.1	3,258.6	8,174.5	15,373.5	17,305.4	15,240.5
Interest paid on MSBs	175.4	266.9	185.9	355.2	207.6	152.0	656.6	1,404.2	2,066.9	1,980.0
M2	15,671.1	19,904.2	22,938.1	24,705.6	28,565.2	33,833.1	40,279.5	48,938.8	58,638.0	68,707.5
M1	3,982.4	5,799.3	6,783.4	6,820.7	7,557.8	8,808.9	10,151.4	12,151.4	14,329.0	15,905.3
MSBs outstanding/M2 (%)	0.2	0.0	0.7	2.3	1.8	9.6	20.3	31.4	29.5	22.2
MSBs outstanding/M1 (%)	0.8	0.1	2.3	8.3	6.7	37.0	80.9	126.5	120.8	95.8

Source: Bank of Korea, *Annual Report* (1991).

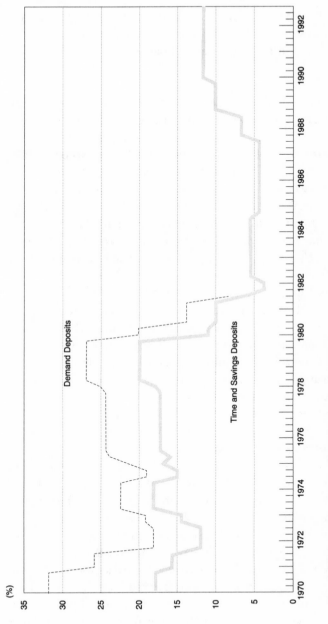

Note: A unified reserve requirement ratio was introduced on July 1, 1981.

Source: Bank of Korea, *Economic Statistics Yearbook* (1992).

Figure 6-2. Reserve Requirement Ratio

loans relied on the practice of borrowing from the Bank of Korea to meet reserve deficiencies. Taking this fact and the profitability of commercial banks into account, the central bank lowered the ratios on several occasions after 1980. Even before that, the Bank of Korea had regularly paid interest on reserve deposits, sometimes as high as 15 percent, to relieve the financial burden of commercial banks.

Rediscounts

The Bank of Korea makes loans and discounts to commercial banks. This discount policy has played a very important role in monetary control in Korea because commercial banks there have traditionally relied on borrowing from the Bank of Korea for funds. The Bank of Korea supplies credit to banks through two channels: policy loans, extended to encourage banks to support specific sectors in industry (examples are rediscounts of commercial paper and loans for export financing, agriculture and fisheries, and particular sectors, such as heavy and chemical industries), and general loans available to banks that have participated in preferential financing (Type A loans) or used mostly to control bank reserves (Type B).

The Bank of Korea can affect the availability and cost of funds for banks by changing the loan allotments or discount rates; customarily, the rediscount rate is set lower than commercial bank rates, which are also fixed below market rates. In addition, much of the bank's lending was to support policy loans made by the commercial banks, and when there were rediscount applications, most of them were automatically approved. This situation has limited the effectiveness of discount policy as an instrument for monetary control.

Direct Control over Domestic Credit

The most commonly used direct instrument of monetary policy in Korea is control over domestic credit. Formally, the Monetary Board is allowed by the Bank of Korea Act to set ceilings on the aggregate volume of loans for each banking institution in periods of excessive monetary expansion. The Bank of Korea may also specify the maximum loan period and types of collateral for each banking institution and the amount of loans that can be made. From time to time, banks have been asked to stop new lending until there is further notice from the monetary authorities. These direct controls are very effective in achieving monetary growth targets quickly.

Direct control over domestic credit has been used as a key instrument for monetary control in Korea since 1950 when it was adopted for the alleviation of wartime inflation and economic reconstruction. When the government introduced interest rate reforms in September 1965, it announced its intention to discontinue the direct control over bank credit and to depend more on indirect methods. Nevertheless, direct control has persisted, in part due to the difficulty of controlling the money supply effectively with traditional indirect instruments given the underdevelopment of the financial markets.

The Monetary Stabilization Account

The Monetary Stabilization Account, along with monetary stabilization bonds (MSBs), is one of the major instruments in Korea for liquidity control.[11] It is a special account placed in the Bank of Korea for controlling the quantity of money in the short term. The bank is authorized to require banking institutions to deposit an assigned amount of money into the account when a contraction in the quantity of money is desired. When an increase in the quantity of money is desired, it allows them to withdraw money from the account. Since deposit in the account is compulsory, its effects on liquidity control are as strong as those of reserve requirements. However, operations of the account differ from the reserve requirement system in that it need not be universal and can be conducted selectively and flexibly, with attention being paid to the reserve position of each bank. Therefore, it has been used as an instrument for liquidity control when there have been significant disparities of liquidity positions among banks.

Interest Rate Policy and Credit Rationing

Except for briefly starting in 1965, monetary authorities in Korea fixed bank interest rates at very low levels in real terms (Table 6-5). Formally, the Monetary Board sets the maximum interest rates on each loan and deposit by banking institutions as well as on loans from the Bank of Korea. The Banker's Association or an individual bank is supposed to decide the actual or effective rate within the bounds set by the maximum rate. Since the board sets the upper limits on rates far below market clearing levels, ceiling rates have typically become the effective rates. To guarantee the profitability of the banking business, the board sets bank deposit rate ceilings lower than loan rate ceilings by some constant spread and fixes most of the Bank of Korea rediscount rates lower than the commercial bank deposit rates.

This policy of setting low real rates has induced chronic excess demand for bank loans by business firms and, in turn, excess demand

Table 6-5. Nominal and Real Interest Rates, 1962–1990 (in percentage per annum)

Year	Nominal Rate of Time Deposit[a]	Inflation Rate[b]	Real Rate
1962	15.0	18.4	−3.4
1963	15.0	29.3	−14.3
1964	15.0	30.0	−15.0
1965	18.8	6.2	12.6
1966	30.0	14.5	15.4
1967	30.0	15.6	14.4
1968	27.6	16.1	11.5
1969	24.0	14.8	9.2
1970	22.8	15.6	7.2
1971	22.2	12.5	9.7
1972	15.7	16.7	−1.0
1973	12.6	13.6	−1.0
1974	14.8	30.5	−15.7
1975	15.0	25.2	−10.2
1976	15.5	21.2	−5.7
1977	16.2	16.6	−0.4
1978	16.7	22.8	−6.1
1979	18.6	19.6	−1.0
1980	22.9	24.0	−1.1
1981	19.1	16.9	2.2
1982	11.0	7.1	3.9
1983	8.0	5.0	3.0
1984	9.3	3.9	5.4
1985	10.0	4.2	5.8
1986	10.0	2.8	7.2
1987	10.0	3.5	6.5
1988	10.0	5.9	4.1
1989	10.0	5.2	4.8
1990	10.0	8.9	1.1

[a]Average annual rate of one-year time deposits.
[b]Rate of change in GNP deflator (annual rate).
Source: Bank of Korea, *Economic Statistics Yearbook* (1992).

for Bank of Korea loans by commercial banks. Although nominal interest rates for one-year time deposits (which, with the rate on general bank loans, can be considered as a representative interest rate in Korea) have been high, real interest rates were negative in twelve of the twenty years between 1962 and 1981 due to high inflation.

There are two opposing schools of thought on how interest rate policy in Korea should be implemented. One school is greatly influenced by the ideology of the free market and is composed mostly of American-educated scholars both in and out of government. They believe the low interest rate policy has distorted the allocation of resources and led to the waste of scarce funds. Furthermore, they argue, this policy is unfair as well as unproductive. Credit rationing inevitably favors large, well-established firms with sufficient collateral over small- to medium-sized industries that lack collateral but may have high growth potential. Most adherents of this school have advocated not the introduction of a completely flexible interest system but a gradual rise in interest rates in several stages, or a flexible system starting with call markets, which is analogous to the federal funds market in the United States. To support their argument, the liberals usually cite the studies of Brown, McKinnon, Shaw, and Fry.[12]

The other school is composed of business economists and government officials, in particular those in the Ministries of Trade and Industry and of Finance. Higher interest rates, they argue, would increase the burden of interest payments and the cost of production, which would be passed on to consumers in the form of higher prices. Cost and price increases would worsen the competitiveness of domestic goods and services in international markets, a particularly undesirable outcome given that export-oriented growth has been the country's basic strategy. This school seems to have been influenced by the success of Japan, which ruled Korea for thirty-five years prior to 1945 and whose economic policy after World War II can be characterized as one of high investment and exports coupled with low interest rates. Except for the five-year period starting in 1965 when an interest rate reform was introduced, this school has dominated the formulation of interest rate policy. Instead of being used as a means of allocating funds and controlling liquidity and aggregate demand, interest rates were raised or lowered in accordance with changes in the cost and profit environment.

An extreme case was the lowering of bank rates in 1977. At that time, it was evident that interest rates should be adjusted upward. Money supply and domestic credit were growing rapidly, and inflationary pressures were strong. To appease business circles antagonistic to the introduction of a value-added tax system, the Monetary Board lowered bank rates on the pretext of relieving business firms of the additional cost burden that might be caused by the new tax system.

Another characteristic of Korea's interest rate policy is its rigidity. Changes have been made in bank interest rates only infrequently, even in comparison to neighboring countries that have also employed low interest rate policies. Table 6-6 summarizes the frequency of changes in bank loan rates in Korea, Japan, and Taiwan from 1966 to 1988. Between 1966 and 1977, the interest rate was adjusted only six times in Korea, in contrast with twenty-one times in Japan and sixteen times in Taiwan. From 1973 to 1977, when the world and domestic economies were experiencing severe fluctuations, the Bank of Korea changed the rate

Table 6-6. Number of Bank Loan Rate Changes, 1966–1988

Country	1966–1977[a]	1978–1988
Korea	6 (1)	10
Japan	21 (12)	Flexible rates
Taiwan	16 (11)	25

[a]Numbers in parentheses are for the period 1973–1977.
Source: Bank of Korea, *Monetary Policy in Korea* (1978).

just once in comparison with twelve times in Japan and eleven times in Taiwan. From the late 1970s on, interest rate policy became more flexible, but the number of interest rate adjustments was fewer than half that of Taiwan.

A partial liberalization of interest rates began after 1980. The interest rates for call transactions between banking institutions were liberalized, and those for issuances and loans of certificates of deposit were liberalized in March 1983. The Ministry of Finance removed ceilings on most lending rates of financial institutions as well as those on a few long-term deposit rates on December 15, 1988.

Credit Rationing

Economic theory tells us that the counterpart of government efforts to control interest rates is disequilibrium and the emergence of rationing and a black market. The Korean financial market is a typical example, though the task of rationing was not the business of commercial banks but of government. In addition to setting interest rates, the government has also intervened extensively in the allocation of financial resources.

Bank loans have been broadly divided into policy loans and general loans, with policy loans made with money earmarked in the direction of government industrial policy and usually carrying concessional interest rates. Long-term government plans (the five-year plans) stipulate broadly which industries should be given priority, and the annual financial stabilization program and government or Monetary Board directives specify how much money should be earmarked for specific sectors cr industries.

In the 1960s, export industries were the most favored. Not only was the interest rate for export financing the lowest among bank lending, but there was no availability problem since qualified export loan applications were automatically approved. In the 1970s, government directed more resources to the machinery, shipbuilding, shipping, and chemical industries, among others. According to calculations by Nam, the share of policy loans among all bank credits was more than 40 percent throughout the 1970s, although it was lowered to 35 percent in the 1983–1988 period.[13]

Even residual funds were not completely at the disposal of commercial banks due to Monetary Board regulations and guidelines, the most important of which is the Regulation on the Use of Funds in the Banking Sector. Policy loans and other loans that conform to the directives of the Monetary Board were eligible for rediscount at low interest rates from the Bank of Korea; others were not. In rationing whatever was left, commercial banks favored, for profitability and safety, conglomerates and firms with collateral over small- and medium-sized firms and firms with no collateral, giving rise to the charge that credit rationing contributed to industrial concentration.

Monetary Targeting

A low interest rate policy leads to an increase in demand for bank credit. Meeting the greater demand means a rapid increase in the money supply, contributing to pressures on prices. As a result, Korea has periodically suffered from bouts of high inflation. Despite the long history of favoring industrial growth through its credit policy, Korea also has a long history of monetary targeting.

Defining Monetary Targets

Various monetary indicators have been chosen by the Korean monetary authorities as an appropriate intermediate target of monetary policy: M1 (narrowly defined money), the reserve base, domestic credit, or M2 (broadly defined money). Selection of a monetary indicator, or the related issue of the definition of money, has been one of the most controversial issues in monetary economics for a long time. In the 1950s, there was just one definition of money: the sum of currency and demand deposits. When the government announced its first annual stabilization program in 1957 in accordance with an agreement with U.S. aid officials, it set the target growth rate for M1.

Twelve years later, M1 was replaced by the reserve base, or high-powered money, which is the monetary liability of the central bank, that is, currency and reserve deposits. The change was based on the argument that high-powered money was easier to control and monitor than broader aggregates and that the money supply (whether defined as M1 or M2) is in any case indirectly determined by the reserve base and the money multiplier.

Change in the reserve base can be attributed to government, financial, foreign, and other sectors. Monetary control through regulation of the reserve base means that monetary authorities regulate the components of change in base money by sector. Usually the most important sector in this approach is the financial sector. It turned out, however, that volatility in the government or foreign sectors also seriously affected base money, impeding efficient liquidity management. When the reserve base started to jump in 1970 due to increased foreign capital inflows, monetary authorities substituted domestic credit for reserve money as a monetary indicator.

Domestic credit is defined as total credit supplied to all nonbank domestic economic units by deposit money banks and the central bank; domestic credit is conceptually closer to M2 than M1. Domestic credit regulation is based on the idea that the liquidity level of the whole economy can be maintained at a desirable level by controlling bank credit, ignoring foreign and other sectors or assuming they are neutral.

When domestic credit is adopted as a means of monetary control, monetary authorities are looking at the asset side of the balance sheet of monetary institutions, not the liability side. This scheme is based on the contention that the control of excessive demand for money should start with the regulation of financial institutions. Direct credit control by the central bank therefore became much more important.

Since the mid-1970s, the importance of domestic credit seems to have declined, and gradually it became unclear whether domestic credit or M1 was the main monetary indicator. There were discussions on the importance of broadly defined money as an indicator.[14] When government introduced a comprehensive stabilization program in 1979, it announced that the new monetary indicator would be M2.

Procedures for Targeting

Setting the target growth rate should take into account such factors as the expected real GNP growth rate, the tolerable inflation rate, and expected changes in velocity. Proponents of monetary targeting have argued that velocity is stable or predictable, but in Korea, at least, velocity turned out to be quite volatile. As a result, before the annual stabilization program or economic management program is completed, there has typically been heated debate on the target growth rate for money. Usually, the minister of trade and industry and the private sector think that the preliminary target growth rate set by the Ministry of Finance and Bank of Korea is too low. Either the minister of the Economic Planning Board or the senior presidential counselor will play the role of coordinator to reach a compromise. From the 1960s through the 1970s, the target rates were also periodically subject to International Monetary Fund (IMF) consultation.

At the Bank of Korea, both micro and macro methods have been employed in setting target growth rates. At the macro level, the EC

(European Community) method or a modified version of the Fisher equation was used to calculate the target rates.[15] More complicated forms of money demand equations were also employed for this purpose, making use of expected changes in real and financial variables. At the micro level, the bank prepared tables on the sources and uses of funds, which represented expected demand for funds in major sectors for the coming year.

The target rate that is set is announced around the end of the year, together with other economic goals of the government. The Bank of Korea employs all its instruments to keep to the targets. Until the mid-1980s, one of the biggest headaches for monetary authorities in setting the monetary target and implementing monetary control was the deficit financing of borrowing from the Bank of Korea by the Grain Management Fund and Fertilizer Account, which function to support prices for agricultural products and fertilizers, respectively. The size of borrowing by these accounts was large and unpredictable (Table 6-7).[16] On the average, borrowing from the Bank of Korea by the fund and the account together accounted for as much as 12.1 percent in the growth of money supply (M1) between 1979 and 1983. From 1984, however, the government shifted these accounts to the budget and discontinued their borrowing from the central bank, as a component of its stabilization efforts.

There are a number of additional peculiarities of monetary targeting in Korea that are worth noting. First, it is worthwhile to distinguish between the Park Chung Hee era and the 1980s. Before 1980, Park was more concerned about economic growth than price stability, and even when it was necessary to fight inflation, measures other than restrictive monetary policy were considered first. As Table 6-8 suggests, setting the monetary target was one thing; keeping it was quite another.

In the 1980s, President Chun Doo Hwan followed a different course. Influenced by his senior economic adviser, Jae-Ik Kim, Chun gave price stability top priority, and monetary targeting was more strictly enforced. To propagate his objectives and gain general public acceptance of stabilization efforts, a special program of economic education was introduced. Efforts were made to advance the benefits of price stability and monetary control, and greater attention was given to monetary growth rates, which were announced monthly. The concern of the Ministry of Finance and the Bank of Korea shifted to keeping monetary growth under its target level. Even with such strong efforts, actual growth rates of M2 deviated from the targets, particularly as a result of the need to come to the rescue of troubled banks and firms.

Despite these deviations, it can be argued that monetary control in Korea in the 1980s was handled in a myopic way. In principle, monetary

Table 6-7. Operations and Effects of the Grain Management Fund and Fertilizer Account

	Borrowings from Bank of Korea (billion won)		Contribution to M1 Growth (%)[a]
	Grain Management Fund	Fertilizer Account	
1973	50	9	11.4
1974	160	–23	18.8
1975	230	90	33.8
1976	130	—	11.0
1977	150	100	16.2
1978	154	30	8.5
1979	200	—	7.4
1980	130	30	4.9
1981	220	100	8.4
1982	200	100	7.5
1983	250	100	6.0

[a]Grain Management Fund + Fertilizer Account/M1 change.
Source: Sang-Woo Nam, "Liberalization of the Korean Financial and Capital Markets," mimeo (Korea Development Institute, Seoul, 1989), reprinted with permission.

Table 6-8. Target and Actual Growth of Monetary Indicator (in percentage)

Year	Policy Indicator	Target Growth Rate	Actual Growth Rate
1969	RB[a]	27.5	38.3
1970	DC[b]	27.0	26.5
1971	DC	28.0	31.1
1972	DC	24.0	30.4
1973	DC	24.0	31.7
1974	DC	33.7	54.2
1975	DC	35.3	32.2
1976	DC	17.3	21.7
1977	DC	24.7	23.6
1978	DC	34.2	45.9
1979	M2	25.0	24.6
1980	M2	20.0	26.9
1981	M2	25.0	25.0
1982	M2	20.0–22.0	27.0
1983	M2	18.0–20.0	15.2
1984	M2	11.0–13.0	7.7
1985	M2	9.5	15.6
1986	M2	12.0–14.0	18.4
1987	M2	15.0–18.0	19.1
1988	M2	18.0	21.5
1989	M2	15.0–18.0	19.8
1990	M2	15.0–19.0	17.2
1991	M2	17.0–19.0	21.9

[a]RB = Revenue base.
[b]DC = Deposits and currency.
Source: Bank of Korea, *Annual Report* (various issues).

targeting is a long-term policy based on the hypothesis that there exists a stable relationship between inflation and the monetary growth rate. Many economists, therefore, have argued that trying to keep to the target in the short run is meaningless. This was not well appreciated in Korea in the 1980s, however, and each month, the actual growth rate of the monetary indicator was announced comparing the current figures with the ones in the same month in the previous year. When the actual growth rate deviated from the target rate, it made big headlines in the mass media, followed by immediate corrective policy actions: changes in interest rates, changes in Bank of Korea rediscount facilities, or in extreme cases, suspension of new bank lending for a specific period of time.

The problem was compounded by the fact that target growth rates were expressed in terms of point targets in some years as opposed to ranges, the common practice in the United States. The logic behind this system was that under the low interest rate regime, the excess demand for bank credits cannot be met even within the upper limits of the target range. Therefore, even if a target range were announced, the lower bound would be meaningless, and only the upper limit would be considered the real target.

Given the conflicting imperatives between a strong demand for credit and periodic efforts to stabilize, it was not rare for monetary authorities to resort to expediency or "window dressing" in order to keep to targets. When M1 was the monetary indicator, new savings deposits with high interest rates were introduced periodically. These accounts had all the characteristics of demand deposits except for the interest rate but were not counted as a component of M1. The shift of funds from existing demand deposits to the newly introduced ones would depress the growth of M1. When M2 was the main indicator, certificates of deposit and bank trust accounts were introduced for the same purpose. These financial liabilities of the banking institutions were classified outside M2.

In other cases, commercial banks were ordered to ask their customers to repay part of their loans through compensating balances. This practice would lead to cuts in bank deposits and thereby lower M2, loosening the relationship between monetary indicators and nominal gross national product (GNP), and thereby weakening the usefulness of the monetary targeting.

The Stance of Monetary Policy
The government's monetary policy stance has changed over time, with the major shift away from an accommodative policy coming in the early

1980s. The history of monetary policy since the first oil shock can be reviewed briefly.

When the Korean economy was confronted with the first oil crisis, the government put growth and employment objectives ahead of controlling inflation. M2 grew 26.1 percent in 1974.[17] There was no upward adjustment of interest rates, signaling no intention of belt tightening. Wholesale prices went up by 42.1 percent in 1974, and the trade deficit widened to almost $2 billion from $566 million in 1973 (half the increase coming from the nearly fourfold rise in crude oil prices in 1974). However, real GNP growth was not affected, registering 8.1 percent. As the government implemented its ambitious program for the promotion of heavy and chemical industry in the late 1970s, monetary policy inevitably continued to be accommodative. The M2 growth rate soared to 39.3 percent in 1978 from 27 percent in 1975.

To fight accelerating inflation and to regain the competitiveness of Korean products, the government introduced the Comprehensive Stabilization Program in April 1979. The M2 growth rate was cut to 26.8 percent in 1979. When the second oil crisis hit in 1980, the post-Park government chose not to repeat its strategy toward the first crisis, and the monetary growth rate was cut even further. By 1984, the M2 growth rate had fallen to 10.7 percent.

This shift did not mean that the government was straightforward and rigid in the implementation of monetary policy. When a scandal in the curb loan market forced two large firms into bankruptcy, causing shock waves to the financial market in May 1982, government came to the rescue by expanding the money supply and lowering interest rates. The growth of M2 jumped to as high as 32 percent in the third quarter of 1982 compared to the same period in the previous year. In addition, bank interest rates on both deposits and loans were cut by an average of 4 percentage points. Once the shock subsided, the government resumed its stabilization efforts, and monetary growth slowed to 27 percent by the end of the year.

New Developments
Before 1986, Korea had a chronic trade deficit, and the foreign sector played the role of absorbing liquidity. For the purpose of controlling the money supply, the payments deficit provided a relief to policymakers in that it squeezed bank credits. Since 1986, thanks to the decline in oil prices, lower international interest rates, and the strong yen, there has been a considerable improvement in the country's balance of payments. As the current account surplus grew, the excessive supply of liquidity through the foreign sector put the monetary authorities in a difficult situation (Table 6-9).

Table 6-9. Monetary Expansion by Sector (in percentage)

	1982	1984	1986	1988
M2 growth	27.0	7.7	18.4	21.5
Sectoral contribution				
Government	2.7	−0.2	0.6	−5.4
Private	32.5	18.5	23.1	22.9
Foreign	−13.1	−4.8	5.5	22.0
Other	4.9	−5.8	−10.7	−18.0

Source: Bank of Korea, *Annual Report* (1985, 1989).

To diffuse these pressures, the authorities depended on instruments that were seldom employed before. International policy reversed. The authorities restricted the inflow of foreign capital and encouraged overseas investment and repayment of foreign debt. Furthermore, efforts to liberalize and internationalize domestic financial markets were strengthened. The government relaxed foreign exchange controls, and in late 1988 interest rates on loans were finally liberalized, marking a big step toward full financial deregulation.

At the same time, the Bank of Korea engaged in active open market operations by issuing and selling MSBs to absorb liquidity. The ratio of outstanding MSBs to M2 jumped from 1.8 percent in 1985 to 31.4 percent in 1988. Although the monetary authorities more or less succeeded in keeping monetary growth within the target rate, there was a cost. Since the MSB was issued at market interest rates, the Bank of Korea had to pay a large amount of interest to bondholders, which constituted an addition to the supply of high-powered money.

The rapid increase in the issuance of MSBs disrupted the money market. In addition, questions were asked whether MSBs, which are short-term liabilities of the central bank, are significantly different from other types of monetary liabilities; the old issue of defining money was raised again. These new developments also forced the monetary authorities to pay more attention to issues such as the liberalization of financial markets and the need for greater dependence on indirect methods of monetary control such as open market operations.

Impact of Monetary Policy

Monetary targeting is based on the idea that changes in monetary aggregates lead to changes in both real economic activity and prices in the short run but over the long run only to changes in prices. In this connection, two questions should be addressed: the transmission mechanism of monetary policy in Korea and the estimated effects of changes in monetary growth on real income and prices in both the short and long runs.

A typical restrictive monetary action would be to ask commercial banks to suspend lending temporarily. Business firms would turn to the short-term finance companies or curb loan markets for working funds. Long-term investment would be adjusted because of the credit constraint. At the same time market interest rates would rise, affecting both investment and consumption. However, in Korea the availability of credit or the liquidity constraint seems to dominate interest rate effects, since the capacity of the finance companies and the curb market to raise funds is limited, and official lending rates were moved little and infrequently.

How important money is in controlling inflation in Korea is a difficult question because the government employed strong supply-side measures to fight inflation, including an incomes policy and administrative control of the prices of major manufactured goods, which resulted in repressed inflation. Therefore, it is not clear whether cuts in money supply growth alone were mainly responsible for the relatively stable prices in the 1980s or whether falling raw material prices together with strong wage controls were also important.

The Korean monetary authorities have always emphasized the importance of money, arguing that there exists a stable and close relationship between the growth of money and the inflation rate. However, Cheong and other economists have argued that Korean inflation in the past two decades has been mainly caused by supply-side factors, although later accommodated by monetary growth.[18] Figure 6-3 shows that velocity of M2 has not been stable in the past two decades.

In an attempt to detect the impact of changes in money, Ro and Sakong built a St. Louis–style monetarist model of the Korean economy.[19] According to their simulations, a 1 percentage point increase in M2 would cause a 0.6 percentage point increase in nominal GNP, which would be divided into a 0.5 percentage point increase in real GNP and a 0.1 percentage point increase in prices after one year. Two years later, nominal GNP would go up by 0.7 point, with a 0.28 point growth in real GNP and a 0.42 point change in prices. Real GNP would continue to grow at that rate in the following three years. Thus, even after five years and even when the most powerful analytic tools of monetarists are employed, money was not neutral and had real effects in Korea, implying that the long-run Phillips curve is not vertical.[20]

Source: Bank of Korea, *Economic Statistics Yearbook* (1992).

Figure 6-3. Inflation Rate, Growth, and Velocity of M2

169

Features of Financial Markets

It is indisputable that Korea's financial sector has contributed to the country's rapid economic growth of the past three decades. However, government intervention has caused distortions in the financial markets, including the substantial degree of dualism that came to exist in the structure of the financial system. This section reviews the effects of government policy on the evolution of the Korean financial markets.

One of the most important features of the Korean financial system is the existence of a sizable curb loan market. Transactions in the curb market are made without the intermediation of formal financial institutions. Formally, curb lending is illegal, prohibited by the General Banking Act and other laws.[21] However, credit rationing at the bank and high interest rates of the curb market, usually more than double bank interest rates, have attracted many lenders and borrowers. Figure 6-4, which contains the curb market interest rates estimated by the Bank of Korea, shows that these rates have been much higher than banks' general loan rates, which were fixed by the monetary authorities.

The only public and consistent estimate of the size of the curb loan market comes from the flow-of-funds account compiled and published by the Bank of Korea. Making use of tax data, this captures only the tip of the iceberg of the private loans made to business firms by households and does not contain any information about lending activities among firms or among households. According to this estimate, the curb market was around one-tenth of the DMB loan market during the period 1963 to 1972. Starting in 1972, when presidential emergency measures to abolish the curb market took effect, the size of the market shrank drastically. In 1980, it was less than 2 percent of the DMB loan market.

The Bank of Korea estimate, however, has been criticized as severely underestimating the actual size of the market since most transactions are unreported in order to evade income taxes. In many cases, lenders demand that loans go unreported and borrowers have no choice but to oblige.

There have been several attempts, most of them based on survey data, to estimate the volume of curb loans more accurately. Shim and associates estimated that the curb market was three times bigger than reported by the Bank of Korea in the 1960s and early 1970s.[22] Park and Cole's estimate of curb loan transactions among households and loans to unincorporated firms as well as to corporations falls between those by Shim and associates and the Bank of Korea.[23]

More recently, Lee and Han attempted to measure the market size by a different method.[24] Making use of the divisia index method of

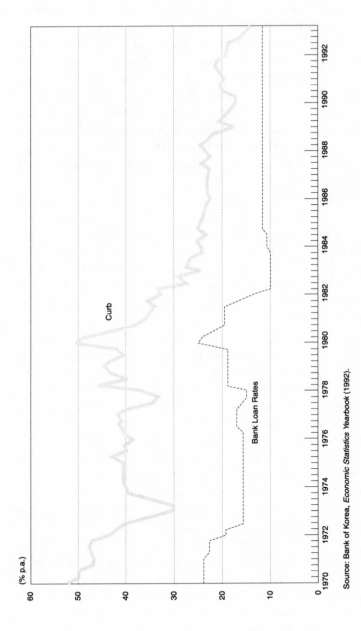

(% p.a.)

Source: Bank of Korea, *Economic Statistics Yearbook* (1992).

Figure 6-4. Curb and Bank Loan Rates

171

monetary aggregation pioneered by Diewert and Barnett, they estimated that the size of the curb market was much bigger than thought, and in 1978 and 1979 it was even bigger than the official financial market, including banking and nonbanking sectors.[25] However, the relative size decreased in the 1980s, and in 1986, the final year of estimation, it was about 20 to 30 percent of the official market. With government efforts to abolish the curb market strengthening in the 1970s and 1980s, the relative size of the pure curb market seems to have shrunk. Newly established financial institutions, and short-term finance companies in particular, have attracted private lenders by offering handsome interest rates for their deposits. These institutions have flourished but have been criticized for employing curb market practices, charging borrowers effective rates almost as high as in the curb market.[26]

In general, the government has regarded the market as a necessary evil. It seems to understand that due to the fixed low interest rate, there has been little room for an organized short-term money market whereby firms can borrow flexibly to meet their working fund needs and that the curb market worked as a substitute. Restricting this market would cause complaints from lenders and borrowers, which include major business firms with some influence, and might even lead to financial panic.

Sporadically, however, the government has attempted to reduce or abolish the market. In 1965, it introduced an interest rate reform, raising the annual rate on general loans from 16 percent to 26 percent and that of time deposits with a maturity of one year from 15 percent to 26.4 percent. In an effort to absorb funds from the curb market, a new longer-term time deposit with a maturity of eighteen months or more was created with a high annual interest rate of 30 percent. However, it was not just the interest rate differential that caused the curb market to flourish. Through bureaucratic bank lending practices and strict qualifications, many firms have been denied access to bank loans and have had no recourse but to rely on private loans. Therefore, even with interest rate reform, the curb market did not shrink in size.

On August 3, 1972, President Park issued a special decree designed to freeze curb market transactions: It required all curb loans to business firms to be reported by both lenders and borrowers. From that time on, outstanding loans were frozen for three years and interest rates were set at 1.35 percent per month, well below monthly interest rates on curb loans and bank loans of 3.2 percent and 1.58 percent, respectively. The volume of curb loans reported by business firms amounted to 345.6 billion won, approximately 80 percent of M1 at that time.

These drastic measures practically suspended curb market transactions for a while. It was inevitable that the market would reappear under a system whereby bank interest rates were arbitrarily fixed at low levels, and in fact, the revival started about a year later, during the first oil crisis.

Short-term finance companies and others helped shrink the curb market by offering attractive financial assets in the 1980s. However, these are nonbank financial institutions and lie beyond the direct control of the central bank, weakening the efficacy of the monetary policy, just like the curb loan market. Firms could still borrow from these finance companies even when bank loans were squeezed. Disintermediation, or substitution between bank deposits and nonbank financial assets, has reduced the usefulness of M2 as monetary indicator.

The effects of the low interest rate policy can also be approached from the demand side by looking at the relationship between financial institutions and firms (Table 6-10). With insufficient corporate savings, Korean firms have depended heavily on external funds to finance their ambitious investment projects. Since bank loan rates were fixed below a market clearing level, they did their best to borrow as much as possible, resulting in high leverage ratios. In the 1970s, the ratio of liabilities to net worth was around four to one in a typical nonfinancial company.

Some business firms were favored over others in securing bank credits because they engaged in strategic activities such as exporting and, in the 1970s, heavy and chemical industry production. Making full use of secured money, they grew into conglomerates, accounting for the

Table 6-10. Source of Funds in Business Sector (in percentage)

	1970	1975	1980	1985	1986	1987	1988	1989	1990
Internal funds		21.6	16.9	38.6	39.9	41.1	41.0	26.3	
External funds		78.4	83.1	61.4	60.1	58.9	59.0	73.7	
External funds									
Indirect Financing	39.7	27.7	36.0	56.2	38.8	36.1	24.2	35.5	40.3
From Deposit Money banks	30.2	19.1	20.8	35.4	29.0	17.2	17.1	14.8	15.6
From OFI	9.5	8.6	15.2	20.8	9.8	18.9	7.1	20.7	24.7
Direct financing	30.7	42.5	47.4	43.0	61.2	63.9	75.8	64.5	59.7
Securities	15.1	26.1	22.9	30.3	31.4	32.9	52.6	53.8	40.7
Governmental bonds	0.1	0.8	0.9	0.8	0.7	1.2	4.8	2.8	2.8
Papers	3.0	1.6	5.0	0.4	8.8	−1.9	5.4	13.3	4.1
Corporate Bonds	1.1	1.1	6.1	16.1	8.5	6.6	6.6	12.8	20.1
Equities	13.9	22.6	10.9	13.0	13.4	27.0	35.8	24.9	13.7
Others	15.6	16.4	24.5	12.7	24.8	31.4	17.6	11.2	11.6
Borrowing from abroad	29.6	29.8	16.6	0.8	5.0	−0.5	5.6	−0.5	7.4

Source: Bank of Korea, *Flow of Funds Account in Korea* (1987, 1992).

lion's share not only of bank credits but of investment, production, and employment in the Korean economy. Once these firms grew big enough, banks became hostages to them; when they were in trouble, the government was forced to intervene to bail them out. In times of tightening bank credit, the largest, and often the weakest, companies were the last to be affected, thereby weakening the efficacy of the policy.

To cope with this problem of concentration of economic power among a few conglomerates, the Monetary Board required banking institutions to earmark a certain amount of loanable funds for small- and medium-sized firms. In addition, starting in 1974, the government introduced a credit control system according to which large business groups required approval from designated banks for any new investment projects or purchase of real estate. From February 1984 on, ceilings of bank credit were set for each conglomerate, which banks were forced to observe. As a result, the share of the thirty biggest business groups in total bank credit declined from over 40 percent in the early 1980s to 16.8 percent in 1990.

Another constraint on monetary policy in connection with bank lending practices was that bank loans in Korea were authorized mostly for long-term purposes such as facility investment, although loan terms were typically for only one year. In some cases, loans could be used for the purchase of land required to build factories. Bond and stock markets were still at an early stage of development even in the first half of the 1980s, so commercial bank loans were the major source of long-term funds. The implications of this system were, first, that it was customary for banks to roll over outstanding loans, and second, that bank lending to an individual firm tended to increase over time. These rigidities made it hard for the monetary authorities to introduce restrictive policy actions even when necessary.

At the macro level, finally, it appears that excessive government control and interference has been detrimental to financial development and deepening. It is difficult to measure the degree of financial development, but the Goldsmith ratio, or the financial interrelation ratio has been frequently used for this purpose. This is the ratio of the total value of financial assets to the total value of physical assets, or when data on physical assets are unavailable, the ratio of financial assets to nominal GNP.[27] Figure 6-5 shows that the ratio was stagnant in the 1970s when financial repression was severe but increased in the 1980s. Figure 6-6 shows that a positive relationship exists between an increase in the real value of financial assets and real interest rates, which is a representative measure of financial repression.

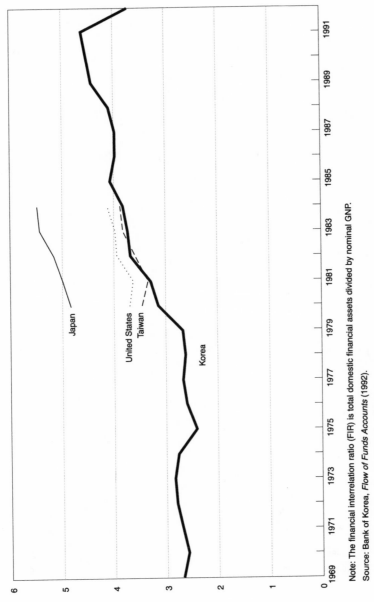

Note: The financial interrelation ratio (FIR) is total domestic financial assets divided by nominal GNP.

Source: Bank of Korea, *Flow of Funds Accounts* (1992).

Figure 6-5. Financial Interrelation Ratio

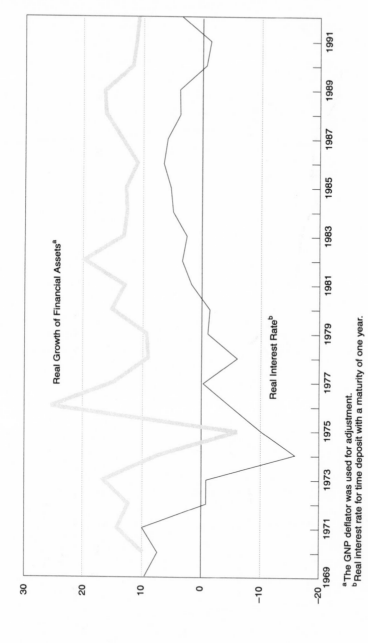

Real Growth of Financial Assets[a]

Real Interest Rate[b]

[a]The GNP deflator was used for adjustment.
[b]Real interest rate for time deposit with a maturity of one year.

Source: Bank of Korea, *Economic Statistics Yearbook* (1992).

Figure 6-6. Real Growth of Financial Assets

Evidence of financial underdevelopment can be found in the existence of a large curb loan market. Another indicator is the poor performance of formal banking institutions. Government control and intervention reduced innovation and initiative in the financial sector. Protected by entry barriers on the one hand and controlled by the government on the other, bankers have made little effort to improve investment or loan analysis techniques or to introduce new types of products.

In the 1960s and 1970s, government intervention was so tight as to lead to virtual uniformity among commercial banks.. For a long time, nationwide banks had been almost identical in asset and capital size, numbers of branches and employees, and even profit figures and dividend capital ratios.

Government intervention in credit allocation and the obedient attitude of the commercial banks also resulted in a huge amount of nonperforming assets beginning in the late 1970s. On the recommendation of the government, banks generously provided loans and guarantees to the shipping, shipbuilding, and overseas construction companies, which started to grow very fast. The second oil crisis, however, caused financial difficulties for some of these firms. Government did not allow the ailing business firms to fail for fear of enormous losses to the banks and wider economic repercussions. The commercial banks continued to supply loans to these companies even though they could not pay interest on time. Banks were, in turn, supported by subsidized loans from the central bank. According to a study by Kim, nonperforming assets of the five nationwide banks were almost 3 trillion won in 1986, equivalent to 8.5 percent of their total loans and discounts.[28] The significant size of the nonperforming assets has been an obstacle to the flexible implementation of monetary policy and has delayed financial liberalization.

The low interest rate policy can also be held responsible for the delayed development of the capital market. Although the Korea Stock Exchange was opened in 1956, the role of the securities market in mobilizing private savings for corporate financing had been quite limited until the mid-1980s. Business firms, which should have played the role of the supplier of stocks and bonds, shied away from the capital market because low-rate bank loans were available. Not until 1986 did the stock market begin to grow rapidly (Table 6-11).

New Issues and Prospects

Since the mid-1980s, two significant events have been changing the environment under which monetary and other economic policies are

Table 6-11. Growth of the Korean Capital Market (in billion won)

	1975	1980	1985	1990
Number of listed companies	189	352	342	669
Total annual financing (equity and bonds)	156	1,135	3,471	14,001
Market value of listed stocks	1,436	2,527	6,570	79,020
(percent of GNP)	(14.2)	(6.9)	(9.0)	(46.9)
Value of listed bonds	220	2,545	12,001	51,117
Price earnings ratio	5.3	2.6	5.2	12.8

Source: Bank of Korea, *Economic Statistics Yearbook* (1992).

formulated and implemented: the emergence of balance-of-payments surpluses and democratization. Korea had been a chronic deficit country, with a high foreign debt, until 1985. Aided by favorable changes in the international economy—the drastic fall in oil prices, the decline in foreign interest rates, and the strong yen—the trade account recorded a surplus for the first time in the country's modern history in 1986.

The new phenomenon of a payments surplus brought about two formidable issues for the monetary authorities. Monetary pressures coming from the foreign sector demanded a new policy of sterilization. The authorities responded hastily by issuing a large amount of MSBs, which are by nature short-term liabilities of the central bank and cannot be relied upon in the long term. Forcing financial institutions to purchase large amounts of the bonds disturbed financial markets, raising interest rates. Although the surplus has subsequently declined, more effective means and methods of sterilization are clearly needed.

The problem has been complicated by the growing size of overseas borrowing by the banking sector. Since 1967, five nationwide commercial banks have been elevated to Class A foreign exchange bank status with eligibility to borrow from the international money market. However, several factors kept them from depending heavily on the overseas money market until the late 1980s. In most cases, borrowing from abroad required approval from the minister of finance in accordance with the Foreign Exchange Control Act of 1961. Many restrictions and interest rate ceilings were imposed on lending with the borrowed foreign funds. There were shortages of bank personnel experienced in international banking. By comparison, the government-established special banks, such as Korea Exchange Bank, Korea Export-Import Bank, and Korea Development Bank, have played a major role in borrowing from abroad. With the liberalization of the capital and foreign exchange markets in the late 1980s, commercial banks started to engage in the international banking business and increased their borrowing from the international money market.[29]

With the emergence of the trade surplus, Korea has been facing ever-increasing pressures from the United States and other advanced countries to open both commodity and financial markets and to abolish foreign exchange controls. The Ministry of Finance announced its master plan for the internationalization of the financial market in December 1988, but that plan was extremely gradual: The capital market would be opened in several stages starting in 1992. The expected inflow and outflow of foreign capital and freer exchange rate movements will further complicate monetary control.

Democratization has also affected the environment for monetary policy. The general public has been demanding greater equity and additional measures to correct the concentration of economic power among the conglomerates. The argument for tighter control on bank credits to these firms has been persuasive. The problem is that many of these firms need money for further investment to compete effectively with foreign firms, particularly as the domestic market opens. Policymakers are being asked to produce measures that satisfy these contending arguments.

With democratization, demands for deregulation in the financial market naturally followed. There are, however, some problems to be addressed before the government can go ahead with liberalization. First, the nonperforming assets of commercial banks are a serious stumbling block. In most cases, government is responsible for this and has been helping banks with subsidized Bank of Korea loans. Still, it will take several years until banks recover from these losses.

Second, the Korean financial market is severely segmented and needs greater integration through restructuring before full liberalization is introduced. Commercial banks, short-term finance companies, merchant banks, and stock brokerage companies all compete for deposits by offering similar financial assets. "Big bang"–type full liberalization might solve the segmentation problem in one shot, but policymakers are considering restructuring in several steps to reduce the shocks and uncertainties to the financial market.

Third, there seems to be a need for the introduction of deposit insurance before the financial market is fully deregulated. The government has typically stood behind financial institutions, and as a result bank runs and failures have never occurred. With the abolition of government intervention, an insurance system needs to be developed to guarantee a stable financial market during times of distress. In addition, the bank supervision and examination system needs to be overhauled to prevent unsound banking practices from leading to failures of financial enterprises during the transition.

Besides these problems, the authorities will find monetary control much more difficult when deregulation is in full swing. There will be less room for direct credit control or window guidance. Volatilities in the financial market may be amplified.

Another new issue that has become politically sensitive is the independence of the Bank of Korea. The dispute between the Ministry of Finance and the central bank became quite serious when the latter demanded more independence and a revision of the relevant laws in 1988. The bank even staged a campaign to obtain the signatures of 1 million people sympathetic to its cause. The ministry responded that since the government is finally responsible for the results of economic policies, it should control monetary policy. Public opinion was divided, and heated debates raged until a truce was arranged. There was also criticism that the rivalry between the two institutions delayed financial liberalization because both were preoccupied with their own interests. There is no question, however, that through this process, the Bank of Korea has become more independent. The independence issue is expected to resume when the next administration is sworn in.

NOTES

1. A. Bloomfield and J. Jensen, *Banking Reform in South Korea* (New York: Federal Reserve Bank of New York, 1951).

2. Although the Ministry of Finance gained in terms of monetary policy, it lost the more powerful instrument of fiscal policy. Preparing the national budget became the responsibility of a newly established super-ministry, the Economic Planning Board.

3. In the past forty years, except for a few occasions, the ministers of finance have typically not attended Monetary Board meetings, knowing that the board would not make any decision that would displease them.

4. According to the Bank of Korea Act, seven non–ex officio members are to be recommended to the president by financial institutions and other economic ministers, including the ministers of the Economic Planning Board, Trade and Industry, and Agriculture. Board members are supposed to represent various sectors, but the minister of finance effectively controls appointments.

5. Some policy actions have been announced by the government even before they were discussed by the board.

6. Voting rights of large, private shareholders of nationwide commercial banks were restricted by law, creating room for government manipulation.

7. In Korea, a swap agreement is a repurchase contract between foreign banks and the Bank of Korea. In selling foreign exchange to the Bank of Korea, foreign banks preserve the right to repurchase foreign currencies in the future at the current rate and thereby are able to avoid exchange risk.

8. Commercial banks are supervised and examined by the Office of Bank Supervision and Examination (OBSE) of the Bank of Korea. Specialized banks and development institutions are formally supervised by the minister of finance, but examinations are carried out by the OBSE. Investment, savings, and development institutions are supervised by the minister of finance but examined by the OBSE, life insurance companies are overseen by the Securities Supervisory Board, and the postal savings system is managed by the minister of communications.

9. The government had an incentive to depend on the Bank of Korea. It could borrow at an especially low rate of 2 percent per annum, when the general lending rate of the commercial banks was 15 to 20 percent.

10. Banks pay preferentially high rates of interest on Worker's Savings Accounts. To compensate partially bank losses caused by handling the accounts, smaller reserves are required.

11. When the Monetary Stabilization Account was introduced in 1967, there was no provision in the Bank of Korea Act empowering the Monetary Board to establish or require deposits into the account. No commercial bank, however, dared to challenge the board. Ten years later, when there was an amendment to the act, regulation of the account was formally included.

12. See G. Brown, *Korean Pricing Policies and Economic Development in the 1960s* (Baltimore: Johns Hopkins University Press, 1973); R. McKinnon, *Money and Capital in Economic Development* (Washington, D.C.: Brookings Institution, 1973); E. Shaw, *Financial Deepening in Economic Development* (New York: Oxford University Press, 1973).

13. Sang-Woo Nam, "Liberalization of the Korean Financial and Capital Markets," unpublished paper (Seoul: Korea Development Institute, 1989).

14. Bank of Korea, *Monetary Policy in Korea* (Seoul, 1976) (in Korean).

15. According to the EC (European Community) method, monetary growth rate should be set to be the same as the sum of the real GNP growth rate and a tolerable or target inflation rate. The method ignores the possibility of changes in velocity.

16. There are, of course, ceilings on government borrowing. The Bank of Korea Act stipulates that loans to the government and subscriptions

of government bonds by the central bank should "not exceed the amount of the indebtedness which, together with any borrowing done by the government from other banking institutions and the public, has been authorized by the National Assembly."

17. M2 grew 38.8 percent in 1973, partly to accommodate the unusually high growth of exports and GNP. The rapid monetary expansion was also due partly to the shift of the curb market funds into the banks, which resulted from presidential emergency measures to freeze the curb loan market in August 1972.

18. Mun-Kun Cheong, "The Process of Korean Inflation since 1980," *Journal of Korean Economic Studies* (May 1979): 94–108 (in Korean).

19. Sung-Tae Ro and Eun-Duk Sakong, "A St. Louis Model of the Korean Economy," *Korea Development Review* (Spring 1988): 19–35 (in Korean).

20. Sang-Woo Nam and Duckhoon Lee, "Monetary Transmission Mechanism and Recommendations for Monetary Policy," *KDI Quarterly Economic Outlook* (Second Quarter 1989) (in Korean) employed a different model of reduced-form equations and came up with somewhat different results. A one percentage point increase in M2 would cause a 0.24 point increase in real GNP two years later. The real impact of money supply would decline gradually, to a 0.15 point increase in GNP after seven years. Their model seems to be subject to the degree-of-freedom problem, since it is an annual model and the observation period is from 1967 to 1988.

21. More recently, some banks and investment finance companies seem to have become involved in curb loan activities. A lender and a borrower reach an agreement, and the lender makes a deposit at the bank on the condition that deposited money should be lent to a specific borrower. In addition to the interest income from the bank, the lender receives interest from the borrower under the table. In this way, lenders feel safer, borrowers pay the same effective interest as before, and banks get the interest rate differential.

22. Byung-Koo Shim et al., *A Study of Preferential Interest Rate Structure— The Korean Experience* (Seoul, 1972).

23. D. Cole and Yung Chul Park, *Financial Development in Korea, 1945–1978* (Cambridge: Harvard University Press, 1983).

24. Tong-Hun Lee and Han Sil, "On Measuring the Relative Size of the Unregulated to the Regulated Money Market over Time," unpublished paper (Seoul: Ilhae Institute, 1987).

25. W. Diewert "Exact and Superlative Index Numbers," *Journal of Econometrics* 4, 2 (1976): 115–146; W. Barnett, "Economic Monetary Aggregates: An Application of Index Number and Aggregation Theory," *Journal of Econometrics* 14, 1 (1980): 11–48.

26. Investment finance companies, better known as short-term finance companies, have engaged in practices that are similar to the compensating balances in commercial banks. Borrowers have been asked to purchase designated financial assets with part of the borrowed money.

27. R. Goldsmith, "Financial Structure and Economic Growth in Advanced Countries," in *Capital Growth and Economic Growth* (New York: NBER, 1955).

28. Joonkyung Kim, "An Overview of Readjustment Measures against the Banking Industry's Nonperforming Loans," *Korea Development Review* (Spring 1991) (in Korean).

29. As of February 1993, most of the headquarters and major branches of all types of banks were registered as Class A foreign exchange banks, totaling 548.

7

Wage Policy and Labor Market Development

Choongsoo Kim

Recently academic and public attention has focused on developments in the Korean labor market. Many scholars and policymakers see the rapid wage growth and increase in labor disputes of the late 1980s as serious obstacles to continued economic growth. In fact, the sudden change in labor market conditions—and the attention given to labor—is mainly attributable to the transition to democracy that occurred in 1987–1988. Previously, labor market issues received relatively little attention as a component of macroeconomic policy. As in most other underdeveloped economies, a constant excess supply of labor existed in Korea, and policy emphasized the creation of employment opportunities rather than macroeconomic ends.

Several stages of growth and policy can be distinguished. When Korea was in its initial phase of export-led development in the 1960s, growth was fueled largely by labor-intensive light manufacturing industries which did not require highly skilled workers. There was an excess supply of labor, and the labor market was able to supply needed labor at relatively low wages.

Following the shift in industrial policy toward fostering capital-intensive heavy manufacturing industries in the mid-1970s, a shortage emerged of skilled blue-collar workers, technicians, and engineers. This shortage led to substantial wage hikes for skilled labor, brought about a widening of wage differentials among workers of different occupations and educational levels, and became an important source of inflation.

In the early 1980s, the Korean government changed its policy objectives once again, emphasizing stabilization policies aimed at curbing the chronic inflation that had persisted since the mid-1970s, and even before. It implemented implicit wage guideline policies together with tight monetary and fiscal policies. Although the government considered wage increases a major source of inflation, other policies were also pursued to maintain the relative balance between income for work and return to capital.

This chapter describes labor market developments in Korea over the 1970s and 1980s and discusses the causal relationships among wages, employment, productivity, and government policies, with particular emphasis on wage determination and its impact on other macroeconomic variables. We will examine the puzzle of how real wages and employment increased simultaneously, as well as the hypothesis that Korea's successful economic performance was attributable to a low-wage policy.[1]

The relationship between the change in industrial strategy in the mid-1970s and labor market developments is a major theme of this chapter, particularly the effect of wage increases on inflation. In the 1980s, the government devalued the currency in order to improve the international competitiveness of exporting firms. Nonetheless, real wages continued to rise. We will endeavor to explain how such seemingly unusual results came about and assess the policy implications of the findings for other developing countries.

A Statistical Overview

Continuous economic growth requires the size of the labor force to increase more rapidly than the size of the population. The Korean labor market has more than satisfied this condition (Table 7-1). Since the early 1960s, except for a few years, the labor force's growth rate has always exceeded the population's growth rate; the average population growth rate was 2.3 percent per year between 1964 and 1973, while the average labor force growth rate was 3.4 percent per year. Moreover, the gap between the two rates widened during subsequent years as the Korean economy achieved higher economic growth rates.

The three main sources of labor force growth in Korea have been population increases, migration from rural to urban areas, and increases in female labor force participation. Population increases were the main source of labor force increases, especially until the early 1970s. However, the population growth rate began to drop rapidly beginning in the early 1970s due to effective birth control policies.[2] The rising rate of female labor force participation is a relatively recent phenomenon, reflecting women's declining fertility rates and rising educational levels. On the other hand, continuous industrialization policies induced migration from rural to urban areas, contributing to an increase in the nonagricultural labor force.[3]

Table 7-1. Labor Force and Unemployment (in percentage)

Year	Population	Labor Force	Employment[a]		Unemployment Rate[b]		Real Wage[c]
1964	2.65	1.27	1.79	(3.57)	7.7	(14.4)	-5.7
1965	2.58	4.85	5.38	(11.55)	7.4	(13.5)	4.3
1966	2.55	2.39	2.63	(5.40)	7.1	(12.8)	6.0
1967	2.36	2.47	3.59	(10.13)	6.2	(11.1)	10.5
1968	2.35	3.79	5.07	(9.81)	5.1	(9.0)	14.6
1969	2.29	2.50	2.47	(6.64)	4.8	(7.8)	19.4
1970	2.21	3.15	3.58	(8.38)	4.5	(7.4)	9.2
1971	1.99	3.36	3.42	(9.35)	4.5	(7.4)	2.3
1972	1.89	4.85	4.35	(2.92)	4.5	(7.5)	2.2
1973	1.78	4.95	5.42	(8.73)	4.0	(6.8)	14.3
1974	1.73	4.14	4.38	(6.92)	4.1	(6.8)	8.7
1975	1.70	2.15	2.37	(6.17)	4.1	(6.6)	1.5
1976	1.61	5.84	6.16	(7.52)	3.9	(6.3)	16.8
1977	1.57	2.91	3.22	(8.80)	3.8	(5.8)	21.5
1978	1.53	3.66	4.68	(9.31)	3.2	(4.7)	17.4
1979	1.53	1.97	1.42	(4.64)	3.8	(5.6)	8.8
1980	1.57	1.75	0.60	(3.68)	5.2	(7.5)	-4.6
1981	1.56	1.77	2.49	(3.45)	4.5	(6.5)	-1.0
1982	1.49	2.52	2.54	(7.98)	4.4	(6.0)	7.0
1983	1.24	0.32	0.88	(4.51)	4.1	(5.4)	8.5
1984	0.99	-0.95	-0.52	(4.43)	3.8	(4.9)	5.7
1985	0.93	3.80	3.75	(6.80)	4.0	(4.9)	7.3
1986	0.95	3.38	3.57	(5.38)	3.8	(4.7)	6.2
1987	0.96	4.70	5.48	(7.34)	3.1	(3.8)	8.3
1988	0.97	2.56	3.16	(4.65)	2.5	(3.0)	11.7
1989	0.97	3.85	3.80	(5.05)	2.6	(3.0)	18.3
1990	0.97	2.87	3.00	(4.58)	2.4	(2.9)	10.7
Average							
1964–1973	2.27	3.36	3.77	(7.65)	5.6	(9.8)	7.7
1974–1980	1.61	3.20	4.04	(6.72)	4.0	(6.2)	10.0
1981–1990	1.11	2.48	2.82	(5.42)	3.6	(4.5)	8.6

[a]Figures in parentheses are the employment growth rate in the nonagricultural sector.
[b]Figures in parentheses are the unemployment rate in nonfarm households.
[c]Nominal wage in manufacturing sector deflated by the consumer price index.
Sources: Economic Planning Board, *Monthly Statistics of Korea* (March 1991), and *Annual Report on the Economically Active Population Survey* (various issues).

An important characteristic of Korean growth is that while the size of the labor force increased continuously, the unemployment rate fell during the same period, implying a higher growth rate in employment opportunities than of the labor force. The average unemployment rate in nonfarm households dropped from 9.8 percent between 1964 and 1973 to 6.2 percent between 1974 and 1980, and to 4.5 percent between 1981 and 1990.

Employment Expansion and Real Wage Increase

Employment expansion and real wage increases generally have an inverse relationship, particularly in the short run. In the Harris-Todaro model of wage and employment determination in labor-surplus developing economies, wage differentials between urban and rural sectors widen, resulting in increased unemployment rates in urban sectors as workers migrate from rural to urban sectors. A market-clearing equilibrium wage rate is reached with a reduced employment probability (that is, rising unemployment) in urban areas.

In the long run, however, if the economy grows at a reasonably high rate, both real wages and employment can increase simultaneously. One important condition for achieving this result is that labor productivity growth is high enough relative to real wage increases that the economy can absorb additional entrants into the labor force. Indeed, this line of causal relationship—from high labor productivity growth, to high economic growth, to high labor absorption—has been maintained by the Korean economy.

Under these conditions, the Harris-Todaro model does not hold. While real wage growth rates were higher, and thus urban-rural wage differentials were larger during the period 1974 to 1980 than the period 1964 to 1973, unemployment rates were lower over the period 1974 to 1980 than from 1964 to 1973.[4] The achievement of employment expansion and real wage simultaneously is one important piece of evidence against the hypothesis that the success of the Korean economy is mainly attributable to the maintenance of low wages.

Changes in Employment Structure

Rapid industrialization has caused the composition of employment by industry to change rapidly in Korea (Table 7-2). The most noticeable change is the dramatic reduction in the percentage of agricultural employment. The proportion of agricultural employment fell from over 60 percent in the early 1960s to below 20 percent in the late 1980s.

Employment in the manufacturing sector increased rapidly until the mid-1970s, reflecting the leading role of that sector in Korea's economic growth. The rate has slowed somewhat since then. Specifically, the average share of employment in the mining and manufacturing sector was 12.9 percent during the period 1963 to 1973, increased sharply to 20.7 percent between 1974 and 1980, and rose modestly to 25.5 percent from 1981 through 1990. Considering the relatively high economic growth of the manufacturing sector during the 1980s as compared to that of the 1970s, the increasing rate of employment share of the 1980s may be regarded as modest.[5] The slowdown is mainly attributable to the shift in industrial policy during the mid-1970s when huge investments

Table 7-2. Percentage Distributions of Employment and GNP, by Industry

Year	Agriculture		Mining and Manufacturing		Social Overhead Capital and Others	
	Employment	Composition of GNP[a]	Employment	Composition of GNP[a]	Employment	Composition of GNP[a]
1963	63.1	41.1	8.7	9.7	28.2	49.2
1964	61.9	43.5	8.8	9.8	29.3	46.7
1965	58.6	40.7	10.4	11.0	31.0	48.3
1966	57.9	40.3	10.8	11.2	31.3	48.5
1967	55.2	35.4	12.8	12.7	32.0	51.9
1968	52.4	32.3	14.0	14.0	33.6	53.7
1969	51.3	31.3	14.3	14.7	34.4	54.0
1970	50.4	28.7	14.3	16.4	35.3	54.9
1971	48.4	27.2	14.2	17.5	37.4	55.3
1972	50.6	26.5	14.2	18.7	35.2	54.8
1973	50.0	24.7	16.3	21.0	33.7	54.3
1974	48.2	24.6	17.8	22.4	34.0	53.0
1975	45.9	24.2	19.1	23.5	35.0	52.3
1976	44.6	23.2	21.8	25.1	33.6	51.7
1977	41.8	21.1	22.4	25.8	35.8	53.1
1978	38.4	17.7	23.1	29.8	38.5	52.5
1979	35.8	17.5	23.7	30.4	40.5	52.1
1980	34.0	15.1	22.6	32.0	43.4	52.9
1981	34.2	17.4	21.3	32.4	44.5	50.2
1982	32.1	16.9	21.9	32.0	46.0	51.1
1983	29.7	16.1	23.3	32.1	47.0	51.8
1984	27.1	14.9	24.2	33.8	48.7	51.3
1985	24.9	14.8	24.5	33.3	50.6	51.9

Table 7-2 (continued)

Year	Agriculture		Mining and Manufacturing		Social Overhead Capital and Others	
	Employment	Composition of GNP[a]	Employment	Composition of GNP[a]	Employment	Composition of GNP[a]
1986	23.6	13.8	25.9	34.6	50.5	51.6
1987	21.9	12.2	28.1	37.0	50.0	50.8
1988	20.6	11.8	28.5	37.5	50.9	50.7
1989	19.5	9.8	28.2	37.3	52.3	52.9
1990	18.3	8.5	27.3	36.8	54.4	54.7
Average						
1963–1973	53.8	31.9	12.9	15.5	33.3	52.6
1974–1980	39.7	19.9	20.7	27.1	40.1	53.0
1981–1990	24.9	12.6	25.5	35.9	49.6	51.5

[a]In constant prices.
Sources: Bank of Korea, *National Accounts* (1991); Economic Planning Board, *Annual Report on the Economically Active Population Survey* (various issues); and *Monthly Statistics of Korea* (March 1991).

in the heavy and chemical industries were initiated. These policies lowered the capacity of industry to absorb employment, and from the mid-1970s on, employment in the tertiary sector rose rapidly.

The changes in employment structure are detailed in Tables 7-3 through 7-5, with some highlights noted here. The percentage of permanent employees plus daily or temporary workers has more than doubled during the past three decades, although the ratio of 60.2 percent in 1990 was still far below the 74.8 percent of Japan in 1986 and the 87.5 percent of West Germany in 1985.[6] The share of unpaid family workers has fallen correspondingly.

Table 7-3. Employment Composition by Position (in percentage)

	Self-Employed	Family Workers	Daily Workers	Permanent Employees
1963	37.2	31.3	12.7	18.8
1964	37.0	32.4	11.1	19.5
1965	36.8	31.1	10.4	21.7
1966	36.2	30.5	10.9	22.4
1967	36.2	28.6	10.9	24.3
1968	35.1	27.4	11.4	26.1
1969	34.9	27.0	10.9	27.2
1970	34.1	27.0	10.6	28.3
1971	34.2	26.5	10.5	28.8
1972	34.3	27.3	11.2	28.2
1973	34.5	27.7	10.6	27.2
1974	34.6	26.5	9.6	29.3
1975	33.9	25.5	9.6	31.0
1976	34.0	24.7	9.1	32.2
1977	33.2	22.2	11.1	33.5
1978	33.0	20.4	10.8	35.8
1979	33.5	18.8	10.4	37.3
1980	33.9	18.8	9.5	37.8
1981	33.7	19.1	8.8	37.4
1982	34.1	18.3	8.7	38.9
1983	33.7	16.8	8.0	41.5
1984	31.7	15.4	9.0	43.9
1985	31.3	14.5	9.3	44.9
1986	31.4	14.2	9.4	45.0
1987	30.5	13.4	9.3	46.8
1988	30.2	12.8	8.9	48.1
1989	28.9	12.0	9.8	49.3
1990	28.3	11.5	10.1	50.1
Average				
1963–1973	35.3	28.6	11.0	25.1
1974–1980	33.7	22.2	10.0	34.1
1981–1990	31.3	14.7	9.1	44.9

Source: Economic Planning Board, *Annual Report on the Economically Active Population Survey* (various years).

Table 7-4. Employment Composition by Occupation (in percentage)

Year	Professional, Technical, Managerial	Clerical	Sales	Service	Agriculture	Production
1963	3.2	3.5	10.0	5.4	62.9	5.0
1964	2.8	3.8	10.9	6.0	61.6	14.9
1965	2.8	4.0	11.9	6.5	58.5	16.3
1966	3.1	4.7	11.7	5.7	58.1	16.7
1967	3.6	4.6	12.6	5.5	55.0	18.6
1968	3.9	4.4	13.4	6.1	52.3	19.9
1969	4.5	5.2	13.1	5.7	50.8	20.7
1970	4.7	5.9	12.3	6.5	50.3	20.3
1971	4.9	6.8	12.8	7.7	48.3	19.5
1972	3.7	6.4	11.6	6.8	50.7	20.7
1973	3.0	6.0	12.1	6.9	50.2	21.8
1974	3.3	6.5	12.6	6.7	48.3	22.6
1975	3.5	6.3	12.9	7.2	46.0	24.1
1976	3.4	6.8	11.8	7.1	44.8	26.1
1977	4.2	7.6	12.2	6.7	41.8	27.5
1978	4.6	8.2	12.6	6.9	38.3	29.3
1979	5.1	8.7	13.2	7.2	35.7	30.1
1980	5.3	9.3	14.5	7.9	34.0	29.0
1981	5.6	9.0	14.6	8.5	34.0	28.2
1982	5.5	9.7	15.4	9.9	31.8	27.7
1983	6.1	10.5	15.5	10.1	29.4	28.4
1984	6.7	11.4	14.7	10.3	26.8	30.0
1985	7.3	11.5	15.5	10.8	24.6	30.3
1986	7.5	11.6	15.0	10.8	23.4	31.6
1987	7.5	11.5	15.2	10.9	21.7	33.4
1988	7.8	12.0	14.7	10.8	20.5	34.2
1989	8.3	12.4	14.7	10.8	19.3	34.5
1990	8.7	13.0	14.5	11.1	18.1	34.6

Source: Economic Planning Board, *Annual Report on the Economically Active Population Survey* (various years).

Employment composition also changed dramatically. As noted, the proportion of laborers in agriculture and related occupations has fallen significantly. In line with a deepening industrial structure, the percentage of professionals, technicians, and production workers has more than doubled, although the percentage of production workers has not increased since the late 1970s.

Finally, it is worthwhile to note the stability of employment in industry. The ratio of employees to total employment, here termed the employee ratio, in the mining and manufacturing industry increased rather rapidly, from 65.8 percent in 1963 to 86.7 percent in 1990. The counterpart of this development was a decline in the share of unpaid family workers and self-employed workers. Considering that the employee ratio in Japan's mining and manufacturing industry in 1986 was 85.7 percent, the Korean mining and manufacturing industry can be

Table 7-5. Employment Status

Year	All	Wage Workers as a Share of Total Employment			Permanent Workers as a Share of Total Employment		
		Agriculture and Fishing	Mining and Manufacturing	Social Overhead Capital and Others	Total	Male	Female
1963	31.5	14.9	65.8	57.9	59.6	61.9	52.3
1964	30.6	13.8	62.9	56.4	63.6	65.5	57.3
1965	32.1	14.1	66.3	54.8	67.7	68.4	65.2
1966	33.3	4.2	67.7	56.8	67.3	68.7	62.8
1967	35.2	14.6	69.9	56.9	69.0	71.0	62.6
1968	37.5	14.8	72.4	58.3	69.5	71.4	64.0
1969	38.1	15.0	71.9	58.4	71.4	72.4	68.7
1970	38.9	15.1	71.3	59.7	72.8	74.4	68.5
1971	39.3	16.0	65.6	59.5	73.3	75.6	67.3
1972	38.4	14.5	71.9	59.5	71.2	71.3	71.0
1973	37.8	13.1	73.3	57.2	72.1	71.8	72.8
1974	38.9	12.6	76.7	56.4	75.2	75.2	75.4
1975	40.6	12.5	78.7	56.6	76.4	76.1	77.0
1976	41.4	11.9	77.8	57.0	77.8	77.7	78.2
1977	44.6	15.0	79.1	57.5	75.1	75.4	76.3
1978	46.6	13.7	80.4	59.3	76.7	76.3	77.6
1979	47.7	12.6	81.2	59.1	78.1	77.9	78.3
1980	47.3	11.8	80.0	58.1	79.9	80.4	78.8
1981	47.2	10.8	81.7	58.5	81.4	81.4	81.2
1982	47.6	13.8	81.3	55.1	81.6	82.5	79.9
1983	49.5	12.7	83.3	56.0	83.8	85.1	81.2
1984	52.9	12.0	85.8	59.3	83.0	85.2	78.7
1985	54.2	11.7	86.1	59.6	82.8	85.8	77.3
1986	54.4	11.0	83.4	59.8	82.8	85.2	78.1
1987	56.2	11.1	83.8	60.9	83.4	86.4	78.1
1988	57.0	9.4	83.5	61.4	84.4	87.1	79.8
1989	59.1	8.3	86.5	63.4	83.4	87.3	77.0
1990	60.2	7.8	86.7	64.5	83.7	87.0	79.4

Source: Economic Planning Board, *Annual Report on the Economically Active Population Survey* (various years).

regarded as having an industrialized employment structure. On the other hand, the employee ratio in the social overhead capital (SOC) and services industry has remained at about the same level for the past three decades, indicating a proportionate increase in self-employed workers and unpaid family workers in that sector. This suggests that due to the heavy emphasis on industry in the government's plans, the formal component of the tertiary sector did not expand as much as those of manufacturing industries.

Wage Growth by Industry

The data on wage growth by industry (Table 7-6) show that wage differentials among industries have narrowed over time.[7] The coefficient of variation, a measure of wage dispersion among industries, shows a

Table 7-6. Wage Growth Rates by Industry (in percentage)

Year	All	Mining	Manufacturing	Gas	Construction	Sales	Transportation	Finance	Services	Coefficient of Variation[a]
1971	16.9	19.4	16.2	27.4	9.7	10.2	14.9	16.5	19.3	31.2
1972	16.0	13.4	13.9	7.7	20.1	16.0	26.9	19.3	22.4	36.3
1973	11.5	21.0	18.0	20.3	14.8	17.0	6.9	15.8	4.2	57.3
1974	31.9	35.0	35.3	20.2	19.7	21.8	26.4	20.8	27.3	26.7
1975	29.5	33.1	27.0	41.6	40.0	46.1	24.7	30.5	41.9	32.4
1976	35.5	20.9	34.6	27.8	85.5	42.7	41.3	27.8	47.1	55.0
1977	32.1	42.1	33.9	28.2	35.2	20.3	38.7	23.8	33.5	21.6
1978	35.0	36.1	34.3	23.2	44.2	36.8	33.7	35.5	23.6	19.2
1979	28.3	30.1	28.6	17.5	11.3	27.6	32.5	19.4	30.3	28.3
1980	23.4	22.3	22.7	14.3	4.0	33.7	28.8	14.3	30.1	40.7
1981	20.7	19.9	20.1	26.2	24.1	17.2	17.1	20.6	24.6	15.6
1982	15.8	10.2	14.7	17.6	14.4	14.8	13.9	14.2	19.2	16.7
1983	11.0	6.6	12.2	15.3	5.8	9.6	7.7	7.6	10.1	30.9
1984	8.7	3.6	8.1	2.8	-1.7	9.3	9.4	14.9	0.5	67.5
1985	9.2	9.5	9.9	15.4	5.2	9.5	7.1	8.3	7.0	31.1
1986	8.2	9.3	9.2	11.3	3.8	8.1	9.1	6.2	8.1	25.8
1987	10.1	8.3	11.6	9.3	9.0	11.2	9.9	11.1	6.5	16.8
1988	15.5	16.1	19.6	6.9	11.2	7.6	12.3	7.9	9.7	37.7
1989	21.1	18.6	25.1	9.2	17.8	16.1	13.3	11.6	17.0	32.1
1990	18.8	14.1	20.2	16.9	25.6	17.3	11.8	15.5	15.6	23.1
Average										
1971–1973	14.8	17.9	16.0	18.5	14.9	14.4	16.2	17.2	15.3	84.8
1974–1980	30.8	31.4	30.9	24.7	34.3	32.7	32.3	24.6	33.4	75.4
1981–1990	13.9	11.6	15.1	13.1	11.6	12.1	11.2	11.7	11.9	14.4

[a]Coefficient of variation = Standard deviation/Mean × 100.
Source: Ministry of Labor, *Report on Monthly Labor Survey* (various years).

decreasing trend. During the 1980s, however, the coefficient of variation remained stable, perhaps reflecting the effects of the government's attempt to propagate wage guidelines.

Given that the manufacturing sector typically enjoys higher labor productivity growth than the service industry, it is often expected that wages in manufacturing will increase more rapidly than in the service sector. In Korea, this has not been the case. Wage growth in manufacturing has been about the same as the average growth rate for wages in all industries, suggesting that wage growth has not been directly related to labor productivity growth.

Korea's inflation in the 1970s can be attributed to a combination of cost and demand factors. In addition to the two large increases in world oil prices, the heavy industry push, the construction boom in the Middle East, and the expansion of domestic infrastructure investment resulted in a shortage of construction workers. In the 1980s efforts were made to ease the inflationary pressures from wage increases. Nominal wage growth during the 1980s dropped to almost one-third of that during the mid-1970s. Wage increases in the nontradable sectors in particular were kept in check through a government wage guidelines policy.

Labor Turnover

A high turnover rate, as is characteristic of Korea (Table 7-7), typically indicates a competitive labor market. Like most other Asian nations with a Confucian social tradition, however, hiring and firing practices are different from Western nations. Even during a recession, layoffs are quite rare and firms are likely to retain excess workers. Although Korea does not have the lifetime employment system visible in Japan's largest firms, employers are still reluctant to fire employees, and the separation rate thus represents mostly voluntary separation.

The turnover rate in the manufacturing sector has always been higher than that of other industries.[8] It increased in the late 1970s, during the heavy industry push, when wage growth was high and unemployment rates falling. In contrast to the advanced industrial states, where high turnover is associated with unemployment, job change was not necessarily associated with job loss. Employers of heavy industries scouted highly skilled laborers from other firms, suggesting that high turnover reflected job changes within manufacturing, and wages rose substantially.

This explanation is consistent with the changing pattern of labor accession rates presented in Table 7-8. During the high separation period, accession rates were also high, supporting the argument that job change was voluntary. In all industries, the separation rates have declined since

Table 7-7. Labor Separation Rate by Industry

Year	All	Mining	Manufacturing	Construction	Gas	Sales	Transportation	Finance	Services
1970	5.1	6.0	6.0	3.0	2.2	2.6	3.9	1.7	2.6
1971	4.6	6.6	5.4	2.3	1.6	3.9	3.4	1.5	2.2
1972	4.0	5.3	4.5	4.8	1.9	3.8	2.6	2.2	2.4
1973	3.9	3.7	4.5	4.0	2.4	2.2	2.1	2.1	1.9
1974	4.0	3.5	5.1	3.0	1.1	2.9	2.3	2.1	1.7
1975	3.7	2.6	4.4	3.2	1.1	2.8	2.2	2.4	2.1
1976	3.8	2.7	4.4	3.2	1.7	3.7	2.1	2.5	2.1
1977	4.4	2.9	5.1	3.4	2.1	3.6	2.6	2.5	2.0
1978	5.1	3.2	5.9	4.1	2.5	3.9	3.0	2.7	2.4
1979	5.3	3.2	6.3	4.1	3.4	4.0	3.2	2.6	2.2
1980	4.8	3.7	5.6	4.9	1.5	3.5	3.8	2.5	2.0
1981	4.7	3.6	5.4	5.8	1.7	3.4	3.4	2.4	2.0
1982	4.3	3.1	5.0	5.1	1.2	3.4	3.0	2.5	1.8
1983	4.3	2.7	5.0	4.9	1.5	3.4	2.8	2.4	1.9
1984	4.5	3.4	5.4	4.4	1.3	3.5	3.5	2.1	1.8
1985	3.9	3.1	4.5	4.7	1.3	3.1	3.0	2.2	1.7
1986	3.5	2.8	4.2	4.0	1.8	3.2	2.3	2.2	1.5
1987	3.6	2.6	4.3	3.9	1.1	3.1	2.2	1.9	1.4
1988	3.7	3.0	4.5	2.8	1.0	3.0	2.0	2.1	1.8
1989	3.2	2.5	3.8	2.9	1.1	3.1	1.9	2.1	1.8
1990	3.2	3.2	3.8	2.4	0.9	3.2	2.2	2.1	1.7

Note: Separation rate = Workers separated that month/Workers as of last day of previous month × 100. Numbers are monthly averages.
Source: Ministry of Labor, *Yearbook of Labor Statistics* (various issues).

Table 7-8. Monthly Labor Accession Rate by Industry

Year	All	Mining	Manufacturing	Construction	Gas	Sales	Transportation	Finance	Services
1970	4.7	4.9	5.4	3.4	3.2	2.0	4.2	1.9	2.0
1971	3.9	4.9	4.5	2.9	1.6	3.0	2.9	1.8	1.5
1972	4.0	3.2	4.6	3.0	3.2	3.0	3.0	2.2	2.4
1973	4.8	4.0	5.8	4.1	2.3	2.5	2.2	2.2	2.2
1974	4.1	4.9	4.8	2.9	1.8	2.9	2.7	2.4	2.0
1975	4.4	3.3	5.2	5.3	1.4	3.1	2.5	2.3	2.4
1976	4.5	2.5	5.2	5.2	2.2	4.3	2.6	2.7	2.3
1977	5.0	3.1	5.5	7.9	2.1	4.1	3.0	3.1	2.5
1978	5.5	2.7	6.3	5.6	2.3	4.4	3.6	3.2	2.9
1979	5.1	3.2	5.7	5.2	3.3	3.7	3.6	3.1	2.6
1980	4.4	3.8	4.9	4.9	1.7	3.2	3.5	2.6	2.3
1981	4.8	3.5	5.5	4.9	1.5	3.6	3.5	3.0	2.4
1982	4.3	2.8	4.8	5.8	1.4	3.4	3.2	3.7	2.1
1983	4.6	2.5	5.5	4.9	1.1	3.4	3.0	2.8	2.1
1984	4.5	3.7	5.4	4.4	1.3	3.6	3.8	2.3	2.0
1985	3.7	3.2	4.3	3.7	1.5	3.1	2.9	2.0	1.9
1986	4.0	2.8	4.8	3.8	1.7	3.4	2.7	2.4	1.7
1987	3.8	2.5	4.6	3.4	1.2	3.5	2.3	2.1	1.7
1988	3.7	2.2	4.4	2.8	1.4	3.4	2.1	2.3	2.1
1989	3.0	2.1	3.4	3.3	1.4	3.0	2.0	2.7	2.0
1990	3.0	2.6	3.3	3.1	1.4	3.2	2.3	2.4	2.1

Note: Accession rate = Workers hired that month/Workers as of last day of previous month × 100.
Source: Ministry of Labor, *Yearbook of Labor Statistics* (various years).

the late 1970s. Part of the reason may be economic stabilization policies, under which wage growth rates have remained stable across industries, reducing the incentives for workers to move.

Labor Share

An inappropriate real wage can significantly distort a country's trade pattern.[9] For a country like Korea with abundant labor, the wage-rental ratio should be relatively low, a point directly related to the low-wage hypothesis for Korea's success. The proper way to evaluate this argument, however, is not cross-nationally but by asking whether Korean workers have been appropriately compensated for their contributions to economic growth. In order to determine the welfare implications of real wage changes, we examine the changing patterns of labor shares of gross national product (GNP) by decomposing GNP growth rates into shares of real wage increases and employment changes. Labor's share, defined as the ratio of employee compensation to national income in current prices, increased dramatically from 40.6 percent in 1971 to 59.7 percent in 1990 (Table 7-9).

The speed of this increase can be assessed by comparing it to statistics for Japan and West Germany.[10] In Japan, it took about twenty-five years for the labor share to increase by 19 percentage points, from 50.3 percent in 1961 to 69.3 percent in 1986. In West Germany, the labor share increased by only 3 percent over the past two decades, from the much higher base of 66 percent in 1965 to 69 percent in 1987. In Korea, the labor share increased significantly, especially during the 1970s, leaping by more than 10 percent, from 41.1 percent in 1971 to 51.9 percent in 1980. By the end of the 1980s, labor's share of national income in Korea still remained substantially below that in Japan or Germany.

In order to investigate the changing patterns of labor share, the GNP growth rate is decomposed into wage and employment growth rates based on the following relationship,

$$GNP = vL + rK,$$

where L and K denote labor and capital, and v and r represent the wage rate and rental cost of capital. By differentiating this equation with respect to time, we find that labor's share, wL/GNP, remains constant if and only if the sum of the growth in real wage (w) and employment (e) is equal to the GNP growth rate (g).

Here, we construct an index, $w/(g - e)$, that measures the relative wage growth after controlling for the effects of employment growth. If the value of the index exceeds one, labor's share of output has increased,

Table 7-9. Trend of Labor Share and Its Components (in percentage)

Year	Labor Share[a]	GNP Growth Rate (g)	Real Wage Changes (w)[b]	Employment Changes (e)	$\frac{w}{g-e}$
1971	41.1	8.6	3.9	3.3	0.83
1972	40.5	5.1	−1.0	4.9	−5.00
1973	40.8	13.2	−1.8	5.5	−0.23
1974	39.2	8.1	1.2	4.0	0.29
1975	40.4	6.4	4.1	2.1	1.78
1976	41.9	13.1	14.1	6.1	2.01
1977	44.0	9.8	15.5	3.0	2.28
1978	46.3	9.8	12.2	4.3	2.22
1979	48.8	7.2	8.6	1.3	1.46
1980	51.9	−3.7	−0.5	0.1	—
1981	51.6	5.9	3.7	2.5	1.09
1982	52.7	7.2	8.9	2.5	1.89
1983	54.0	12.6	5.9	0.9	0.50
1984	53.5	9.3	4.8	−0.5	0.49
1985	53.2	7.0	5.0	3.7	1.52
1986	51.8	12.9	5.5	3.6	0.59
1987	52.8	12.9	6.5	5.5	0.88
1988	54.2	12.4	9.6	3.2	1.04
1989	56.6	6.7	16.4	3.8	5.66
1990	59.7	9.0	9.8	3.0	1.63
Average					
1971–1973	40.8	9.0	0.4	4.6	0.09
1974–1980	44.6	7.2	7.9	3.0	1.88
1981–1990	54.0	9.6	7.6	2.8	1.13

[a]Ratio of compensation of employees to national income in current prices.
[b]Nominal wage change minus change in GNP deflator.
Sources: Bank of Korea, *National Accounts* (1990); Economic Planning Board, *Annual Report on the Economically Active Population Survey* (various issues) and *Monthly Statistics of Korea* (March 1991); Korean Development Institute database.

and that increase is mainly attributable to wage rather than employment increases. Since the index value varies greatly from year to year, we compare average index values. We find that the average value was highest during the mid-1970s, reflecting the high wage increases during that period. The average value still exceeded one during the 1980s. This finding casts doubt on the low-wage hypothesis; real wages in Korea have seen sustained growth.

Trends in Labor Productivity Growth

Among the many factors explaining Korea's rapid economic growth, labor productivity growth and sustained employment expansion may be the two most important. An important point to note about Korea is that these two developments went hand in hand, a phenomenon not usually observed in other economies.

There are several ways to construct a labor productivity index. One frequently used method for international comparisons is the purchasing-power-parity estimation method.[11] An international comparison of productivity for the manufacturing industry shows that Korea has recorded a remarkable productivity growth (Table 7-10). The productivity of Korean manufacturing was only 24 percent of that of the United States in 1970; by 1985, it was 36 percent. The productivity gaps between the Korean manufacturing industry and the Singaporean and Taiwanese manufacturing industries have also narrowed, though the gap with Japan has widened slightly.

Table 7-11 contains an industry-specific labor productivity trend, with labor productivity defined as value-added per employed person.[12] Even with substantial employment expansion during the past two decades, labor productivity increased continuously. The labor productivity growth rates of the manufacturing, construction, gas, and electricity industries were higher than those in other industries. Table 7-12, using an output-based labor productivity measure, shows similar trends.

Labor productivity growth rates during the 1980s turned out to be substantially higher than those of the 1970s. The productivity differentials between the 1970s and the 1980s were mainly attributable to changes in employment rather than economic growth rates. The average real GNP growth rate in the manufacturing industry between 1974 and 1980 was 13.9 percent, which is 1.6 percent higher than during the period 1981 through 1990, but the labor productivity growth rate was lower during the former period than during the latter, primarily due to substantial employment expansion during the 1970s and relatively slower employ-

Table 7-10 International Comparison of Labor Productivity: Manufacturing

	1970	1975	1980	1985
Korea	100.0	100.0	100.0	100.0
Japan	214.0	204.1	204.1	226.8
Taiwan	159.6	132.8	128.2[a]	118.0
Singapore	281.5	215.4	173.4[a]	165.2
Hong Kong[b]	90.3	75.6	86.5	103.3
United States	420.8	370.5	287.3	281.8

[a]The exchange rate was used.
[b]Data from 1971 and 1984 were used for 1970 and 1985, respectively.
Note: The purchasing-power-parity method was applied.
Source: Korea Productivity Center, *International Comparison of Productivity* (December 1987).

Table 7-11. Value-Added Based Labor Productivity Growth by Industry (in percentage)

Year	All	Mining	Manufacturing	Construction	Gas	Sales	Transportation	Finance	Services
1971	3.3	-4.6	6.6	38.4	7.3	2.1	4.8	3.8	-10.8
1972	4.6	0.3	8.7	7.8	27.0	5.7	3.5	-4.3	2.1
1973	2.8	32.0	4.8	18.2	32.7	0.9	17.1	6.0	0.8
1974	0.3	-4.9	3.1	13.2	-14.4	6.2	4.8	-0.9	1.7
1975	2.2	0.3	2.6	15.2	-9.2	3.0	9.0	10.8	-2.7
1976	-2.4	-8.2	0.5	22.3	4.9	-7.1	12.3	10.0	-8.6
1977	1.6	-7.0	2.4	-3.0	-11.2	-13.8	13.2	4.1	-0.9
1978	8.0	18.6	12.1	21.3	-5.5	-5.9	9.0	-3.9	8.6
1979	-3.8	-12.3	1.4	-16.4	-11.8	-24.0	0.6	-15.0	-11.6
1980	1.5	-8.5	2.6	19.4	-6.8	-7.8	-1.2	4.7	-7.5
1981	3.7	16.6	7.4	9.3	2.0	6.0	3.9	-13.2	-0.1
1982	1.7	4.8	0.9	-6.9	4.3	-4.2	2.0	5.8	-9.4
1983	5.3	6.8	7.7	28.0	18.2	0.6	-3.3	-8.3	-0.0
1984	8.5	6.2	11.1	24.3	4.4	8.3	3.2	9.1	13.2
1985	8.6	3.4	6.8	17.4	15.0	6.7	6.4	16.4	-1.5
1986	11.0	2.9	13.3	19.6	11.5	15.0	7.6	12.2	6.0
1987	9.8	1.2	9.8	18.7	19.8	9.9	6.7	12.9	5.3
1988	10.8	7.7	12.2	11.5	3.7	6.4	10.3	12.5	7.8
1989	9.0	-0.3	7.9	11.0	6.1	3.2	8.6	6.9	9.4
1990	10.3	1.7	10.7	10.1	17.6	7.5	9.6	0.2	4.1
Average									
1971–1973	3.6	9.2	6.7	21.5	22.3	2.9	8.5	1.8	-2.6
1974–1980	1.1	-3.2	3.5	10.3	-7.7	-7.0	6.8	1.4	-3.0
1981–1990	8.0	5.1	8.7	14.3	10.2	6.0	5.5	5.4	3.5

Sources: Bank of Korea, *National Accounts* (1990), and *Monthly Bulletin* (various issues); Ministry of Labor, *Report on Monthly Labor Survey* (various issues).

201

Table 7-12. Output-Based Labor Productivity Growth (in percentage)

Year	All	Mining	Manufacturing	Electricity
1971	9.4	–3.3	10.9	14.4
1972	7.1	–5.0	8.8	15.4
1973	5.2	17.7	4.3	19.3
1974	–2.5	–5.0	–2.7	12.9
1975	4.4	0.2	4.5	7.0
1976	4.2	–1.2	4.3	17.9
1977	4.3	6.8	4.5	4.7
1978	2.2	–0.5	2.1	30.9
1979	9.4	–4.0	10.5	2.1
1980	8.9	–6.8	8.6	12.5
1981	14.0	–2.4	14.5	12.4
1982	6.6	11.7	7.5	3.3
1983	13.9	13.5	13.4	25.7
1984	11.8	0.9	11.6	17.5
1985	8.0	–4.8	8.0	8.0
1986	15.1	2.1	15.0	15.6
1987	10.7	–2.4	11.6	5.5
1988	12.6	5.6	13.0	3.4
1989	8.7	6.1	8.1	7.3
1990	15.8	19.8	14.9	10.8
Average				
1971–1973	7.2	3.1	8.0	16.4
1974–1980	4.4	–1.5	4.5	12.6
1981–1990	12.1	4.6	12.5	6.0

Source: Korea Productivity Centre, *Labor Productivity Indexes* (various years).

ment growth in the 1980s. As indicated earlier, until the late 1980s, Korean economic growth was led by labor-intensive manufacturing. As the focus of industrial policy shifted in the late 1970s toward fostering heavy industries, the absorption of labor declined due to the high capital and technological intensity of heavy industries. Therefore, even with high economic growth rates, employment growth has not been that high during the 1980s.

Labor productivity growth rates in nontradable industries, such as sales, finance, and service, are considerably lower than those in the tradable sectors due to the lack of domestic and international competition in the former. On the other hand, wage increase rates were about the same among industries. This phenomenon is widely viewed as one cause of high domestic inflation during the 1970s.[13]

Change in industrial competitiveness is generally measured by unit labor costs defined as nominal wage increases minus labor productivity gains. Table 7-13 shows the changing patterns of unit labor costs by industry.

Table 7-13. Growth in Unit Labor Cost by Industry (in percentage)

Year	All	Mining	Manufacturing	Construction	Gas	Sales	Transportation	Finance	Services
1971	13.6	23.9	9.6	-11.0	2.3	8.1	10.1	12.8	30.1
1972	11.3	13.1	5.3	-0.2	-6.8	10.3	23.4	23.6	20.2
1973	8.7	-11.0	13.2	2.1	-17.9	16.1	-10.2	9.8	3.4
1974	31.6	39.9	32.2	7.0	34.1	15.6	21.6	21.7	25.6
1975	27.3	32.8	24.5	26.4	49.3	43.1	15.7	19.8	44.6
1976	37.9	29.1	34.1	5.5	80.6	49.7	28.9	17.8	55.7
1977	30.5	49.1	31.5	31.1	46.4	34.1	25.5	19.7	34.4
1978	27.0	17.4	22.2	1.9	49.6	42.7	24.7	39.3	15.0
1979	32.1	42.4	27.3	34.0	23.1	51.5	31.9	34.3	42.0
1980	21.9	30.9	20.2	-5.2	10.8	41.4	30.0	9.6	37.6
1981	16.9	3.2	12.8	16.9	22.1	11.2	13.2	33.8	24.8
1982	14.1	5.4	13.8	24.5	10.2	19.0	11.8	8.4	28.6
1983	5.7	-0.2	4.5	-12.7	-12.4	9.0	11.0	15.8	10.2
1984	0.2	-2.5	-2.9	-21.5	-6.1	1.0	6.2	5.8	-12.7
1985	0.6	6.1	3.2	-1.9	-9.8	2.7	0.7	-8.1	8.5
1986	-2.8	6.4	-4.1	-8.3	-7.7	-6.9	1.5	-6.0	2.1
1987	0.3	7.1	1.8	-9.4	-10.8	1.3	3.3	-1.8	1.2
1988	4.7	8.4	7.4	-0.3	3.2	1.2	2.0	-4.6	1.9
1989	12.1	18.9	17.2	6.8	3.1	12.9	4.7	4.7	7.6
1990	8.5	12.4	9.5	15.5	-0.7	9.8	2.2	15.3	11.5
Mean	15.1	16.6	14.2	5.1	13.1	18.7	12.9	13.6	19.6
Standard deviation	12.1	15.9	11.3	15.0	25.8	17.7	11.5	13.0	17.2
Coefficient of variation	80.2	95.6	80.1	296.5	196.8	94.6	89.1	95.8	87.8
Average									
1971–1973	11.2	8.7	9.3	-3.0	-7.5	11.5	7.8	15.4	17.9
1974–1980	29.8	34.5	27.4	14.4	42.0	39.7	25.5	23.2	36.4
1981–1990	6.1	6.6	6.4	0.9	-0.9	6.1	5.6	6.3	7.5

Sources: Bank of Korea, *National Accounts* (1990), and *Monthly Bulletin* (various issues); Ministry of Labor, *Report on Monthly Labor Survey* (various issues).

Throughout most of the period until 1987, unit labor costs of the manufacturing industry increased more slowly than the average unit labor costs of all industry, though relatively slow increases in unit labor costs in the social overhead capital sectors might have also played an important supporting role in increasing the international competitiveness of Korean manufacturing. Slowly rising unit labor costs is a major reason for the continued growth of the manufacturing industry and particularly of manufactured exports. Recently, however, there has been an indication that this pattern may have been reversed. Since 1987, unit labor costs of the manufacturing industry have risen more rapidly than those of other sectors, partly because of the relatively low labor productivity increases. This may indicate a relatively strong growth of sectors oriented primarily toward the domestic economy compared to export industries in coming years.

Unit labor costs in the nontradable sectors rose substantially more than those in the tradable sectors throughout the whole period, particularly during the mid- to late 1970s, contributing to rising domestic inflation. The gap in unit labor costs between these sectors, however, shrank in the 1980s, which is consistent with the stable inflation rate that the Korean economy has experienced recently.[14]

Finally, the international competitiveness of the manufacturing industries in Korea, Japan, and Taiwan measured by unit labor costs in U.S. dollar terms is compared in Table 7-14. In terms of domestic currency, Korea has been losing its edge against major international competitors throughout the entire period. To improve international price competitiveness, the government continuously depreciated the currency in nominal terms until 1987, while Japan and Taiwan, two major competitors, more or less appreciated their currencies. Even taking into consideration the foreign exchange depreciation, Korean manufacturing industry lost international competitiveness against its counterparts during the 1970s, particularly during the mid-1970s. However, the Korean manufacturing industry began gaining international competitiveness against Japanese and Taiwanese manufacturing industries during the 1980s, primarily as a result of foreign exchange policies (which are discussed in Chapter 9).

Changing Patterns of Wage Differentials

The widening of wage differentials in the 1970s was primarily the result of the labor shortage in certain categories of skilled labor as a result of the push of heavy industry. These differentials became the focus of policy

Table 7-14. International Comparison of Growth in Unit Labor Costs
(in percentage)

	Korea		Japan		Taiwan	
	ULC	ULC$	ULC	ULC$	ULC	ULC$
1971	9.6	−2.2	8.5	11.5	−0.6	−0.6
1972	5.3	−7.9	4.0	17.2	12.3	12.2
1973	13.2	11.8	10.8	21.2	26.4	30.9
1974	32.2	30.6	25.7	18.2	44.0	44.7
1975	24.5	4.9	12.7	11.1	14.8	14.8
1976	34.1	34.1	−0.2	−0.1	3.8	3.8
1977	31.5	31.5	2.9	12.4	16.4	16.4
1978	22.2	22.2	−2.3	19.3	−4.5	−2.0
1979	27.3	27.3	−1.2	−5.3	26.4	29.1
1980	20.2	−5.3	−0.4	−3.9	14.5	14.6
1981	12.8	0.6	2.8	5.5	10.7	8.4
1982	13.8	6.5	−1.2	−14.2	8.9	2.7
1983	4.5	−1.6	−4.6	0.1	3.5	1.0
1984	−2.9	−6.8	−5.4	−5.4	10.5	11.7
1985	3.2	−4.8	−2.5	−2.9	−5.7	−6.3
1986	−4.1	−5.4	2.1	31.4	−0.2	4.8
1987	1.8	8.5	−6.3	7.9	3.2	19.0
1988	7.4	18.8	−5.6	3.5	5.1	15.3
1989	17.2	24.8	N.A.	N.A.	6.6	4.5
1990	9.5	4.0	N.A.	N.A.	N.A.	N.A.
Average						
1971–1973	9.3	0.6	7.8	16.6	12.7	14.1
1974–1980	27.4	20.8	5.3	7.4	16.5	17.3
1981–1990	6.4	4.5	−2.6	3.2	4.7	7.9

Note: ULC = Nominal wage increase − Labor productivity.
ULC$ = ULC − Foreign exchange rate change against U.S. dollar.
Sources: Various issues of the following publications: Bank of Korea, *National Accounts* and *Monthly Bulletin;* Ministry of Labor (Korea), *Report on Monthly Labor Survey;* Office of Economic Cooperation and Development, *National Accounts;* Bank of Japan, Statistics Department, *Economic Statistics Annual;* Bureau of Statistics (Japan), *Japan Statistical Yearbook;* Republic of China, Director General of Budget, Accounting, and Statistics, *Statistical Yearbook of the Republic of China;* Republic of China, Council for Economic Planning and Development, *Taiwan Statistical Databook.*

and public attention beginning in the mid-1970s as income distribution deteriorated because they were thought to be the main cause. Wage differentials among industries were also thought to be a cause of inflation.

Labor turnover rates in the Korean labor market, especially in the manufacturing industry, were high during the period under review. If wage differentials are stable across time and space, as Dickens and Katz stress,[15] and if they reflect rent sharing behavior that can be explained within the theoretical framework of the efficiency wage hypothesis,[16] then the high turnover rates of Korean industries may be viewed as a consequence of wide wage gaps among industries and occupations.

Wage differentials by industry are presented in Table 7-15. We find that manufacturing wages have been lower than those of any other

Table 7-15. Wage Differentials by Industry

Year	All	Mining	Manufacturing	Gas	Construction	Sales	Transportation	Finance	Services	Coefficient of Variation
1970	100.0	104.2	80.2	208.4	136.3	111.1	103.9	212.6	136.6	33.6
1971	100.0	106.3	79.7	227.0	127.8	104.7	102.1	211.9	139.3	36.7
1972	100.0	103.9	78.3	210.7	132.4	104.7	111.7	218.0	147.0	34.6
1973	100.0	112.8	82.8	227.5	136.3	109.9	107.1	226.4	137.3	36.0
1974	100.0	115.5	85.0	207.5	123.8	101.5	102.7	207.4	132.6	32.9
1975	100.0	118.8	83.4	226.9	133.8	114.5	98.9	209.2	145.3	33.9
1976	100.0	105.9	82.8	213.9	183.2	120.6	103.1	197.2	157.8	31.5
1977	100.0	114.0	84.0	207.6	187.6	109.8	108.3	184.9	159.5	29.8
1978	100.0	114.8	83.5	189.4	200.3	111.3	107.2	185.6	146.0	29.3
1979	100.0	116.5	83.8	173.5	173.7	110.7	110.7	172.7	148.3	24.2
1980	100.0	115.5	83.3	160.7	146.4	119.9	115.6	159.9	156.4	19.8
1981	100.0	114.7	82.9	168.1	150.5	116.4	112.2	159.9	161.5	21.6
1982	100.0	109.2	82.2	170.8	148.8	115.4	110.3	157.7	166.3	22.9
1983	100.0	104.9	83.0	177.4	141.7	113.9	107.0	152.8	164.9	23.8
1984	100.0	100.0	82.6	167.7	128.2	114.5	107.7	161.5	152.5	22.9
1985	100.0	100.2	83.2	177.3	123.5	114.7	105.5	160.1	149.4	24.0
1986	100.0	101.3	83.9	182.3	118.4	114.6	106.4	157.1	149.2	24.4
1987	100.0	99.5	85.0	180.8	117.2	115.7	106.2	158.5	144.2	24.1
1988	100.0	100.1	88.1	167.5	112.9	107.8	103.3	148.1	137.0	21.2
1989	100.0	98.1	90.9	150.9	109.8	103.3	96.6	136.4	132.4	18.0
1990	100.0	94.2	92.0	148.5	116.1	102.0	90.9	132.7	128.7	18.0
Average growth rate per year	20.0	19.4	20.8	17.9	20.0	19.7	19.4	17.1	19.9	—
Mean	100.0	107.2	83.8	187.8	140.4	111.3	105.6	176.7	147.3	—
Standard deviation	—	7.3	3.2	24.8	25.8	5.6	5.6	27.4	10.8	—
Coefficient of variation	—	6.8	3.7	13.2	18.4	5.0	5.3	15.5	7.3	—

Source: Ministry of Labor, *Report on Monthly Labor Survey* (various issues).

industry throughout the entire period since 1970. This observation has also been cited as supporting evidence for the low-wage hypothesis. Dornbusch and Park, in particular, argue that Korean wages are exceptionally low by international standards considering the skill level of the labor force.[17] Comparing hourly wages for Korean manufacturing workers with those of industrialized nations and other Asian newly industrializing countries (NICs), they argue that even the hourly rates in high-wage industries such as the steel and motor vehicle industries are slightly lower than or about the same as those in Taiwan.

This apparently important argument is, at worst, misleading and at best trivial, however. According to Dornbusch and Park, the hourly wage in the Korean manufacturing industry in 1988 was $1.39 (in U.S. dollars), $1.66 in Taiwan, $2.23 in Singapore, and $1.88 in Hong Kong. If we assume that a nation's technology and production capacity is represented by per capita GNP, we find that the wage gaps between Korea and the other Asian NICs are substantially smaller than the income gaps between them.[18] Given per capita GNP, Korea's wage level is relatively higher than that of its counterparts.

The crucial issue in this discussion of wages is the growth rate rather than the absolute level; we cannot define certain industries as low-wage industries simply by comparing their wage levels because the composition of the labor force in terms of age, tenure, experiences, and skill is different among them. The lower wage in manufacturing mainly stems from compositional differences in its labor force. Labor-intensive light manufacturing firms constitute a significantly high proportion of Korean manufacturing industry, and they employ primarily young laborers who are relatively new to the labor force. Moreover, the percentage of females in the labor force whose lifetime work tenures are relatively short is very high in Korean manufacturing, because female workers typically leave the workplace on marriage.

The average age and tenure of workers in manufacturing, the two most important determinants of the wage rate, are substantially lower than in the service industry, although the average growth of wages is approximately the same among all industries (Table 7-16). Considering that the average worker in the manufacturing industry is about five to six years younger than in the service industry and that the average annual growth rate of wages is about 20 percent, the wage differentials between the two sectors can be explained by differences in these two determinants.[19] In this respect, the manufacturing industry cannot be categorized as a low-wage sector simply because of intersectoral wage differences.

Table 7-16. Average Age and Tenure of Workers in the Manufacturing and Service Industries (in number of years)

	Age		Tenure	
	Manufacturing	Services	Manufacturing	Services
1972	26.6	31.8	2.3	3.2
1978	26.0	33.0	3.2	6.1
1987	29.5	35.3	3.2	6.2
1989	30.7	36.4	3.4	6.4

Source: Ministry of Labor, *Report on Occupational Wage Survey* (1972, 1978, 1987, 1989).

If the size and the composition of the labor force remain the same, then the growth of wages and the growth of the total wage bill will be the same. However, the share of manufacturing employment in total employment has expanded continuously, from 14 percent in 1970 to 27 percent in 1990 (see Table 7-2). If the composition of the labor force has changed to include a larger concentration of low-wage young workers, the growth rate of wages to low-wage workers must be higher than the average wage growth rate of all workers. Otherwise, wages in industry would be growing more slowly than in other sectors, and this is not the case.

An examination of the coefficients of variation of interindustry wage differentials, a measure of dispersion of wage differentials, reveals a declining trend, particularly during the recession of 1979–1980. The coefficients of variation, which remained over 30 during the early 1970s, dropped below 30 during the mid- to late 1970s and to below 20 in 1980.

This result implies that high-wage sectors respond more quickly to cyclical changes than do low-wage sectors. This finding is somewhat contrary to that of Wachter, who argued for the United States that the lagged response of wage changes to the cycle was attributable to an implicit wage contract.[20] The different result is not surprising, however, considering that labor unions in Korea, in contrast to those in the United States, have not been strong enough to influence wage determination. During the 1980s, the dispersion was much smaller than in earlier periods, and the coefficient of variation dropped significantly, primarily because of the strengthening of the labor movement in the late 1980s.

Wage differentials by occupation and educational attainment status are reported in Table 7-17. As was the case for interindustry wage differentials, the wage gaps among occupations and different levels of educational attainment have narrowed since the late 1970s. The strong price stabilization policy undertaken by the government during that time

Table 7-17. Wage Differentials by Occupation and Educational Attainment (total = 100.0)

	By Occupation				By Education		
	Professional, Technical	Clerical	Service	Production	Middle School	High School	College
1971	179.9	151.6	69.2	78.1	88.3	131.2	229.9
1972	193.8	142.4	72.6	80.5	77.9	115.6	210.7
1973	187.6	150.1	75.2	75.9	78.5	120.9	225.0
1974	165.7	150.1	73.1	80.1	80.7	115.6	229.1
1975	198.1	160.1	77.3	74.6	75.3	121.6	260.8
1976	211.5	161.2	74.4	72.5	67.2	113.7	261.2
1977	203.2	154.2	74.8	74.9	69.6	114.9	264.9
1978	203.1	136.6	74.2	75.3	70.1	112.3	259.3
1979	184.5	128.4	75.1	79.1	71.0	107.7	248.6
1980	176.4	117.5	76.5	78.4	71.9	104.5	238.7
1981	167.3	117.6	75.7	79.5	71.9	104.2	234.5
1982	173.3	114.5	76.9	78.2	71.2	101.8	225.6
1983	168.9	110.7	75.4	77.9	71.5	98.6	223.0
1984	167.8	110.4	76.6	79.2	72.5	97.3	220.6
1985	166.6	110.4	75.3	78.7	72.0	96.4	218.5
1986	163.1	108.7	73.5	79.3	72.7	93.7	208.0
1987	169.0	106.8	74.0	80.8	77.8	92.1	192.7
1988	153.6	106.1	78.1	83.8	79.6	92.9	177.4
1989	144.9	103.9	73.4	85.3	80.8	92.7	169.0
Mean	177.8	128.5	74.8	78.5	74.8	106.7	226.2
Standard deviation	17.4	20.3	2.0	3.0	5.1	11.2	26.4
Coefficient of variation	9.8	15.8	2.6	3.8	6.8	10.5	11.7

Source: Ministry of Labor, *Report on Occupational Wage Survey* (various years).

may be the force responsible for this shrinkage. On the other hand, the shift of industrial policy toward fostering capital- and technology-intensive heavy and chemical industries during the mid-1970s resulted in widened wage differentials between professional and production workers and between college graduates and middle school graduates. To a certain extent, this phenomenon reflected the excess demand for skilled and educated workers that characterized the labor market of that time.

The introduction of the minimum wage system in 1988 and the increase in the minimum wage level of over 25 percent in 1989 definitely reduced wage differentials among workers with different occupations and levels of educational attainment. During its first year, the minimum wage system covered only firms in the manufacturing industry that employed more than ten regular employees. The estimated number of workers affected by the minimum wage law was about 4.2 percent of manufacturing employees. In 1989, when the coverage expanded to include

Table 7-18. Wage Differentials by Skill Level

Skill Level[a]	1975	1980	1983	1986	1987	1988	1989
Total Cash Earnings Index							
A	100.0	100.0	100.0	100.0	100.0	100.0	100.0
B	204.3	199.4	185.1	177.3	176.1	173.5	161.9
C	306.1	312.0	307.1	292.0	287.4	255.6	237.2
Average	119.0	130.7	137.7	140.4	139.6	136.1	133.7
Composition of Employed Persons (percentage)							
A	83.0	80.1	71.5	65.5	65.2	63.9	60.6
B	6.1	7.7	14.2	18.0	17.9	18.1	20.2
C	9.2	9.7	11.0	12.2	12.3	12.9	13.5
Total	100.0	100.0	100.0	100.0	100.0	100.0	100.0

[a]Group A: elementary and middle school graduates, and high school graduates with less than five years of work experience. Group B: high school graduates with five or more years of work experience. Group C: university graduates.
Source: Ministry of Labor, *Reports on Occupational Wage Survey* (various years).

mining and construction workers, the share of workers affected by the minimum wage law was estimated to be about 10.7 percent.

Another interesting issue is how wage differentials by skill level have changed over time. Table 7-18 divides workers into three skill groups based on educational attainment and work experience: Group A is the low-skill group, B the middle-skill group, and C the high-skill group.[21] The gap between the wage rate of the low-skill group and the average wage rate of all groups widened until the mid-1980s but has narrowed since then. The ratio of the average wage rate of all workers over the wage rate of low-skill group was about 1.2 in 1975, increasing to about 1.4 in 1986 and then decreasing somewhat to 1.3 in 1989.

On the other hand, a comparison of wage rates among different skill groups shows that the gaps between low- and middle-skill groups and between low- and high-skill groups have narrowed over time. Specifically, the ratio of the wage rate of the middle-skill group over the low-skill group decreased from over 2.0 in 1975 to 1.6 in 1989. The wage gap between high-skill and middle-skill groups remained about the same or even slightly widened during that time.

A final issue of wage differentials, which has also become politically salient, is related to urban-rural differences. This issue also has particular relevance to the "turning-point" hypothesis. The relative slowdown of employment expansion in manufacturing industries, together with a sharp increase in real wages, are frequently cited as supporting evidence for the turning-point hypothesis.[22] This hypothesis argues that until the mid-1970s, economic growth was led mainly by labor-intensive light industries, the supply of unskilled labor being almost unlimited. Following the shift in industrial policy toward the fostering of capital-intensive heavy industries, the demand for skilled and educated labor increased. The lack of skilled labor resulted in substantial wage increases, and by the mid-1970s it was no longer appropriate to argue that Korea was a labor-surplus economy.

Regional cost of living and consumer price indexes are not available in Korea. Further, since income components differ between urban and rural households, the real incomes between the two sectors may not be directly comparable. Therefore, we focus on the changing pattern of the urban-rural income ratio. Urban household income is defined to include salaries and wages from business and work at home, as well as other income such as interest, dividends, and rents received. Rural household income is defined to include both agricultural and nonagricultural income, but agricultural management expenditures are subtracted. Monthly income statistics are reported in Table 7-19.

Table 7-19. Urban versus Farm Household Monthly Income (income in thousand won)

Year	Urban Income (A)	Farm Income (B)	A/CPI(× 100) (C)	B/FPI(× 100) (D)	B/A(× 100)	D/C(× 100)
1970	28.2	21.3	126.9	136.6	75.6	107.6
1971	33.3	29.7	132.3	166.8	89.1	126.1
1972	38.1	35.8	135.5	175.4	94.0	129.4
1973	40.4	40.1	139.2	179.6	99.2	129.0
1974	47.8	56.2	132.4	187.3	117.6	141.5
1975	65.5	72.7	145.0	196.1	111.0	135.2
1976	88.3	96.4	169.4	208.1	109.2	122.8
1977	105.9	119.4	184.5	220.3	112.7	119.4
1978	144.5	157.0	220.0	222.7	108.7	101.3
1979	194.7	185.6	250.6	231.5	95.3	92.3
1980	234.1	224.4	234.1	224.4	95.9	95.9
1981	281.0	307.3	231.6	239.2	109.4	103.3
1982	317.1	372.1	243.7	257.9	117.4	105.8
1983	364.0	427.4	270.6	273.6	117.4	101.1
1984	402.3	462.4	292.4	308.1	114.9	105.4
1985	431.2	478.0	305.8	326.5	110.9	106.8
1986	481.0	499.6	333.6	343.4	103.9	102.9
1987	561.7	544.6	378.2	368.0	97.0	97.3
1988	657.2	677.6	413.2	424.7	103.1	102.8
1989	804.9	786.4	478.6	453.4	97.7	94.7
1990	943.3	N.A.	516.5	N.A.	N.A.	N.A.

Notes: CPI: consumer price index (1980 = 100). FPI: index of prices paid by farmers (1980 = 100).
Sources: Economic Planning Board, Bureau of Statistics, *Monthly Statistics of Korea* (various issues); Ministry of Agriculture, Forestry, and Fisheries, *Report on the Results of Farm Household Economy Survey* (various issues).

Urban-rural income differentials are compared in both nominal and real terms. The statistics on income ratios reveal that the relative level of farm household income increased significantly during the mid-1970s. At the beginning of the third five-year economic development plan (1972–1976) and after the initiation of the Yushin Constitution, the Korean government launched the *Saemaul* (New Village) movement, whereby new village roads were constructed and factories built in rural areas. This movement, successfully executed in its early years, was the main source of rising farm incomes.

Rising rural incomes are often used as supporting evidence for the turning-point hypothesis.[23] If we take a sample period that ends with the 1970s, improvements in the relative earnings of farm households may be regarded as consistent with the turning-point hypothesis. However, the relative level of farm incomes began to decline at that time; the phenomenon is particularly pronounced in nominal terms in recent years. Further study may be needed to conclude that the Korean labor market has already passed the turning-point, which implicitly assumes a labor shortage.

Mention should be made of the fact that Korea is frequently singled out for its long working hours—considerably longer than those in Japan and Taiwan (Table 7-20). For example, average weekly working hours in the manufacturing industries of Korea and Taiwan were about the same until the mid-1970s; then they began increasing in Korea while declining in Taiwan.

It is generally expected that an inverse relationship exists between income level and the number of working hours. As a result, the continuing trend toward longer working hours from the early 1970s to the mid-1980s constitutes an interesting puzzle. The increase might be attributed to a rise in wage rates, but several alternatives are worth exploring. One possible explanation is that due to the low level of income, the income effect of rising wages on demand for more leisure has not become apparent until recently. On the other hand, because wages are low, workers demand overtime work, which pays a rate typically 50 percent higher than the regular rate. Employers benefit as well from overtime work since it is less costly than hiring more employees.

To a certain extent, rising working hours in the Korean manufacturing industry may also reflect the effects of changing industrial policies. The shift toward promoting heavy and chemical industries exposed a lack of skilled technicians and engineers, resulting in longer working hours for that group at a time of rapid economic expansion.

Table 7-20. Weekly Hours of Work in Various Industries

	Korea					Taiwan	Japan
	All Industry	Manufacturing	Sales	Transportation	Services	Manufacturing	Manufacturing
1970	51.6	53.4	48.6	53.9	50.2	43.2	—
1971	50.6	52.0	50.7	55.6	49.9	42.4	—
1972	50.9	51.7	50.5	51.7	51.5	42.2	—
1973	50.7	51.4	52.4	51.5	46.3	41.9	52.3
1974	49.6	49.9	50.7	51.9	47.0	39.9	50.0
1975	50.0	50.5	49.3	51.0	48.2	38.6	50.7
1976	50.7	52.5	49.1	50.5	46.7	40.0	51.3
1977	51.4	52.9	50.9	49.5	46.2	40.2	51.3
1978	51.3	53.0	50.8	49.4	46.4	40.4	50.9
1979	50.5	52.0	49.4	49.5	45.9	41.0	50.7
1980	51.6	53.1	50.5	50.4	47.2	41.0	50.9
1981	51.9	53.7	50.4	50.9	47.0	40.8	48.4
1982	52.2	53.8	51.0	51.9	47.4	40.8	48.1
1983	52.5	54.4	50.9	52.4	47.3	41.0	48.1
1984	52.4	54.3	49.9	53.4	46.8	41.6	48.6
1985	51.9	53.8	50.0	53.2	46.6	41.4	47.4
1986	52.5	54.7	49.7	52.8	46.2	41.0	48.1
1987	51.9	54.0	49.5	51.9	46.1	41.2	48.1
1988	51.1	52.6	49.6	51.6	46.6	41.7	47.6
1989	49.2	51.1	48.0	50.3	45.0	41.3	47.1
1990	48.2	49.8	47.5	48.9	44.6	N.A.	N.A.

Sources: Ministry of Labor, *Report on Monthly Labor Survey* (various issues); *Monthly Statistics of Japan* (various issues); *Statistical Yearbook of the Republic of China* (1989).

Labor Markets, Wage Policy, and Inflation

Historical Overview of Wage Policy

Policymakers did not place a high priority on wage issues until the mid-1970s, primarily because there were no serious social and economic pressures for wage hikes. It is not surprising to find weak labor organization and lack of pressure for wage increases when half of Korea's total employed persons were farmers (as of 1970), the ratio of employees to total employment was less than 40 percent, and generally the supply of labor exceeded the demand. Under such circumstances, the policy priority was on employment expansion. The lack of social pressures for high wage increases was helpful for employment expansion, but no artificial effort to repress wage rises was needed because of the excess supply of labor. Low wages reflected labor market conditions rather than a wage policy.

As labor shortages appeared in certain sectors of the labor market as a result of the heavy industry push, wages rose in skill-intensive sectors.

These increases had spillover effects, bringing about overall wage hikes across all industries. This phenomenon motivated the government to consider wage guidelines for the first time.

In fact, Korea never officially announced a wage guideline policy, but several measures were undertaken to control substantial wage rises, directly or indirectly. Large wage increases were generally initiated by big enterprises with monopoly power in the market, so that the burden of these increases could be passed on relatively easily to consumers by price increases. The first wage policy announcement appeared in a statement made by the deputy prime minister, Duck-Woo Nam, in February 1977. He stated that if price increases were requested to cover the costs of wage increases for "monopolistic" and "oligopolistic" products, over which the government had some control, then the only acceptable increase in wage rates would be within a range of 15 to 18 percent.[24] The effectiveness of such an announcement was ambiguous, however, given the lack of competition and the relatively closed nature of the domestic market.

A more specific measure of wage control policy was enforced beginning in the early 1980s as a component of the price stabilization effort. In 1981 and 1982, two policy measures were undertaken. First, the Bankers' Association of Korea was instructed to restrict credit to firms that increased wages despite losses, firms that were not expected to yield profit for some time, or firms whose increase in wage rates exceeded the firm's productivity growth rates.[25] Second, the government attempted to induce lower wage increases in private firms by keeping wage increases of public service employees low. For example, while the salary increases of public servants amounted to 20 percent in 1978 and 15 percent in 1979, the government announced that the increase in salaries would be 9 percent in 1982 and 6 percent in 1983; it declared a freeze in 1984.

The efforts by the government to control the wage-price spiral by indirect wage guidelines may have affected inflation expectations to some extent. However, since wage changes basically represent supply and demand conditions in the labor market, wage drift soon prevailed. The wage drift ratio, which compares actual wage payments to negotiated wage settlements, turned out to be significantly high during the period 1982 through 1984 when wage guideline policies were imposed (Table 7-21).

The wage restraint policy, designed to improve the international competitiveness of the export industry, was especially persuasive because the labor-intensive industries constituted a high proportion of Korea's export industries. Furthermore, since wage costs were the main source of total costs for final goods and services, curbing wage inflation was considered a prerequisite for containing overall price inflation.

Table 7-21. Wage Drift (in percentage)

	Negotiated Wage Increase *(A)*	Actual Increase *(B)*	Wage Drift Rate: *(B − A)/A*
1977	36.0	32.1	−10.8
1978	29.7	35.0	17.8
1979	26.8	28.3	5.6
1980	21.5	23.4	8.8
1981	16.1	20.7	28.6
1982	9.5	15.8	69.9
1983	6.9	11.0	59.4
1984	6.4	8.7	35.9
1985	7.5	9.2	22.7

Source: Se-Il Park, *Wage Policy in an Open Economy: The Case of Korea* (Seoul: Korea Economic Research Institute, 1987) (in Korean), reproduced with permission.

The informal wage guideline policy produced some positive effects on moderating price inflation, but it also yielded some negative effects. First, because of the government's strong initiation and execution of a wage policy, the practice of voluntary negotiation between workers and employers was not established. Owners of firms became reluctant to initiate wage negotiations and tended to rely on the government to keep wage increases in check. Partly as a result, workers' distrust of government began to grow. Second, a distortion in the relative wage structure between private and public service employees emerged. The government could control the salary increases of government workers effectively, and these were kept artificially low in order to serve as a wage guideline for the private sector; private sector workers, however, frequently received wage increases that exceeded government guidelines.

The Role of Unions

Wage increases are in principle determined by negotiations between employers and labor unions. Although the influences of Korean labor organizations on wage determination during the past economic development period were not so strong as those of developed nations, labor unions did play some role in improving worker welfare. Upon the liberation of Korea in 1945, several labor organizations were created. In order to counter radical and militant left-wing labor organizations, right-wing groups allied with the government to form a union in March 1946. That organization was subsequently named the Federation of Korean Trade Unions (FKTU) in November 1960 and is still active.

Due to the FKTU's weak leadership, strong government interventions, and slack labor market conditions, the FKTU's attempts to improve worker welfare had limited effect. During the 1960s, collective bargaining was permitted, but after a presidential decree on national security was issued in 1971, labor strikes were practically banned.

In early 1981 under the new Chun Doo Hwan government, labor laws were amended to include three major provisions. First, the right to bargain was transferred from the industrial federations of unions to the enterprise-level unions. Second, so-called third parties were prohibited from participating in any activities related to labor disputes or organizing labor. Third, the union-shop system was replaced by an open-shop system.[26]

The FKTU did not play a significant role in improving the overall welfare of workers, but it exerted some influence on wage negotiations. It announced the desired rate of wage increase at the beginning of each year, and this rate usually served as the basis for wage negotiations. The FKTU generally claimed that the increase it sought should be viewed as a minimum, incorporating increases in the cost of living. However, the method and basic statistics for such computations were never presented to the public.

The FKTU's counterpart, the Korea Employers' Federation (KEF), established in July 1970, also announced its desired rate of wage increases for the year. KEF claimed that its suggested rate was computed by the so-called productivity wage formula: real GNP growth rate plus expected inflation minus expected increases in the employment rate. KEF reasoned that if wages increased by this rate, labor's share would remain constant. Basically, KEF argued that because wage increases constituted the main source of price inflation, they had to be limited to the growth rate in productivity.

The FKTU argued that the effects of wage increases on price inflation were rather small compared to the effects of aggregate demand and foreign exchange policies and suggested that workers had to be compensated for the previous year's inflation to maintain their real standard of living. Table 7-22 sets out the demanded rate by FKTU, the suggested rate by KEF, and actual increases. In some years, a range of rates, instead of a single rate, was announced, with the condition that the negotiated rate had to correspond to the firm's profitability. The actual rate of increase turned out to be approximately the average of the demanded and suggested rates of the FKTU and KEF.

Wages and Price Inflation

Wage inflation is specified as a function of expected price inflation and labor market conditions, proxied by the unemployment rate. Price inflation

Table 7-22. Comparisons of Wage Increase Rates (in percentage)

	Rate Demanded by FKTU	Rate Suggested by KEF	Actual Increase
1971	—	—	16.9
1972	34.0	—	16.0
1973	17.0–45.8	—	11.5
1974	40.0	—	31.9
1975	57.5	—	29.5
1976	48.8	—	35.5
1977	49.3	18.0–18.7	32.1
1978	48.4	28.2	35.0
1979	57.7	19.2	28.3
1980	49.1	10.0–15.0	23.4
1981	58.3	—	20.7
1982	27.5	—	15.8
1983	—	6.4	11.0
1984	13.4	3.0–4.0	8.7
1985	12.7	5.2	9.2
1986	—	5.0	8.2
1987	7.5	6.0–7.0	10.1
1988	29.3	7.5–8.5	15.5
1989	26.8	8.9–12.9	21.1
1990	17.3–20.5	7.0	18.8
1991	17.5	—	—

Note: KEF announced that it would not suggest the wage increase rate from 1991.
Sources: Korea Labor Institute, *Collective Bargaining and Wage Increase* (1989) and *Wage Related Statistics Book* (1990).

is determined by changes in factor costs, wage increases net of productivity growth, and aggregate demand. (A detailed discussion of the conceptual background and empirical specifications of the models are presented in the chapter appendix.)

The estimated result of the wage equations indicates that a 1 percent increase in expected price inflation brings about a 0.5 percent increase in wages. An inverse relationship between wage inflation and unemployment rate was found; a 1 percent increase in unemployment was shown to reduce wage inflation by 1.3 percent. By examining the lag structure, we found that price inflation has more prolonged effects on wage inflation than unemployment. That is, the impact of labor market conditions on wage increases is more immediate than the effects of price inflation. The changes in the unemployment rate during the previous two quarters affected wage increases in the current quarter, while changes in inflation during the previous four quarters exerted an effect on current wage increases. The effect of unemployment on wage increases proved stronger in recent years than had previously been the case.

An attempt was made to determine whether any relationships existed between wage inflation and three different price variables: the wholesale price index (WPI), the consumer price index (CPI), and the GNP deflator (GDF). First, wage increases exerted a significant impact on all three price variables. The impact of these increases on price inflation is particularly significant for the WPI and GDF in the short run; substantial and statistically significant effects lasted for only about two quarters.

On the other hand, although the effect of wage hikes on the CPI is as substantial as that on the WPI, the effect lasted longer, and the magnitude of impact was rather evenly distributed during the time period. This finding implies that wage increases affect the production side first and only later hit services prices, which comprise a relatively higher proportion of the CPI than other price variables.[27] A 1 percent increase in the wage rate increased the WPI by 0.3 percent and GDF by 0.5 percent during the same quarter.

While unit labor costs, defined as nominal wage increases net of labor productivity growth, are usually introduced in price equations, wage increases and productivity growth were introduced separately because their effects on prices were assumed to be asymmetric.[28] The estimated results turned out to support our conjectures. For the WPI, the overall effects of productivity growth, somewhat surprisingly, were larger than those of wage increases. However, the estimated results indicate that the immediate impact on price inflation is larger for wage increases than for productivity growth in absolute terms.

In contrast to the WPI, however, the effects of productivity growth on the CPI and GDF turned out to be significantly smaller than those of wage increases. This is an expected result given the relatively higher proportion of service prices in the CPI and GDF than in the WPI. As in the case of the WPI, the impact of labor productivity growth has a longer distributive lag than wage increases.

Along with wage increases and productivity growth, import prices and the exchange rate are known to be important cost-push factors. As expected, changes in import prices in U.S. dollar terms had an important effect on changes in producer prices; in fact, the magnitude of the effects of wage increases and import prices is about the same. This finding implies that in order to stabilize inflation as measured by the WPI, the Korean currency has to be appreciated as much as changes in the wage rate, other things being equal. However, since labor productivity will rise, the magnitude of appreciation should be determined by the relative effects of wage increases and labor productivity growth, as measured by the relative magnitude of their influences.

To illustrate, assume that all other variables remain constant and that wage rates and labor productivity rise by 5 and 3 percent a quarter, respectively. The Korean currency has to be appreciated by 1 percent to stabilize WPI in the long run. And in order to keep the WPI at the same level during the current quarter, the Korean currency has to be appreciated by over 4 percent, which will eventually reduce the WPI. As is the case for labor productivity growth, the effects of a rise in import prices in dollar terms are substantially smaller for the CPI and GDF than for WPI.

A final finding concerns the interest rate on the curb market, which captures the effects of capital costs. This variable produces a significant but negative impact on the CPI, a rather unexpected result. Theoretically, there should be a positive relationship since a rising interest rate indicates increasing factor costs, which will affect inflation positively. The negative relationship may reflect reduced consumption behavior due to increased household savings given the higher interest rate.

Recent Labor Market Developments

In the last three years of the 1980s, government policy placed high priority on addressing labor market issues, largely the result of the transition to democracy that occurred after mid-1987. Following Roh's declaration of democratization in June, strong labor movements emerged and violent labor disputes erupted. Nominal wages rose more than 20 percent per year, about three times the average wage increase during previous years. Wage increases were cited as the main cause for weakening international competitiveness, rising inflation, and unemployment. Due to continued economic growth, led by domestic consumption increases and a boom in construction, unemployment did not become a policy issue. However, high wages contributed to a rapid increase in investment in labor-saving automation in the manufacturing sector.

If we consider possible future changes in the Korean labor market, distinguishing the demand and supply sides, we find that a disequilibrium will persist in the labor market unless substantial efforts are made to create a sufficient number of employment opportunities for new entrants into the labor market. Supply-side pressures in the labor market are likely to increase continuously, at least during the next five to ten years, primarily because the largest age cohort of the baby-boom generation has been entering the labor market only since the late 1980s. A doubled enrollment quota of colleges in the early 1980s has also resulted in a sharp increase in the supply of college graduates. The female labor force participation rate will also continue to rise as the total fertility rate declines and educational attainment grows. We can easily foresee that significant social pressures for employment will be exerted from the supply side of the labor market.

On the other hand, the demand for labor is likely to grow much more slowly in the future. In order to improve the international competitiveness of the economy, the government's industrial policy will emphasize the development and application of new technologies, many of which will be labor saving. The recent surge of wage increases originating from labor strikes and disputes has induced firms to accelerate the adoption of automated processes, which will contribute further to the decline of the capacity of the economy to absorb labor.

It is also likely that imbalances will occur between the demand and supply of highly skilled labor. Since it takes a long time to produce well-trained workers in a rapidly changing technological environment, the supply of labor with specific-skill training may not sufficiently meet the industrial demands for educated and skilled labor. This is particularly true because about half of Korea's college graduates concentrated in the humanities and social sciences and thus do not meet the types of labor demanded by industries.

Public and political concern about unemployment went through a cycle in the second half of the 1980s. In late 1985, rising unemployment emerged as one of the more important social concerns and received much public attention. The same factors already mentioned were cited as the main reasons for rising unemployment: entrance of the baby-boom generation to the labor market, an increase in female labor force participation rates, and a doubling of college enrollment quotas in 1981. Due to favorable external conditions such as falling oil prices, the weakening of the U.S. dollar, and falling international interest rates,[29] Korea achieved an economic growth of 12 percent per year between 1986 and 1988. Corresponding to this remarkably high growth, employment in the same period expanded significantly: It increased by 1.9 million persons, more than three times the increase of the previous period (600,000 persons between 1982 and 1985). Because of this substantial climb in employment, the unemployment issue became somewhat less pressing. But as economic growth slowed to a real growth rate of 6.7 percent in 1989 and wage rates continued to rise by about 20 percent, employment ceased to increase, a situation that once again brought public attention to unemployment issues.

Korea's labor markets in the late 1980s were characterized by substantial wage hikes at a time when the supply of labor continued to increase. The increased supply of labor stems mainly from the increase in the size of the age cohorts entering the labor market, while rising wages are caused by noneconomic factors such as labor disputes and strikes following the transition to democracy.

The magnitude of the cohort of new entrants to the labor market, as measured by the size of the age group of those 20 to 24 years old, is anticipated to reach a peak in 1993. That is, the supply-side pressure in the labor market could be expected to increase in the early 1990s and then recede. Table 7-23 shows that the size of the this age group in 1993 was about 4 percent larger than that in 1990, implying that unless additional employment opportunities for new entrants are created, unemployment rates are likely to rise in the future.

Two further features of Korean wage trends between 1987 and 1990 are important (Table 7-24). On the one hand, the average rate of wage increases was more than twice that of previous years. The manufacturing wage increased by about 25 percent in 1989, in contrast to increases of less than 10 percent during 1985, 1986, and the first half of 1987. On the other hand, a substantial change in the wage distribution occurred at the same time. The wage rate of production workers increased much more substantially than that of clerical and managerial workers, and the wage differential between them narrowed. Also, the wage rate of the workers employed in larger firms rose more than that of the workers employed in smaller firms, which resulted in widening the wage differentials between these firms. This trend is not surprising because larger firms have relatively more powerful labor unions than do smaller firms.

A couple of comments are in order regarding the rapid rise in manufacturing wages. First, the wage surge in the manufacturing sector weakened the international competitiveness of Korean exporters, particularly labor-intensive firms. The unit labor costs of the manufacturing industry in U.S. dollar terms increased substantially—by 16.5 percent in 1987, 24.4 percent in 1988, and 37.2 percent during the first half of 1989—compared to Korea's chief competitor in the export market, Taiwan. Unit labor costs in Taiwanese manufacturing increased by 14.4 percent in 1987, 14.6 percent in 1988, and 12.3 percent during the first half of 1989. During the first half of 1989 alone, the unit labor costs of Korea's manufacturing industry rose by more than three times that of the Taiwanese manufacturing.

Table 7-23. Population Size of those Aged 20 to 24 (in thousands)

1985	1990	1993	1995	2000
4,274	4,368	4,562	4,434	3,900
(97.8)[a]	(100.0)[a]	(104.4)[a]	(101.5)[a]	(89.3)[a]

[a]1990 = 100.
Source: Economic Planning Board, *Korea Statistical Yearbook* (various issues).

Table 7-24. Wage Growth (in percentage)

	1985	1986	1987[c]	1988	1989	1990
All industry	9.2	8.2	10.1	15.5	21.1	18.8
Manufacturing industries	9.9	9.2	11.6	19.7	25.1	20.2
Production workers	9.9	10.6	12.5	21.2	26.0	21.3
Clerical/Managerial	7.7	7.0	9.1	11.0	16.2	15.5
Smaller Firms[a]	13.3	7.8	8.6	10.1	16.2	19.2
Larger Firms[b]	10.0	8.3	10.3	16.2	21.8	19.5

[a]Fewer than thirty employees.
[b]Thirty or more employees.
[c]In 1987, wages began rising from the fourth quarter.
Source: Ministry of Labor, *Report on Monthly Labor Survey* (various issues).

Second, Korean manufacturing industry can no longer be classified as a low-wage sector. With recent wage increases, the ratio of manufacturing wages over the average wage of all industries improved from 83.2 percent in 1985 to 90.9 percent in 1989 (Table 7-25). Taking into account the fact that the average manufacturing worker is 1.7 years younger than workers in all industries, the manufacturing wage is now considered at least as high as that of the average wage of all industries.

A final interesting comparison is of recent labor market conditions in Korea with those of Japan in the early 1970s, when it experienced the challenge of rising real wages. Korean manufacturing wages increased by about 25 percent in 1989, as did Japanese manufacturing wages in 1973–1974, before returning to a slower growth trend during the recession induced by the oil crisis. In Japan, rising wages played a significant role in promoting industrial restructuring by weeding out low-productivity industries.

Although rising wages are similar in the two countries, the developmental path of the economy after following the shift to higher wages may differ, primarily because the supply side of the labor market is quite dissimilar in the two cases. The labor market was rather tight in Japan during the early 1970s, when the entrance of the baby-boom generation to the labor market was complete and the size of the age cohort entering the labor market began to decrease. The opposite appears to be the case

Table 7-25. Relative Wage Trends (in percentage)

	Manufacturing Wage / Average Wage	Production Worker / Clerical/Managerial Owner	Smaller Firm / Larger Firm
1985	83.2	54.5	94.2
1989	90.9	68.7	83.5

Source: Ministry of Labor, *Report on Monthly Labor Survey* (various issues).

in Korea, where rising real wages are coupled with slack labor market conditions. If tightness of the labor market is a prerequisite for the success of a high-wage policy in accelerating industrial restructuring, we have yet to see how Korea will fare.

Appendix: Explanation of Wage and Price Equations

Perhaps the most widely used specification for wage equations is the expectations-augmented Phillips curve:

$$w_t = \alpha_0 + \sum_{i=0}^{k} \beta_i U_{t-i} + \sum_{i=1}^{m} \gamma_i p_{t-i} + \varepsilon_1 ,$$

where w and p are percentage increases in wages and prices, respectively, U is the unemployment rate, and ε_1 is a disturbance term. The distributed lag structure was introduced for U and p because it generally takes time for firms to make necessary adjustments to the changes in labor market conditions. In the traditional Phillips curve analysis, the distributed lag structure is generally used for p but not for U. In practice, when firms negotiate with labor unions on wages, expectations for future labor market developments are taken into account. Past experiences, estimated by distributed lag structure, generally form the basis of future expectations. Thus, if a distributed lag structure is not introduced, it imposes unnecessary restrictions on the estimations. The direct effect of U on w is captured by the sum of β_i's, but there is, in fact, an indirect impact that is transmitted from the price equation. Generally, the price equation may be specified as follows:

$$p_t = \delta_0 + \delta_1 m + \delta_2 (w - q) + \delta_3 D + \varepsilon_2$$

where m represents the increasing rate of factor costs except wages, q is productivity growth, D denotes aggregate demand, and ε_2 is a disturbance term. If we insert the price equation into the wage equation, we find that the lag structure of p simply represents an infinite lag structure of U, which indeed captures the indirect effect of U on w. We use the CPI changes for p for empirical estimations.

The analysis focuses mainly on the following. The U variable is replaced by the *UGAP* variable defined below, and the coefficient on *UGAP* is assumed to be a function of time, that is, $\beta(t)$ rather than a fixed β. This is to examine the changing relationship between wage increases and labor market conditions over time. The *UGAP* variable is defined as $U - Un$, where Un represents a full employment unemployment rate or a nonaccelerating inflation rate of unemployment.[30] The *Un* variable was constructed by removing the impact of the short-run cyclical component of unemployment, while the effect of cyclical swings due to demographic changes is incorporated—specifically, from

$$lnU_i = \alpha_0 + \alpha_1 \, lnUPM + \alpha_2 \, lnRPy,$$

where *UPM* represents the unemployment rate of prime-age males (24–49 years old) and *RPy* is the ratio of population aged 20–24 over total population. *RPy* is used to capture the effect of changing demographic composition on unemployment. As *RPy* increases due to the overflow of the younger generation in the labor market, unemployment is expected to rise. An average of 2.5 percent was inserted instead of actual values to calculate *Un*. The selection of 2.5 percent as a benchmark value for *UPM* was made with the assumption that, historically, wage rates have accelerated when *UPM* has been below 2.5 percent. Therefore, this value was chosen as a minimum level that does not accelerate wage inflation.

The estimated wage equations using the quarterly statistics from 1970 through 1988 are reported in Table 7A-1. Considering that the dependent variable is a rate of change rather than an absolute level, the explanatory power of the equations is fairly strong. The serial correlation problem does not appear to be serious. The first equation is a basic one. It indicates that as prices rise by 1 percent, wages increase by about 0.53 percent over the next quarter. There is a trade-off between unemployment and inflation in that a 1 percent increase in the unemployment rate causes a 1.3 percent reduction in wage inflation.

By substituting *UGAP* × *t* (*t* for time variable that has a value of one for the first quarter of 1970 and the increment of *t* by quarter is one) for *UGAP* in the second equation, we find that the magnitude of the coefficient on the *UGAP* × *t* variable becomes more significant and the explanatory power of the equation increases. One possible explanation for this finding is that the Phillips curve might have shifted upward over time. For example, during stagflation, we frequently observe that both *U* and *w* increase over time, confounding the theoretically expected inverse relationship between the two variables. Furthermore, the strengthened power of labor organizations would make the slope of *U* in the wage equation steeper. The estimated result indicates that the impact of increase in the unemployment rate on the reduction in wage inflation has increased over time.

In the third equation, the distributed lag structure was introduced for both the *UGAP* × *t* and *p* variables.[31] The *U* variable indicated that labor

Table 7A-1. Wage Equations

Variable	Equation 1	Equation 2	Equation 3
Constant	5.6679	5.8795	5.5646
	(6.11)	(6.82)	(5.13)
UGAP	−1.3024	—	—
	(−2.25)		
$(UGAPxt)_t$		−0.0366	−0.0155
		(−3.47)	(−1.35)
$t-1$			(−0.0117
			(−2.72)
$t-2$			−0.0084
			(−2.34)
$t-3$			−0.0055
			(−0.94)
$t-4$			−0.0032
			(−0.51)
$t-5$			−0.0014
			(−0.31)
Σ			−0.0456
			(−3.240)
p_{t-1}	0.5317	0.4980	0.2069
	(3.65)	(3.60)	(1.63)
$t-2$			0.1583
			(2.71)
$t-3$			0.1153
			(2.75)
$t-4$			0.0780
			(1.35)
$t-5$			0.0463
			(0.77)
$t-6$			0.0203
			(0.49)
Σ			0.6250
			(3.19)
$D1$	−7.2207	−7.1734	−7.9713
	(−6.52)	(−6.95)	(−7.48)
$D2$	−0.9069	−0.8390	0.3043
	(−0.83)	(−0.83)	(0.31)
$D3$	1.8427	1.9364	2.5068
	(1.70)	(1.90)	(2.51)
R^2	0.7173	0.7447	0.7572
SEE	2.9982	2.8490	2.8257
D.W.	2.0238	2.0539	2.1237

Note: Numbers in parentheses are t-statistics.

market conditions during the past two quarters affected wage inflation in the current quarter while the length of the lag period is about twice as long for price inflation as for *U*. In other words, in the wage determination process, workers' efforts to maintain their real wages by being compensated for price inflation are more strongly incorporated, while labor market conditions have a relatively shorter-term impact.

Explaining the changing pattern of price inflation is perhaps the most difficult task because price is an endogenous variable determined by the interaction of commodity, money, and labor market equilibrium conditions. In Table 7A-2, the estimated results for the wholesale price index (WPI), consumer price index (CPI), and GNP deflator (GDF) are presented. Explanations of variables are as follows: OPR is the manufacturing operation ratio index, W is the average nominal wage of all industries, Q is the economy-wide value-added labor productivity index, p^f is the import price index, e is the foreign exchange rate, r is the interest rate in the curb market, and Ds are seasonal dummies. Since all variables take logarithmic transformations, the estimated coefficients represent elasticities. The overall explanatory power of the estimated equations turned out to be very high.

Table 7A-2. Price Equations

Variable	ln WPI	ln CPI	ln GDF
Constant	−6.3188	−3.6687	−6.7927
	(−13.16)	(−9.97)	(−13.72)
$ln\ OPR$	−0.1124	−0.1424	0.1672
	(−1.31)	(−2.16)	(1.89)
$ln\ W_t$	0.3146	0.0734	0.5054
	(6.79)	(2.07)	(10.57)
$t-1$	0.1776	0.1055	0.2698
	(10.43)	(8.08)	(15.36)
$t-2$	0.0744	0.1199	0.0947
	(9.47)	(19.92)	(11.69)
$t-3$	0.0050	0.1166	−0.0198
	(0.28)	(8.40)	(−1.06)
$t-4$	−0.0305	0.0955	−0.7380
	(−1.46)	(5.95)	(−3.42)
$t-5$	−0.0322	0.0566	0.0672
	(−2.16)	(4.95)	(−4.37)
Σ	0.5089	0.5675	0.7090
	(17.33)	(25.21)	(23.42)
$ln\ Q_t$	−0.1552	−0.0885	−0.1491
	(−3.01)	(−2.23)	(−2.80)
$t-1$	−0.1501	−0.0800	−0.1297
	(−6.94)	(−4.83)	(−5.73)
$t-2$	−0.1368	−0.0690	−0.1052
	(−8.38)	(−5.52)	(−6.25)
$t-3$	−0.1150	−0.0555	−0.0811
	(−4.66)	(−2.94)	(−3.19)
$t-4$	−0.0850	−0.0395	−0.0555
	(−3.24)	(−1.97)	(−2.05)
Σ	−0.6888	−0.3537	−0.5474
	(−9.70)	(−6.49)	(−7.47)
$ln\ (P^f xe)_t$	0.2504	0.0269	0.1147
	(8.08)	(1.38)	(4.37)

Table 7A-2 (continued)

Variable	*ln* WPI	*ln* CPI	*ln* GDF
$t-1$	0.1341 (12.51)	0.0364 (4.43)	0.0619 (5.60)
$t-2$	0.0777 (9.58)	0.0403 (6.49)	0.0226 (2.71)
$t-3$	0.0360 (2.96)	0.0387 (4.14)	−0.0032 (−0.27)
$t-4$	0.0092 (0.71)	0.0314 (3.17)	−0.0156 (−1.17)
$t-5$	−0.0028 (−0.32)	0.0185 (2.70)	−0.0145 (−1.58)
Σ	0.4596 (12.98)	0.1921 (7.08)	0.1659 (4.54)
ln γ_t	−0.0006 (−1.34)	−0.0011 (−3.04)	−0.0004 (−0.75)
$t-1$	−0.0002 (−0.65)	−0.0008 (−3.51)	0.0004 (−1.30)
$t-2$	0.0001 (0.40)	−0.0005 (−2.51)	−0.0004 (−1.35)
$t-3$	0.0003 (0.93)	−0.0003 (−1.42)	−0.0003 (−1.10)
$t-4$	0.0003 (1.14)	−0.0002 (−0.80)	−0.0003 (−0.92)
$t-5$	0.0002 (1.24)	−0.0001 (−0.44)	−0.0002 (−0.81)
Σ	0.0001 (0.09)	−0.0030 (−2.95)	−0.0019 (−1.40)
D1	−0.0092 (−0.48)	−0.0149 (−1.01)	0.0572 (2.87)
D2	−0.0300 (−1.24)	−0.0172 (−0.93)	0.0300 (1.20)
D3	−0.0508 (−1.89)	−0.0278 (−1.35)	−0.0059 (−0.21)
R^2	0.9986	0.9991	0.9987
SEE	0.0251	0.0192	0.0259

Note: Numbers in parentheses are t-statistics.

NOTES

1. R. Dornbusch and Yung Chul Park, "Korean Growth Policy," *Brookings Papers on Economic Activity*, 2 (1987): 389–454.

2. The total fertility rate reached its peak, 6.2, in the early 1970s, but since then it has decreased consistently. In recent years, it has fallen to about 1.6.

3. The urbanization rate, defined as a percentage of urban population over total population, increased from 50.1 percent in 1970 to 68.7 percent in 1980 according to the official statistics of the Economic Planning Board. The rate rose continuously to 77.8 percent in 1988.

4. In the Harris-Todaro model, the rural wage is assumed to be fixed due to excess supply of labor. Thus, real wage growth in urban sectors implies a widening wage differential between urban and rural sectors.

5. The average annual growth rates in GNP of manufacturing industry were 19.9 percent during the period 1964–1973, 13.9 percent during 1974–1980, and 12.3 percent during 1981–1990.

6. International Labor Organization (ILO), *Yearbook of Labor Statistics* (Geneva: ILO, 1986).

7. Collection of industry-specific wage data was initiated by the Ministry of Labor only in 1970.

8. The separation rate in the Korean manufacturing sector is even higher than the combined layoff and quit rates in U.S. manufacturing. For example, the annual average layoff rate was 1.4 and the quit rate was 2.3 between 1966 and 1975 for the U.S. manufacturing industry.

9. A. Krueger, *Trade and Employment in Developing Countries: Synthesis and Conclusions* (Chicago: University of Chicago Press, 1983).

10. ILO, *Yearbook of Labor Statistics.*

11. The choice of an appropriate foreign exchange rate plays a very important role in the comparison of labor productivity among nations. The level of foreign exchange rate basically represents the relative purchasing power of tradable goods. However, the domestic relative price structure between tradable and nontradable goods cannot be compared directly among different nations due to the different degrees of market openness and industrialization. Generally, the relative price of services in a developing nation is undervalued as compared to a developed nation, and the foreign exchange rate of developing nations is frequently overvalued. In order to correct for these deficiencies in using official exchange rates in computing international competitiveness, the purchasing-power-parity method was devised. In this method, commonly specified items are chosen among the concerned nations, and productivity gains in producing these items are compared. For a detailed discussion, see "International Comparison of Productivity," unpublished paper, Seoul: Korea Productivity Center, December 1987.

12. The official labor productivity statistic is measured as output per production worker. This definition has some drawbacks. First, statistics are available only for the mining, manufacturing, and electricity industries. Thus, the statistics cannot be used for productivity comparisons between tradable and nontradable industries. Second, productivity data are generally used as criteria for wage increases for the next year. In this regard, a value-added index may be more relevant than an output-based one because wages are more directly related to value-added than to

output production. A common deficiency in computation of both value-added and output-based labor productivity is that changes in working hours are not taken into account. The reason is that data of working hours are collected only for limited occupations of workers, including production workers of manufacturing industry. Generally, working hours of white-collar workers of all industries are not collected.

13. The output-based labor productivity growth rate is presented in Table 7-12. Since both the numerator and denominator of this productivity measure are different from those of the value-added index, the magnitude of change differs between the two indexes. However, we find that the pattern of change is similar. For both indexes, for example, productivity growth rates in the manufacturing industry were lower during the late 1970s than during the early 1970s and were higher during the 1980s than during the 1970s.

14. Unit labor costs in Japan show similar patterns to those in Korea. The unit labor costs of the manufacturing sector were generally lower than those of the nontradable sectors. However, the gap in unit labor costs between the two sectors has narrowed recently. One distinct feature is that since the first oil crisis in 1973, unit labor costs in the manufacturing sector have been very low, indicating that labor productivity growth always exceeded wage growth. The low unit labor costs of all industries might have played an essential role in moderating inflation in Japan during the past decade.

15. W. Dickens and L. Katz, "Inter-Industry Wage Differences and Theories of Wage Determination," Discussion Paper 1324, Cambridge: Harvard Institute of Economic Research, June 1987.

16. A. Krueger and L. Summers, "Efficiency Wages and the Inter-Industry Wage Structure," *Econometrica,* 56, 2 (March 1988): 259–93.

17. Dornbusch and Park, "Korean Growth Policy."

18. Per capita GNP in 1986 was $2,300 for Korea, $3,759 for Taiwan, $6,949 for Singapore, and $6,841 for Hong Kong. *International Financial Statistics* (Washington, D.C.: International Monetary Fund, 1987).

19. The average wage of the service industry was 56 percent higher than the average wage of the manufacturing industry in 1988, the equivalent of about three years' increase in wages.

20. M. Wachter, "The Wage Process: An Analysis of the Early 1970s," *Brookings Papers on Economic Activity,* 2 (1984): 507–24.

21. See note *a* to Table 7-12 for a definition of groups.

22. See, for example, Moo-Ki Bai, "The Turning Point in the Korean Economy," *The Developing Economies,* 20 (1984): 117–40.

23. R. Minami, *The Economic Development of Japan* (New York: Macmillan, 1986).

24. For a detailed discussion about Korea's wage guideline policy, see Jae-Won Kim, "Wage Policy: A Historical Review of the Past Forty Years," unpublished paper, Seoul: Korea Employers' Federation, 1988 (in Korean); Soo-Kon Kim, "Income Equalization Policy in the Context of the Korean Industrial Relations System," *Korea Development Review*, 5, 3 (1983) (in Korean); Sang-Woo Nam, "Korea's Stabilization Efforts since the Late 1970s," Working Paper 8405, Seoul: Korea Development Institute, March 1984; Se-Il Park, *Wage Policy in an Open Economy: The Case of Korea* (Seoul: Korea Economic Research Institute, January 1987) (in Korean).

25. Since there were many other regulations on bank credit to firms, it is not easy to identify the source of bank credit. In practice, firms that did not produce profits but nevertheless increased wages were not penalized as long as their increasing rates were lower than average wage growth.

26. See M. Bognanno, "Korea's Industrial Relations at the Turning Point," Working Paper 8816, Seoul: Korea Development Institute, December 1988.

27. Wage costs consist of about 12 percent of total factor costs in the manufacturing industry, and the wage bill comprises about 47 percent of the industry's total value-added. In this respect, if all firms transmit all wage increases to price rises instantaneously, the elasticity would be around 0.5. In reality, price transmission behavior takes place with a time lag. Therefore, the short-run price elasticity with respect to wage increases is generally considered bounded by 0.5.

28. Lowercase letters represent percentage changes.

29. Low international interest rates exert two effects on the Korean economy: On the one hand, it induces inflows of foreign capital due to higher domestic interest rates, which contributes to a surplus of balance of payments. On the other hand, the lower international interest rates lessen the burden of paying interest on foreign borrowing. Remember that Korea was the fourth largest foreign indebted country in the world at the time, with foreign debt amounting to about US$ 45 billion

30. This section tests empirically the model developed in J. Perloff and M. Wachter, "A Production Function–Nonaccelerating Inflation Approach to Potential Output: Is Measured Potential Output Too High?" Discussion Paper 20a, Department of Economics, University of Pennsylvania, 1978. They use the UGAP variable in testing Okun's Law for the U.S. economy.

31. The Almon distributed-lag estimation method was used. A quadratic form with a lag of six quarters was used, and restriction on the far side was imposed.

8

Saving, Investment, and External Balance in South Korea

Susan M. Collins

This chapter focuses on the domestic counterpart to current account imbalance: the gap between domestic (public and private) saving and investment. Prior to 1986, Korea's deficits emerged as investment exceeded savings, while the 1986–1989 surpluses were the external counterpart to a large excess of saving over investment. This saving-investment perspective on external imbalance is especially useful in distinguishing between the roles of government and the private sector.

External imbalances have played an important role in the formulation of Korea's economic policy. Despite the government's continuing ability to finance current account deficits by borrowing externally, large deficits, particularly those associated with slowdowns in export growth, were of great concern. During 1970–1971, the emergence of large current account deficits and a rising debt service ratio led to devaluation and a debate over whether monetary and fiscal restraint was appropriate. During 1974–1975, current account deficits and a growing debt burden contributed to the postponed implementation of the big push to develop heavy and chemical industries. Similarly, concern about large deficits and heavy external debt burdens was a major impetus for devaluation and other changes in economic policy during the early 1980s. Finally, the large current account surpluses of 1986–1988 created a new set of difficulties for economic policymakers.

An analysis of Korea's current account since the mid-1960s points to some unusual features. The most striking is the rapid increase in saving, especially household saving. World Bank data show that Korea's national saving rose from just 8 percent of gross domestic product (GDP) in 1965 to 38 percent in 1988. The rise accounts for Korea's ability to convert its large current account deficits to surpluses by the late 1980s, while maintaining high rates of investment and prepaying external debt obligations. Korea stands in sharp contrast to many other developing countries in which domestic saving has declined sharply. As external financing became unavailable after 1982, these countries were forced to slash investment so as to shift from current account deficits to surpluses. Although there is no one-to-one correlation between investment and growth, Korea's consistently high rates of capital accumulation help to explain persistently rapid growth.[1]

Table 8-1 compares gross domestic saving, investment, and real growth in Korea, other high-growth Asian economies, and comparator country groups: middle-income developing countries, high-income countries (Korea is middle income, aspiring to become high income), and the severely indebted developing countries, included because Korea was the fourth largest debtor country in the early 1980s. Korea (like Singapore) had a low saving rate in 1965 compared with other countries (prompting a study entitled, "Why Do Koreans Save 'So Little'?").[2] By 1988, Korea's saving rate was among the highest in the world; it was substantially above those for both middle- and high-income countries and even above the high rates of Japan and Hong Kong. Korea's average annual growth rose from 9.6 percent during the 1965–1980 period to 9.9 percent during the 1980–1988 period. In the earlier period, Korea's growth was comparable to rates in some other Asian countries but above average for developing economies. During the 1980s, however, Korea stands out for maintaining its high growth, when growth rates were declining throughout the developed and the developing world. Korea's investment as a share of GDP doubled between 1965 and 1988 from 15 percent—low by international standards—to 30 percent—high by international standards but

Table 8-1. Country Comparisons of Saving, Investment, and Growth (in percentages of GDP)

	Saving		Investment		Real Growth	
	1965	1988	1965	1988	1965–1979	1980–1988
Korea	8	38	15	30	9.6	9.9
Hong Kong	29	33	36	28	8.6	7.3
Singapore	10	41	22	37	10.1	5.7
Taiwan[a]	21	35	23	23	9.8	8.1
Japan	28	33	27	31	6.5	3.9
Middle income	21	27	21	25	6.1	2.9
High income	21	22	20	22	3.7	2.8
Severely indebted	22	25	21	22	6.0	1.5

[a]Percentage of GNP.
Sources: The World Bank, *World Development Report* (1990); Republic of China, Council for Economic Planning and Development, *Taiwan Statistical Data Book* (1992).

comparable to investment levels elsewhere in Asia. However, the investment increase—smaller than the rise in saving—was accomplished by a shift from a substantial current account deficit to a large surplus.

Why do Koreans now save "so much"? The question is important for at least three reasons. First, the rise in saving is one of the keys to understanding Korea's economic growth. Second, the large swings in the current account balance, often of great concern to policymakers, were due primarily to swings in saving. Finally, identifying the causes of Korea's shift from a low saver to a high saver may contain useful lessons for policymakers in other developing countries.

This chapter discusses external imbalances and highlights the differences between the Korean experience and the typical experience of developing-country debtors. It empirically examines saving and investment behavior in Korea, and scrutinizes household saving, using data from income and expenditure surveys of urban households to attempt an explanation of the dramatic rise in Korean savings.

The Anatomy of External Deficits

A number of developing countries have undergone a cycle of growing external deficits, a balance-of-payments crisis when sources of foreign exchange financing dry up, and subsequent macroeconomic adjustment. These countries tend to follow a typical pattern, beginning, in the run-up to crisis, with a rise in government dissaving (revenues net of current expenditures), often accompanied by high rates of investment and an economic boom. At the same time, a fixed nominal exchange rate leads to an increasingly overvalued currency. Export growth stagnates; imports mushroom, associated in part with domestic capital formation; the current account deficit is financed by borrowing abroad; and as growing debt service ratios signal the coming balance-of-payments crisis, capital flight reduces available domestic resources. The crisis is reached when the country can no longer finance the external deficit—reserves are depleted and sources of borrowing have dried up—without major domestic policy changes. The adjustment that follows entails devaluation, together with tight monetary and fiscal policies. Typically, public investment is cut, and private investment declines in the midst of high interest rates and poor prospects for domestic demand growth over the short to medium term.[3]

Korea's experience in each of its three "crises" (1966–1969, 1974–1975, and 1979–1982) was quite different from this pattern.[4] To illustrate the points, Table 8-2 shows the behavior of key variables during the

Table 8-2. Crisis and Adjustment

	1978	1979	1980	1981	1982	1983	1984	1985
Real GDP growth (%)	9.71	7.43	-2.02	6.72	7.30	11.78	9.41	6.93
Budget deficit[a]	-1.66	-1.54	-2.53	-3.85	-3.17	-0.92	-1.04	-5.38
Government saving[b]	5.77	5.95	5.62	5.73	5.93	6.92	6.64	5.97
Total saving[c]	27.49	26.58	20.45	19.76	20.89	25.29	26.90	27.31
Current account[d]	-4.78	-8.35	-10.84	-9.12	-6.73	-3.78	-3.52	-2.15
Gross domestic fixed capital formation	32.51	33.76	32.14	27.96	28.37	29.25	28.91	28.25
Change in stocks	0.54	2.24	-0.41	1.51	0.22	-0.48	0.92	1.03
Debt (US$ million)[e]	17,301	22,886	29,480	32,989	37,330	40,419	42,098	47,158

Note: All variables are in percentage of GDP unless otherwise noted.
[a] General government deficit: central government plus local government.
[b] Current revenue less current expenditures.
[c] GDP less private consumption less government consumption.
[d] Calculated from national accounts data.
[e] All creditors; long- and short-term debt, including International Monetary Fund credit.
Sources: Economic Planning Board, *Korea Statistical Yearbook* (various years); World Bank, *World Debt Tables* (various years).

1979–1982 crisis and subsequent adjustment.[5] First, although Korea has had budget deficits, government saving has remained positive throughout Korea's recent development. Certainly there have been fluctuations in the government savings rate as a percentage of GDP; for example, saving of the general government ranged between 4.5 percent and 7.2 percent of GDP between 1978 and 1988. But these fluctuations have been relatively small compared to the swings in the current account balance as a percentage of GDP—from –10.8 percent of GDP in 1980 to a high of 6.9 percent in 1988. Further, the increase in the budget deficit came after the crisis had begun. It was not a major factor in explaining the 1978–1980 current account deterioration that preceded the crisis. There is also no evidence of a decline in government saving, either in the years preceding the crisis or in the subsequent adjustment.

Second, although investment did rise in the late 1970s and was reduced somewhat during 1980–1981, domestic fixed capital accumulation was not slashed during the adjustment. Korea has seen a trend increase in investment from 15 percent of gross national product (GNP) in the mid-1960s to 30 percent by the end of the 1980s. Fixed capital formation rose from 28 percent of GDP in 1977 to nearly 34 percent in 1979 before returning in 1981 to the 1977 level. It remained at about 28 or 29 percent of GDP until 1989, when it rose to 31 percent. These high rates of investment help to explain Korea's strong growth performance during the adjustment. Additionally, an unexpected accumulation of inventories during the economic downturn and a slowdown in export growth—not a surge in public sector capital formation—account for a large part of the high 1979 total investment.

Third, most of the swing in the current account—from a deficit of 2.1 percent of GDP in 1977 to a deficit of 10.8 percent of GDP in 1980 and back down to 2.1 percent in 1985—is associated with swings in private saving. The balance-of-payments crisis coincided with a sharp drop in private saving (4.7 percent of GDP between 1979 and 1980). Increased investment is only part of Korea's crisis story, and rising government dissavings emerges only during the second part of the story, the adjustment phase. Similarly, most of the decline in the current account deficit over the 1980–1985 period and the emergence of surpluses during the 1986–1988 period were associated with rising private savings.

Fourth, Korea did not appear to face a borrowing constraint, but retained the ability to borrow throughout the crisis. Although policymakers at the time grew concerned because foreign funding was less easily obtained during this period, the fact that they continued to be able to finance external deficits by accumulating debt between 1980 and 1982 opened up a wider set of options to Korean policymakers than the options available to countries having debt servicing difficulties after 1982. In particular, the ability to borrow during the first phase of the adjustment is one of the main factors that enabled Korea to undertake expansionary monetary and fiscal policies in the first stage of policy adjustment and to postpone the traditional macroeconomic stabilization policies until after 1982. It also helps to explain why Korean investment remained high during the adjustment, even before private saving had recovered.

Finally, the major use of funds that Korea borrowed abroad from 1966 to 1985 was to finance current account deficits. Although some of the resources were used to augment the stock of foreign exchange reserves, Korea differs from many Latin American debtors in that little of the debt appears to have been offset by private capital flight. Between 1966 and 1978, virtually all of the foreign capital inflows from external borrowing and foreign direct investment can be accounted for by financing of the cumulative current account deficit together with accumulation of foreign exchange reserves (Table 8-3). There is no evidence of either capital flight or accumulation of other foreign assets by the private sector as the counterpart to external debt during this period. During the 1979–1982 economic crisis, financing of current account deficits was equivalent to 84 percent of the external borrowing while foreign exchange accumulation accounts for an additional 5 percent of the debt accumulation.[6] By the 1983–1985 period, however, external deficit finance and reserve accumulation accounted for just 45 percent of the increased debt and direct investment inflows. Over half of these capital inflows financed accumulation of other types of external assets.

Table 8-3. Uses of External Debt (US$ million)

	1966–1978	1979–1982	1983–1985	1986–1988
Sources of funds				
Increase in debt	12,404	20,029	9,828	−10,002
Foreign direct investment	650	−7	216	1,463
Uses of funds				
Current account deficit finance	8,729	16,768	3,865	−28,632
Increase in foreign reserves	4,403	1,076	514	6,112

Sources: World Bank *World Debt Tables* (various issues); International Monetary Fund, *International Financial Statistics* (various issues).

Saving and Investment Behavior

A central feature of Korea's growth experience is a rapid rise in savings, and high levels of investment. Between 1970 and 1988, saving rates dropped during periods of slow growth—1971, 1974–1975, and 1980–1982—but it rose strongly during the periods of high growth (Figure 8-1).[7] Investment also rose, on average, during the 1970s, but was relatively constant during the 1980s. The excess of domestic investment over domestic saving was financed by foreign saving, and in each of the three periods, Korea faced a large external deficit. (Note that foreign saving is equal to the current account deficit plus net transfers from the rest of the world.) Initially, the deficit arose from a combination of high investment and a drop in saving. In the second period, investment declined; however the saving-investment gap remained until saving rates recovered, and began to grow once again. Between 1986 and 1988, the result was a large external surplus because the saving rate increases were not matched by further rises in investment.

Figure 8-1 overstates the role played by planned investment in accounting for external deficits. Figure 8-2 plots both total gross domestic investment, which includes accumulation or deccumulation of stocks,

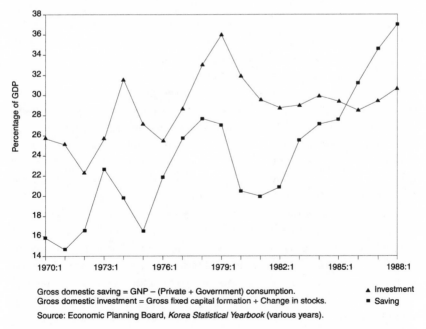

Gross domestic saving = GNP – (Private + Government) consumption.   ▲ Investment
Gross domestic investment = Gross fixed capital formation + Change in stocks.   ■ Saving

Source: Economic Planning Board, *Korea Statistical Yearbook* (various years).

Figure 8-1. Gross Domestic Saving and Investment (as percentage of GDP)

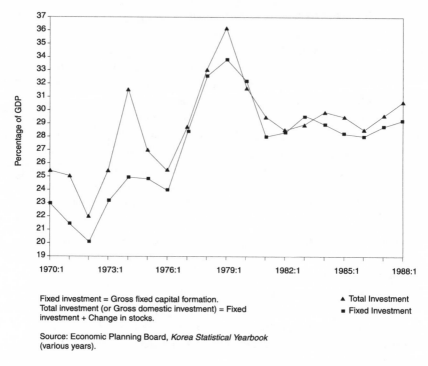

Fixed investment = Gross fixed capital formation.
Total investment (or Gross domestic investment) = Fixed
investment + Change in stocks.

▲ Total Investment
■ Fixed Investment

Source: Economic Planning Board, *Korea Statistical Yearbook*
(various years).

Figure 8-2. Total and Fixed Investment (as percentage of GDP)

and fixed capital formation, which does not. It shows that in 1974–1975
and again in 1979, part of the observed surge in total investment came
from inventory accumulation, much of it unplanned.

Figure 8-3 separates the private from the general government component of fixed capital formation. It shows that private investment
accounted for most of the rise in investment during the 1970s and for
most of the variability of it. (General government here refers to the central
and local governments.) Government investment was relatively low and
relatively constant, averaging 3.9 percent of GDP and ranging between
a low of 2.7 percent in 1964 and a high of 5.1 percent in 1970. There is
little evidence of public investment surges' contributing significantly to
Korea's large swings in external imbalance. However, public investment data
may understate the government's role in total domestic investment
behavior. Subsidized loans to targeted industries and firms were a central
feature of government policy, especially to promote heavy and chemical
industries during the big push. These credit policies appear to have
contributed to the rise in private investment during the late 1970s and
the associated current account deterioration.

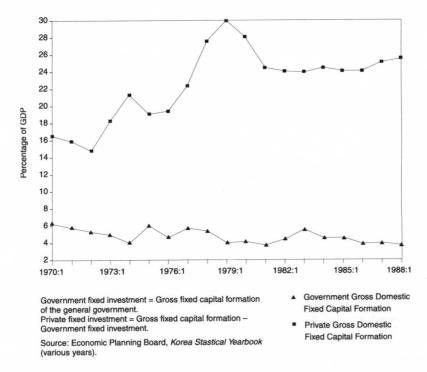

Government fixed investment = Gross fixed capital formation
of the general government.
Private fixed investment = Gross fixed capital formation –
Government fixed investment.

Source: Economic Planning Board, *Korea Stastical Yearbook*
(various years).

▲ Government Gross Domestic
Fixed Capital Formation

■ Private Gross Domestic
Fixed Capital Formation

Figure 8-3. Fixed Investment: Private and Government (as percentage of GDP)

When Korean gross domestic saving as a percentage of GDP since 1970 is decomposed into saving by the general government and saving by the private sector, we see that government saving (current revenue less current expenditure) was positive throughout the period and relatively stable (Figure 8-4). Although it declined from nearly 7 percent of GDP in 1970 to 2.1 percent in 1974, it recovered in the second half of the 1970s, averaging 5.9 percent over 1978–1982 and 8.6 percent during the span 1983–1988. It then fell sharply to 4.9 percent in 1989. Clearly, government saving can account for neither the trend rise nor the large cyclical swings in total domestic saving. Both of these developments are attributable to private saving.

A striking feature of the swings in private saving is that they tended to follow closely on changes in real economic growth. Figure 8-5 looks more closely at the cyclical variation in private saving, plotting deviations of real growth from the average growth rate over the period and deviations of private saving from trend.[8] The figure illustrates the high positive relationship between the two series. Private saving tends to be

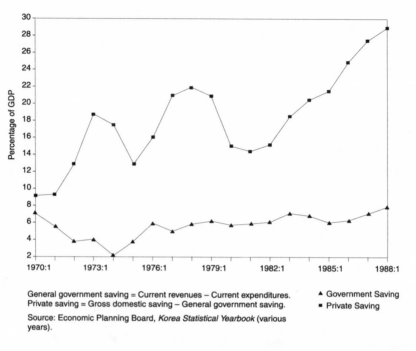

General government saving = Current revenues – Current expenditures.
Private saving = Gross domestic saving – General government saving.

Source: Economic Planning Board, *Korea Statistical Yearbook* (various
years).

▲ Government Saving
■ Private Saving

Figure 8-4. Saving: Private and Government (as percentage of GDP)

high relative to trend in years when the growth rate is above average and
low relative to trend when real growth is below average, suggesting that
the trend of saving growth is associated with average or anticipated real
income growth. This would be true, for example, if households do not
increase consumption expenditures to reflect fully rising real income
levels. The figure also suggests that deviations of saving from trend are
associated with unanticipated income growth. The relationship between
saving and growth is explored further below.

Determinants of Saving

Life-cycle models imply that real income growth should be an important
determinant of national saving.[9] That there have been large fluctuations
in real income growth in Korea suggests that saving may respond
differently to anticipated rises in real income, which are perceived as
reflecting permanent increases, than to unanticipated swings in real
income, which are perceived as reflecting one-time changes in real
income.[10] Life-cycle theory would predict that the propensity to save out
of unanticipated, transitory income should be larger than the propensity
to save out of anticipated and relatively permanent income. Thus,

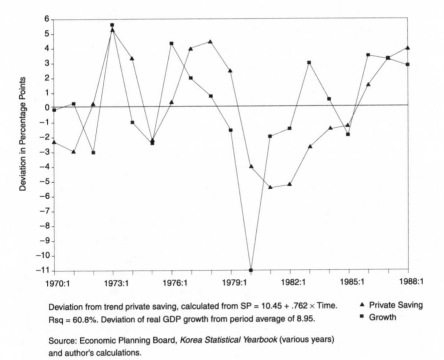

Deviation from trend private saving, calculated from SP = 10.45 + .762 × Time.　　▲ Private Saving
Rsq = 60.8%. Deviation of real GDP growth from period average of 8.95.　　■ Growth

Source: Economic Planning Board, *Korea Statistical Yearbook* (various years)
and author's calculations.

Figure 8-5. Cyclical Variations in Private Saving and Real GDP

unanticipated growth in real income should be associated with rises in the ratio of national saving to GDP.

Anticipated real income growth could also raise the national saving GDP ratio. In a life-cycle framework, this would be true if, for example, additional income is disproportionately distributed to groups of households with relatively high saving rates. But if household consumption is not well described by life-cycle theory—if it does not increase as expected lifetime income rises, perhaps because of historical or cultural factors or credit rationing—then anticipated income growth would be associated with increased saving rates. In fact, equations that distinguish between anticipated and unanticipated real income do fit Korean saving data significantly better than formulations that simply include real income growth. Thus, the saving equations reported later in this chapter include both income variables.[11]

Theory also suggests that the percentage of income saved may be related to real interest rates. A higher real interest rate increases the price of current consumption relative to future consumption, and thus should tend to increase saving, if substitution effects are dominant. Wealth effects may lead to the opposite result. There is a large literature that examines the interest elasticity of saving in developing countries; not surprisingly, it is inconclusive. For example, Giovannini has found negligible effects for a large sample of countries.[12] Still, Korea's 1965 interest rate reform has often been cited as one example in which an interest rate increase (implying that real interest rates rose from negative to positive levels) led to a jump in saving.

Have real interest rates played an important role in the more recent increases in Korean saving? Figure 8-6 shows that saving rose during some periods when real interest rates were falling—for example, 1970–1973 and 1982–1985. Interest rates clearly cannot account for most of the dramatic rise in Korean saving over the past two decades. These data appear more consistent with the view that stable positive real interest rates are consistent with rising saving than the view that increasing real interest rates are necessary to increase private saving.[13]

One potential difficulty in relating saving and real returns is that easily observable interest rates may provide poor measures of true returns to saving (and to investing). The concern is often raised by those who refute the evidence that interest elasticities are statistically or economically insignificant. The empirical work in this chapter focuses on real deposit

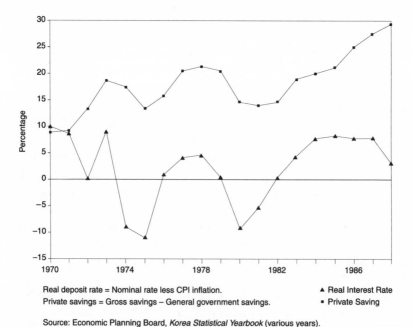

Real deposit rate = Nominal rate less CPI inflation. ▲ Real Interest Rate
Private savings = Gross savings – General government savings. ■ Private Saving

Source: Economic Planning Board, *Korea Statistical Yearbook* (various years).

Figure 8-6. Private Saving/GDP and Real Interest Rates

rates (one-year bank deposit rates less the current consumer price index [CPI] inflation). Other alternatives do not appear to generate a stronger relationship between interest rates and saving. For example, Fry uses a shadow real interest rate.[14] Since the current account is identically equal to the difference between saving and investment, he derives a reduced-form expression for the shadow real interest rate as a function of the world real interest rate and Korea's net foreign assets relative to GDP. However, both variables are insignificant in all of his saving function estimates.

Two additional variables were explored as determinants of saving. The first is the growth in domestic credit relative to GDP. Many have expressed concern that the Korean private sector is credit constrained from time to time. If so, increased credit growth would tend to raise consumption and reduce saving. The second additional variable is population growth. Increased population growth arises primarily because of an increase in the birth rate or a decrease in the death rate. In either case, the economy's dependency ratio (percentage of the population under age 15 or over 65) rises. Since these groups are expected to have negative saving in the life-cycle framework, dependence ratios are expected to be negatively related to national saving. The empirical relationship between dependency ratios and national saving is another issue that has been extensively studied.[15] To date, the empirical results are inconclusive. In fact, neither the population nor the domestic credit variable exhibited a statistically significant relationship to saving. Both are excluded from the regressions reported below.

Table 8-4 reports the estimation results, including lagged saving, to allow for gradual adjustment of saving. In interpreting the results, we focus on the total saving equation. The results for private savings are qualitatively similar. The estimates show a large and significant difference between anticipated and unanticipated income in explaining saving. A 1 percent increase in anticipated real income raises saving by just 0.05 percent of GDP, and a 1 percent increase in real income that is unanticipated raises the saving rate by more than ten times as much—0.6 percent. Saving does appear to adjust gradually, with an adjustment coefficient of a little less than one-half (1.0–0.54) per annum. These three variables are all strongly significant for total saving; however, only unanticipated income changes have a significant effect on private saving (anticipated income changes do not enter significantly).

That increases in both anticipated and unanticipated real income have a larger (and statistically more significant) effect on total saving than on private saving alone suggests that public saving rises strongly with

Table 8-4. Determinants of National Saving, 1971–1988 (OLS regressions)
Dependent Variables: Total and Private Saving as Percentages
of GDP

	Total	Private
Constant	−41.25	−14.04
	(14.68)	(17.38)
Anticipated log (real GDP)	4.70	1.79
	(1.56)	(1.80)
Unanticipated log (real GDP)	61.39	39.46
	(12.59)	(16.31)
Real interest rate	0.19	0.24
	(0.06)	(0.09)
Saving (−1) as a percentage of GDP	0.61	0.73
	(0.12)	(0.15)
Adjusted R^2	0.95	0.90
Durbin-Watson	2.06	2.09

Note: Standard errors in parentheses.
Source: Economic Planning Board, *Korea Statistical Yearbook* (various years); author's calculations.

real income, as revenue increases are matched less than one-for-one with increases in current expenditure. The result could be interpreted as a reflection of Korea's fiscal conservatism.

The estimates also show a positive and statistically significant relationship between saving and real interest rates. However, in economic terms, the effect is quite small. The estimates imply that if real interest rates were to double from 5 percent to 10 percent, total saving would increase by relatively little—just under 1 percent of GDP. However, private saving appears to be somewhat more sensitive to real interest rate changes.

Based on these estimation results, the overwhelming reason for the sharp rise in Korean saving since 1970 has been the rapid rise in real income. In the short run, Koreans appear to have responded to above-average income growth as transitory and to have saved most income gains. Total saving has also risen with increases in permanent income. Two possible explanations for this relationship between saving and income are explored below using more detailed information about Korean households' saving behavior.

Determinants of Investment
The investment functions are based on a standard accelerator model, with both total and private investment as percentages of GDP used as dependent variables.[16] The accelerator model assumes a positive relationship between investment and real GDP growth. (Distinguishing between

anticipated and unanticipated growth did not improve the fit of the investment equations.) Gradual adjustment is built in through inclusion of lagged investment ratios.

Three other variables are potentially important determinants of investment. First, investment should be negatively related to the real cost of capital. Domestic real interest rates are used as a proxy. Second, investment may be positively related to profitability. Given the large share of intermediates and capital goods in Korea's exports and the concentration of investment in export sectors, the terms of trade provide one indicator of the profitability of investment.[17] Percentage changes in the terms of trade are included as a proxy for changes in the price of capital goods relative to final goods. Finally, investment may be related to the availability of credit. If firms are credit constrained and domestic capital markets work imperfectly, credit expansion—again scaled by nominal GDP—should enable firms to raise their investment expenditures.

Neither real interest rates nor the terms-of-trade variable were significant in any of the investment equations. The estimation results, excluding these two variables, are reported in Table 8-5. The investment functions fit reasonably well, though not as well as the saving functions. Additionally, the results for total investment and private investment are very similar, reflecting the fact that nearly all of the changes in total investment are due to changes in private investment.

The estimates imply large and significant effects of real growth on domestic capital formation. For example, a 1 percent increase in real GDP growth raises investment by 0.5 percent of GDP. The estimates also support the hypothesis that private investment expenditures are constrained by credit availability. Private capital formation rises significantly

Table 8-5 Determinants of National Investment, 1971–1978 (OLS regressions)
Dependent Variables: Total and Private Fixed Capital Formation as Percentages of GDP

	Total	Private
Constant	−2.77	−4.51
	(5.14)	(3.72)
Real GDP growth	0.45	0.45
	(0.22)	(0.19)
Domestic credit/GDP (% change)	0.17	0.21
	(0.11)	(0.09)
Investment (−1) as a percentage of GDP	0.94	0.97
	(0.15)	(0.12)
Adjusted R^2	0.75	0.83

Note: Standard errors are in parentheses.
Source: Economic Planning Board, *Korea Statistical Yearbook* (various years); author's calculations.

with a domestic credit expansion. Finally, the large coefficient estimates on the lagged dependent variables suggest relatively slow adjustment of investment over time. (In fact, the null hypothesis that these coefficients are one cannot be rejected.)

Household Saving

This examination of the saving behavior of urban households uses annual data from Korea's income and expenditure survey, which has been conducted since 1962.[18] The characteristics of the sample have been altered a few times since it was initiated; in particular, new sampling criteria and a larger sample were introduced in 1977. Most of the discussion here focuses on the data since 1977, since data from previous years are not strictly comparable.

The household survey data are especially useful for two reasons. First, national income and product account (NIPA) data suggest that household saving accounts for most of the trend rise and the cyclical variation in private saving. However, the NIPA disaggregation of private saving into household and corporate is suspect given the large share of family-owned businesses and the active informal credit markets in Korea. There is also a difficulty of distributing the capital consumption allowance between the household and corporate sectors. Many analysts remain skeptical of the accuracy of the decomposition. However, the household surveys are designed to focus on purely household transactions and are likely to provide relatively accurate measures of saving behavior for the types of households sampled.

The second reason for focusing on the survey data is that they provide additional information on household characteristics that are relevant to an analysis of saving behavior. In particular, these data make it possible to divide households by the age of the household head, a key distinction in models of life-cycle or permanent income consumption. It is also possible to separate out the relatively wealthy from the relatively poor households, a division that may be important if poor households that do not have access to credit markets have different consumption and saving behavior from wealthier households that can borrow and lend.

Both household saving (defined as household saving relative to disposable income) and private saving since 1970 exhibit a strong rising trend, but the survey data do not show the 1987–1988 surge in saving rates that is evident from the NIPA data (Figure 8-7). One possible explanation is that the increase in saving from the NIPA data is from the

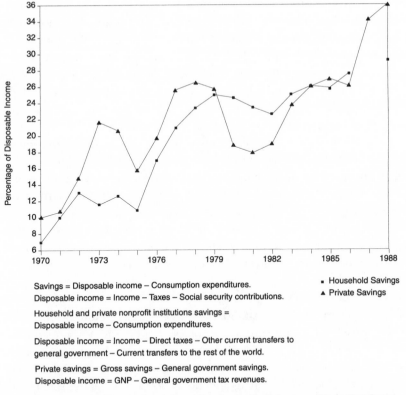

Savings = Disposable income − Consumption expenditures.
Disposable income = Income − Taxes − Social security contributions.

Household and private nonprofit institutions savings =
Disposable income − Consumption expenditures.

Disposable income = Income − Direct taxes − Other current transfers to
general government − Current transfers to the rest of the world.

Private savings = Gross savings − General government savings.
Disposable income = GNP − General government tax revenues.

Sources: Economic Planning Board, *Annual Report on the Family Income and Expenditure Survey*
(various years); Economic Planning Board, *Korea Statistical Yearbook* (various years); Bank of Korea,
National Accounts (various years).

Figure 8-7. Survey Household and Private Savings (as percentage of disposable income)

corporate, not the household, sector. Also, although the household saving from surveys does show some cyclical variability, it is not nearly as pronounced as the cyclical variability in aggregate private saving.[19]

Possible Explanations for the Rise in Household Saving

Two alternative explanations may account for the observed strong rise in Korea's household saving rates since the 1960s: a life-cycle or permanent income explanation and a "sluggish consumption" adjustment explanation.

Consider first the life-cycle model of household consumption behavior. This approach assumes that household consumption decisions are based on expected income to be received over the household's entire lifetime, and that prior to retirement, households save so as to finance consumption after retirement. Thus, other things equal, wealthier households (those with greater anticipated lifetime incomes) will tend to consume more during each phase of their lives than poorer households (those with smaller expected lifetime incomes). Similarly, wealthier households will tend to save more while they are working so as to finance larger consumption during retirement than poorer households.

An alternative approach focuses on household consumption decisions based on relatively stable, perhaps culturally determined, patterns and closely tied to current—not expected lifetime—income. This view would assume that a generally known life-style is expected by households with given real income levels. Households that anticipate high future income may resist consumption behavior that suggests they are living outside their means—based on societal norms from previous generations. Thus, it would not be surprising to find households with similar current incomes but very different expected lifetime incomes following similar consumption patterns. We turn next to the data to see which of these better explains Korean saving behavior.

Age and Household Saving

The life-cycle model of consumption implies three testable propositions about household saving and the age of the head of the household. First, the oldest households should consume more than their current incomes. Second, in a rapidly growing economy, young households have larger expected lifetime incomes than older households. Thus, if this framework is appropriate for Korea, increasing saving of young households should more than offset increasing dissaving of older households—even if the number of households is not growing—and should be a major factor in explaining the rise in total household saving. The third implication concerns the relative consumption growth rates of young and old households over time in an economy like Korea's, in which income growth was stagnant for a period of time and then consistently high. If consumption is tied to lifetime income, consumption of younger households, which benefit from rapid growth throughout their lifetimes, should rise more rapidly than consumption of older households, which benefit from rapid growth during only part of their lifetimes.[20]

To examine the first two propositions, we look at the age profile of household saving to see whether old households dissave and whether growing saving of the young accounts disproportionately for the rise in total household saving. The date for 1978 and 1988 for saving as a percentage of disposable income yield a humped shape of saving rates—lower for young and old households than for middle-aged households (Table 8-6). Studies have shown that Japanese saving exhibits such

Table 8-6. Saving and Age of Household Head

Age of Head of Household	1978			1988		
	Saving as a Percentage of Disposable Income	Saving as a Percentage of Total Saving	Percentage of Total Households	Saving as a Percentage of Disposable Income	Saving as a Percentage of Total Saving	Percentage of Total Households
24 and under	13.40	4.17	8.38	27.84	3.83	5.33
25–29	23.37	17.26	17.12	30.19	17.13	17.86
30–34	26.12	27.51	22.65	31.25	28.12	25.55
35–39	20.92	19.41	19.66	29.29	18.88	16.96
40–44	19.28	14.49	14.52	24.31	12.65	13.21
45–49	16.11	8.49	9.18	22.83	8.77	9.77
50–54	16.80	4.64	4.99	21.34	6.54	6.94
55 and over	19.84	3.44	3.49	24.72	3.97	4.37
Total	20.90	100.00	100.00	27.61	100.00	100.00

Sources: Economic Planning Board, *Income and Expenditure Survey* (various issues); author's calculations.

a hump shape, while saving of households in the United States does not.[21] In 1978, saving rates were highest for 30- to 34-year-old household heads and then declined. The 1988 saving rates show a similar pattern, also peaking for 30- to 34-year-olds, although rates increased for all age groups, with the largest increases for households under age 24, 25–29, and 35–59, so that the hump flattened out. But even so, the oldest households are not dissavers. In fact, households with heads who were aged 55 or older saved more on average than those whose heads were aged 40 to 54.

Table 8-6 also shows the percentage of total household saving accounted for by each age group and the percentage of households in each age group. The contribution of each age group to total saving can be decomposed into three factors: (1) the size of the age group (the percentage of households), (2) the average income of households in the age group relative to average income overall, and (3) the saving rate of the age group.

In 1978, the youngest group of households accounted for just 4 percent of total saving, although they were 8 percent of total households. However, this group had both a lower saving propensity and earned lower-than-average income. Households with heads aged 25 to 34 accounted for 64 percent of total saving slightly more than their share of households. Households with heads aged 40 or more accounted for 32 percent of total saving and 32 percent of total households. The pattern was nearly identical in 1988, with those aged 25 to 34 still accounting for 64 percent of total saving. Young households accounted for a slightly smaller percentage of total household saving, despite the jump in their average saving rate. This is because these young households declined from 8.4 percent of total households to just 5.3 percent.

It is not surprising, then, that the increase in saving between 1978 and 1988 was distributed across age groups in about the same way that 1978 saving was distributed across age groups: The households with heads under age 40 accounted for 68 percent of the rise, and households with heads over age 40 accounted for 32 percent of the rise in saving and 34 percent of total households. These figures provide little support for the hypothesis that younger households account disproportionately for the rise in saving, the primary explanation for why aggregate saving should rise in an economy with positive real income growth, according to the life-cycle model.

We now turn to the third proposition: that consumption of younger households should have been rising more rapidly than consumption of older households. The figures in Table 8-7 show consumption growth

Table 8-7. Average Annual Consumption Growth by Age of Head of Household, 1978–1988

Age	Consumption Growth	Per Capita Consumption Growth
24–29	15.8	17.1
50–54	16.4	18.7

Note: Consumption per capita is consumption expenditures divided by the number of persons in households.
Source: Economic Planning Board, *Income and Expenditure Survey* (various years).

between 1978 and 1988 for two groups of households—those with heads aged 25 to 29 and those with heads aged 50 to 55—and consumption growth rates per capita, scaling household consumption by the number of household members each period. The figures are not consistent with the life-cycle model, which would imply that consumption growth should be greater for younger households. Instead, consumption growth rates and per capita consumption growth rates have been slightly greater for older households than for younger households, suggesting that differences in expected lifetime income across age cohorts have not been a major determinant of differences in consumption behavior.

Thus, none of the three propositions from the life-cycle model about the relationship between household age and saving appears to be borne out by the survey data. In particular, the large trend rise in Korean private saving since 1970 cannot be attributed to a surge in the relative saving of younger households as their expected lifetime income rises.

Saving and Income Decile

We look next at saving behavior of different income groups, inquiring about the rise in saving from an average of 22.5 percent of disposable income in 1982 to an average of 27.5 percent in 1988.

In 1982, the poorest households consumed substantially more than their current income, and the wealthiest households saved 35 percent of their disposable income (Table 8-8). By 1988, saving rates had increased for all income deciles, with larger increases (in saving as a percentage of disposable income) for the poorer income groups.

Not surprisingly, the wealthiest households accounted for most of total saving in both 1982 and 1988; however, their share declined. In 1982, the wealthiest 40 percent of households accounted for 78.7 percent of total saving; by 1988, this share had fallen to 70.5 percent. Similarly, the wealthiest households accounted for most of the increase in total household saving between 1982 and 1988.

Table 8-8. Household Saving by Income Decile

Income Decile	1982					1988				
	Saving as a Percentage of Disposable Income	Saving as a Percentage of Total	Real Disposable Income[a]	Average Age of Head of Household		Saving as a Percentage of Disposable Income	Saving as a Percentage of Total	Real Disposable Income[a]	Average Age of Head of Household	
1	-31.03	-4.13	92.4	36.3		-15.67	-1.81	165.6	36.6	
2	1.70	0.04	151.8	34.4		14.72	2.74	261.9	34.8	
3	7.74	2.09	187.0	34.6		20.48	4.59	315.5	34.2	
4	15.46	4.82	216.1	35.0		24.43	6.27	361.3	34.2	
5	17.45	6.20	246.4	35.9		25.21	7.34	409.6	34.3	
6	21.81	8.75	278.4	36.4		27.32	9.01	464.0	35.2	
7	21.88	10.02	317.6	37.3		28.57	9.42	528.7	36.2	
8	25.86	13.80	370.1	37.6		30.41	13.30	615.6	36.7	
9	27.88	18.22	453.5	39.4		31.91	17.25	760.7	37.6	
10	35.04	36.69	726.5	40.0		35.47	30.62	1,214.8	39.8	
Total	22.49	100.00	308.5	36.7		27.61	100.00	509.7	36.0	

[a]Thousands of won, 1982 prices.
Sources: Economic Planning Board, *Income and Expenditure Survey* (various issues); author's calculations.

Almost all of the rise in saving of households in different income deciles between 1982 and 1988 can be explained by noting that wealthier households consistently saved more (that is, consumed smaller shares of the income) and that average real incomes for each income decile rose between 1982 and 1988. In fact, there is a remarkably stable relationship between real consumption and real income (deflated by the consumer price index), which can be seen by looking at the relationship between saving rates and real income or at the relationship between real consumption and real income.

The equation that follows shows the results of a regression of real consumption *(Cr)* on real disposable income *(Yr)*. There are twenty observations (ten income deciles in two years, 1982 and 1988). The regression estimates separate intercept terms in the two years (*D*82 and *D*88) and allow for the slope coefficient to differ between 1982 and 1988 (*D*88 × *Yr*):

$$Cr = \frac{65.88}{(4.67)} \times D82 + \frac{72.62}{(4.71)} \times D88 + \frac{0.56}{(0.01)} \times Yr + \frac{0.02}{(0.02)} \times D88 \times Yr$$

Adjusted R^2: 99.8

In fact, there is little evidence in the data that the marginal propensity to consume out of real income changed between 1982 and 1988. There is weak evidence that households in 1988 tended to consume more than households in 1982, given their income levels, but the intercept terms are not significantly different from one another.

This linear consumption function implies a saving rate that increases steeply as real income rises initially but that is increasingly less sensitive to real income at higher and higher real income levels. The saving rate approaches 44 percent (1 − 0.56) asymptotically as real income rises. Such a relationship accurately describes the relationship between saving rates and real income in Korea (Figure 8-8). The differences in Korean household saving across income decile and over time can be well explained by differences in real disposable income.

This behavior is not consistent with a strict life-cycle model of consumption and saving as an example will show. The average household in the eighth income decile in 1982 had a disposable monthly income of 370,000 won, consumed 273,100 won, and had a household head who was 37.6 years old. The average household in the fourth income decile in 1988 had nearly the same disposable income of 361,300 won (adjusted for CPI inflation between 1982 and 1988) and nearly the same consumption of 273,100 won, but this household head was 34.3 years old, three years younger. Given Korean economic growth, the latter

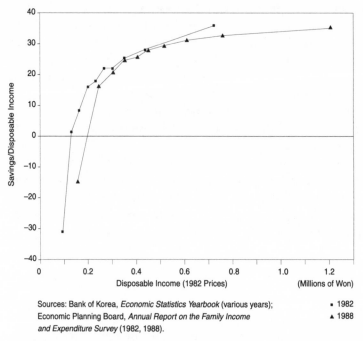

Sources: Bank of Korea, *Economic Statistics Yearbook* (various years); ■ 1982
Economic Planning Board, *Annual Report on the Family Income* ▲ 1988
and Expenditure Survey (1982, 1988).

Figure 8-8. *Household Saving and Real Income*

household had a higher expected lifetime income than the former household.[22] The fact that both households followed nearly identical consumption behavior is not consistent with a life-cycle mode; however, it is consistent with the alternative view of Korean consumption as being primarily culturally determined at each real income level.

Conclusion

Korea underwent a dramatic transition from persistent external deficits to large external surpluses between 1970 and 1988, and saving and investment are key elements of its macroeconomic performance. Although Korea did have periods of large external deficits financed by rapid debt accumulation, the anatomy of these external deficits was quite different from the pattern frequently observed in other developing countries: rising government dissaving and high investment—often public investment—preceding a balance-of-payments crisis, followed by an adjustment period that entails sharp cuts in public investment, declines in private investment, and stagnant or negative income growth rates. In contrast, Korea was able to maintain high rates of physical capital formation and strong rates of growth during adjustment periods. A central part of the explanation for this difference appears to be that government dissaving and surges in public investment played little, if any, role in causing Korea's external deficits. Instead, the data show that growth slowdowns are associated with drops in private saving and with increased inventory accumulation, leading to current account deterioration. The fact that investment rates do not collapse helps to explain why Korean growth rates do not stagnate during adjustment.

A related point is that the trend increases in Korean saving and investment, as well as the variations in saving and investment, came almost exclusively from the private sector. Korea's fiscal conservatism has led to stable government saving and government investment, which account for very little of the movements in national saving and national investment. Thus, Korea's striking transition from current account deficits to surpluses during the 1980s is attributable primarily to a dramatic trend rise in private saving rates. This rise emerges as a key to Korea's impressive macroeconomic performance.

The empirical examination of the determinants of investment and saving in this chapter showed that private investment rates rose strongly with real income growth and with expansions in domestic credit. The results suggest that credit availability constrained private investment activity. On the saving side, real income increases were the most important factor in explaining the rise in saving rates over the past two decades and that the large variations in income growth help to explain the large swings in Korea's private saving. Although saving is positively related to real interest rates, the effect is quite small. The trend rise in saving cannot be attributed to real interest rate increases.

An examination of the survey data on saving by urban households shows little support for standard life-cycle theories of household consumption and saving behavior. It was not a rise in the saving of the relatively young households that accounted for the observed increases in aggregate saving, and differences in household consumption by age group were not consistent with differences in expected lifetime incomes. Instead, observed saving behavior of Korean households appears to be better explained by a slow adjustment of consumption patterns over time, with household consumption for given current levels of real income based on historical or societal norms. Thus, consumption did not increase to reflect fully rising expected lifetime incomes. Of course, if new generations become used to higher income levels and if perceptions of appropriate consumption erode over time, the aggregate saving rate could begin to decline, with implications for the level of domestic investment that can be financed internally. Thus, Korean saving behavior promises to be a central but difficult-to-forecast determinant of future macroeconomic performance.

NOTES

1. Kwang-Suk Kim and Jun-Kyung Park, *Sources of Economic Growth in Korea: 1963–82* (Seoul: Korea Development Institute, 1985).
2. J. Williamson, "Why Do Koreans Save 'So Little'?" *Journal of Development Economics* 6, 3 (1979): 343–362.
3. J. Sachs, *Introduction to Developing Country Debt and the World Economy* (Chicago: University of Chicago Press and NBER, 1989), provides a discussion of the pieces of this typical pattern of a number of heavily indebted developing countries.
4. See S. Collins and Won-Am Park, "External Debt and Macroeconomic Performance in Korea," in J. Sachs and Susan M. Collins, eds., *Developing Country Debt and Economic Performance* (Chicago: University of Chicago Press, 1989), vol. 3, for a detailed discussion of these three periods.
5. Note that the data in Table 8-2 come from the national accounts. The difference between national saving and investment is foreign saving, which is equal to the current account deficit plus net transfers from the rest of the world.
6. The current account may be underestimated in official statistics for the early 1980s because of underreporting of imports. The large errors and omissions in the balance-of-payments statistics suggest that financing the current account deficit may account for an additional 5 percent of the external borrowing.
7. Korean national income and product account (NIPA) statistics have been revised, following the United Nations System of National Accounts, back to 1970. The previous NIPA data, which are not directly comparable with the post-1990 data, are available only through 1984.
8. Over the period 1970–1988, private saving as a percentage of GDP rose by about 0.76 percent per year, and real GDP growth averaged 8.95 percent per year. The estimated time trend in private savings as a percentage of GDP *(ps)* was:

$$ps = \frac{10.46}{(3.54)} + \frac{0.76}{(0.15)} \times \text{time}$$

Adjusted R^2: 0.61; Number of Observations: 19

(Standard errors in parentheses)

9. There are a number of interesting and informative studies of saving in developing countries. M. Gersovitz, "Saving and Development," in H. Chenery and T. N. Srinivasan, eds., *Handbook of Development Economics,* vol. 1. (Amsterdam: Elsevier, 1988), pp. 381–424; A. Deaton, "Saving in Developing Countries: Theory and Review," *Proceedings of the World Bank Annual Conference on Development Economics,* 1989 (Washington, D.C.: World Bank, 1989), and V. Corbo and K. Schmidt-Hebbel, "Public Policies and Saving in Developing Countries," *Journal of Development Economics* 36, 1 (1991): 89–115, provide recent overviews. S. Collins, "Saving Behavior in Ten Developing Countries," in B. Douglas Bernheim and J. Shoven, eds., *National Saving and Economic Performance* (Chicago: University of Chicago Press, 1991), pp. 349–75, focuses on saving behavior in Asian countries. The following publicatons look at Korea's experience: S. Yusuf and R. Kyle Peters, "Savings Behavior and Its Implications for Domestic Resource Mobilization: The Case of Korea," World Bank Staff Working Paper 628, Washington, D.C.: World Bank, 1984; Sang-Woo Nam, "The Determinants of the Korean National Saving Ratio: A Sectoral Accounting Approach," unpublished manuscript, Washington, D.C.: World Bank, 1988; and Maxwell Fry, "Saving and Investment in South Korea" unpublished manuscript, International Finance Group, University of Birmingham, England, 1991.

10. See, for example, the discussion in Yung Chul Park, "Korea's Experience with External Debt Management," in G. Smith and J. Cuddington, eds, *International Debt and the Developing Countries* (Washington, D.C.: World Bank, 1985), pp. 289–328.

11. Anticipated real GDP (in logs) was estimated with a simple auto-regression. The fitted values were used as the anticipated income series, and the residual was used as the unanticipated income series.

$$Log\,(GDP) = \frac{4.39}{2.22} + \frac{0.92}{(0.26)} \times Log\,(GDP-1) - \frac{0.36}{(0.26)} \times (Log\,GDP-2) + \frac{0.04}{(0.02)} \times \text{TimeTrend}$$

Adjusted R^2: 0.99; D.W. 1.88; Sample: 1971–1988

(Standard errors in parentheses)

12. A. Giovannini, "Saving and the Real Interest Rate in LDCs," *Journal of Development Economics* 18, 2 (1985): 197–218.

13. R. Dornbusch and A. Reynoso, "Financial Factors in Economic Development," NBER Working Paper 2889, Cambridge: NBER, 1989.

14. Fry, "Saving and Investment in South Korea."

15. See A. Mason, "Saving, Economic Growth and Demographic Change," *Population and Development Review* 14, 1 (1988): 113–44; Collins, "Saving Behavior in Ten Developing Countries."

16. See L. Serven and A. Solimano, "Private Investment and Macroeconomic Adjustment: A Survey," *World Bank Research Observer* 7, 1 (1992): 95–114, for a review of recent theories of investment behavior and empirical studies of investment in developing countries. S. Yusuf and R. Kyle Peters, "Capital Accumulation and Economic Growth: The Korean Paradigm," World Bank Staff Working Paper 712, Washington, D.C.: World Bank, 1985, an analysis of gross domestic investment in Korea over 1970–1982, yields results similar to those reported here. See also Fry, "Saving and Investment in South Korea." M. Dailami, "Financial Policy and Corporate Investment in Imperfect Capital Markets: The Case of Korea," PRE Working Paper WPS 409, Washington, D.C.: World Bank, 1990, and M. Dailami and E. Han Kim, "The Effects of Debt Subsidies on Corporate Investment Behavior," PRE Working Paper WPS 727, Washington, D.C.: World Bank, 1991, provide interesting analyses of determinants of corporate investment in Korea, focusing on alternative means of finance.

17. The Korean government offered extensive investment incentives as part of its export promotion strategy. See, for example, the discussion in Il Sakong, *Korea in the World Economy* (Washington, D.C.: Institute for International Economics, 1993).

18. See K. Schmidt-Hebbel, S. Webb, and G. Corsetti, "Household Saving in Developing Countries: First Cross-Country Evidence," *World Bank Economic Review* 6, 3 (1992): 529–547, for a cross-country study of household saving behavior.

19. Table 8-7 suggests that much of the cyclical variation in aggregate private saving is due to corporate saving or rural household saving, or both. This is consistent with studies of rural household consumption that show a large cyclical component to saving, associated with accumulation and depletion of farm inventories.

20. The point can best be made with a simple example. Assume households (each associated with a worker who is the household head) earn income from age 20 to age 60. Before 1965, workers earned an annual income of w. Each year since 1965, annual income has grown by 8 percent. Under these assumptions, it is straightforward to show that households with heads who are 25 years old in 1988 have a lifetime income equal to roughly 2.2 times the lifetime income of households whose heads were 25 in 1978. However, households with 55-year-old heads in 1988 have lifetime incomes equal to 1.8 times the lifetime income of households with 55-year-old heads in 1978. The increase is smaller because part of the lifetime income of older households was accumulated before the period of growth began.

21. See, for example, Fumio Hayashi, "Why is Japan's Saving Rate so Apparently High?" in S. Fischer, ed., *NBER Macroeconomics Annual* (Cambridge: MIT Press, 1986), pp. 147–210.

22. The following example illustrates that a household with a 34-year-old head should have a greater expected lifetime income than one with a 37-year-old head. Suppose that household i has a lifetime income of

$$L_i = \sum_{k=20}^{60} (W_i \times K)$$

where k = age of household, and real annual income grows at rate g: $W_{i,k+1} = W_{i,k}(1 + g)$. If at each age k, household A earns what household B earned at age $k + 3$, $L_A/L_B = (1 + g)^3$. For $g = 0.5$, L_A is about 16 percent greater than L_B. For $g = 0.8$, L_A is about 25 percent greater than L_B.

9

Korea's Balance of International Payments

Richard N. Cooper

When Korea's basic development strategy was formulated and put into place in the 1960s, the prevalent intellectual doctrine among those concerned with development was that shortage of foreign exchange was the most decisive constraint on economic development. This view arose partly out of the experience of Europe during the reconstruction from World War II. The shortage of hard currency was apparently overcome through Marshall Plan aid from the United States, combined with concerted export drives and trade discrimination against imports from hard currency countries. This prevailing view concerning the foreign exchange gap was one factor in the adoption of import-substituting development strategies in Latin America and other developing countries.

In the 1960s, Korea seemed too poor and too small to base an industrial strategy on import substitution; its lackluster growth under the highly protectionist policies of the late 1950s confirmed that. But the conviction that foreign exchange was the key to development and that extensive aid was bound to end sooner or later (as the U.S. government, the major donor, kept reminding Korean officials) left only the alternative of a policy of export promotion, which Korea embraced. Concern with the balance-of-payments constraint on growth has been a preoccupation of Korean officials ever since, even through the large current account surpluses of the late 1980s.

In fact, it is unlikely that Korea faced an effective balance-of-payments constraint at any time during the 1970s or 1980s, with the possible exception of 1971–1972. Although it ran persistent and often substantial current account deficits until 1986, it had no trouble financing those deficits, and indeed could have financed even larger deficits had it chosen to do so. This was true despite the world debt crisis that started in 1982.

The major reason that Korea had no serious trouble borrowing abroad was precisely because of its demonstrated success at raising exports year after year, thus earning the foreign exchange with which to service foreign currency debt. As is usual in the world of finance, those who need to borrow least have the least difficulty borrowing.

This chapter will review briefly the history of Korea's balance of payments over the past two decades; discuss in sequence the reasons for Korea's strong export performance, Korea's exchange rate policy, Korea's import policy insofar as it was influenced by the balance of payments, and Korea's approach to external debt; and conclude with a discussion of appropriate exchange rate and debt policies.

A Brief History of Korea's Balance of Payments

Korea spent forty years as a Japanese colony, was divided in half at the end of World War II (with the bulk of industry in the north and the principal agriculture in the south), and then became a battleground when North Korea invaded in 1950. South Korea turned to serious reconstruction after the cease-fire was negotiated in 1953, but throughout the 1950s it was heavily dependent for its sustenance on foreign aid, especially from the United States. As late as 1960, foreign aid was the equivalent of over 70 percent of Korea's total import bill and 7 percent of gross national product (GNP). Much of the foreign aid was in goods to be resold in Korea, generating counterpart funds that accounted for over half of the Korean government's budgetary revenues.

Korea undertook a number of economic reforms between 1964 and 1967 that anticipated the decline of economic assistance and laid the basis for its subsequent strong economic performance.[1] It devalued the won and unified the exchange rate, reduced and rationalized tariffs, and liberalized the granting of credit (although not to the point at which credit rationing ceased) and raised interest rates correspondingly. A number of special incentives for exporters, mainly tax concessions and subsidized credit, were also introduced.

Exports and domestic investment rose sharply, aided in considerable measure by the economic boom in the United States related to the military buildup in Vietnam between 1965 and 1967. The dollar value of exports grew 37 percent a year from 1965 through 1970. Net borrowing abroad on a substantial scale began in 1968, facilitated by government institutions and government guarantees, helping to finance an investment boom.

Gross investment increased by 6.6 percentage points of GNP between 1967 and 1969. This boom, combined with an effective real appreciation of the won, especially for imports, and the 1970–1971 recession in the United States, worsened the Korean current account.[2] Despite its strong export performance, Korea found itself in payments difficulty in 1971, with a current account deficit equal to 10 percent of GNP, up from 9 percent in 1970. Foreign aid continued to fall, and international reserves fell for the first time in eight years.

A major fiscal retrenchment was undertaken in 1972, price and import controls were tightened, the won was devalued in 1971 and again in 1972 by a total of 23 percent, and export incentives were greatly strengthened. Korean exports almost doubled in value between 1972 and 1973, aided by the world economic boom of the latter year. By 1973, the current account deficit had dropped to 3.7 percent of GNP.[3]

In May 1973, the Park administration announced an ambitious program for restructuring the Korean economy toward heavy and chemical industries (HCI), defined to include both ferrous and nonferrous metals, transport equipment (especially shipbuilding), and machinery (especially electrical generating equipment). This program had several motivations (see Chapter 3). Perhaps most important in the mind of President Park was the desire to lay the basis for a domestic defense industry in view of the U.S. withdrawal from Vietnam and the spirit of the 1969 Nixon Doctrine, which called for greater regional self-reliance.[4] Second, the Koreans thought that the stimulus to growth from light industry—largely textiles and apparel—would soon be exhausted and that the next stage of development, using Japan as a guide, was steel, metal products of various kinds, and chemicals.

Continuing concern about the balance of payments constituted a third motive. The plan sought to substitute domestic production for products that were accounting for a rapid growth in imports, while laying the groundwork for new export industries. It was recognized from the beginning that many of these activities were subject to economies of scale and that to reduce costs would require exportation.

The sharp improvement in Korea's balance of payments in 1973 was rudely interrupted by the threefold increase in oil prices decided by the ministers' meeting of the Organization of Petroleum Exporting Countries (OPEC) in Tehran in December 1973. Korea imports all its oil, and the OPEC price increase raised Korea's total import bill by $700 million—over 15 percent. In addition, Korea's investment rebounded from the depressed level of 1972 by over 7 percentage points of GNP; the two factors together raised Korea's current account deficit to 12 percent of GNP. Like many other prices, oil had been subject to government control and had been held down as part of the 1972 program. Nonetheless, Korea responded at once with an emergency decree, which, among things, sharply raised oil prices to world levels, a move that was extremely unusual among developing countries.

Korea negotiated a standby with the International Monetary Fund (IMF) in May 1974 and subsequently drew not only from the ordinary resources of the IMF but also from the newly created oil facility, designed to help countries cover their increased oil import bills temporarily. Korea devalued the won in December 1974 by 22 percent, to 484 won to the U.S. dollar, where it remained fixed for five years. Exports grew by 14 percent in dollar value during 1975, despite a severe world economic downturn. The current account deficit fell slightly from $2.0 billion in 1974 to $1.9 billion in 1975, and then dramatically to $0.3 billion in 1976 and essentially to balance in 1977 (Table 9-1).

The large deficits in 1974–1975 entailed borrowing not only from the IMF and the usual suppliers of export credit, but also from foreign commercial banks. A syndicated loan for $200 million was finally arranged in March 1975. There was also a modest drawdown of foreign

Table 9-1. Korea's Balance of Payments (in US$ million)

	Merchandise Exports	Current Balance	Direct and Portfolio Investment	Other Long-Term Capital	Short-Term Capital	Change in Reserves
1973	3,284	−299	93	507	3	353
1974	4,516	−2,019	105	939	697	−173
1975	5,003	−1,889	53	1,291	1,123	374
1976	7,814	−310	149	1,183	534	1,313
1977	10,046	12	143	1,257	−10	1,355
1978	12,711	−1,085	103	2,008	18	710
1979	14,705	−4,151	24	3,047	2,282	896
1980	17,214	−5,321	33	1,954	3,983	350
1981	20,671	−4,646	120	3,517	1,090	−244
1982	20,879	−2,650	−61	1,858	2,159	74
1983	23,204	−1,606	131	1,660	524	−171
1984	26,335	−1,372	406	2,606	−189	527
1985	26,442	−887	1,182	1,113	−333	158
1986	33,913	4,617	626	−3,197	−1,422	77
1987	46,244	9,854	305	−8,777	−462	2,104
1988	59,648	14,161	238	−3,645	−847	9,316
1989	61,408	5,056	424	−4,328	1,278	3,120
1990	63,123	−2,172	706	2,263		−1,208

Source: IMF, *International Financial Statistics* (various years).

exchange reserves during 1974, one of the rare years in which that occurred.

Full launching of the HCI program was delayed by the first oil shock but began in earnest in 1976. Gross fixed investment as a percentage of GNP rose from 24.1 percent in 1976 to 32.8 percent in 1979, an astounding increase of nearly 9 percentage points in three years. The surge put considerable strain on the Korean economy. The current account deficit rose from 2.5 percent of GNP to 8.8 percent over the same period of time, after briefly touching balance in 1977. The second oil shock began in December 1978 with a labor strike in the Iranian oil fields, and oil prices rose for over two years, reaching $33 a barrel in early 1981, nearly three times the price at the end of 1978. Once again Korea faced a large increase in oil prices, superimposed on a domestic investment boom. The current account deteriorated further in 1980 to $5.3 billion, or 11 percent of GNP. This was a slightly lower ratio than in 1974, and it would have been still lower if GNP had not fallen by 5 percent in 1980, due mainly to an extremely bad harvest.

In January 1980 the government devalued the won by about 20 percent and shifted from fixity against the U.S. dollar to a heavily managed float linked to a basket of currencies. By year-end, the won had depreciated a further 14 percent, and it continued to depreciate against the dollar until late 1985. An IMF program was introduced in March 1980 and again in February 1981, both involving some policy commitments and large loans to Korea. After a brief period of fiscal stimulus in late 1980 and 1981, Korea adopted a stringent stabilization program, designed mainly to reduce the high rate of inflation. Among other things, planned investment was cut back substantially, such that the rate of fixed capital formation declined about 4 percentage points of GNP from its peak in 1979 to 1981 and rose only slowly thereafter.

The combined effects of all these actions, along with modest growth in the world economy from the 1982 recession—the deepest since World War II—was a steady improvement in Korea's current account position from its deficit of $5.3 billion in 1980 through 1985 and the emergence of a surplus in 1986 that grew to $14.2 billion in 1988 before declining sharply in 1989 and returning to deficit in 1990. Outstanding external debt continued to grow as long as Korea ran a current account deficit and added to its foreign exchange reserves, but Korea began to prepay its debt in 1986, and at a rate in 1987–1988 that probably left it as a net creditor with respect to the rest of the world by the end of 1989.

The central point here is that Korea borrowed heavily through its two terms-of-trade-driven balance-of-payments crises and used the temporary relief provided from the second crisis to install a longer-term adjustment program.

Promotion of Exports

The outstanding characteristic of the Korean economy is its extraordinary growth in exports. In dollar terms, exports increased 21.3 percent a year over the fifteen years 1973 through 1988. Some of this increase in value was due to world inflation during the period, but even in volume terms, Korean exports increased 14.7 percent a year on average, a record that is matched only by Taiwan over such a long period. World trade (measured in U.S. dollars) during this period grew at an average rate of 11 percent, so Korea's share rose sharply. It is true that a substantial and increasing proportion of Korea's exports involved processing imported materials or parts, so that the growth in gross value does not measure the contribution to Korean income and output. Park estimates that the direct and indirect import content of exports grew from 26 percent to 38 percent over the period 1970 through 1980.[5] Applying these coefficients to the growth in export receipts over the period 1973 through 1988 still leaves a growth in export value-added—the contribution of exports to GNP—of 19 percent a year.

The strong export performance was not accidental or fortuitous. Starting in the 1960s, Korea introduced a variety of devices to stimulate exports: "preferential credit; indirect tax exemptions on inputs into export production and export sales; a 50 percent reduction in income tax on export earnings (abolished in early 1973); tariff exemption on imported raw materials and equipment for export production; wastage allowances on imported raw materials for export production; and government support for export marketing activities."[6]

An attempt to quantify the major export incentives was made in 1977 by Westphal and Kim. They find that in 1973 the combination of internal tax exemptions, customs duty exemptions, and interest rate subsidies totaled 94 won per dollar of export earnings, or about 24 percent of the prevailing exchange rate of 398 won per dollar. This total was down from 28 or 29 percent in the late 1960s, and it fell further to 17 percent in 1975 (81 won of implicit subsidy on the new exchange rate of 484 won to the dollar after December 1974). Of the export incentives of 94 won per dollar in 1973, 64 won were due to customs duty exemptions (down to 34 won by 1975), 22 won to tax exemptions (up to 34 won in 1975), and 7 won to preferential interest rates (up to 13 won by 1975).[7]

These calculations suggest that interest rate subsidies were relatively minor, amounting to just 2.7 percent in 1975, and even less earlier.[8] Probably much more important as a stimulus to exports was the credit allocation system, which for many years strongly favored exporting firms. This preference was tempered once the HCI program was fully launched, when many small- and medium-sized export firms in light industry found themselves at a disadvantage in receiving credit as compared with the newly favored activities.

One calculation of the effect of export incentives on the cost of capital to exporting firms suggests that the total impact of both financial and tax incentives peaked in 1969, amounting to a reduction in the cost of capital of 39 percent. This incentive declined to a low of 30 percent in 1973 but rose again to 38 percent by 1979. In short, the incentive was quite high throughout the 1970s. It declined sharply to 12 percent in 1981 with rationalization of the credit and tax systems, followed by a further gradual decline to 5 percent by 1986.[9]

Probably more important, export targets were established for the country as a whole, for each industry, and for major firms within industries. President Park met monthly with his key economic officials and typically asked for reports on export performance. If exports seemed to be falling short of targets, he wanted to know the reasons and what was being done to overcome them. This pressure was no doubt transmitted down the line and showed up not only in credit allocation but also in ease in dealing with the tax authorities on controversies over tax liability within their range of discretion, and perhaps even in land use approvals and other areas where governmental cooperation is needed for business firms to function effectively and profitably.

Export volume continued to grow at a dramatic pace, undeterred by the deep world recessions of 1975 or 1982, both of which seemed to affect Korean imports more than exports, perhaps because of large inventory adjustments of imported goods. The only decline in Korean export volume occurred in 1979, when domestic demand boomed, and a substantial real appreciation of the won took place due to domestic inflation that substantially exceeded inflation in Korea's major export markets, plus some appreciation of the U.S. dollar (to which the won was pegged) against the yen.

The major change in the basic structure of exports had already taken place before 1973, when manufactured goods accounted for 83 percent of Korean exports, up from 17 percent in the early 1960s. Among manufactures, the pattern between 1973 and 1988 showed both continuity and further change. Apparel remained the leading export category over the fifteen-year period, with textiles and apparel together accounting for 38 percent of total exports in 1973, 27 percent in 1980, and 23 percent in 1987. Steel rose sharply in relative importance during the 1970s, from 6 to 9 percent of total exports, but then declined to below 5 percent by 1987, receding to seventh place, behind consumer electronics, footwear, and automobiles (Table 9-2).[10] Like steel, export of ships also grew dramatically in the 1970s but declined in relative importance in the 1980s. Fish and plywood declined in relative importance throughout the period, as did tires and fertilizers in the 1980s. In 1973 exports of wigs were nearly as great as exports of fish and shellfish. Automobiles were the big new entrant of the 1980s, followed by office machines (personal computers, copying machines, and the like) and toys.

Krueger summarizes the export regime of the mid-1970s by saying that there was a clear bias in Korean trade policy favoring exports after the mid-1960s, that this bias did not change dramatically over the course of the 1970s, and that it depended more on destination of sale (overseas versus domestic) than on product category, although some differentiation among products did occur. Krueger then concludes that the bias toward exports was more moderate than many others have claimed, but it was a bias toward exports, in contrast to the bias against imports prevailing in many other developing countries.[11]

Westphal and Kim find an average effective subsidy to exports of manufactures of 8.9 percent in 1968, compared with an average "subsidy"

Table 9-2. Leading Export Sectors (in US$ million)

	1973		1980		1987	
	Value	Rank	Value	Rank	Value	Rank
Total	3,225		17,500		47,300	
Apparel	792	(1)	2,950	(1)	7,537	(1)
Textiles	453	(2)	1,778	(2)	3,382	(3)
Iron and steel	182	(4)	1,569	(3)	2,158	(7)
Footwear	106	(5)	874	(4)	2,756	(4)
Consumer electronics	33		839	(5)	3,608	(2)
Ships	24		618	(6)	1,138	(11)
Fish and shellfish	97	(6)	596	(7)	1,195	(10)
Thermionic valves	N.A.		517	(8)	2,396	(6)
Rubber tires	19		477	(9)	642	
Fertilizers	5		344	(10)	167	
Plywood	273	(3)	304	(11)	80	
Telecommunications	N.A.		248	(12)	1,369	(9)
Toys	N.A.		209	(13)	1,120	(12)
Office machines	N.A.		89		1,599	(8)
Autos	—		50		2,748	(5)

Source: Bank of Korea, *Economics Statistics Yearbook* (various issues).

on domestic sales of –6.5 percent, for a differential of about 15 percent in favor of exports. The highest effective export subsidy is 26 percent, applicable to intermediate products such as cotton yarn, pig iron, steel ingots, lumber, plywood, and petroleum products. Interestingly, consumer nondurable goods (including footwear and apparel) had an effective export subsidy of 4.1 percent and consumer durables a subsidy of 1.9 percent. Transport equipment (such as ships and autos) had an effective export subsidy of –5.6 percent, being one of the few areas (with consumer durables) in which the incentive for domestic sales was higher than for exports.[12]

One of the interesting facts to emerge from the Westphal-Kim study, which included detailed market price observations, is that the effective protection afforded by import tariffs was much less than the often high tariffs would suggest. This was in part because exporters were granted customs duty exemptions on their imported inputs, including capital equipment, along with a "wastage allowance" that often was far in excess of the actual loss of inputs during processing. The excess could be sold into the local market, thus lowering the effective import duty.

One aspect of Korea's export promotion policy deserves special mention. Following the first oil shock, incomes in all oil-exporting countries rose sharply, and these countries typically undertook substantial increases in public construction. A number of them, especially those in the Persian Gulf, were labor-short economies, so they had to import not only the construction materials but the skilled and unskilled labor as well. Korea took advantage of this new opportunity by fielding a number of construction teams that offered turnkey construction. The Korean firms would undertake the full responsibility for completing the project—for housing, port expansion, airport construction, and others—and then turn it over to the purchaser in running order. By 1977 overseas construction earnings were contributing nearly 4 percent of GNP. In 1983 overseas construction contributed $1.7 billion (2.2 percent of gross domestic product, GDP) to Korea's export receipts, and nearly 160,000 Koreans were working in construction overseas. By 1987 this figure had dwindled to 40,000. Weakening of the overseas construction market, combined with overexpansion and poor financial planning by some of the Korean construction firms, became in 1983 a source of embarrassment to the Korean banks that had lent them funds.

By 1983 preferential interest rates for export-related activities had been eliminated, although directed credits continued to account for 17 percent of total loans and discounts by financial institutions to the private sector. This figure had dropped to 11 percent by 1987. However, the share of export-related loans, including loans to foreign buyers by the Korean Export-Import Bank, rose from about 50 to 60 percent between these two years. Export credits to large firms were eliminated in February 1988, and those to small firms were reduced by about a third (per dollar of exports). Refunds of duties on imported inputs, which had been converted from exemptions to drawbacks in 1974, were also reduced from 100 to 70 percent. These were the equivalent of 7 percent of export value in 1983, about the same as in 1975, but had fallen below 6 percent by 1987.

In summary, Korea relied heavily throughout the period under study on export promotion, using a variety of techniques: directed credit, low interest rates, tax breaks, generous treatment with respect to imported inputs, and just plain exhortation. Over time these incentives were both rationalized and reduced, but as we shall see, export promotion remains a key element of Korea's development strategy and of overcoming potential balance-of-payments problems.

Exchange Rate Policy

Until 1980 Korea pegged the won to the U.S. dollar. From 1964 to 1974 it was devalued on average every two years. Then in December 1974 it was fixed for a period of over five years, until January 1980, and then devalued again. At the same time, the government moved to a formula for fixing the exchange rate that involved a weighted average of the U.S. dollar and four other currencies (Japanese yen, German mark, British pound, and French franc), adjusted by an alpha factor used by the authorities to allow for other considerations that might be relevant to setting the external value of the currency. In practice, this arrangement entailed a cumulative depreciation of the won against the dollar by 84 percent between the end of 1979 and the end of 1985, from 484 to 890 won to the dollar.

Since the U.S. dollar appreciated sharply against most other currencies from 1979 until February 1985, the depreciation of the won against other leading currencies was considerably less than against the dollar during this period. Indeed in 1982 the won actually appreciated slightly against the Japanese yen (Table 9-3). By the same token, when the won was fixed to the dollar during the late 1970s, it depreciated with the dollar in 1977 and 1978 against the yen and leading European currencies.

A depreciation of about 8 percent against the dollar occurred in 1985, even after the dollar began its sharp descent relative to the yen and the

Table 9-3. Exchange Rates and Trade Volume

| | Nominal Exchange Rates won per | | Real Effective Exchange Rate[a] (1980–82 = 100) | Exports | | Imports | | Terms of Trade (1985 = 100) |
	US$	yen		Value (US$ billion)	Volume (1980 = 100)	Value[b] (US$ billion)	Volume (1980 = 100)	
1972	393	1.30	93.7	1.7	23	2.3	37	142
1973	398	1.47	79.1	3.3	37	3.8	47	128
1974	404	1.38	80.1	4.5	40	6.5	49	96
1975	484	1.63	80.0	5.0	49	6.7	50	100
1976	484	1.63	88.5	7.8	67	8.4	62	110
1977	484	1.80	89.0	10.0	79	10.5	75	116
1978	484	2.30	86.5	12.7	91	14.5	98	126
1979	484	2.21	95.3	14.7	90	19.1	110	117
1980	607	2.68	95.9	17.2	100	21.6	100	96
1981	681	3.09	101.2	20.7	118	24.3	111	95
1982	731	2.94	102.9	20.9	125	23.5	111	97
1983	776	3.27	97.3	23.2	146	25.0	126	98
1984	806	3.39	95.9	26.3	168	27.4	146	100
1985	870	3.65	88.7	26.4	181	26.5	154	100
1986	881	5.23	76.3	33.9	203	29.7	167	107
1987	823	5.69	75.6	46.2	253	38.6	202	104
1988	731	5.71	82.3	51.6	284	48.2	229	104
1989	671	4.87	92.4	61.4	266	56.8	268	107
1990	708	4.89	85.2	63.1	276	65.1	303	112

[a] A decline in the index signifies real depreciation.
[b] f.o.b.

Sources: IMF, *International Financial Statistics* (various years); Morgan Guaranty, *World Financial Markets* (various years).

mark in February of that year, but then the won began to appreciate against the dollar, by a cumulative 25 percent between the end of 1985 and the end of 1988, while still continuing to depreciate against the yen until 1989.

This history suggests that Korea has had a proclivity toward fixed exchange rates long after the exchange rate features of the Bretton Woods system ceased to be operative in 1973. The won was fixed against the U.S. dollar until 1980, then to the dollar and the SDR from 1980 to 1988, with a tilt toward nominal depreciation of the won against the yen, the currency of Korea's leading model and competitor.

The nominal exchange rate does not reflect competitiveness insofar as inflation rates differ among countries. Much of the depreciation of the won over the years has served merely to offset a higher rate of inflation in Korea than obtained in the United States, Japan, or Europe.

There is no standardized method for computing real effective exchange rates, which try to take into account both inflation differentials among countries and the likelihood that in a world of floating currencies, the exchange rates among the currencies of a country's major competitors or markets may themselves have changed. Morgan Guaranty Bank computes a real effective exchange rate with respect to forty of Korea's trading partners, weighted by Korea's trade with them, and adjusted for relative movements in wholesale prices of manufactured goods. It is reported in the third column of Table 9-3.[13]

Perhaps not surprising, the real effective exchange rate has moved much less than the nominal rate, suggesting that most of the depreciation of the won merely corrected for higher inflation rates in Korea. Nonetheless, there are significant movements in the real effective rate, most notably the sharp appreciations in 1976 (from what perhaps was a very competitive rate) and again in 1979, when Korean exports actually fell in volume. Even more apparent is the sharp depreciation over the two years 1984 through 1986, a factor that no doubt played a major role in the emergence of the large Korean trade surpluses in the late 1980s, and the closely related pressure from the U.S. Treasury for appreciation of the won (Figure 9-1).

Given Korea's strong commitment to encouraging exports, it might be thought that Korean policy throughout this period was to maintain an undervalued currency (assuming that expression can be given meaning). This was not the case. On the contrary, in 1974, 1980, and 1985, the Korean government resisted IMF suggestions for larger devaluations than it undertook on these occasions. President Park also resisted advice for currency devaluation during the late 1970s, preferring instead a strong

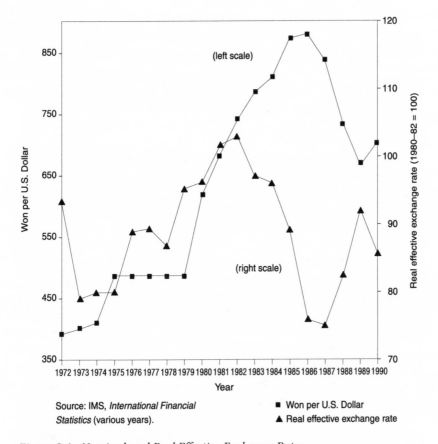

Figure 9-1. Nominal and Real Effective Exchange Rates

anti-inflation policy even when that entailed cutting back on HCI investment, to which he was strongly committed.

Several factors played a role in the 1979 stabilization program, and to some extent they were mutually reinforcing. Concern with loss of export competitiveness, brought about by accelerating prices and wages and manifest in declining export volumes, was certainly an important factor, but it cannot have been the only one, since currency devaluation would have been an obvious solution. President Park was committed at this stage to a fixed exchange rate, however, in part because of concern about the impact of a devaluation on domestic inflation. The fact that the dollar, and hence the won, depreciated against the yen in 1978 may also have eased the pressure for devaluation. In any case, devaluation did not finally take place until January 1980, after the recently assassinated Park had been replaced, temporarily, by President Choi Kyu Hah.

Even then, the devaluation was less than that urged by the IMF, and indeed by some economic advisers. The Korean Development Institute (KDI) was using a rate of 630 won to the dollar for its forward projections, and devaluation from 484 was strongly urged. In the end, President Choi reluctantly agreed but decided on the lesser magnitude of 580. Because of the shift to a managed float based on the SDR and subsequent developments, however, a rate of 660 won to the dollar obtained by the end of the year.

Public enterprises apparently did not favor a currency devaluation at this time, in part because they had acquired substantial amounts of foreign currency debt; devaluation would raise their debt-servicing obligations measured in won. Firms with sufficient exports, of course, would gain on the increase of their export revenues in won. Some large private firms and many small exporting firms, with less debt and a relatively greater stake in export markets, favored devaluation.

Jae-Ik Kim, who later became the leading economic adviser to President Chun, did not favor reliance on currency devaluation as a means to promote exports, however. To the contrary, he apparently considered it too easy an option because it would relieve exporters of the competitive pressures that were necessary for them to improve their products and their production efficiency.

The most important conclusion to be drawn from this review, however, is that despite the occasional sharp movement in Korea's real effective exchange rate, its variation over time has been relatively low compared with many other developing countries, particularly those in Latin America.[14] This outcome reflects the fact that, at least in comparison with many of the large Latin American newly industrializing countries, Korea kept its inflation under control and, except during the late 1970s, generally adjusted its exchange rate with sufficient frequency to keep it from getting badly out of line.

Import Policies and the Balance of Payments

Korea pursued a highly restrictive import policy during the 1950s, liberalized somewhat in 1961, but soon restricted again following the reemergence of balance-of-payments difficulties. A major liberalization was introduced in June 1967 as part of the redirection of Korean economic policy toward greater reliance on markets and market-determined prices.

These changes must be seen in relative terms. Korea's import policy remained highly restrictive by the standards of developed countries.

Tariffs were actually increased somewhat in 1967, leaving the unweighted average tariff rate at nearly 40 percent. The major liberalizing change was to switch from a positive to a negative list for automatic approval of requests for an import license; that is, after 1967 an import request was automatically approved unless it was specified on a list of restricted items. This change had the effect of increasing nearly fivefold the subcategories of imports subject to automatic approval. It meant that about 60 percent of three-digit Standard International Trade Classification (SITC) categories of potential imports were subject to automatic approval in the latter part of 1967.

This was to be a temporary high point for import liberalization. Items soon began to be added to the restricted list, especially during 1968–1969, 1972, and 1975, the latter two years being ones of substantial balance-of-payments difficulty. (It is noteworthy, however, that import restrictions were not greatly tightened during 1974, the year of the first oil shock.) By 1975 automatic approval had declined to a low of 49 percent of the import categories.[15]

Westphal and Kim calculate effective rates of protection (on the basis of tariff structure) and effective subsidy (taking into account also tax advantages and preferential credits) for 1968, which Krueger judges to have remained relatively unchanged at least until 1975, when her study ended.[16] Pyo reports, in contrast, that effective protection for all manufacturing (import competing as well as export oriented) rose from –1.4 percent in 1968 to 31.7 percent in 1978 and then declined slightly to 28.2 percent in 1982.[17] Direct import restrictions tightened somewhat during the period 1967–1975, especially during the payments difficulties of 1972 and 1975, but were substantially liberalized in 1978.

Resumption of liberalization was strongly influenced by the desire to control inflation, but was suspended during 1980, a year of the second oil shock and the decline in GDP. Liberalization was resumed in 1981 as part of the broader thrust toward economic reform, although the current account deficit remained large. Import liberalization progressed slowly but steadily from 1980 to 1988, during which time the percentage of import categories (7,915, at the eight-digit CCCN level) subject to automatic license approval rose from 69 to 95 percent, with the remaining restrictions falling largely on agricultural products, with only pharmaceuticals and silks among manufactured goods still being restricted (Table 9-4).

Scheduled import tariffs, which have not been the principal form of protection, declined steadily after the import reform of 1967. A new tariff schedule introduced in 1973 reduced (unweighted) average tariff rates from 39 to 31 percent. Further reductions in 1976 lowered the average

Table 9-4. Measures of Import Restrictions (in percentage)

Year	Automatic Approval of License Application[a]	Average Scheduled Duty[b]	Tariff Revenues Relative to Imports
1961	34.4	39.4	13.5
1973	52.1	31.3	4.9
1978	61.3	24.9	8.9
1983	80.4	23.7	7.0
1988	94.8	18.1	6.8
1990	96.3	11.4	5.6
1992	97.7	10.1	4.9

[a]Percentage of import categories subject to automatic approval.
[b]Unweighted.
Source: Bank of Korea, *Economic Statistics Yearbook,* 1993; Office of Customs Administration, *The Customs Journal* (various issues), courtesy of Soogil Young.

to 24 percent by 1983, although a number of individual tariffs were also increased, especially in connection with the HCI program. A new thrust toward import liberalization was promulgated in February 1984, leading to a staged increase in automatic license approvals and a staged reduction in tariffs over the five-year period 1984–1988. By 1988 the (unweighted) average tariff was 18 percent, and only 8.5 percent of tariffs, down from 38 percent, were over 20 percent. Provision was made for the temporary introduction of emergency tariffs to cope with import surges that injured domestic firms, but in fact they were used only sparingly, the main exception being to raise tariffs sharply on crude oil and petroleum products after the steep oil price decline of 1986, but that was governed by energy policy rather than by a desire to protect Korean firms. A new tariff reduction schedule was announced in 1988, designed to reduce Korea's average tariff to 7 or 8 percent by 1993.

Korea gave selected industries and firms many exemptions from import duties along with generous wastage allowances when that was thought to serve public purposes, such as promoting exports or, later, housing. Moreover, lower-duty import quotas were often introduced to combat commodity shortages in local markets or to inhibit inflation, a strategy that might work if the quotas were sufficiently large or if the items in question were subject to price control. As a result, tariff revenues actually collected were only a fraction of the scheduled duties, even after allowing for weighting tariffs by imports. In 1984, for instance, import duties collected amounted to only 7 percent of the value of imports, less than half the import-weighted average tariff of 15 percent. In 1973 duties collected had amounted to only 5 percent of the value of imports. This ratio rose to 7 percent in 1987, partly as a result of the petroleum tax.

In 1987 Korea established a five-member trade commission charged with examining claims by Korean firms for relief against import competition, determining whether injury occurred, and recommending what form of import relief, if any, should be granted. The goal was to make the tariff-adjusting process much more transparent.

In summary, although adjustments in the import regime played some role in Korea's balance-of-payments adjustment policies over the 1970s and 1980s, that role was far less active than is true for most other developing countries. Other developing countries have often relied on compressing imports as their first line of defense when they are in balance-of-payments difficulties but then find it difficult to relax fully the import restraints once the balance-of-payments problem has passed because domestic interests get established behind supposedly temporary import restriction.

Korea cannot be said to have embraced a liberal import regime during most of this period, and indeed it tightened restrictions somewhat in the early 1970s. But liberalizing pressures, particularly from within the government, were constantly present. By the end of the period, they had succeeded in establishing a relatively liberal import regime by developing-country standards. While this was finally established during a period of strong current account surpluses, it was planned and introduced at a time when substantial deficits persisted and the subsequent large surpluses could not have been foreseen. Indeed, substantial import liberalization took place in 1981 and 1982, years of large current account deficits and concern about the maturity of external debt.

Thus, the liberalization was undertaken as part of a program of macroeconomic stabilization, to contribute to reduction in inflation, and as part of the modernization of the Korean economy, one of the attributes of which was to keep Korean firms under competitive pressure so that they would continue to improve their product quality and production efficiency.

Reserves, the IMF, and External Borrowing

Until the late 1980s, Korea relied extensively on foreign resources for its economic growth. Foreign aid, so vital in the 1950s, declined in relative importance over the years and virtually disappeared by the mid-1970s, replaced by loans. Only rarely, until 1983, was the net inflow

Table 9-5. Exports, Imports, Current Balance in Relation to GDP
(in percentage of GDP)

	Exports	Imports	Balance on Goods and Services	Net Factor Receipts
1972	19.6	24.3	−4.7	−0.4
1973	29.1	32.1	−3.0	−0.7
1974	27.4	38.5	−11.2	−0.9
1975	27.9	36.5	−8.5	−1.6
1976	31.8	33.0	−1.3	−1.3
1977	31.6	32.2	−0.6	−1.5
1978	29.7	33.1	−3.4	−1.3
1979	27.9	34.6	−6.7	−1.7
1980	34.0	41.5	−7.4	−3.4
1981	36.5	41.5	−5.0	−4.1
1982	34.5	37.1	−2.6	−4.2
1983	35.6	36.1	−0.5	−3.3
1984	36.0	35.8	0.2	−3.5
1985	36.4	35.9	0.5	−3.4
1986	38.6	32.5	6.1	−3.0
1987	41.5	33.5	8.0	−2.2
1988	39.9	31.7	8.2	−1.4
1989	34.1	31.3	2.8	−0.8
1990	31.6	32.2	−0.6	−0.7

Source: IMF, *International Financial Statistics,* national accounts (various years).

of foreign resources (as measured by the current account deficit) less than 3 percent of GDP, and in a number of years it was above 5 percent, even after the reconstruction period of the 1950s and the formative years of the 1960s (Table 9-5).

Korea used external borrowing not merely to support domestic investment but also to build foreign exchange reserves, which rose from $523 million in 1972 to $12.3 billion in 1988. A reserve target is appropriate for a country with a rapid growth in international transactions that adheres to a (more or less) fixed exchange rate. The large increase in reserves in 1988 was mainly a passive response to other developments, but Korea has deliberately programmed for a steady increase in reserves; the growth to $3.3 billion in 1986, for example, was planned.

Korea's foreign exchange reserves were helpful on several occasions, but it is remarkable how little they were used. A drawdown in reserves to finance payments imbalances occurred in only six years during the 1970s and 1980s: 1971, 1974, 1978, 1980, 1981, and 1983 (see Table 9-1). Furthermore, only in 1974 did the drawdown in reserves exceed 30 percent of the current account deficit, and only in that case did a drawdown seriously deplete total reserves. Korea barely used its reserves betwen 1979 and 1981. So while for many countries reserves are useful and even essential, Korea overwhelmingly relied on borrowed funds to cover the great imbalances of the 1970s and especially those of the 1980s.

One of the sources of funds was the IMF. Korea has been a regular user of IMF credit. Total reliance on this credit increased from nothing in 1973 to SDR 302 million in 1976, declined to SDR 104 million in 1979, and then rose to a maximum of SDR 1,599 (about $1.6 billion) in 1984. Relative to its quota in the IMF, Korea's use of fund resources peaked at 446 percent of quota in 1982 but dropped despite additional borrowing because of a general quota increase in 1983. Throughout the period 1974 through 1986, except briefly in 1979, Korea one way or another borrowed in excess of 100 percent of its quota and more typically borrowed around 300 percent of its quota.

These drawings were made under several different facilities. Korea had ordinary drawings in 1974, 1980, 1981, and 1983, and it arranged a standby against which drawings could have been made in 1985. Such regular use of the fund is desirable, since it defuses public criticism of outside pressure for economic policy changes; use of the IMF never became the sensitive issue in Korea that it unfortunately has in a number of Latin American and African countries. In addition, Korea made use of IMF credit beyond the ordinary drawings through the oil facility created in 1974 to help countries deal with the first large oil price increase, and it borrowed under the compensatory financing facility in 1976, 1980, 1982 (under new provisions allowing drawings for unexpected need to finance imports of cereals), and 1984. In each case (except 1982), borrowings were on the grounds that Korea's export earnings fell sufficiently below the projected level of earnings to qualify, even though Korea's export earnings grew in every year, and on average at a remarkable pace.

By the end of 1988, Korea had repaid all its debts to the IMF. But the history suggests that Korea drew on the fund to the maximum extent that was permissible, perhaps because the charges on IMF borrowings have been lower than interest rates that would have to have been paid on borrowings from commercial banks.[18] (See Table 9-6 for outstanding IMF credits.)

Although Korea drew extensively on the IMF, its main sources of funds until the 1980s were trade credits and development loans. Direct investment and portfolio investment (that is, foreign purchases of Korean securities) were not significant sources of funding until the mid-1980s. Korea occasionally sought foreign direct investment actively, but foreign ownership was tightly circumscribed, and the regime under which foreign investors operated was not a generous one until the relaxations of the late 1980s. Korea also borrowed regularly from the World Bank, in amounts that averaged $337 million a year over the period 1975 through 1987.

Sales of bonds abroad began in 1974 but were limited in magnitude, and cash loans to private borrowers—loans, that is, that were not linked to specific import purchases—were generally not approved. Moreover, the government itself did not rely heavily on foreign loans to finance budget deficits until the 1980s, strongly preferring project loans or loans to be relent for specific projects, for example, through the Korea Development Bank.

This practice changed in the 1980s, when the government borrowed extensively from banks under its own name. Government revenues typically exceeded its expenditures during this period, however, so that in a sense, all government borrowing was for the purpose of relending, although not always for specific projects.

Debt, both external and internal, mounted rapidly in the late 1960s and early 1970s, with public plus private external debt (including short-term debt) reaching 34 percent of GNP in 1972.[19] The ratio of debt service (including interest but not repayment of short-term debt) to exports reached 21 percent in 1971.

As we have seen, the size of the current account deficit was of concern in the early 1970s, but the major concern with debt involved private domestic debt, especially to the high-interest curb market. In August 1972 the Korean government took the extraordinary step of nullifying all informal debt contracts and substituting lower interest, longer maturity obligations to reduce the debt burden on domestic firms.

At no point, however, did the Korean government raise doubts about its determination to pay international obligations. The external debt receded relative to GNP in 1973–1974 but rose sharply to 40.6 percent in 1975, due in part to the 1974 devaluation of the won, which increased by 20 percent the won counterpart of external debt denominated in dollars and other foreign currencies. Following a decline to 34.5 percent in 1978, it resumed its rise with the large deficits of 1979 and subsequent years (see Table 9-6). It reached 54.4 percent in 1982 and a peak of 56.8 percent in 1985 before declining sharply with the large repayments of the late 1980s. The debt service ratio, which is not so sensitive as the debt-to-GNP ratio to sharp changes in exchange rates, declined steadily from 21 percent of exports in 1971 to 11 percent in 1977, before rising year by year again to 21 percent in 1985, the 1971 level. The further rise in 1986 is artificial, since it reflects voluntary prepayment of debt in that year, a practice that continued in 1987 and 1988.

Table 9-6. Korea's External Debt (in US$ billion)

Year-end	Debt			Interest Payments[b]	Debt/GNP	Debt Service Ratio[b]
	Long-term[a]	Short-term	IMF Credit		percent	
1970	2.0	0.4	—	0.1	28.7	20.5
1973	3.6	0.6	—	N.A.	31.6	N.A.
1974	4.7	1.1	0.1	0.2	32.0	11.0
1975	6.3	2.2	0.3	0.3	40.6	12.7
1976	7.2	2.7	0.4	0.4	36.7	10.4
1977	8.7	2.9	0.3	N.A.	33.8	N.A.
1978	12.5	4.5	0.3	0.8	34.5	11.3
1979	14.3	6.7	0.1	1.0	32.9	13.7
1980	18.5	10.6	0.7	1.6	49.3	14.0
1981	21.9	10.2	1.1	2.0	50.3	14.7
1982	24.1	12.4	1.3	2.5	54.4	16.1
1983	27.0	12.1	1.4	2.4	50.8	16.3
1984	30.2	11.4	1.6	2.6	52.4	16.3
1985	35.3	10.7	1.5	2.8	56.8	21.3
1986	34.3	9.3	1.5	2.9	47.4	24.4
1987	30.0	9.3	0.5	2.5	31.0	28.9
1988	25.9	9.8	—	2.1	21.1	13.5
1989	23.0	9.8	—	1.9	15.6	10.7
1990	23.2	10.8	—	1.8	14.4	9.6

[a] Over one-year maturity, excluding IMF credit.
[b] Long-term debt only.
Note: Sources are not consistent. Where possible, World Bank data have been used. Long-term debt for 1979 is probably understated, as is short-term debt before 1978.
Sources: World Bank, *World Debt Tables* (1991–1992; 1987–1988; 1985–1986; 1984–1985); Park in G. W. Smith and J. T. Cuddington, eds. *International Debt and the Developing Countries* (Washington: World Bank, 1985) pp. 318–19, reproduced with permission.

Korea's strategy after the first oil shock was to sustain growth, borrow to cover the external deficit, and promote exports to cover the debt service and the increased import bill. It worked. Korea again increased sharply its foreign borrowing in the late 1970s, although the increase began before the second oil shock and was associated first with the increased investment in chemicals and heavy industries and then with some loss of competitiveness of Korean export products. Korean interest rates combined with a credibly fixed exchange rate made overseas borrowing attractive to private and public enterprises alike. Between 1975 and 1978 borrowing rates within Korea were about 10 percentage points above Eurodollar rates in London, for instance, even after allowing for the roughly 1 percentage point premium that Korea paid during this period.

A reevaluation of overall Korean policy and a stabilization program had already been undertaken before the second oil shock hit in force, followed in quick succession by the politically unsettling assassination of President Park, the sharp rise in world interest rates, and the disastrous rice crop in 1980. In these circumstances, Korea had to borrow extensively to avoid an even sharper drop in GNP than it experienced in 1980. Indeed, from the second half of 1980 through 1982, Korea pursued a modestly stimulative macroeconomic policy, with a view to resuming rapid growth, as well as reinforcing its promotion of exports.

Korea's borrowing tactics had several components. First, the government eased the conditions of import finance to Korean firms, for example, by increasing the allowable deferment of payments for imports and reducing the prior deposits required on imports subject to deferred payments. This strategy was based on the generally valid assumption that importers would prefer lower-interest foreign credits to domestic credit. Second, it encouraged the Korea Development Bank, the Korea Exchange Bank (which was well known in foreign banking circles), and the commercial banks (still largely government owned in 1980) to borrow more abroad. The borrowing of these institutions was facilitated by guarantees by the Bank of Korea. Third, the government also relied on drawings from the IMF and increased direct government borrowing overseas.

This approach led to an exceptionally sharp increase in short-term debt in 1979–1980, and by that time an increasing amount of long-term debt was also at floating interest rates, generally linked to the London interbank offered rate (LIBOR).[20] Thus, the substantial rise in interest rates in 1980–1981 added to the current account deficit and the need for financing. Korean officials became concerned about the maturity structure (as distinguished from the total) of external debt even before the Mexican debt crisis of August 1982, which ushered in a worldwide debt crisis focused on, but not limited to, Latin American countries. After the large burst of short-term borrowing in 1979–1980, Korea attempted to stretch the average maturity of the debt and succeeded in reducing the ratio of short-term to total external debt from 36 percent at the end of 1980 to 34 percent by the end of 1982 and 27 percent by the end of 1984, even while total debt was rising substantially.

After August 1982 the question of external debt became front-page news around the world, and Koreans were not immune to concerns about large and growing external debt. In particular, politicians in the government party began to raise questions about the external debt in 1983, and by late 1984 the question of Korea's large external debt—it stood fourth in the world, after Brazil, Mexico, and Argentina—had become a major campaign issue of the opposition parties for the parliamentary elections of February 1985.[21]

Nonetheless, Korea does not seem to have had any difficulty borrowing during this period. Raising external funding was a major preoccupation of some officials in the Ministry of Finance. In the early 1980s, bankers came to them. By 1984 they had to travel to the major financial centers, which reflected an important change in tone in the market for bank loans.[22] But by describing its situation, current policies, and plans for the future, Korea was able to borrow readily. Indeed, after the Mexican debt crisis, Korea found it somewhat easier to borrow. Banks were flush with incoming funds. Although OPEC surpluses had declined from their peak in 1980, they were still substantial and had to be recycled through the world's leading banks. Moreover, bankers had become much more cautious about the major borrowers of Latin America and were looking for new clients in Asia.

Y. C. Park argues that the policy of expansion plus borrowing that Korea followed in 1974–1975 after the first oil shock was not "a viable alternative" in 1980–1981. "The foremost reason was the questionable availability of the external finance needed to lengthen the adjustment period. Indeed, it is rather obvious that any further deterioration in the current account could seriously undermine Korea's credit standing in international financial markets and cripple its ability to borrow."[23]

This judgment, written in early 1984, must be given some weight in view of Park's subsequent role as a Blue House adviser, but it does not seem to be supported by the evidence. The premium that the Korea Development Bank had to pay over LIBOR for its syndicated bank loans rose to nearly 2 percent following the first oil shock but had dropped below 1 percent by 1978 and to 0.5 percent in 1982. It then rose by 0.25 percent or less following the Mexican debt crisis (Table 9-7).

Total loans to Korea from U.S. banks did indeed decline after 1983 (Table 9-8), but this decline is more than explained by the drop in loans with less than one year maturity. Reducing such loans by lengthening the maturity of the debt was planned by Korea, although no doubt some banks welcomed it. Korea substituted some longer-term loans from non-U.S. banks for the reduced short-term loans, and total commercial bank loans reached their peak at the end of 1985, when Korea was moving into current account surplus.

No doubt there is some path of Korea's current account deficit that would have raised questions in international financial circles about Korea's ability to service its external debt. But it also seems as though Korea could have borrowed some billions more than it did without jeopardizing its credit standing.

Table 9-7. Bank Syndicated Borrowings, Korea Development Bank

Signing Date	Amount (US$ million)	Life in years	Spread over LIBOR (%)[a]
1970	25	5	2
1974	80	10	1
1976	80	5	1.875
1978	250	10	0.875
1979	600	10	0.625(5)/0.75(5)
1980	600	8	0.875
1981	500	8	0.5(4)/0.625(4)
1982	300	8	0.5
1983	300	8	0.75(6)/0.875(2)
1984	400	8	0.625(3)/0.75(5)
1985	409	8	0.625(4)/0.75(4)

[a]The number in parentheses indicates the number of years the spread was applicable, in cases where the spread was stepped up.
Note: The bank issued two floating rate notes (FRNs) in 1985 and 1986. Both issues were US $100 million with fifteen years to final maturity and spread over LIBOR of 37.5 basis points. First put dates were five and nine years away, respectively.
Source: Morgan Guaranty.

A comparision of the twenty largest debtor countries at the end of 1983 shows that Korea was the fourth largest debtor, but in terms of its ability to service the debt, as measured by the debt service ratio, Korea stood fifteenth on the list, well below all of the problem countries (Nigeria's debt problems emerged later and arose mainly because of the very large amount of short-term debt) and even below some countries, such as Thailand, that were not perceived to be problem countries (Table 9-9). Korea's dramatic success at exporting—exports grew right through the deep 1982 recession—also permitted it to borrow readily.

Nonetheless, public concern in Korea about the growing debt burden led to a revision in April 1984 of the fifth five-year development plan,

Table 9-8. Commercial Bank Claims on Korea by Maturity (US$ billion)

Date	U.S. Banks Up to One Year	Total	All Banks Up to One Year	Total
December 1982	8.3	11.0	13.9	23.2
December 1983	8.3	11.5	14.5	25.7
December 1984	6.7	10.0	13.0	26.0
December 1985	5.9	9.2	13.7	28.7
December 1986	3.7	6.0	12.4	27.2
December 1987	3.0	3.8	13.0	23.8
December 1988	3.3	3.9	12.5	21.5

Sources: Federal Reserve, *Country Exposure Lending Survey;* Bank for International Settlements, *The Maturity and Sectoral Distribution of International Bank Lending* (various issues).

Table 9-9. Debt Indicators for the Twenty Largest Debtor Countries, 1983

	Total External Debt[a]		Debt-to-Exports Ratio[b]		Debt-to-GDP Ratio		Debt Service Ratio[c]	
	Amount	Country Rank	Percentage	Country Rank	Percentage	Country Rank	Percentage	Country Rank
Mexico	89.8	1	320.7	5	69.9	6	42.5	5
Brazil	89.0	2	365.6	2	29.5	17	52.3	3
Argentina	44.8	3	459.1	1	64.8	8	69.3	1
Korea	40.2	4	132.4	16	53.6	11	18.8	15
Venezuela	35.1	5	203.2	11	61.0	9	31.0	11
Indonesia	29.6	6	149.0	15	37.3	13	17.5	18
Philippines	23.9	7	294.1	6	70.4	4	34.2	9
India	23.4	8	199.1	12	12.8	20	15.1	19
Egypt	22.9	9	209.7	10	70.1	5	29.6	13
Israel	22.7	10	228.4	9	90.4	1	37.2	7
South Africa	21.9	11	102.0	19	26.4	19	19.0	16
Nigeria	17.7	12	150.7	14	26.5	18	18.5	17
Chile	17.1	13	356.6	3	88.3	2	55.6	2
Turkey	16.8	14	233.4	7	32.9	14	33.4	10
Yugoslavia	16.6	15	122.2	17	38.1	12	31.0	12
Malaysia	15.9	16	97.2	20	53.9	10	9.5	20
Algeria	14.8	17	108.6	18	30.2	16	36.3	8
Portugal	14.4	18	229.5	8	69.6	7	37.5	6
Thailand	12.9	19	153.5	13	31.5	15	24.9	14
Peru	12.4	20	323.9	4	76.9	3	46.1	4

[a]In billions of U.S. dollars.

[b]Ratio to exports of goods and services.

[c]Debt service comprises amortization of medium- and long-term debt and interest payments on debt of all maturities. Data refer to actual debt service payments (i.e., net of the effect of debt rescheduling).

Note: Data include all private and public external debt of all maturities.

Source: Aghevli, B. and J. Márquez-Ruarte, *A Case of Successful Adjustment: Korea's Experience During 1980–84*, Occasional Paper No. 39 (Washington, D.C.: International Monetary Fund, August 1985), p.21, reproduced with permission.

which covered the years 1982–1986. The revision called for a new target export growth over the remainder of the plan of 10 percent a year, an increase in the savings rate by 4.6 percentage points of GNP from the 24 percent obtained in 1983, and a ceiling on external debt of $50 billion by the end of 1986, the last change having apparently been reduced by President Chun from an initially proposed $60 billion. In fact debt reached only $45 billion by the end of 1986, in part due to the unforeseen "three blessings" of 1986: the sharp drop in oil prices, the sharp drop in the value of the dollar relative to the yen (thus increasing Korean export competitiveness with respect to Japan), and a further decline in world interest rates. Exports in 1986 grew by 13 percent in dollar terms and 12 percent in real terms, and the current account position swung by 4 percent of GNP, a measure of the improvement in national savings net of investment. These developments occurred even though Korea (modestly) missed meeting its target current account deficit of only $1.0 billion in 1984.

The sixth five-year plan, publicly released in early 1986 to cover the years 1987–1991, envisioned that Korea would run a current account surplus averaging $4 billion a year over the five years of the plan, or about 2.5 percent of GNP, for the purpose of reducing external debt.

Indeed, during 1986, before the sixth plan was to take effect, Korea began to repay its external debt, with initial emphasis on the short-term debt, which had peaked in 1982 and dropped by $1.5 billion during 1986. In 1987–1988 extensive prepayments were also made on long-term debt, especially by the Korea Development Bank, the Korean Export-Import Bank, and the Korea Long-Term Credit Bank, for which purpose they were given special loans from the Bank of Korea when they could not induce their own debtors to prepay.[24] The Bank of Korea also lent to private enterprises at attractive interest rates to induce them to prepay their external debt.

Debt had become such a sensitive public issue that little resistance was met by public enterprises that were able to prepay; their officials enhanced their reputations by reducing their outstanding indebtedness. From a macroeconomic perspective, prepayment was desirable if it could be done out of current earnings, for it helped to reduce the inflationary impact of the unexpectedly large current account surpluses.

Thus, Korea chose to build up external debt heavily during the difficult years 1979 through 1981, drawing very little on its foreign exchange reserves. During this period, Korea experienced unusual political uncertainty following the assassination of President Park in 1979, and it also experienced a harvest-driven recession in 1980. But funds were amply available in the world money market despite a severe tightening of monetary policy in the United States in November 1979, thanks in part to large surpluses by most oil-exporting nations, so Korea had no trouble borrowing abroad even during its expansionary policies of 1980–1981. Korea launched a program of adjustment, focused on the currency depreciations of 1980–1981, reinforced by wage guidelines and from mid-1982 by stringent fiscal and monetary policy. Exports responded smartly. The current account deficit declined by $2 billion in 1982, despite the world recession, and by another $1 billion in 1983. Korea's actions and performance were visible as the world moved into the debt crisis in late 1982, and despite its large outstanding debt, Korea appeared to be a relatively good credit risk as bank credits to Latin American countries dried up.

Conclusion: An Assessment of the Balance-of-Payments Constraint

How should we evaluate Korea's experience over the past two decades with respect to the alleged balance-of-payments constraint? Ex post, there clearly was no effective constraint, in that Korea has not since 1971 reduced domestic demand or investment explicitly for balance-of-payments reasons, as has so often been the case in many other developing countries. Moreover, Korea's growth during this period has been outstanding by comparison with all other countries except the three other Asian tigers (Hong Kong, Singapore, and Taiwan), which have experienced comparable growth.[25] Thus, it is difficult to argue that the constraint was binding. But was it present at all, in the sense that policymakers had to take it into account in framing the country's overall policy?

This is a difficult question to answer without further specification, since any country, even one that can borrow readily, can eventually reach a point at which its ability to service outstanding debt with surplus production of tradable goods may be called into question. But within the domain of Korean experience in the 1970s and 1980s, there was no doubt about Korea's ability to service its existing debts and even somewhat larger ones.[26] As Table 9-9 shows, Korea stood sixteenth among major debtor countries in the ratio of debt to exports, with a ratio well below those of the problem countries.

Moreover, most Korean debt was carried, directly or indirectly, by operating enterprises rather than by the government. This meant that the other possible constraint on ability to service external debt, the taxing capacity of the government, was not brought into play. About 80 percent of the long-term debt was government guaranteed in the mid-1980s; most of that was not a direct charge on the government's taxing powers but rather represented on-lending to revenue-generating enterprises, public and private. As a result, there was no effective fiscal constraint, real or perceived, due to government guarantees.[27]

The major reason Korea could borrow readily was its attentiveness to macroeconomic stability and the competitiveness of its exports. The periods of macroeconomic restraint in Korea's recent history, 1979 and 1983–1984, were governed more by a desire to reduce inflation and to improve the competitiveness of exports than they were by a market-driven need to improve the balance of payments. Indeed, Korea continued to borrow abroad during its expansionist actions of late 1980–1981. Public concern about the growth of external debt expressed in the mid-1980s, which led to a policy of debt reduction, ironically probably made Korea even more creditworthy.[28]

What about exchange rate policy? Balassa and Williamson argued in mid-1987 that the Korean won should be appreciated, on a real effective basis, by 10 to 15 percent.[29] In general terms, although not in detail, their position was also taken by the U.S. Treasury, which pressed for won appreciation and indeed opened special bilateral talks in 1989 on the subject.

By comparison with many other developing countries, Korea has had a relatively stable real effective exchange rate.[30] But it is possible to argue in retrospect that the sharp depreciation during 1985 was a mistake. Why was the won encouraged to depreciate against the dollar even while the dollar was dropping rapidly against the yen and the European currencies? This issue was discussed in more detail in Chapter 4, but the main answer seems to lie in a compromise among Korean policymakers. Businessmen complained of economic sluggishness during 1984 (a year of fiscal austerity, with the objective of reducing inflation) and called for economic stimulus. They would have preferred lower interest rates, which would reduce directly one of their important costs, but the authorities feared that might bring the stabilization program into question. As export orders began to slacken with the slowdown in the growth of world trade in 1985 and export volume actually declined briefly in the first quarter of 1985, the notion of accelerated currency depreciation became attractive, both to improve the cash flow of (export-oriented) business firms and to position them (through new investment) to take advantage of the faster growth in world trade that was forecast for 1986.

As a result of these calculations, the won was substantially depreciated during the course of 1985 and Korean exports did respond smartly to the trade opportunities of 1986: Korean exports jumped 28 percent in dollar terms. Currency depreciation in 1985 thus served in part as an instrument of stabilization policy, designed to pick up what seemed to be a slackening in aggregate demand. It also contributed to the current account surplus of that year, which, however, was larger than planned or expected due to the unexpected declines in world oil prices and world interest rates.

It seems likely that Korea shifted its basic macroeconomic strategy in late 1984 or early 1985. Previously, Korea had relied mainly on fiscal policy for the stabilization of domestic demand and output, and on export promotion, including currency depreciation, and (earlier) import restrictions to help correct external imbalances. In 1985–1986 it looks as though Korea relied on currency depreciation at least in part to stimulate total demand and output of the economy. In short, the extent of Korea's currency depreciation during this period smacks of competitive devaluation, an action that runs against IMF rules.

While it seems clear in retrospect that this depreciation was a mistake, even if the drop in oil prices had not occurred, that was perhaps less evident at the time. The IMF staff felt that if anything, the won was overvalued, and in the consultations leading to the IMF standby of July 1985, they urged an even greater depreciation than occurred, as they had done also in 1974 and 1980. Although Korean officials may be accused of engaging in competitive devaluation during 1985, this is a judgment that would have to be leveled as well at the IMF officials whose responsibility it is to discourage such actions.

NOTES

1. See S. Haggard, R. Cooper, and Chung-In Moon, "Policy Reform in Korea," in R. Bates and A. Krueger, eds., *The Politics of Economic Policy Reform* (Oxford: Basil-Blackwell, 1993).
2. See A. Krueger, *The Developmental Role of the Foreign Sector and Aid* (Cambridge: Harvard University, Council on East Asian Studies, 1979), p. 123.
3. Figures on the ratio of current account to GDP are from the national accounts. Figures drawn from the balance-of-payments accounts differ in detail but show the same general pattern.
4. A close reading of the doctrine, however, would not in any way exclude continuing U.S. military support for Korea, since the Nixon Doctrine specifically did not apply to countries with which the United States had defense commitments by treaty. See H. Kissinger, *White House Years* (Boston: Little, Brown, 1979), pp. 224–25.

5. Yung Chul Park, "Korea's Experience with External Debt Management," in G. Smith and J. Cuddington, eds., *International Debt and the Developing Countries* (Washington, D.C.: The World Bank, 1985), p. 294.

6. From Kwang-Suk Kim and M. Roemer, *Growth and Structural Transformation* (Cambridge: Harvard University, Council on East Asian Studies, 1981), pp. 46–47, citing C. Frank Jr., Kwang Suk Kim, and L. Westphal, *Foreign Trade Regimes and Economic Development: South Korea* (New York: National Bureau of Economic Research, 1975).

7. L. Westphal and Kwang-Suk Kim, "Industrial Policy and Development in Korea," World Bank Staff Working Paper 263, Washington, D.C.: World Bank, 1977, cited by Krueger, *Developmental Role,* pp. 48, 87, 122.

8. However, the differential interest rate for the rediscount of export paper as opposed to domestic commercial paper at Korean banks was 8.88 percent in 1975, 7.50 percent versus 16.38 percent. See Hak Kil Pyo, "The Preferred Order of Liberalization: The Korean Experience during the 1980s," unpublished paper, Washington, D.C.: International Monetary Fund, 1989, Table 1. This suggests Krueger's calculation may be low.

9. Results from a 1988 study by Taewon Kwack, cited by Kwang Choi, "Tax Policy and Tax Reforms in Korea," unpublished paper, Washington, D.C.: World Bank, 1990.

10. The ranking in Table 9-3 obviously depends on the definition of each commodity category, but the categories are fairly standard, and in any case they give some idea of the change in structure over time.

11. Krueger, *Developmental Role,* pp. 176–98.

12. The Westphal-Kim data are cited in ibid., Tables 48–50.

13. R. Lynn and F. Desmond McCarthy, "Recent Economic Performance in Developing Countries," World Bank Staff Working Paper 228, Washington, D.C.: World Bank, 1989, report a real effective exchange for Korea—and many other countries—for 1978–1988, citing the IMF as source, but they do not give the basis for the calculation. It broadly moves as the series in Table 9-3. However, the IMF database, presumably related to the figures used by Lynn and McCarthy, shows a substantially greater real appreciation of the won (21 percent) between 1975 and 1978 than do the Morgan Guaranty figures (8 percent). This is potentially significant in interpreting the reasons for the stabilization program of March 1979.

14. Among eighteen major developing countries, for instance, Korea's real effective exchange rate (IMF version) had the lowest coefficient of variation, with Mexico having twice and Argentina four times the variation. See R. Cooper, *Economic Stabilization and Debt in Developing Countries* (Cambridge: MIT Press, 1992), Table 3.4.

15. Krueger, *Developmental Role,* p. 129. There are 1097 import categories at the four-digit customs nomenclature (CCCN) level.

16. Westphal and Kim, World Bank Staff Working Paper 263, cited by ibid., p. 177.

17. Hak Kil Pyo, "The Preferred Order of Liberalization: The Korean Experience during the 1980s," unpublished manuscript, International Monetary Fund, Washington, D.C., 1989.

18. In 1982 the IMF charged a 0.5 percent service fee plus an interest rate of 6.6 percent for ordinary drawings. This compares with a London interbank offer rate (LIBOR) at that time of nearly 12 percent. Borrowings under the Fund's Supplementary Financing Facility were charged the Fund's borrowing cost—which would be less than the rate at which Korea or most other countries could borrow—plus 0.2 percent for loans up to three and a half years in maturity.

19. Various sources of data on external debt do not agree in detail. The disagreements arise in part from differences in coverage (e.g., whether short-term debt is included, whether the debt has been disbursed or only committed), and, when it comes to comparing debt with GNP or exports, what conventions are used for taking the ratio, since debt is a stock recorded at the end of the year, while GNP and exports are flows recorded over a calendar year. Also, external debt is denominated in foreign currency, whereas GNP is measured in domestic currency, thus requiring some convention for making the conversion, a matter that is especially important when, as in 1974 and 1980, there are discrete changes in the official exchange rate. But the general trends are what is important here, so we rely on Yung Chul Park, "Korea's Experience with External Debt Management," in Smith and Cuddington, *International Debt and the Developing Countries,* pp. 318–20 for the early 1970s, and the World Bank's *World Debt Tables, 1990–1991* (Washington, D.C.: World Bank, 1991) for the period since 1975.

20. In 1980 28 percent of Korea's public external debt was at variable interest rates. This was to grow to 49 percent by 1985. See World Bank, *World Debt Tables, 1987–88* (Washington, D.C.: World Bank, 1988), p. 207.

21. Not counting Canada, which is never mentioned in this connection, even though it is a larger external debtor than any of those countries; or the United States, which ran a current account deficit of $104 billion in 1984 and thus was beginning the process that in a few years would make it the world's largest debtor country.

22. This change in tone, reflected also in the nature of the questions bankers began to ask, apparently wounded Korean pride and led some

Korean officials to resolve to reduce the current account deficit in order not to be beholden to foreign banks. France went through a similar experience in 1982–1983, and it played some role in President Mitterrand's decision to reverse France's expansionist economic policy in April 1983. See R. Cooper, "External Constraints on European Growth," in R. Lawrence and C. Schultze, eds., *Barriers to European Growth* (Washington, D.C.: Brookings Institution, 1987), pp. 540–601.

23. Park, "Korea's Experience," p. 307.

24. Prepayment of debt is not as easy as it might sound, since, as with borrowing, there is a conflict of interest between debtor and creditor. If the outstanding debt carries a below-market fixed interest rate, the creditor is pleased to receive prepayment. But the debtor would prefer to prepay debts with above-market rates, debts that the creditor would prefer to remain outstanding. Korea had to negotiate with the World Bank and other creditors over the mix of debts to be prepaid, striking a compromise between the interests of debtor and those of creditor.

25. Only Singapore and Taiwan had higher growth rates over the period 1963–1985, and only Singapore had a higher growth in per capita income.

26. In an econometric analysis by D. McFadden, R. Eckaus, G. Feder, V. Hajivassiliou, and S. O'Connell, "Is There Life after Debt? An Econometric Analysis of the Creditworthiness of Developing Countries," in Smith and Cuddington, *International Debt,* pp. 179–212, McFadden and colleagues showed that in 1981 Korea was a more serious risk than many other countries that later developed debt problems, such as Argentina, Mexico, and the Philippines. But that study is marred by the fact that it identifies credit problems in terms of likelihood of developing arrears, requiring rescheduling, or borrowing from the IMF. As we have seen, Korea did borrow from the IMF, an appropriate action under the circumstances, and such an action is inappropriately lumped with arrearages and rescheduling as signifying debt problems by McFadden et al.

27. Furthermore, even if it were, the government had by no means reached the limits of its ability to raise taxes if necessary.

28. Still, it is difficult to avoid the judgment that repayment of outstanding debt by Korea, at least on the scale undertaken, was a mistake. The emergence of a large current account surplus in 1986 was in part a surprise, a consequence of the three blessings, and prepayment of debt out of such a windfall in current income is understandable and even desirable. But to encourage prepayment of foreign debt in exchange for higher domestic credit made little sense beyond the symbolic gain of reducing outstanding external debt. The average interest rate on Korea's outstanding long-term debt in 1986 was 8.0 percent. That represented

the average "saving" on prepayment of external debt. Yet returns to investment within Korea were roughly twice that rate. Although productive investment cannot always be undertaken on short notice, it can be geared up in a year or two. Especially in view of the rapid rise in wages, due in part to the export-led boom, Korea will want to undertake substantial labor-saving investment in the coming years.

29. B. Balassa and J. Williamson, *Adjusting to Success: Balance of Payments Policy in the East Asian NICs* (Washington, D.C.: Institute for International Economics, June 1987), p. 47. The authors rightly emphasize that import liberalization, including invisibles, should occur as well. Their estimate for the appropriate currency appreciation is conditioned on that action and on the assumption that Korea should run a modest current account deficit of $1–2 billion in the long run (p. 41).

30. According to Lynn and McCarthy, "Recent Economic Performance," Korea had a smaller variation in its real effective exchange rate over the period 1978–1988 than every country in Latin America except Honduras and Panama, and it tied for eleventh place out of sixteen countries of Asia. Most of Korea's variation arises from the 20 percent depreciation between 1984 and 1986.

10

Epilogue

Stephan Haggard and Richard N. Cooper

For the most part, the analysis of this book has covered the period of Korea's Fourth and Fifth republics, 1973–1988. With the inauguration of President Roh Tae-Woo in February 1988 began the Sixth Republic, which restored democracy with open, contested elections. This epilogue sketches the main events of the Roh administration (1988–1992) as they had a bearing on the formulation and execution of macroeconomic policy. We find some strong elements of continuity with the previous two decades but also some important modifications in the direction of economic policy (Table 10-1).

The principal political innovation was contested elections: for president in December 1987 and 1992, for the National Assembly in April 1988 and March 1992, and for local and provincial assemblies in March and June 1991, respectively. Mayors and provincial governors continue to be appointed by the president.[1]

The main issues of political contention, apart from personalities, concerned (1) the detailed nature of governance in the Sixth Republic, including the principles of electoral representation and the rights of individuals to organize; (2) the pursuit and rectification of corruption from the Fifth Republic; (3) distributional equity and the closely related issues of land prices and the role of the *chaebol;* and (4) macroeconomic questions, in particular the inflation of 1990–1991 and the economic slowdown in 1992. Under strong pressure from student groups, rapprochement with North Korea also became an important political issue with which the government had to deal.

Following the 1987 presidential election, attention turned to the issue of the electoral system. The system under Chun Doo Hwan was a direct descendant of the authoritarian Yushin system, based on a combination of two-member districts and a national list that heavily favored the ruling party. Moreover, district boundaries were drawn to favor conservative

Table 10-1. Korea Economic Indicators, 1987–1992 (in percentage)

	1987	1988	1989	1990	1991	1992
Real GDP growth	12.0	11.5	6.2	9.2	8.4	4.8
Consumer price index	3.0	7.2	5.6	8.6	9.7	6.2
Money growth	14.7	20.2	17.9	11.0	36.8	13.0
Export growth	36.4	29.0	3.0	2.8	10.2	8.0
Current account/GDP	8.0	8.2	2.8	−0.6	−2.6	−1.0
Budget surplus/GDP	0.4	1.6	0.2	−0.7	−1.7	−0.9
Exchange rate (won/$)	823	731	671	708	733	781
Money market rate	8.9	9.6	13.3	14.0	17.0	14.3
Monthly wages	11.7	19.8	25.2	20.0	16.9	13.8
Manufacturing employment	15.4	5.7	3.7	0.3	1.7	−3.4

Source: IMF, *International Financial Statistics* (various years).

rural voters. A complex and lengthy process of negotiation ensued that not only pitted the ruling Democratic Justice party (DJP) against the opposition but continued to divide the three main opposition leaders: Kim Young Sam's Reunification Democratic party (RDP); Kim Dae-Jung's Party for Peace and Democracy (PPD); and Kim Jong-Pil's New Democratic Republican Party (NDRP). The final proposal contained both electoral rules and redistricting provisions that the DJP believed to be in its favor and was passed in a surprise vote at 2:00 A.M. without reaching a final consensus with the opposition negotiators.[2]

Nonetheless, the system marked a reform. A proportional representation component was retained and districts remained gerrymandered, but the share of the total number of seats allocated to the national list was reduced from one-third to one-quarter, and their distribution was less biased. The two-member district system, through which the Chun government had captured two seats in conservative rural districts and the second seat in urban districts where the opposition was divided, was replaced by a single-member district system. The DJP had come to the conclusion that such a system would favor it because of divisions in the opposition; in fact, it tended to favor the opposition parties because of their strong regional bases. The DJP's share of the total vote dropped by only 2.6 percent, to 34 percent, but this translated into only 39 percent of the seats in the assembly. As a result, Roh Tae-Woo initially had to contend with the problems of divided government.

Yet he did this from a position of substantial executive power. The press law was relaxed and student organizations were permitted in early 1988. Trade unions and collective bargaining were allowed in November 1988. However, the National Security Law gave the government broad powers to arrest and detain anyone accused of forming or participating in antistate organizations, and a restrictive Law on Assembly and Demonstration was not amended until early 1989; the powers in the National Security Law in particular were used liberally in the offensive against dissidents and labor that began in 1989. The formal powers of the president in regard to the legislature also remained impressive, particularly with respect to the formulation of economic policy. Although the National Assembly deliberates on the budget bill, it does not have the power to increase any particular budget item or to create any new expenditure lines.

Roh's power was rooted not only in formal institutional capabilities, however, nor in the continuing power of conservative forces in the state and private sector. Despite the turmoil on the surface of Korean politics, Roh was also able to draw on substantial electoral and social support. His June 1987 reform speech as presidential candidate had been extremely popular, and during the campaign he played effectively on concerns about national security and the prospect of domestic instability were the opposition to win.

The economy, buoyed by strong export performance and then substantial investments in preparation for the 1988 Summer Olympics, was an obvious plus, permitting Roh to distance himself from his predecessor by outlining a more progressive social agenda. One of Roh's most ambitious, and economically controversial, proposals was a pledge to construct 2 million new housing units to respond to the rapid inflation of housing costs. The DJP introduced amendments into the labor law that guaranteed collective bargaining, collective action, and the freedom to form new unions, and it moved quickly to institute a minimum wage and a national worker pension program. Roh's campaign platform also converged with the opposition's in calling for the elimination of policy loans, progressive taxation of large landholders, and the implementation of a "real name" financial transaction system that would force disclosure of the ownership of financial assets and provide a means for more effective taxation. In general, rhetoric suggested a reduction of preferential treatment for big business.

Finally, Roh sought to preempt the upsurge of public support for reunification by announcing in July 1988 a new "Nordpolitic" aimed at reopening dialogue with the North and actively courting contacts with the Soviet Union, China, and Eastern European countries. His administration received a substantial boost from these policies following the historic summit on June 4, 1990, between Roh and Mikhail Gorbachev in San Francisco and the rapid move toward normalization that followed in September, well before the collapse of the Soviet Union in the fall of

1991. A reconciliation agreement was reached with North Korea in December 1991, which among other things was to proscribe aggression and permit family travel and commercial contacts. Normalization with the People's Republic of China, entailing severance of formal relations with Taiwan (and a subsequent boycott by that country), was achieved in August 1992. North Korea signed the Non-Proliferation Treaty but announced (and subsequently suspended) its intention to withdraw in early 1993 after International Atomic Energy Agency inspectors showed excessive curiosity about some North Korean nuclear facilities. U.S. nuclear weapons were withdrawn from South Korea in the fall of 1992. As of mid-1993, however, North Korea still had not agreed on the modalities for international inspections that had been agreed in principle in December 1991.

Roh began to move in a decidedly more conservative political direction by the end of 1988. Student demonstrations were muted in the first four months of the year by a tacit truce surrounding the Olympics, but after September antigovernment demonstrations began in earnest and became a persistent, and often violent, feature of Korean political life. The combination of labor strife and student unrest clearly alienated portions of the middle class that initially supported the political transition. With a cabinet reshuffling in December 1988, signs began to emerge that the government was moving toward a tougher position regarding social protest. Arrests of students, activists, and labor leaders increased, and the government sided openly with management in breaking several important strikes.[3]

The confrontation on the streets was matched by deadlock in the legislature that contributed to perceptions of government weakness. The opposition was completely preoccupied with addressing the legacy of the Fifth Republic, leaving a number of important issues in legislative limbo.[4] The perception of drift was heightened by the fact that in the second half of 1989, growth slowed, inflation increased, and the stock market began a long and politically contentious drop that was to take it to little over half of its peak value by August 1992.

In mid-December 1989, Roh reached an eleven-point agreement with the opposition on the major Fifth Republic issues, eased by a costly and ultimately unsuccessful scheme to support stock prices (stock prices rose briefly but subsequently resumed their decline). This paved the way for a surprising merger of the DJP not only with Kim Jong-Pil's conservative NDRP but also with Kim Young Sam's RDP. The result was the creation of the new Democratic Liberal Party (DLP), which despite some defections effectively controlled more than two-thirds of the seats in the legislature. This democratic coup not only froze out Kim Dae-Jung and his PPD—the only party with any appeal to the Left—but provided the political backing for a more extensive crackdown on both labor and the Left and for a complete turnaround in the pattern of legislative politics. In July 1990, the new party flexed its muscles by ramming through a cluster of bills that had been blocked by the stalemate existing prior to the merger; similarly, the DLP majority was used in 1991 to limit the extent of reform in legislation governing the police and in the revision of the much-reviled National Security Law.[5]

The power of the new ruling party was tested twice in 1991 in separate local elections in March and June. Despite low turnout, the DLP won large majorities of the contested seats in both elections, even in Seoul, where the opposition traditionally did well. The provincial election in June came on the heels of weeks of violent student protests. Strong support for the DLP was interpreted broadly as representing a backlash against the Left.

The March 1992 legislative elections, however, revealed clearly that support for the DLP was not equal to the support for its constituent parts. The party captured only 38.5 percent of the popular vote and was thus once again denied a clear majority in the National Assembly, holding 149 of 299 seats. Yet the conservative nature of Korean politics was under-lined by the fact that the most surprising gainer was not Kim Dae-Jung's new Democratic party, which had already moved sharply toward the center, but a quickly formed party on the Right led by business leader Chung Ju-Yung. An attempt to form a genuine leftist party in 1990 failed miserably, proving unable to capture a single seat. Despite substantial internal conflict within the DLP, culminating in Roh Tae-Woo's adopting a neutral stance in the election, Kim Young Sam won both the party's nomination and the presidency with a strong showing (41 percent of the popular vote against 33 percent for Kim Dae-Jung and 16 percent for Chung Ju Yung) in the election of December 1992 and was inaugurated president in February 1993.

Korea had experienced a strong economic boom over the 1986–1988 period, due in part to the "three blessings" of lower oil prices, lower world interest rates, and a stronger yen. How the government coped with the externally generated boom and the unexpected large current account surpluses has been discussed in earlier chapters. The government ran a large budget surplus and, partly in response to U.S. pressure, allowed the won to appreciate against the U.S. dollar through 1988.

In the spring of 1989 a series of major strikes occurred, starting with the Seoul subway workers. Political and economic demands were mixed, but organized labor pressed strongly for higher wages and improved conditions of work. Nominal wages rose during 1989 by over 25 percent, and by another 20 percent in 1990, compared with an increase of 12 percent in 1987; these increases were far greater than increases in productivity. Market interest rates rose steadily throughout the year. Profits were squeezed, but export prices also rose by about 5 percent, and Korea experienced a decline in the volume of its exports for the first time since 1979, despite strong world demand. Gross domestic product (GDP) growth fell by nearly 50 percent from the (admittedly high) growth of 1988, and industrial production grew by less than 3 percent—exceptionally low for Korea.

By the second half of 1989, the question arose of how the government would respond to conflicting political pressures on its economic program in the context of slower growth. The answer came very soon after the formation of the grand coalition. In March 1990, Roh reshuffled his cabinet, removing the three most important economic ministers, men who had been identified with a policy of stable growth, rapid liberalization of the economy, greater distance between business and government, and a concentration on issues of social justice and equity. Their successors emphasized their pro-business, growth-oriented credentials by announcing a new set of stimulus measures in April that included an easing of credit and interest rates and a corresponding breach in monetary targets. Previous efforts to get the largest firms to disgorge their land holdings were softened, as was the effort to move toward a "real name" financial system and greater taxation on property holdings. New financial supports were extended to exporters over the next year as part of a revitalization of industrial policy. Fiscal policy also changed, amid charges that the government was seeking to influence the outcome of the 1991 and 1992 elections. Proposed government budgets for 1991 and 1992 called for 10 percent real increases in expenditure, with greater targeting toward public investments in housing and the environment that had a strong pork barrel component.

Yet what is striking about Korea—and contrasts with a number of Latin American countries—is that the government moved to contain inflationary pressures despite looming elections. Even after the announcement of the April 1990 stimulus, internal policy debates centered on whether stabilization was required or whether the level of inflation was tolerable given the structural adjustments Korea required. Although the pro-growth faction prevailed initially, the acceleration of inflation in 1990 strengthened the hand of the stabilizers, particularly as critics of the administration began to charge that Roh was using macroeconomic policy to increase the probability of a DLP victory in the presidential elections.

In February 1991, the cabinet was once again reshuffled, bringing in a more conservative economic team. Roh's hand was strengthened in taking difficult policy measures by his surprising adoption of a neutral posture toward both the DLP nomination process and the election itself. Monetary and credit policy tightened in the second half of 1991, with market interest rates reaching over 19 percent, and a sharply contractionary budget for 1992 was submitted in the fall of 1991. The liberalization of trade and the financial markets followed a slow and circuitous route, but the general direction of policy was clearly toward a deepening of the market-oriented reforms initiated by Chun Doo Hwan.

The economy slowed markedly during 1992, partly related to a weak world economy (exports to the United States and Japan actually fell but were modestly overcompensated by exports to Southeast Asia and Europe). Industrial production grew less than 2 percent during the course of the year, and manufacturing employment had reached its peak in early 1991. The rate of inflation (consumer price index) dropped to 4.7 percent, half that of the previous year. Real GDP growth also declined to 4.7 percent, compared with 8.2 percent the preceding year. The year-over-year volume of imports fell for the first time since 1980, reflecting the weak overall domestic demand.

In a number of important ways, democratization altered the course of economic policymaking as the executive and technocrats lost the insulation they had enjoyed under Chun Doo Hwan. Business-government relations became decidedly more strained. Even following the policy shift of 1989, the government did not retreat from the effort to distance itself from big business; antibusiness measures were simply targeted more carefully at the largest industrial groups.[6] It is also clear that the new democratic government produced a substantial change in the composition of government spending, with a relative decline in the share going to defense and a greater orientation toward social spending. After a period of decline, the share of government expenditure in GDP began to rise again, from 16.0 percent in 1987 to 17.3 percent in 1991, and net lending by government rose rapidly, especially in connection with the housing program. Political sensitivity to farmers slowed import liberalization of agricultural products, and the government was decidedly more sensitive to workers than it had been in the past.

It is also plausible to argue that electoral politics imparted an inflationary bias to Korean macroeconomic policy during the Roh years, even when controlling for the positive external shocks of the mid-1980s. The government's commitment to a vast housing program, the stock market support effort, credit policy, and the ouster of pro-stabilization technocrats in 1990, along with large wage increases, had produced nearly double-digit inflation by 1991.

Yet when we view Korea from the perspective of the new democracies elsewhere in the world, the striking feature is the strong continuity in the most central features of economic policy, a continuity that can be traced to institutional features of the Korean system and, more important, the social base that had been created by two decades of export-led growth. At the broadest level, the government maintained and deepened the country's outward orientation, in part through selective liberalization, in part through a revival of industrial policy. A countercyclical macroeconomic policy and the aggressive use of the exchange rate as a tool were certainly not new, but these were associated with strong executive control over fiscal policy and a willingness to undertake difficult stabilization measures when required. Despite the tensions with the private sector, the overall stance of the government was clearly pro-business, reflected particularly in credit policy and an increasingly pro-management stance with respect to labor disputes.

The extent of this conservative consensus is clear in the role that economic issues played in the presidential election of 1992, a year of weak economic performance.[7] Kim Young Sam's platform called for a gradual reform of financial markets, including freeing of interest rates, slightly looser money, and tight fiscal policy. Deregulation would proceed gradually, with controls on big business and more support for small enterprises. Yet the proposals of Kim Dae-Jung—presumably the candidate on the Left—contained policy proposals not normally associated with the Left. He argued for a strengthening of the central bank, an immediate freeing of interest rates, conservative fiscal policy, and rapid deregulation, although with strong controls on the activities of the *chaebol* and a substantial easing of monetary policy. Business candidate Chung espoused a platform not very different. There is perhaps no clearer evidence of the strong underlying consensus that characterizes economic policy in the country, despite the apparently deep and contentious policy debates and political divisions.

NOTES

1. For an overview of the transition process, see Manwoo Lee, *The Odyssey of Korean Democracy: Korean Politics 1987–1990* (New York: Praeger, 1990).
2. There is debate about the determinants of the final outcome, a single-member district system that the ruling party initially opposed. D. Brady and Jongryn Mo, "Electoral Systems and Institutional Choice: A

Case Study of the 1988 Korean Elections," *Comparative Political Studies* 24, 4 (1992): 405–429, argue that the DJP gradually turned to the single-member district model on the assumption that it would divide the opposition, but they miscalculated its actual electoral effects. Tun-Jen Cheng and Mihae Lim Tallian, "Bargaining over Electoral Reform in the Republic of Korea: Evaluating Rational Choice Determinants of Political Decision-Making in Democratic Transition" (paper prepared for the American Political Science Association Convention, Chicago, September 1992), believe that Roh was pressured to move toward a fairer system by the same forces that had led him to call for political change in his ground-breaking June 29 speech. We find the Brady-Mo argument more compelling, but in either case it is clear that the government had substantial power to impose its preferences and that the formal properties of the electoral system proved less important for the direction of Korean politics than the realignment of the party system that occurred in late 1989.
3. For details of this shift to the right, see Asia Watch, *Retreat from Reform: Labor Rights and Freedom of Expression in South Korea* (New York: Asia Watch, 1990); Manwoo Lee, *Odyssey of Korean Democracy*, pp. 118–20.
4. The agenda of Fifth Republic issues included assigning responsibility for the 1980 coup and subsequent political persecution, and allegations of corruption on the part of Chun and members of his family.
5. Shim Jae Hoon, "Violent Clashes Reduce Parliament to Shambles," *Far Eastern Economic Review*, July 26, 1990, p. 13.
6. Chung-In Moon, "Bringing Politics Back In: State-Business Relations in South Korea since 1980," in A. MacIntyre, ed., *Government-Business Relations in Industrializing East Asia* (Sydney: Allen and Unwin, forthcoming).
7. E. Paisley, "Pocketbook Poll: Economic Woes Dominate Voters' Choice," *Far Eastern Economic Review*, December 10, 1992, pp. 20–22.

Select Bibliography

Aghevli, B., and J. Márquez-Ruarte. 1985. A case of successful adjustment: Korea's experience during 1980–84. Occasional Paper 39, IMF, Washington, D.C.

Amsden, A. 1989. *Asia's next giant.* New York: Oxford University Press.

Asia Watch. 1990. *Retreat from reform: Labor rights and freedom of expression in South Korea.* New York: Asia Watch.

Bai, Moo-Ki. 1984. The turning point in the Korean economy. *The Developing Economies* 20: 117–140.

Balassa, B., and J. Williamson. 1991. *Adjusting to success: Balance of payments policy in the East Asian NICs.* Washington, D.C.: Institute of International Economics.

Ban, Sung Hwan, Pal Yong Moon, and D. Perkins. 1980. *Rural development.* Cambridge: Harvard University Press.

Bates, R., and A. Krueger, eds. 1993. *The politics of economic policy reform.* Oxford: Basil Blackwell.

Bloomfield, A., and J. Jensen. 1951. *Banking reform in South Korea.* New York: Federal Reserve Bank of New York.

Bognanno, M. 1988. Korea's industrial relations at the turning point. Working Paper 8816, Korea Development Institute, Seoul.

Brady, D., and Jongryn Mo. 1992. Electoral systems and institutional choice: A case study of the 1988 Korean elections. *Comparative Political Studies* 24 (4): 405–429.

Brown, G. 1973. *Korean pricing policies and economic development in the 1960s.* Baltimore: Johns Hopkins University Press.

Casse, T. 1985. The non-conventional approach to stability: The case of South Korea: An analysis of macro-economic policy, 1979–1984. Research Report 5, Centre for Development Research, Copenhagen.

Cheng, Tun-Jen, and Mihae Lim Tallian. 1992. Bargaining over electoral reform in the republic of Korea: Evaluating rational choice determinants of political decision-making in democratic transition. Paper prepared for American Political Science Association Convention, Chicago.

Cheong, Jum-Kun. 1979. The process of Korean inflation since 1980 (in Korean). *Journal of Korean Economic Studies:* 94–108.

Cho, Lee Jay, and Yoon Hyung Kim, eds. 1991. *Economic development in the republic of Korea: A policy perspective.* Honolulu: University of Hawaii Press.

Cho, Soon. 1992. *The dynamics of the Korean development model.* Washington, D.C.: Institute of International Economics.

Choi, Byung-Sun. 1987. Institutionalizing a liberal economic order in Korea: The strategic management of economic change. Ph.D. diss., Harvard University.

Choi, Jang Jip. 1983. Interest conflict and political control in South Korea: A study of the labor unions in manufacturing industries, 1961–1980. Ph.D. diss., University of Chicago.

Choi, Kwang. 1990. Tax policy and tax reforms in Korea. World Bank. Typescript.

Choue, Inwon. 1988. The politics of industrial restructuring: South Korea's turn toward export-led heavy and chemical industrialization, 1961–1974. Ph.D. diss., University of Pennsylvania.

Cole, D., and Yung-Chul Park. 1983. *Financial development in Korea, 1945–1978.* Cambridge: Harvard University Press.

Cooper, R. 1992. *Economic stabilization and debt in developing countries.* Cambridge: MIT Press.

Corbo, V., and K. Schmidt-Hebbel. 1991. Public Policies and Saving in Developing Countries. *Journal of Development Economics* 36 (1): 89–115.

Corbo, V., and Sang-Mok Suh, eds. 1992. *Structural adjustment in a newly industrialized country: The Korean experience.* Baltimore/London: Johns Hopkins University Press, a World Bank publication.

Cotton, J. 1992. Understanding the state in South Korea: Bureaucratic authoritarian or state autonomy theory? *Comparative Political Studies* 4 (4): 512–31.

Dailami, M. 1990. Financial policy and corporate investment in imperfect capital markets: The case of Korea. PRE Working Paper: WPS 409. World Bank.

Deyo, F., ed. 1987. *The political economy of the new Asian industrialism.* Ithaca: Cornell University Press.

Dornbusch, R., and Yung-Chul Park. 1987. Korean Growth Policy. *Brookings Papers of Economic Activity* 2: 389–454.

Economic Planning Board. *Economic survey: Annual report of the Korean economy.* Various Issues. Seoul: Economic Planning Board.

Federation of Korean Industries. 1983. *Chungyungryun Isipnyonsa* [History of FKI: twenty years]. Seoul: FKI.

Fields, G. 1993. Changing labor market conditions and economic development in Hong Kong, Korea, Singapore and Taiwan. Cornell University. Typescript.

Fields, K. 1991. Developmental capitalism and industrial organization: Business groups and state in Korea and Taiwan. Ph.D. diss., University of California, Berkeley.

Frank, C., Kwang-Suk Kim, and Larry Westphal. 1975. *Foreign trade regimes and economic development: South Korea.* New York: National Bureau of Economic Research.

Fry, Maxwell. 1990. Saving and investment in South Korea. International Finance Group, University of Birmingham, U.K. Typescript.

Haggard, S. 1990. *Pathways from the periphery: The politics of growth in the newly industrializing countries.* Ithaca: Cornell University Press.

Haggard, S., and Chung-In Moon. 1990. Institutions and economic growth: Theory and a Korean case study, *World Politics* (42) 2: 210–37.

Haggard, S., Chung-In Moon, and Byung-Kook Kim. 1991. The transition to export-led growth in Korea 1954–1966. *Journal of Asian Studies* 50 (4): 850–73.

Haggard, S., and S. Webb., eds. Forthcoming. *Voting for reform: The politics of adjustment in new democracies.* New York: Oxford University Press for the World Bank.

Im, Hyug Baeg. 1987. The rise of bureaucratic authoritarianism in South Korea. *World Politics* 39 (2): 231–57.

Jones, L., and Il Sakong. 1980. *Government, business, and entrepreneurship in economic development: The Korean case.* Cambridge: Harvard University Press.

Kim, Jae-Won. 1988. Wage policy: A historical review of the past forty years (in Korean). Seoul: Korea Employers' Federation. Typescript.

Kim, Joonkyung. 1991. An overview of readjustment measures against the banking industry's nonperforming loans (in Korean). *Korea Development Review,* Spring 1991.

Kim, Kwang-Suk, and Jun-Kyung Park. 1985. *Sources of economic growth in Korea: 1963–82.* Seoul: Korea Development Institute.

Kim, Kwang-Suk, and M. Roemer. 1981. *Growth and structural transformation.* Cambridge: Harvard University, Council on East Asian Studies.

Kim, S. K. 1988. Business concentration and government policy: A study of the phenomenon of business groups in Korea. Ph.D. diss., Harvard Business School.

Kim, Soo-Kon. 1983. Income equalization policy in the context of the Korean industrial relations system (in Korean). *Korea Development Review* 5(3).

Kim Wan-Soon, and K. Y. Yun. 1988. Fiscal Policy and Development in Korea, *World Development* 16(1): 65–83.

Koh, B. C. 1985. The 1985 Parliamentary Election in South Korea. *Asian Survey* (25) 9: 883–97.

Korea Productivity Center. 1987. International comparison of productivity. Seoul. Typescript.

Korean Development Institute. 1982. *Gyungje Anjunghwa Sichaek Jaryo Jip* [Collection of materials on economic stabilization policies]. Seoul: Korea Development Institute.

Krause, L., and Kihwan Kim, eds. 1991. *Liberalization in the process of economic development.* Berkeley: University of California Press.

Krueger, A. 1979. *The development role of the foreign sector and aid.* Cambridge: Harvard University, Council on East Asian Studies.

Krueger, A. 1983. *Trade and employment in developing countries: Synthesis and conclusions.* Chicago: University of Chicago Press.

Kuznets, P. 1982. The dramatic reversal of 1979–80: Contemporary economic development in Korea. *Journal of Northeast Asian Studies* 1 (3): 71–87.

Lee, Manwoo. 1990. *The odyssey of Korean democracy: Korean politics 1987–1990.* New York: Praeger.

Lee, Tong-Hun, and Han Sil. 1987. On measuring the relative size of the unregulated to the regulated money market over time. Ilhae Institute, Seoul. Typescript.

Lindauer et al. 1991. Korea: The strains of economic growth. Harvard Institute for International Development, Cambridge. Typescript.

Mason et al. 1980. *The economic and social modernization of the Republic of Korea.* Cambridge: Harvard University Press.

McKinnon, R. 1973. *Money and capital in economic development.* Washington, D.C.: Brookings Institution.

Ministry of Finance. 1978. *Jaijung Gumyung Samsipnyonsa* [Thirty-year history of finance and banking]. Seoul: Ministry of Finance.

Moon, Chung-In. 1988. The demise of the developmentalist state? The politics of stabilization and structural adjustment. *Journal of Developing Societies* 4: 67–84.

Moon, Chung-In. 1983. Political economy of third world bilateralism: The Korean-Saudi Arabian connection, 1973–84. Ph.D. diss., University of Maryland.

Moon, Pal-Yong, and Bong-Soon Kang. 1989. *Trade, exchange rate, and agricultural pricing policies in the Republic of Korea.* Washington, D.C.: World Bank Comparative Studies.

Nam, Sang-Woo. 1984. Korea's stabilization efforts since the late 1970s. Working Paper 8405. Korea Development Institute, Seoul.

Nam, Sang-Woo. 1988. The determinants of the Korean national saving ratio: A sectoral accounting approach. World Bank, Washington, D.C. Typescript.

Nam, Sang-Woo. 1989. Liberalization of the Korean financial and capital markets. Korea Development Institute, Seoul. Typescript.

Nam, Sang-Woo, and Duckhoon Lee. 1989. Monetary transmission mechanism and recommendations for monetary policy (in Korean). *KDI Quarterly Economic Outlook,* Second Quarter 1989.

Park, Chung Hee. 1963. *Our Nation's path: Ideology of social reconstruction.* Seoul: Hollym.

Park, Se-Il. 1987. *Wage policy in an open economy: The case of Korea* (in Korean). Seoul: Korea Economic Research Institute.

Park, Yung-Chul. 1986. Foreign debt, balance of payments, and growth prospects: The case of South Korea, 1965–1988. *World Development* 14 (8): 1019–58.

Pylo, Hak Kil. 1989. The preferred order of liberalization: The Korean experience during the 1980s. IMF. Typescript.

Rhee, Jong-Chan. 1991. The limits of authoritarian state capacities: The state-controlled capitalist collective action for industrial adjustment in Korea, 1973–87. Ph.D. diss., University of Pennsylvania.

Ro, Sung-Tae, and Eun-Duk Sakong. 1988. A St. Louis model of the Korean economy. *Korea Development Review* Spring: 19–34.

Sachs, J. 1985. External debt and macroeconomic performance in Latin America and East Asia. *Brookings Papers on Economic Activity* 2: 523–64.

Sachs, J., and S. Collins, eds. 1989. *Developing country debt and economic performance.* Chicago: University of Chicago Press.

Sakong, Il. 1993. *Korea in the world economy.* Washington, D.C.: Institute for International Economics.

Shaw, E. 1973. *Financial deepening in economic development.* New York: Oxford University Press.

Song, Byung-Nak. 1990. *The rise of the Korean economy.* Hong Kong: Oxford University Press.

Stern et al. 1992. Industrialization and the state: The Korean heavy and chemical industry drive. Harvard Institute for International Development, Cambridge. Typescript.

Tan, A., and B. Kapur, eds. 1986. *Pacific growth and financial interdependence.* Sydney: Allen & Unwin.

Yusuf, S., and R. Kyle Peters. 1984. Savings behavior and its implications for domestic resource mobilization: The case of Korea. World Bank Staff Working Paper No. 628. World Bank, Washington, D.C.

Yusuf, S., and R. Kyle Peters. 1985. Capital accumulation and economic growth: The Korean paradigm. World Bank Staff Working Paper No. 712. World Bank, Washington, D.C.

West, James W., and Edward J. Baker. 1988. The 1987 constitutional reforms in South Korea: Electoral process and judicial independence. *Harvard Human Rights Yearbook.* Spring.

Whang, In-Joung. 1986. Korea's economic management for structural adjustment in the 1980s. Paper presented at the World Bank/Korea Development Institute Working Party Meeting on "Structural Adjustment in the NICs: Lessons from Korea," 19–20 June, at World Bank, Washington, D.C.

Williamson, J. 1979. Why do Koreans save 'so little'? *Journal of Development Economics* 6 (3): 343–62.

Woo, Jung-Eun. 1991. *Race to the swift.* New York: Columbia University Press.

World Bank. 1987. *Korea: Managing the industrial transition.* Washington D.C.: World Bank.

Index

Agricultural subsidies, 57
Agriculture, 9
  decline of, 186
  labor force in, 189–90
  wages in, 210–12
Algeria, external debt of, 285
Argentina, external debt of, 282, 285
Asian Development Bank, 125
Assembly and Demonstration, Law
    on, 297
Asset growth, 176

Balance of payments, 14–15, 38
  exchange rates and, 270–74
  exports and, 266–270
  external borrowing and, 277–87
  history of, 262–66
  imports and, 274–77
  table of, 1973–1990, 264
Bank credit, allocation of, 52
Bank of Korea, 10, 11, 12, 27, 59,
    63, 92, 113, 138, 170
  charter of, 151–52
  control over credit, 156
  earnings of, 123
  and external borrowing, 282
  Fertilizer Account in, 164
  functions of, 121–24
  independence of, 180
  interest rate regulation by, 160
  and monetary policy, 145–46,
    147, 151–53
  and monetary targeting, 163
  open market operations of, 167
  rediscounts and, 156
  reserve requirement of, 153, 155,
    156

  stabilization efforts by, 133
Banker's Association, 157
Bankruptcy, avoidance of, 138
Banks
  commercial, 149, 283–84
  privatization of, 12
  types of, 147–49
Bloomfield, Arthur, 125
Brazil, external debt of, 282, 285
Bretton Woods, 31, 272
Brown, G., 159
Budget
  breakdown of, 113–15
  deficits in, 9, 124–26
  governance of, 115–16
  influence on distribution, 127–29
  influence on economic growth,
    127
  influence on economic stabiliza-
    tion, 129–34
  of 1987, 113–15
  as policy instrument, 126–41
  role of, 111
Business-government nexus
    (*chungkyung yuchak*), 25

Caltex Oil Co., 37
Capital markets, 178
Chase Manhattan Bank, 39
Cheong Mun-Kun, 168
Chief executive, economic role of,
    6–7
Chile, external debt of, 285
China, normalization of relations
    with, 298
Choi Byung-Sun, 60
Choi Kyu Hah, 67, 273, 274

Chong Jae-Sok, 62
Chun Doo Hwan, 6, 7, 8, 17, 50,
    51, 56, 67, 76, 68, 94, 95,
    101, 118, 132, 138, 286, 301
  electoral system under, 295–96
  labor laws of, 216
  macroeconomic policy of, 78–94
  monetary policy of, 163, 165
  philosophical stance of, 79
  repression under, 79
Chung Ju-Yung, 96, 299
Chung Seung-Hwa, 67
Cole, D., 170
Collins, S., 40
Colombia
  fiscal tradition of, 141
  taxation in, 115
Comprehensive Stabilization Pro-
    gram, 166
Consultative Group on Develop-
    ment Assistance to Korea, 37
Consumer Price Index 1980–1984,
    88
Corbo, V., 40
Cost of borrowing, 52
Credit
  constraint of, 243
  domestic, 162
  policy uses of, 11–12
  rationing of, 158–59, 160–61
  See also Loans
Credit expansion, 31
Credit policies, 90–91
  in 1985, 95
Curb lending, 170, 172–73
  rates of, 171
  reasons for, 177
  scandals in , 85–86, 91, 166
Currency devaluation, 31, 50, 78,
    97, 264, 265, 270, 274

Debt. *See* Credit; Domestic debt;
    External debt; Loans
Debt interest, 113, 114
Defense expenditures, 113, 114,
    136–37, 139
Deficits
  external, 233, 235–36
  justifications for, 112
Democratic elections, 295
Democratic Justice Party, 80, 93,
    296, 298
Democratic Liberal Party, 298, 299

Democratic Party, 299
Democratization, 8, 93–94, 179, 296
  effects of, 219, 301
  labor movements in, 219
Devaluation, currency, 31, 50, 78,
    97, 264, 265, 270, 274
Distribution systems, 127–29
Domestic credit, 67
  defined, 162
  government control over, 156–57
Dornbusch, R., 207

Economic development
  advantages of, 140
  budgetary role in, 127
  costs of, 113, 114
  government role in, 140
Economic indicators, 25, 26, 29–30
  1976–1980, 50
  1978–1986, 84
  1979–1985, 76
  1984–1988, 95
  1987–1992, 296
Economic performance, 4
Economic and Science Examination
    Council, 63
Economic Planning Board (EPB), 6,
    10, 67, 68, 79, 129
  budgetary role of, 115–16
  and monetary policy, 146
Economic Stability and Growth,
    Emergency Measures regard-
    ing, 32
Education expenditures, 113, 114,
    137
Egypt, external debt of, 285
Electoral system
  democratic, 295
  under Chun Doo Hwan, 295–96
Employment
  composition by occupation, 192
  composition by type of work, 191
  expansion of, 187–88
  growth in 1991, 301
  status of workers, 193
Employment structure, 188–89
Exchange rates, 31, 77, 270–74, 281
  computation of, 272
  in 1984–1986, 97
  nominal vs. real, 273
  and trade volume, 271
Exports, 262–65
  importance of, 266

promotion of, 266–70
related to GDP, 278
types of, 267–68
volume of, 267
External debt, 9, 14, 54, 234,
    235–36, 277–87, 285
  borrowing strategies for, 282
  to build reserves, 278
  as campaign issue, 282
  commercial banks and, 283, 284
  IMF and, 278–79
  increase in 1979–1980, 282
  1970–1990, 281
  1979–1982, 87
  servicing of, 285–87
  World Bank and, 280
External deficits, 233, 235–36
External shocks to economy
  in 1974, 15–16
  in 1979–1981, 15–16, 17

Federation of Korean Industries,
    31, 32, 82, 91, 92
Federation of Korean Trade
    Unions, 27, 101, 215–16
Fifth five-year plan, 80
Fifth Republic, 7
Financial institutions, 147–51
  banking, 147–49
  government control over, 151
  nonbank, 150
Financial interrelationship ratio, 175
First oil shock, 23–24, 265
  economic effects of, 37–38
  government response to, 29–30,
    35–41
Fiscal impulse, 130–32
Fiscal policy, 9–10
Fiscal policy reform, 11, 12
Fiscal structure, 89
Fiscal tradition, 141
Foreign debt. *See* External debt
Foreign exchange
  development loans and, 279–80
  external debt and, 278
  foreign investment and, 279
  See also Exchange rates
Foreign travel restrictions, 133
Foreign Exchange Control Act, 178
Fry, 159

GDP growth, 234
  growth in 1991, 301

General Agreement on Tariffs and
    Trade, 133
General Banking Act, 149
General trading companies (GTCs),
    53
Germany
  employment in, 191
  fiscal tradition of, 141
  labor share in, 198
GNP growth in 1980–1984, 88
Gorbachev, Mikhail, 297
Government expenditures, 9, 113, 114
  in 1973–1988, 118–21
Government investments, 34–35
Government revenues, 9, 11
  in 1973–1988, 118–21
Grain Management Fund, 27, 61,
    83, 89, 100, 113
  function of, 128
  operations of, 164
Growth
  advantages of rapid, 140
  budgetary role in, 127
  costs of, 113, 114
  government involvement in, 140
  rate, 1970–1980, 169
Guam Doctrine, 33
Gulf Oil Co., 37

Han Sil, 170
Harris-Todaro model, 187–88
Heavy and Chemical Industry Plan
    (HCI), 7, 11, 13, 23–24, 33,
    41, 86, 112, 121, 126, 127,
    263, 265
  details of, 51–54
  effects of, 40, 49
  financing of, 54–56
  imports and, 276
  investment credit and, 267
  justifications for, 64
  macroeconomic policy during,
    56–59
Heavy and Chemical Industry Plan-
    ning Council, 34
Hong Kong
  economic growth of, 287
  investment in, 232
  labor productivity of, 200
  real growth rate in, 232
  savings in, 232
Household savings, 246
  age and, 248–51

Household savings *(continued)*
consumption and, 247–48
income level and, 251–54

Imports
and balance of payments, 274–77
liberalization of, 274, 275
restrictions on, 276
related to GDP, 278
Income
distribution of, 129
relation to savings, 243–44, 251–54
India
external debt of, 285
fiscal tradition of, 141
Indonesia, external debt of, 285
Industrial centralization, 6
Industrial Rationalization Deliberation Committee, 61
Industrial Rationalization Fund, 61
Industry
growth of, 186, 188
labor force in, 189–90
light manufacturing, 185
Inflation, 12, 25, 49, 56–59, 63, 195
in 1991, 301
curbing, 185
during Big Push, 56–59
politics and, 301
wage increases and, 186, 195,
216–19
Inflation rate, 158
1970–1980, 169
Interest rate, 67, 69, 158, 171, 176,
281
bank, 171
curb, 171
lowering in 1982, 85
1980–1982, 83–84
1986–1988, 100–1
1987–1990, 300
regulation of, 159–60
relation to investments, 245
relation to savings, 242–43
setting of, 157–60
subsidized, 267, 269, 270
International borrowing, 38–40
International exchange, 133, 134
International relations, 297–98
International trade, 3–4, 94–95,
261–93
relation to investments, 245

International Atomic Energy Commission, 298
International Economic Policy
Council, 99
International Monetary Fund, 23,
30, 31, 264, 265
assessment of Korea, 75
conflicts with Korea, 87
convertibility obligations under,
133
Korean dependence on, 55–56
loans to Korea, 126
as source of foreign exchange,
278–79
Investment, 232, 235, 237–40,
244–46
determinants of, 244–46
fixed, 238, 239
gross domestic, 237
growth and, 235
patterns of, 13–14
savings and, 237–40
total, 238
Israel, external debt of, 285

Japan, 31
employment in, 191, 192
financial interrelationship ratio
of, 175
fiscal tradition of, 141
importance of agriculture in, 103
interest rate manipulation in, 160
investment in, 232
labor costs in, 204, 205
labor market in, 222
labor productivity of, 200
labor share in, 198
occupation of Korea, 262
postal savings plan in, 35
real growth rate in, 232
savings in, 232
working hours in, 212, 213
Japan Import-Export Bank, 125
Jeon, Tai-il, 26
Jonghwa (purification), 79
Jung Jai-Suk, 67

Kang Kyung-Shik, 62, 70
Kim Chungsoo, 58
Kim Dae-Jung, 66, 296, 298, 299, 302
kidnapping of, 39
populism of, 28

prosecution of, 80
Kim Jae-Ik, 16, 62, 69, 77, 79–80,
    84, 86, 89, 92, 274
Kim Jong-Pil, 296, 298
Kim Joonkyung, 177
Kim Kihwan, 70, 79, 98, 99
Kim Kwang Suk, 266, 268, 275
Kim Mahn-Je, 31, 62, 96, 99
Kim Yong Hwan, 39
Kim Young Sam, 66, 296, 298, 299,
    302
Korea
  agriculture in, 9
  asset growth in, 176
  balance of payments of, 14–15, 38
  budget deficits in, 9
  budget of 1987, 113–15
  capital markets in, 178
  chief executive's economic role,
    6–7
  conflict with IMF, 87
  Consumer Price Index 1980–1984,
    88
  credit expansion in, 31
  credit policies of, 90–91
  credit policy in 1985, 95
  credit rationing in, 158–59,
    160–61
  currency devaluation in, 31, 50,
    78, 97, 264, 265, 270, 274
  debt in 1979–1982, 87
  debt of, 234
  democratic elections in, 295
  democratic politics in, 93–94
  democratization in, 8, 179
  domestic credit in, 67, 156–57
  economic indicators, 25, 26, 29–30
  economic indicators 1976–1980, 50
  economic indicators 1978–1986, 84
  economic indicators 1979–1985, 76
  economic indicators 1984–1988, 95
  economic indicators 1987–1992,
    296
  economic performance of, 4
  exchange rates of, 31, 77
  exchange rates, 1984–1986, 97
  exports of, 262–65
  external debt of, 9, 14, 235–36, 285
  external shocks to economy in
    1974, 15–16
  external shocks to economy in
    1979–1981, 15–16, 17

Fifth Republic, 7
financial institutions in, 147–51
financial interrelationship ratio
    of, 175
fiscal impulse in, 130–32
fiscal policy in, 9–10
fiscal policy reform in, 11, 12
fiscal structure of, 89
fiscal tradition of, 141
foreign debt of, 54
foreign travel restrictions, 133
GDP growth in, 234
GNP growth in 1980–1984, 88
government expenditures, 9, 113,
    114
government expenditures in
    1973–1988, 118–21
government investments, 34–35
government revenues, 9, 11
government revenues in
    1973–1988, 118–21
growth rate 1970–1980, 169
income distribution in, 129
industrial centralization in, 6
inflation in, 12, 25, 49, 56–59, 63,
    158, 195
inflation rate in, 158
inflation rate 1970–1980, 169
interest rate lowering in 1982, 85
interest rates in, 67, 69, 158, 171,
    176
interest rates 1980–1982, 83–84
interest rates 1986–1988, 100–1
international borrowing of,
    38–40
international exchange, 133, 134
international relations of, 297–98
international trade of, 3–4,
    94–95, 261–93
investment in, 232, 235, 237–40,
    244–46
investment patterns in, 13–14
labor costs in, 204, 205
labor disputes in, 25, 27
labor disputes in 1989 in, 299
labor markets in, 12
labor productivity of, 200
as labor supply for Persian Gulf
    countries, 269
labor unrest in, 101
liberalization of financial markets,
    1983–1988, 98–101

Korea (continued)
  liberalizing influences in, 5
  loan markets in, 170, 172–74, 177
  M2 velocity 1970–1980, 169
  macroeconomic policies in
    1985–1987, 93–102
  macroeconomic policies of, 4–6,
    8–15
  monetary policy of, 10–12, 165–80
  monetary targeting in, 161–65
  nuclear weapons in, 298
  overseas borrowing by, 178
  payment surpluses of 1986–1988,
    16
  political economy analysis of,
    6–8
  political liberalization in 1988,
    296
  price determinants, 58
  public debt in 1971–1989, 152
  public debt of, 113–14, 124–26
  public enterprises in, 117–18
  real growth rate in, 232
  reliance on exports, 15
  rural concerns of, 27–28
  savings in, 231–44, 246–54
  savings patterns during first oil
    shock, 37
  savings patterns in, 13, 14, 54
  stabilization in 1983–1984, 87–93
  state involvement in market
    policies, 5
  surpluses in, 120, 178
  surpluses in 1984–1986, 95–97
  surpluses in 1986–1989, 132
  surpluses in 1987, 114
  tax policy in, 134–39
  tax structure in, 134
  trade balance of, 77
  trade balance with U.S., 98
  trade deficit of, 55–56
  unemployment in, 95
  wage growth in 1987, 101
  wages in, 25, 26–27, 77
  working hours in, 212, 213
  zero-based budgeting in
    1983–1984, 89
Korea Development Bank, 55, 117,
  178
  and external borrowing, 282, 284
Korea Electric Power Co., 117, 118
Korea Employers' Federation, 216

Korea Exchange Bank, 56, 92, 178,
  282
  and external borrowing, 282
Korea Export-Import Bank, 178
Korea Redevelopment Bank, 280
Korea Stock Exchange, 177
Korea Telecommunications
  Authority, 117
Korean Development Institute, 31, 63
Korean Export-Import Bank, 270
Korean Shipbuilding Corp., 26
Korean Traders Assn., 86
Krueger, A., 268
Kukje Group, 92
Kwangju, 27

Labor
  accession rates, 195, 197
  causes of growth of, 186–87
  changing demand for, 220
  changing demographics of,
    219–20, 221
  costs of, 202–4
  demographics of, 207–8
  fueling export-led development,
    185
  growth of, 186–87
  laws regarding, 216
  output-based productivity, 202
  productivity of, 199–204
  recent developments in market,
    219–22
  share of GNP, 198–99
  shortages in, 213–14
  strikes, 101
  strikes in 1989, 299–300
  turnover in, 195–98
  union role in, 215–16
  value-added productivity of, 201
  working hours, 212, 213
Labor costs, 204, 205
Labor disputes, 25, 27
  in 1989, 299
Labor force, 187
  by industry, 189–90
Labor markets, 12
Labor productivity, 200
Labor unrest, 101, 299–300
Latin America
  economic difficulties in, 103
  external debt of, 236

import-substituting strategies in, 261
Lee Hahn Been, 67
Lee Tong-Hun, 170
Liberalization
  financial markets, 1983–1988, 98–101
  import, 274, 275
  influences toward, 5
Loan markets, 170, 172–74, 177
Loans
  curb lending, 166, 170, 172–73
  purposes of, 174, 177
  rates of, 171
  sources of funds for, 173
  subsidized, 238

M2 velocity 1970–1980, 169
Machine Localization Plan, 51
Macroeconomic policy, 4–6, 8–15
  in 1985–1987, 93–102
Malaysia, external debt of, 285
Marshall Plan, 261
Martial law decree of October 1972, 28
Martial law decree of May 17, 1980, 68
McKinnon, R., 159
Mexico
  external debt of, 282, 285
  taxation in, 115
Military expenditures, 113, 114, 136–37, 139
Ministry of Agriculture and Fisheries, 100
Ministry of Commerce and Industry, 41, 63, 67
Ministry of Finance
  friction with Bank of Korea, 180
  and monetary policy, 145–46
Mitsui Corp., 41
Monetary policy, 10–12, 165–80
  Bank of Korea and, 145–46, 147
  expansion, 167
  government control over, 145–51
  instruments of, 151–57
Monetary stabilization bonds (MSBs), 152–53, 154, 157, 167
Monetary targeting, 161–62
  procedures in, 162–65
  theory behind, 167–68
Monetary Board, 121, 146, 147, 174

control over credit, 156
interest rates set by, 157–60
Monetary Stabilization Account, 152, 157
Monopoly Regulation and Fair Trade Law, 81
Morgan Guaranty Survey, 75

Nam Duck Woo, 31, 38–39, 42, 61, 62, 214
Nam Sang-Woo, 40
National Assembly, makeup of, 62
National Investment Fund, 34
National Security and Defense, Law Concerning, 65
National Security Law, 296–97, 299
Netherlands
  fiscal tradition of, 141
  taxation in, 115
New Democratic Party, 28, 62
New Democratic Republican Party, 296, 298
New Korea Democratic Party, 93
New Village (*Saemaul*) Movement, 212
Nigeria, external debt of, 284, 285
Nixon, Richard, 31, 33
Nixon Doctrine, 263
Nixon shock of August 1971, 31
North Korea, 136
  reconciliation agreement with, 298
Nuclear Non-Proliferation Treaty, 298

Office of Monopoly, 114
Office of National Tax Administration, 136
Oh Won Chul, 34
Olympics, Summer 1988, 297
Open market operations, get from MSBs, 152–53, 154, 157, 167

Park Chung Hee, 6, 7, 41, 62, 101, 163, 172, 263, 273, 282
  agricultural bias of, 127
  assassination of, 50, 67, 76
  economic policies of, 23, 24–25, 33, 53, 63
  emergency decrees of, 36
  and first oil shock, 35–41
  labor relations of, 27

Park Chung Hee *(continued)*
 monetary policy of, 146–47
 opposition to, 28
 policies of, 8, 17, 42
 political methods of, 64–65
Park Won-Am, 40
Park Yung Chul, 40, 41, 170, 207, 283
Party for Peace and Democracy,
 296, 298
Payment surpluses of 1986–1988, 16
Peru, external debt of, 285
Philippines, external debt of, 285
Phillips curve, 223
Pohang Iron and Steel Co., 117
Political economy analysis, 6–8
Political liberalization in 1988, 296
Portugal, external debt of, 285
Price determinants, 58
Price stabilization, 32
Price Stabilization and Fair Trade
 law, 59
Price Stabilization Committee, 59
Prices, equations, 226–27
Proportional representation, 296
Public debt, 113–14, 124–26
 1971–1989, 152
Public enterprises, 117–18

Rangoon bombing, 80
Reagan, Ronald, 98
Real growth rate, 232
Recession of 1982, 265
Rediscounts, 156
 rate on, 1986–1988, 100
Reserve requirement, 153, 155, 156
Reunification Democratic Party,
 296, 298
Rhee, Syngman, 10, 141
Rice, distribution of, 128
Ro Sung-Tae, 51, 168
Roh Tae-Woo, 3, 5, 8, 94, 295, 296
 democratization by, 219, 296, 301
 fiscal policies of, 300–1
 political conservatization of, 298
 power base of, 297
Rural areas
 agricultural subsidies, 57
 agriculture, 9
 concerns of, 27–28
 decline of, 186
 labor force in, 189–90
 wages in, 210–12
Ryochun petrochemical plant, 41

Saemaul Movement, 212
Sakong Eun-Duk, 168
Sakong Il, 80, 118
Saudi Arabia, relations with Korea,
 53, 54
Savings, 231–44, 246–54
 cyclical variations in, 241
 determinants of, 240–44
 gross domestic, 237, 239
 household, 246–51
 income and, 243–44, 251–54
 interest rates and, 242–43
 investment and, 237–40
Savings patterns, 13, 14, 54, 239–40
 during first oil shock, 37
Second Oil Shock, 64–69, 77
Seigniorage, 11
 and Bank of Korea, 121–24
Seoul Peace Market, 26
Shaw, E., 159
Shim Byung-Koo, 170
Shin Hyun-Hwack, 62, 63
Singapore
 economic growth of, 287
 investment in, 232
 labor productivity of, 200
 real growth rate in, 232
 savings in, 232
South Africa, external debt of, 285
Soviet Union, relations with Korea,
 297–98
Stabilization and Growth,
 Emergency Decree on, 139
Stabilization of National Life,
 Emergency Measure for, 139
Stabilization Plan of 1979, back-
 ground of, 59–64
State of emergency of December
 1971, 27, 28
Supply Fund, 113
Surpluses, 120, 178
 in 1984–1986, 95–97
 in 1986–1989, 132
 in 1987, 114

Taiwan
 economic growth of, 287
 financial interrelationship ratio
 of, 175
 interest rate manipulation in, 160
 investment in, 232
 labor costs in, 204, 205
 labor productivity of, 200

real growth rate in, 232
relations with, 298
savings in, 232
trade relations with U.S., 98
working hours in, 212, 213
Takeshita, Noboru, 121
Tariffs, rate of, 275, 276
Tax Exemption and Reduction
    Control Law, 51
Tax Exemption and Reduction Law,
    137, 138
Taxes and taxation
    breakdown of, 113, 115
    costs of raising, 112
    economic stabilization and, 139
    elasticity of system, 120
    governance of, 115
    in 1987, 114–15
    incentives, 138
    income, 135
    policy of, 134–39
    purpose of, 135
    response to oil shocks, 36–37
    revenues forgone, 138–39
    revenues from, 135
    structure of, 134
    target revenue approach to, 136
    value-added, 60, 121, 135
Thailand
    external debt of, 284, 285
    taxation in, 115
Third five-year plan, 33
Trade balance, 77
    with U.S., 98
Trade deficit, 55–56
Turkey
    external debt of, 285
    taxation in, 115

Unemployment, 95, 187
    concerns about, 220
Union Oil Co., 37
Unions, labor, 215–16
United States
    dollar exchange of, 270, 272
    economic aid to Korea, 31
    financial interrelationship ratio
        of, 175
    labor productivity of, 200
    monetary policy of, 287
    taxation in, 115
    trade balance with Korea, 98

Value-added tax (VAT), 135
    introduction of, 60, 121
Venezuela, external debt of, 285
Vietnam, 136
    effect of U.S. withdrawal on
        Korean economy, 31
    importance to Korean economy,
        263

Wage(s), 25, 26–27, 77
    control of, 214
    drift of, 215
    equations, 223–25
    growth in, 13
    growth, 1971–1990, 193–95
    growth, 1987, 101
    growth, 1987–1990, 299–300
    hourly, 207
    influence on international trade,
        214
    minimum, 209
    patterns of differential, 204–12
    policies regarding, 213–19
    price inflation and, 216–19
    rates of increase, 207, 217, 220,
        221–23
Wage differentials, 204–12
    demographics of, 208–10
    urban-rural, 210–12
Wage increases
    as cause of inflation, 186
    employment expansion and, 187
Wage and Salary Workers Fortune
        Formation Savings Fund, 137
Westphal, L., 266, 268, 275
Won, devaluation of, 31, 50, 78, 97,
        264, 265, 270, 274
Working hours, 212, 213
World Bank, 31, 125
    as source of foreign exchange, 280

YH Trading Co., 66
Yong Ja Chang, 85
Yugoslavia, external debt of, 285
Yushin Constitution, 7, 23, 28–29
    National Assembly under, 62
Yushin system
    economic aspects of, 33
    justifications for, 64–65

Zero-based budgeting in
        1983–1984, 89